WITHDRAWN

THE CHILD AS VULNERABLE PATIENT

Medical Law and Ethics

Series Editor
Sheila McLean, Director of the Institute of Law and Ethics in Medicine,
School of Law, University of Glasgow

The 21st century seems likely to witness some of the most major developments in medicine and healthcare ever seen. At the same time, the debate about the extent to which science and/or medicine should lead the moral agenda continues, as do questions about the appropriate role for law.

This series brings together some of the best contemporary academic commentators to tackle these dilemmas in a challenging, informed and inquiring manner. The scope of the series is purposely wide, including contributions from a variety of disciplines such as law, philosophy and social sciences.

Other titles in the series

Disclosure Dilemmas
Edited by Christoph Rehmann-Sutter and Hansjakob Müller
978-0-7546-7451-1

Critical Interventions in the Ethics of Healthcare
Edited by Stuart J. Murray and Dave Holmes
ISBN 978-0-7546-7396-5

Law, Mind and Brain
Edited by Michael Freeman and Oliver R. Goodenough
ISBN 978-0-7546-7013-1

Speaking for the Dead
D. Gareth Jones and Maja I. Whitaker
ISBN 978-0-7546-7452-8

The Jurisdiction of Medical Law
Kenneth Veitch
ISBN 978-0-7546-4944-1

The Child As Vulnerable Patient

Protection and Empowerment

LYNN HAGGER
University of Sheffield, UK

ASHGATE

Published by
Ashgate Publishing Limited
Wey Court East
Union Road
Farnham
Surrey, GU9 7PT
England

Ashgate Publishing Company
Suite 420
101 Cherry Street
Burlington
VT 05401-4405
USA

www.ashgate.com

British Library Cataloguing in Publication Data
Hagger, Lynn.
  The child as vulnerable patient : protection and
  empowerment. -- (Medical law and ethics)
  1. Child health services--Law and legislation--England.
  2. Child health services--Law and legislation--Wales.
  3. Pediatrics--Law and legislation--England.
  4. Pediatrics--Law and legislation--Wales. 5. Children's rights.
  I. Title II. Series
  344.4'203219892-dc22

Library of Congress Cataloging-in-Publication Data
Hagger, Lynn.
  The child as vulnerable patient : protection and empowerment / by Lynn Hagger.
    p. cm. -- (Medical law and ethics)
  Includes index.
  ISBN 978-0-7546-7252-4 -- ISBN 978-0-7546-9129-7 (ebook) 1. Child health services--
Law and legislation--England. 2. Children's rights--England. I. Title.

  KD3405.C48H34 2009
  342.4208'772--dc22

2009001726

ISBN 978-0-7546-7252-4 (hardback)
ISBN 978-0-7546-9129-7 (ebook)

Mixed Sources
Product group from well-managed forests and other controlled sources
www.fsc.org Cert no. SGS-COC-2482
© 1996 Forest Stewardship Council
FSC

Printed and bound in Great Britain by
TJ International Ltd, Padstow, Cornwall

Contents

Preface   *vii*
Table of Cases   *ix*

1   The Importance of Protecting and Empowering Children   1

2   The Law and Children's Autonomy   13

3   Parental Responsibility and Children's Health Care Treatment   55

4   Confidentiality and Children   75

5   Genetic Testing and Counselling:
     The Paradigm Case for Family Medicine?   111

6   Negligence and Complaints   131

7   Children in Research   175

8   Children's Participation and Foundation Trusts:
     Some New Opportunities?   213

9   Concluding Remarks   235

Index   *245*

Preface

I have had the benefit of being involved in the National Health Service (NHS) for the last 20 years. I first served on the now defunct patient watchdog body, the Sheffield Community Health Council, as a volunteer for six years. During the remaining period, I worked as a Non-executive Director of NHS Trust Boards, first in an adult hospital and for the last nine years as Chairperson of Sheffield Children's NHS Foundation Trust. It was a privilege being able to witness the skill and commitment of staff who work in the NHS at first hand. In the paediatric setting, their dedication was even more palpable. My own nascent commitment to the rights of children was confirmed through my exposure to paediatric health care practice. I will remain forever indebted to the many conversations I have had with patients, their families and staff who have helped me to further formulate my views. This exposure to clinical practice in the wider NHS context gave me a unique perspective on aspects of medical ethics and health care law in its broadest sense. With this in mind, I have located the law in its practical context. For some time I have wanted to draw together my research interests and add my voice to an already rich debate about the parameters of children's interests and to satisfy practitioners who sometimes struggle to locate relevant material in one place. Medical law moves at a rapid pace and I have sought to state the law as of October 2008.

There are many people for whose support I am very grateful as I wrote this book. Particular thanks are owed to Derek Morgan and Simon Woods whose insights and informed comments have proved invaluable. I am also indebted to colleagues for their willingness to comment on drafts of various chapters (in alphabetical order): Vicky Chico, Samantha Halliday, Norma Hird, Aurora Plomer and Mark Taylor. Thanks also to Professor Sheila McLean for her helpful editorial comments. Without their remarks and advice, this book would be significantly weaker. Any remaining errors are, of course, my own. None of this would have been possible without the emotional and practical support from my family and friends all of whom have enriched my life beyond measure. In particular, I wish to thank my children, Gareth, Megan and Harry and my husband Barry, whose love, support and pride always sustains me and who has made many things possible. It is to him that I dedicate this book.

Lynn Hagger

To Barry

Table of Cases

A v National Blood Authority [2001] 3 All ER 289 159–60

A (A Child) v Ministry of Defence [2004] EWCA Civ 641 136n32

A-G v De Keyser's Royal Hotel Ltd [1920] AC 508 30n125

A-G's Reference (No. 3 of 1994) [1998] AC 245 165n239, 166n240

AB v Glasgow and West of Scotland Blood Transfusion Service (1989) 15 BMLR 91 (Scottish Court of Session) (Outer House) 106

AB v Tameside and Glossop Health Authority (1997) 8 *Medical Law Review* 91 162n219

Airedale NHS Trust v Bland [1993] All ER 821 4n19

Airedale NHS Trust v Bland [1993] AC 789 150n147

Alcock v Chief Constable of South Yorkshire Police [1992] 1 AC 310 141, 162n219

Anderson v Newham College [2003] ICR 212 167n253

Andre Deklerek v Belgium. Application No. 8307/78 DR21, 116 40n211

Ashworth Hospital Authority v MGN [2001] 2 All ER 991 90n96, 91n100, 100n161

Attorney General v Guardian Newspapers Ltd (No 2) [1990] 1 AC 109 83n57, 86–7, 91n99

Ayse Colak and others v Germany (Admissibility Decision) 8 January 2008 91n103, 99–100, 126

B v B [1992] FLR 327 57n16

Barker v Corus UK Ltd [2006] 3 All ER 785 153n168

Barkway v South Wales transport Co Ltd [1950] 1 All ER 392 151n154

Barnett v Chelsea and Kensington HMC [1968] 1 All ER 1068 150n145, 151–2

Barnett v Chelsea and Kensington [1969] 1 QB 428 139n55

Barrett v Ministry of Defence [1995] 3 All ER 87 140n63

Belgian Linguistic case, Series B, No. 3 (1967), 24 June 1965 40n205, 40n206

Bensaid v UK (2001) 33 EHRR 10 42n221

Birmingham CC v O [1983] 1 All ER 497 77n15

Blyth v Birmingham Waterworks Co. (1856) Ex 781 142n77

Blyth v Bloomsbury HA [1993] 4 Med LR 151 136n34

Bolam v Friern HMC [1957] 2 All ER 118 136, 143, 144, 146, 149, 150, 153, 167, 197

Bolam v Friern Management Committee [1957] 1 WLR 582 199, 200

Bolitho v Hackney HA [1997] 4 All ER 771 145, 146, 147, 149, 153–4, 167

Bolitho (Deceased) v City and Hackney Health Authority [1998] AC 232 3n15,
    199, 200
Bonnington Castings v Wardlaw [1956] A.C. 613 152n163
Botta v Italy (1998) 26 EHRR 241 41, 42n221, 225
Bro Morgannwg NHS Trust v 'P' and others [2003] EWHC 2327 (Fam) (Re P)
    35n168, 43, 49n263, 49n265, 52, 68 , 236n8, 239n23, 244
Bull v Devon AHA [1993] 4 Med LR 117 136n37
*Burke v General Medical Council (defendant) and Disability Rights Commission
    (interested party) and the Official Solicitor (intervenor)* [2005] EWCA 103
    150n146
*Burlton v Islington Health Authority, de Martell v Merton and Sutton Health
    Authority* [1993] QB 204 165n238, 167n255, 167n256

C v C [1946] 1 All ER 562 77n11
Campbell v MGN [2004] UKHL 22 76n8, 77n10, 79n29, 87n80, 89–90, 93, 102
Caparo Industries v Dickman [1990] 2 AC 605 140
Capital and Counties v Hampshire CC [1997] Q.B. 1035 140n64
Cassidy v Ministry of Health [1954] 2 KB 343 151
Catherine Urch v Hammersmith Hospitals NHS Trust 173
Cattanach v Mechior [2003] HCA 38 172n284
Cattley v St John's Ambulance Brigade (1998) (Lexis) 148n126
Chatterton v Gerson [1981] 1QB 432 25n79, 199n144
Chester v Afshar [2004] 4 All ER 587 131n1, 155–7
Chester v Afshar [2005] 1 AC 134 199n150, 200n153
Crawford v Board of Governors of Charing Cross Hospital (1953) *The Times* 8
    December, CA 144n92

D v East Berkshire Community Health NHS Trust et al. [[2005] 2 AC 373 142
D v NSPCC [1978] AC 171 104, 105
Daubert v Merrill Dow Pharmaceuticals Inc. 509 US 579 (1993) 149n142
De Freitas v O'Brien [1993] 4 Med LR 281 144n94, 146n116
DF (by her litigation friend and mother CF) v St George's Healthcare NHS Trust
    [2005] EWHC 1327 150n150
Dobson v Dobson [1999] 2 SCR 753 176n256
Donoghue v Stevenson [1932] AC 562 158
Dudgeon v United Kingdom, Series A, No. 45 (1981) 20n207
Dwyer v Roderick (1983) 127 SJ 806 147n123

Early v Newham Health Authority (1994) 5 Medical Law Review 214 150n151
Easson v London and North Eastern Railway [1944] 1 KB 421 151n152
Elaine Ruth Glicksman v Redbridge NHS Trust [2001] EWCA Civ 1097
    146n110
Emeh v Kensington and Chelsea and Westminster AHA [1985] QB 1012
    171n280

F v West Berkshire HA [1989] 2 All ER 545 140n59
Fairchild v Glenhavon Funeral Services [2002] UKHL 22 152–3
Fairchild v Glenhavon Funeral Services [2002] Lloyd's Rep Med 361 153, 157n187
French v Thames Valley Strategic Health Authority [2005] EWHC 459 146n109

Garcia v St Mary's NHS Trust [2006] EWHC 2314 (QB) 137n39
Gascoine v Ian Sheridan & Co [1994] Med LR 437 136n35
Geest plc v Monica Lansiquot [2002] 1 WLR 1311 162n218
Gillick v West Norfolk and Wisbech Area Health Authority [1986] AC 112 5n22, 21n44, 22n53, 26n93, 27n100, 28–32, 34–5, 37–8, 41, 42, 43n233, 48, 50n270, 50n272, 56n5, 57, 59n33, 62, 82, 83–4, 85, 108, 183n44, 205–8, 210, 221n59
Glass v UK [2004] 39 EHRR 15 39n199, 65–6, 69n104
Glass v UK 1 FLR 1019 192n95
Godden v Kent and Medway SHA [2004] EWHC 1629 135n29, 136n33
Gold v Haringey HA [1988] QB 481 143n78
Goodwill v BPAS [1996] 2 All ER 161 139n56
Greenfield v Irwin [2001] 1 WLR 1279 172n285
Gregg v Scott [2005] 2 AC 176 154–5, 157
Groom v Selby [2002] Lloyd's Rep. Med. 1 172n290

H v Royal Alexandra Hospital for Sick Children [1990] 1 *Med Law Rev* 297 144n92
H (A Healthcare Worker) v Associated Newspapers Ltd and N (A Health Authority) [2002] 210 (CA) 100, 101
Hardman v Amin [2000] Lloyd's Rep Med 498 173n292
Hartman v South Essex Mental Health [2005] EWCA Civ 6 141n66
Heil v Rankin [2000] 3 All ER 138 160n206, 160n207
Herczegfalvy v Austria [1992] 15 EHRR 437 39n201
Hotson v E Berkshire [1987] AC 750 154, 155
Houston, Applicant (1996) SCLR 943 48n256, 48n257
Howard v Wessex RHA [1994] 5 Med LR 57, QBD 151n157
Hunter v Mann [1974] QB 767 87n80

In Re Cincinnati Radiation Litig 874 F Supp 796 (SD Ohio 1995) 200n154
Interbrew SA v Financial Times Ltd [2002] 1 Lloyd's Rep 542 104n186

Jones v Manchester Corporation [1952] 2 All ER 125 137n41
Judge v Huntingdon HA [1995] 6 Med LR 223 146n114

Keenan v UK [2001] EHRR 38 36n178, 39n202
Kirkham v Chief Constable of Greater Manchester [1990] 2 Q.B. 283 143n77
Knight and others v Home Office and another [1990] 3 All ER 237 136n36
Knightly v Johns [1982] 1 WLR 349 157n190

KR v Bryn Alyn Community (Holdings) Ltd (In Liquidation) [2003] 3 WLR 107
    161–2

L and P v Reading BC and Chief Constable of Thames Valley Police [2001] EWCA
    Civ 346 142n75
Lee v Taunton and Somerset NHS Trust [2001] 1 FLR 419 173n293, 173n294
Lewis v Secretary of State for Health [2008] EWHC 2196 (QB) 87, 112n5
London Borough Council v (1) Mr & Mrs N [2005] EWHC 1676 128n104
Loveday v Renton (1990) 1 Medical Law Review 117 149n139

Mabon v Mabon et al. [2005] 3 WLR 460 42, 43, 84, 224n77
Mahon v Osborne [1939] 2 KB 14 151
Marriott v West Midlands Health Authority [1999] Lloyd's Med Rep 23 145
Maynard v West Midlands HA [1985] 1 All ER 635 143n82, 144n89, 145n104
McGhee v National Coal Board [1973] 1 WLR 152
McFarlane v Tayside Health Board [2000] 2 AC 59 168n260, 169n266, 171–2,
    173
McKay v Essex AHA [1982] 1 QB 1166 168–9
MG v UK [2002] 3 FCR 413 109n218
Mikulic v Croatia [2002] 1 FCR 720 89n88
Mosley v News Group Newspapers Ltd [2008] EWHC 1777 (QB) 76n8, 90n92
MS v Sweden (1998) 45 BMLR 1 89, 98
Murray v Express Newspapers plc and another [2008] EWCA Civ 446 91–2

*NHS Trust v (1) A (A Child) (Represented by an officer of CAFCASS as Child's
    Guardian) (2) Mrs A (3) Mr A* [2007] EWHC 1696 (Fam) 69n107
NHS Trust v MB [2006] 2 FCR 319 58n24, 66, 69
NHS Trust v Ms T [2004] EWHC 1279 26n87
NHS Trust A v M, NHS Trust B v H [2001] Fam.348 41n217
Nielsen v Denmark Eur Ct HR, Series A, No. 144, Judgement of 28 November,
    1988 39–40
Niemetz v Germany (1993) 16 EHRR 97 42n221
North Glamorgan NHS Trust v Walters [2002] EWCA Civ 1792 141n67, 141n71

Odièvre v France (2004) 38 EHRR 43 89n88
Osman v UK [1999] 1 FLR 193 99n154
Osman v UK (2000) 29 EHRR 245 142n74
Oxford v Moss (1978) 68 Cr App R 183 92n106

Palmer v Tees Health Authority [1999] Lloyd's Rep Med 359 140n58
Palmer v Tees Health Authority [2000] PIQR 1 98
Parkinson v St James and Seacroft University Hospital NHS Trust [2002] QB 266
    168n260, 172, 173
Pearce v United Bristol Healthcare Trust [1999] PIQR 53 199n149

Penney v East Kent Health Authority (2000) 55 BMLR 63 146n108
Phelps v Hillingdon Borough Council [2001] 2 AC 619 142
Portsmouth NHS Trust v Wyatt and Wyatt, Southampton NHS Trust (Intervening)
    [2004] EWHC 2247 64–5
Powell v Boldaz [1997] 39 BMLR 35 140n64
Pretty v United Kingdom (2002) 35 EHRR 1 41, 42n221, 87n84

R v Adomoko [1995] 1 AC 171 137n43
R v Bow Street Metropolitan Stipendiary Magistrate ex p. Government of the USA
    [2000] 2 AC 216 80n31
R v Collins and others; *ex parte S* [1999] Fam.26 46n246
R v Crozier (1990) 12 Cr. App. R. (S) 206 106n196
R v Department of Health ex p. Source Informatics [2000] 1 All ER 786 78n20,
    79, 92–3
R v Dica [2004] EWCA Crim 1231 99n155
R v Hampshire CC, ex p. H [1999] 2 FLR 359 104n184
R v Harrow LBC, ex p. D [1978] AC 171 104n184
R v Mid-Glamorgan FHSA ex p. Martin [1995] 1 All ER 356 92n108, 109n217
R v Portsmouth Hospital NHS Trust ex parte Glass [1999] 2 FLR 905 7n37,
    56n15, 65–6
R (A) v Chief Constable of C [2001] 1 WLR 461 98n148
R (Axon) v Secretary of State for Health (Family Planning Association intervening)
    [2006] EWHC 37 (Admin) 3n16, 42–3, 44n236, 82–5, 224n77, 236n8, 238n22,
    239n23
R (on the application of A, B, X and Y) v East Sussex County Council (No 2) [2003]
    EWHC 167 (Admin) 87n84, 225
R (on the application of Burke) v GMC [2004] EWHC 1879 25n80, 66n81, 208
R (on the application of PS) v G (RMO) and W (SOAD) [2003] EWHC 2335 (Fam)
    36n178, 39n202
R (Williamson) v Secretary of State for Education and Employment and Others
    [2005] 2 FLR 374 68n93
Rand v east Dorset Health Authority [2000] Lloyd's Rep Med 181 173n292
Ratcliffe v Plymouth and Torbay HA [1998] 4 Med LR 162 151n158, 151n159
Re A (Children) (Conjoined twins: surgical separation) [2001] Fam 147 4n19
Re A (male sterilization) [2000] 1 FLR 549 57n21, 197n129
Re B [1997] 2 All ER 206 27n101, 202n167
Re B (a minor) (Wardship: Medical Treatment) [1981] 1 WLR 1421 64n70
Re B (adult: refusal of medical treatment) [2002] 2 FCR 1 24n69, 25n79, 25n81,
    33, 46n246, 51
Re C (adult: refusal of medical treatment) [1994] 1 All ER 819 25n79, 27, 32,
    33n149, 35, 36n174, 38n194
Re C (a child) (immunization: parental rights) [2003] 2 FLR 1095 55n4
Re C (detention: medical treatment) [1997] 2 FLR 180 28n105
Re C (HIV test) [1999] 2 FLR 1004 67–8

Re C (a minor) (care proceedings: disclosure) [1997] Fam 76   104n180
Re C (a minor) (medical treatment) [1998] Lloyd's Rep. Med. 1   150n148
Re C (a minor) (medical treatment) [1998] 1 FLR 384   63n53, 67
Re C (a minor) (medical treatment) (No.2) [1989] 2 All ER 791   82n44
Re D [1976] 1 All ER 326   202n167
Re E (a minor) (wardship: medical treatment) [1993] 1 FLR 386   26n88, 31,
    36n180, 45n239, 47n247, 51–2, 68n95, 68n96, 243
Re F [1990] 2 AC 1   143n85
Re F (mental patient: sterilization) [1990] 2 AC 1   25n80, 27n98, 27n99, 27n103
Re J (a minor) (medical treatment) [1991] Fam 33   57n20
Re J (a minor) (medical treatment) [1992] 2 FLR 165   7n35
Re J (specific issues orders: Muslim upbringing and circumcision) [1999] 2 FLR
    678 61, 62
Re J (wardship: medical treatment) [1991] 2 WLR 140   64n70, 65n71
Re K, W and H (minors) (medical treatment) [1993] 1 FLR 854   30
Re L [2004] EWHC 2713   69n103
Re L (medical treatment: Gillick competency) [1998] 2 FLR 810   25n79, 31–2,
    36n180, 45n239
Re M [1990] 1 All ER 205   103n176
Re M (a child) (refusal of medical treatment) [1999] 2 FLR 1097   32–3, 45n239,
    47n248
Re MB [1997] 2 FLR 426   165n239
Re MB (adult: medical treatment) [1997] 2 FCR 541   24n69, 25n76, 25n79, 26n86,
    26n87, 33–4,
Re O (a minor) (medical treatment) 1993] 2 FLR 149   57n16, 68n92
Re P (a minor) [1982] 8 LGR 30   27n102
Re P (Bro Morgannwg NHS Trust v 'P' and others [2003] EWHC 2327 (Fam)
    35n168, 43, 49n263, 49n265, 52, 68 , 236n8, 239n23, 244
Re R (a minor) [1986] 1 FLR 272   29
Re R (a minor) (blood transfusion) [1993] 2 FLR 757   68n92
Re R (a minor) (wardship: consent to medical treatment) [1991] 4 All ER 177
    CA   28n111, 29n115, 35, 37, 47n249, 182n43, 221n60, 243n46
Re Roddy (a child) (identification: restrictions on Publication) [2004] 2 FLR 949
    42, 224n77
Re S (a child) (identification: restriction on publication) [2004] 4 All ER 683
    101–2
Re S (a minor) (medical treatment) [1993] 2 FLR 1065   31n129
Re S (a minor) (medical treatment) [1993] 1 FLR 376   68n92
Re S (adult: refusal of treatment) [1992] 4 All ER 671   24n68
Re S (adult patient: sterilization) [2001] Fam 15   146n111
Re S (specific issues order: religion: circumcision) [2004] EWHC 1282   62
Re T [1992] 4 All ER 649   199n142, 199n143
Re T (a minor) (wardship: medical treatment) [1997] 1 All ER 906   202n167

Re T (adult; refusal of medical treatment) [1993] Fam 95 15n8, 24n67, 25n76, 26n86, 29n116, 29n117, 36–7, 45n238, 46n246, 50n273

Re T (wardship: medical treatment) [1997] 1 WLR 242 7n37, 63–4, 69

Re W [1993] Fam 64 63n52, 205–6, 208

Re W [2002] EWHC 901 26n86

Re W (a minor) (medical treatment) [1993] Fam 64 24n69, 25n71, 27n94, 29n117, 29n118, 29n119, 29n120, 30n121, 35, 47n249, 50, 183n43, 243n47

Re W (a minor) (wardship: consent to medical treatment) [1992] 4 All ER 627 CA 221n60

Re W (children) (identification: restriction on publication) [2005] EWHC 1564 (Fam) 77n9, 101

Re W (contact: joining child as party) [2001] EWCA Civ 1830 58

Re Y [1997] 2 WLR 556 58n22, 62, 197n130, 202n168

Re Z [1997] Fam 1 55n2, 82n44, 82n45

Rees v Darlington Memorial Hospital NHS Trust [2004] 1 AC 309 168n261, 172n286, 173

Reeve v UK (1994) 24844/94 169n266

Rice v Connelly [1966] 2 All ER 649 105n193

Richards v Richards [1984] AC 174 30n125

Robinson v Post Office [1974] 1 WLR 1176 158

Roe v Minister of Health [1954] 2 All ER 131 144n90

Rogers v Whitaker (1992) 109 ALR 625 145n98, 145n99

S v Gloucestershire County Council [2001] 2 WLR 909 142n75

S v S [1972] AC 24 55n6, 59n34, 202

Salter v UB Frozen and Chilled Foods (2003) S.L.T. 1011 141n66

Sayers v Smithkline Beecham plc [2007] EWHC 1346 (QB) 91

Shakoor v Situ [2001] 1 WLR 410 143n78

Sidaway v Board of Governors of the Bethlehem Royal Hospital and the Maudsley Hospital [1985] AC 871 37n183, 143n83, 156n184

Sidaway v Board of Governors of the Bethlehem Royal Hospital and the Maudsley Hospital [1985] 2 WLR 871 199n146, 200n151

Simms v Simms [2002] 2 WLR 1465 143n86, 145, 146n111, 159n200, 197n129, 201n160

Simms v Simms [2003] 1 All ER 669 201

Sion v Hampstead HA [2002] EWCA Civ 1792 141n70

Smith v Leech Brain Co [1962] 2 QB 405 157–8

South Glamorgan County Council v W and B [1993] 1 FLR 574 30

South West Hertfordshire HA v B [1994] 2 FCR 1051 30n122

St George's Healthcare NHS Trust v S [1999] Fam 26 24n68, 28n113, 33n154, 46n246

Stockdale v Nicholls [1993] 4 Med LR 190 146n115

Swinney v Chief Constable of the Northumbria Police [1996] 3 All ER 449 86n77

Sykes v DPP [1962] A.C. 528 105n188

Tarasoff v Regents of the University of California 5551P.2d 334 (1976) 125
Telles v South West Strategic HA [2008] EWHC 292 (QB) 133n12
Thanke v Maurice [1986] 1 All ER 497 137n44
Thompson v Blake-Jones [1998] Lloyd's Rep Med 187 146n113
Torbay Borough Council v News Group Newspapers [2003] EWHC 2927 82n48

U v Centre for Reproductive Medicine [2002] EWCA Civ 565 195n110

Venables v MGN [2001] Fam 430 82n44, 91n98

W v Edgell [1990] 1 All ER 835 87n80, 94n120, 94n121, 96–7, 127n99
W v Essex CC [2001] 2 AC 592 141n65, 142n75
W v Westminster City Council and others [2005] 1 FCR 39 105n187
Wagon Mound (No. 1) [1961] AC 388 157n191
Wainwright v Home Office [2003] 3 WLR 1137 87n83
Ward v Leeds Teaching Hospitals NHS Trust [2004] EWHC 2106 162n219
Watt v Hertfordshire CC [1954] 2 All ER 368 148n125
Watt v Rama [1972] VR 353 167n255
Weiss v Solomon (1989) Carswell Que 72 200n154
White v Chief Constable of South Yorkshire Police [1999] 2 AC 455 141n66, 141n68
Whitehouse v Jordan [1981] 1 All ER 267 143n84
Whitehouse v Jordan [1981] 1 WLR 246 146n112
Wilsher v Essex AHA [1986] 3 All ER 801 147n123
Wilsher v Essex AHA [1987] QB 730 148n125
Wilsher v Essex AHA [1988] AC 1074 152–3
Wood v Thurston, The Times, 25 May 1951 148n127
Woolgar v Chief Constable of Sussex Police [1999] 3 All ER 604 98
Wyatt and another v Portsmouth Hospital NHS Trust and another [2005] EWCA Civ 1181 58n25, 64–5, 69n103

X v Y [1988] 2 All ER 649 100–101

YL v Birmingham City Council and others (Secretary of State for Constitutional Affairs intervening) [2008] 1 AC 95 129n106

Z v Finland (1998) 25 EHRR 371 77n11, 88
Z v UK (2002) 34 EHRR 97 142n74

Chapter 1
The Importance of Protecting and Empowering Children

Introduction

At a time when the media is full of stories about children having too much power and that parents should exercise more control,[1] it may seem counter-intuitive to propose that children should have greater recognition of their human rights in the paediatric health care setting[2], as an overarching theme of this book. The reality is that even mature children have limited opportunities to exercise their rights appropriately[3] and my argument is that we have become too protective of the younger age group.[4] There appears to be a widespread feeling in young people that they are not respected by adults because their participatory rights are insufficiently recognized.[5] To adopt the position advocated here would address some of these concerns. To listen and respond to children's views, and encourage their involvement in decision-making, will make them feel more respected and facilitate a sense of responsibility.[6] The law has a crucial role here. As James[7] notes:

---

1   E.g. Marrin, M., 'You won't stop violent children now, minister', *The Sunday Times*, 17 February 2008 (http://www.timesonline.co.uk/tol/comment/columnists/minette_marrin/article3382270.ece).

2   The paediatric setting generally deals with children aged 16 and below. Exceptionally, health care for older children may be offered where an immediate transition to adult services is not possible and/or advisable. Some care, e.g. mental health services, may be extended to a wider age group in due course. Mental health provision is beyond the scope of this book

3   See the discussion in Chapters 2 and 9 with regard to self-regarding and other-regarding decision-making in the health care setting respectively.

4   See e.g. Alderson, P., *Young Children's Rights: Exploring Beliefs, Principles and Practice*, London, Jessica Kingsley Publishers, 2008.

5   E.g. this was the conclusion of the Children's Right Alliance's Report to the United Nations Convention on the Rights of the Child presented on 11 June 2008 in Geneva: 'Get Ready for Change: Being a Children's Right Champion', Children's Rights and Participation Conference, Centre for Applied Human Rights, University of York, 1 July 2008 and www.getreadyforgeneva.org.uk.

6   Ibid. *and* Koller, D., '"Making a Difference": Youth Participation in Education and Health Care' presentation at the University of Sheffield, Centre for the Study of Childhood and Youth: 'Childhood and Youth: Choice and Participation' International Conference, 2006.

7   James, A., 'Responsibility, Children and Childhood', in Bridgeman, J., Keating, H. and Lind, C., (eds) *Responsibility, Law and the Family*, Aldershot, Ashgate, 2008.

... law [is] the key mechanism through which social structures (including the social space of childhood) and social practices (including the day-to-day interactions between adults and children that constitute the lived experience of childhood) are linked ... law not only incorporates the principles on which social structures are founded, it also provides the means through which relationships between the State and citizens are ordered and conducted' which .. includes the issues of rights and responsibilities.[8]

Some may believe that raising the issue of children's rights can lead to a sterile debate[9] and that such an approach fails to protect their welfare interests adequately.[10] I contend that the use of human rights language can lead to a change for the better[11] and that human rights frameworks allow a full consideration of all relevant interests, including the need to protect children where appropriate. Of course, establishing where the balance should lie when taking account of a range of interests can be challenging. This book offers some suggestions as to where that might be and emphasizes the significance of the process by which decisions are reached. These propositions should interest both lawyers and health professionals.

Lawyers should note that some chapters will be more relevant to health professionals who wish to access an exposition of the law in certain key areas as it affects children in the health care setting. Indeed, the content of the chapters has been determined with the expressed wishes of paediatric health professionals in mind. Some base-line knowledge of the law and legal systems is assumed on the part of health professionals.[12] All the areas addressed raise questions that are not always clearly answered by the law for reasons that will become apparent. However, there are some topics that require particular attention, and concern lawyers and health professionals alike. The house style of using non-specific pronouns should be noted.

The law plays a part in every aspect of clinical practice. Claims for medical malpractice are of great concern to all health professionals. These perhaps matter more to doctors because they usually carry ultimate responsibility for clinical

---

8   Ibid. at pp. 149–50.

9   Williams, R., Chief Executive Officer of 11 Million (formerly the Office of the Children's Commissioner), 'Key Participation Issues', Children's Rights and Participation Conference, Centre for Applied Human Rights, University of York, 1 July 2008.

10   See e.g. Herring, J., 'The Human Rights Act 1998 and the welfare principle in family law – conflicting or complementary?' (1999) 11 *Child and Family Law Quarterly* at p. 233–43.

11   See further in Chapters 2 and 8 in particular.

12   A useful introductory and comprehensive text, if needed, may be found in Brazier, M. and Cave, E., *Medicine, Patients and the Law*, (4th ed.), London, Penguin Books, 2007.

decisions, hence the predominance of doctors in oft-cited cases.[13] However, other ethico-legal issues are also likely to tax them throughout their careers. The rapid pace of development in medical science continues unabated and it becomes necessary to re-visit longstanding moral dilemmas of. The climate in which health professionals work is also changing. Partly encouraged by Government initiatives and partly fuelled by disillusionment with the health professions, patients have become more demanding. Health professionals often feel under siege with increasing demands from Government and patients[14] at a time when they are subject to unprecedented criticism following high profile scandals.[15] The prevalence of human rights discourse helps to stimulate such an environment. Patients want to be more involved in the decision-making about their care. The extent to which they can do this is, in the final analysis, determined by the parameters of the law.[16] This is not as clear-cut as it sounds. The regulation of health care practice as a whole is derived from a range of domestic and European instruments. For our purposes, the complex interplay between statute, case law, professional guidance and, in some cases, European Union law and European Conventions in relation to the provision of health care to children, also needs to be noted.

Health care law rarely provides a definitive guide to good clinical practice. While some law does provide very detailed reflections,[17] much is left to clinical judgment. Traditionally, politicians have been wary of association with ethically-charged legislation and have preferred to leave guidance in the hands of the judges and professional and statutory bodies, although this is less in evidence now.[18] Even where there are legislative provisions, these tend to provide a framework that requires supplementary guidance in the form of codes of practice. They still require statutory interpretation where there is a lack of clarity or an omission. The law cannot anticipate every situation that might arise and health professionals are likely to have a breadth of knowledge not at the courts' disposal. Nevertheless,

---

13   It should be noted that, although the cases invariably refer to doctors because they are ultimately responsible for clinical decisions made, the principles may be extrapolated to all health professionals.

14   See e.g. the Foundation Trusts' governance structure discussed in Chapter 8 which holds Trusts increasingly to account.

15   See e.g. 'The Report of the Public Inquiry into Children's Heart Surgery at the Bristol Royal Infirmary 1984–95: Learning from Bristol', (Cmnd 5207 (1)) 2001 (the Bristol Inquiry).

16   See *Bolitho (Deceased) v City and Hackney HA* [1998] 4 AC 232, discussed in Chapter 6, where the courts reserve the right to determine standards in the final analysis.

17   See e.g. the Mental Capacity Act 2005 and its accompanying Code of Practice on the steps to be taken to enable decision-making, *R (Axon) v Secretary of State for Health (Family Planning Association intervening)* [2006] EWHC 37 (Admin) and Silber J's exploration of the nature of the mature minor's autonomous interests, discussed in Chapter 2.

18   See e.g. the Human Fertilisation and Embryology Act 1990, the Human Tissue Act 2004 and the Mental Capacity Act 2005.

health professionals need to employ rigorous reasoning when presented with an ethical dilemma that may result in a legal challenge despite their best endeavours. Any decisions will need to be justifiable before the law if they wish their decision to receive judicial support. However, would it be expected that ethical decisions have a 'right' answer? There are contrasting ethical views here[19] but, in my opinion, courts are unlikely to castigate those responsible for decisions made in good faith: they have an understanding of the difficult environment in which health professionals work. Indeed, judges often believe ethical dilemmas are of such magnitude that they should be for Parliament to determine.[20] Nevertheless, where there is any doubt as to the legality of a proposed course of action, it will be necessary, and in some cases mandatory, to seek judicial clarification.

Health professionals will easily recognize that their clinical practice raises issues of fundamental ethical importance: it deals with the nature of life from its very beginning until its end. The law and professional ethical guidance present a potentially bewildering array of sources for the health professional grappling with the ethical challenges they face in everyday practice. This can be even more the case in the paediatric setting. I hope this book will highlight some of the key concerns of health professionals who work with children and illustrate how these might be approached. As a legal academic, I am particularly interested in how medical law and ethics may be used to further the interests of children. In examining the law, it is clear its foundations are derived from deontological ethical perspectives with their focus on the rights and duties of individuals. As far as children are concerned, the focus of modern law and policy has been one of protection. This is partly as a response to historical and more current abuse[21] as well as recognizing that children lack adult capacities at certain stages of their development. While entirely understandable, this has arguably been at the expense of children's interests, especially that of having their autonomy acknowledged appropriately in light of persuasive empirical evidence suggesting that children

---

19   Harris, J., *The Value of Life*, London, Routledge, 1992 takes the view that it is possible to produce the 'right' answer ethically; *cf.* Maclean, A., *The Elimination of Morality*, London, Routledge, 1993, who disputes this believing that philosophical positions merely represent an opinion.

20   See, for example, *Airedale NHS Trust v Bland* [1993] AC789 at 880 per Lord Browne-Wilkinson although Hoffman LJ at 825 noted that '[t]he decision of the court should be able to carry conviction with the ordinary person as being based not merely on legal precedent but also upon acceptable ethical values'. See also *Re A (children) (conjoined twins: surgical separation)* [2001] Fam 147, *per* Ward LJ, where despite his comments that the 'court is a court of law, not of morals' (at 155), he explicitly acknowledges the need to grapple with 'irreconcilable conflicts of moral and ethical values' (at 151).

21   See e.g. Fortin, J., *Children's Rights and the Developing Law*, (2nd ed.) London, Butterworths, 2003, Chapter 15, and the discussion in Chapter 7 in this book on unethical research in children.

are more capable than traditionally thought.[22] The nature of these interests will be explored in the following chapter.

I am a strong advocate for the promotion of children's autonomy and for the freedom for them to exercise this. However, I recognize that this needs to be fettered in some circumstances: some children lack the capacity for autonomy. This constraint may be needed to protect children when they lack competence. There is a need to ensure children's welfare is promoted and maintained, hence the requirement for those caring for children, be they family members or health professionals, to act in their best interests.[23] However, potential restrictions also apply to those children who do have the capacity. A protective stance gradually needs to give way by allowing children to determine what happens to them on their journey to competent adulthood. They need to acquire knowledge and experience life. This 'empowers' children:

> The concept of empowerment simply serves to bring out the fact that many people do not have autonomy or the ability to adequately make choices and determine their own lives. People must therefore be enabled and encouraged to develop autonomy – they must in a word be 'empowered'.[24]

True well-being, or a flourishing human life, will require a measure of control over one's life and being able to develop one's talents. This can be achieved by acquiring life skills and achieving autonomy.[25] Self-determination, self-government, sense of responsibility and sense of development are overlapping aspects of autonomy. The individual cannot be seen as an abstraction from the socio-political context or from their relationships with others.[26] However, autonomy is an ideal towards which we should strive for optimal functioning.[27] On this basis, children must be empowered to make their own decisions, within certain parameters, and accept the consequences of those decisions. Ideal empowerment is a '... process of trusting, affirming and building self-esteem in children'.[28] This '... should make them feel dignified, confident, affirmed respected and admired'.[29] The rationale for

---

22   Discussed in Chapters 2 and 8 in particular.

23   See e.g. *Gillick v West Norfolk and Wisbech Area Health Authority* [1986] AC 112 at 127.

24   Downie, R.S., Fyffe, C. and Tannehill, A., *Health Promotion: Model and Values*, Oxford, Oxford University Press, 1990 at p. 3.

25   Ibid. at pp. 18–19.

26   As will be explained in Chapters 5 and 7 in particular.

27   Ibid. at pp. 138–9.

28   Hymas, J.L., 'Do Children Have Rights?' citing Cullen, S., *Empowering Children*, (1999) www.congcreator.com/ifcw99/cullen2.htm at www.nhsexposed.com/patients/child health/childrights.shtml.

29   Ibid.

this position and how it may be achieved are key themes of this book. We have some way yet to go in order to achieve this standard.[30]

In the paediatric setting there is an increased tendency to focus on the child as an individual with rights independent from those of their family. To what extent these rights should be acknowledged can be very problematic. Health professionals are keenly aware of the tension between the natural inclination to safeguard children's interests so that they may enjoy the best life possible in the future and respecting a child's autonomy which is also a relevant interest. Determining the scope of that respect is very difficult. A stark example of this can be found in the case of older children who suffer from debilitating, chronic conditions. Those caring for them are often struck by the level of mature insight this experience can bring. Only they fully know the effects of their condition and what it means for them. They have a unique perspective. Assuming all efforts have been made to explore a range of options with them, allowing that child to decide they no longer wish to receive even life-saving treatment may be entirely legitimate. That is not to advocate a cavalier approach to such situations but one that is considered as a possibility. It is my belief that a human rights approach can establish the parameters of autonomy to the extent that this is possible. This is where my interests lie, partly fuelled by pragmatic reasoning. I believe we have a mechanism in the Human Rights Act 1998 (HRA), which largely incorporates the European Convention on Human Rights (ECHR),[31] to balance competing claims. For example, the qualified right to private and family life under Article 8(1) of the ECHR protects autonomy. Interference with this right is possible under Article 8(2), broadly in the interests of other individuals and society.[32] Where children are concerned, we must balance the child's right to autonomy with parental and societal interests in protecting that child.

As with competent adults, there may be a need to override autonomy in the interests of others. Apart from some public health measures, the law rarely considers wider interests and this emphasis should change in some circumstances. It has been said that appealing to rights is unduly confrontational and does not form a sound basis for relationships between parents and their children[33] nor between health professionals and patients.[34] In the latter case, it is said that the relationship should be characterized by respect and trust[35] with an acknowledgement that each

---

30   See e.g. UK *Children's Commissioners' Report to the UN Committee on the Rights of the Child*, 2008 at p. 10 with respect to the participatory rights of children.

31   See Schedule 1.

32   See the discussion in Chapters 2, 3, 4, 5 and 7 in particular.

33   Bridgeman, J., *Parental Responsibility, Young Children and Healthcare Law*, Cambridge, Cambridge University Press, 2007, *passim*.

34   Mason, J.K. and Laurie, G.T., *Law and Medical Ethics*, (7th ed.), Oxford, Oxford University Press, 2006 at p. 28.

35   Ibid.

party has an obligation to work towards the ideal.[36] This concern is understandable and the suggested approach has force, particularly where adult patients are concerned. However, the current position of children requires the use of rights language to ensure that their interests are not neglected, partially or otherwise. Whether discussions about rights is constructive or not will depend partly on the skill of those involved. The key point is that the HRA allows a full consideration of everyone's interests including those of the child in their familial and wider social networks. To ignore the ambiguities and uncertainties that characterize social relations in ethical debate will result in unworkable and, possibly, unethical decisions. Reality tells us that problems cannot be reduced to a focus on the individual. Life is much richer, more interesting and messier than that. Health practitioners recognize that treating the child can be a family experience, indeed, the family can be the 'patient'.[37] Relatives are ultimately responsible for caring for the child.[38] As a living instrument, the HRA is also sufficiently flexible to extend the law in accordance with evolving social mores. In light of evidence that children are more capable than we usually give them credit for,[39] the concept of autonomy as it pertains to children does require further development. I intend to demonstrate this throughout the book.

With this book, I wish to offer a source of law and a version of ethics as it relates to children for legal academics and health practitioners alike. While I hope my coverage of relevant law is comprehensive, I will not attempt to provide an exhaustive account of ethical approaches to the issues raised. This is more than adequately dealt with elsewhere.[40] Health professionals are keen to ensure that they are engaged in the highest possible standards of clinical practice because they are driven by strong personal ethical codes. It might be suggested that a health professional's intuition will suffice when a difficult ethical dilemma is presented. However, the role of intuition is often viewed with suspicion not least because some people may be able to justify abhorrent actions on this basis: they believe their unsound intuitions to be right. Most ethicists prefer reasoning and rational thought to form the basis of establishing principles to guide action. Health professionals and scientists are often in despair with intuitive thinking when it manifests itself in the form of the so-called 'yuk' factor prevalent in a range of newspapers when scientific developments are highlighted. A lack of rigorous and rational reasoning

---

36   Ibid., noting Lord Donaldson's remarks in *Re J (a minor) (medical treatment)* [1992] 2 FLR 165 at 172.

37   See the discussion in Chapter 5 especially nn. 84*ff.*

38   See e.g. *Re T (wardship: medical treatment)* [1997] 1 WLR 242 and *R v Portsmouth Hospitals NHS Trust ex parte Glass* [1999] 2 FLR 905 where the importance of the family was explicitly addressed. These cases are discussed further in Chapter 3.

39   See the discussion in Chapters 2 and 7 in particular.

40   See e.g. Gillon, R., *Philosophical Medical Ethics*, Chichester, Wiley Medical Publications, 1986 and Hope, T., Savulescu, J. and Hendrick, J., *Medical Ethics and Law: The Core Curriculum* , (2nd ed.), Oxford, Churchill Livingstone Elsevier, 2008.

has been very evident in media discussions about the use of hybrid embryos for research purposes.[41] Some commentators argue that this phenomenon has a sound anthropological basis.[42] Others propose that it arises more as a function of social conditioning.[43] Intuition *can* constitute a significant obstacle for proper debate. Nevertheless, account must be taken of such responses. Health professionals want guidance that is intuitively correct and accords with their manner of dealing with problems in everyday practice that require speedy resolution. It is highly likely that intuition actually consists of the experience of developing a moral code throughout life whether this has involved an explicit discussion of philosophical perspectives or not. As Mason and Laurie[44] point out:

> Intuitions may point in the direction of a value which may not always be articulated formally but which may none the less be very important.'[45]

Understandably, there may be resistance to examining closely one's belief system which may be thought adequate for the task of effecting clinical decision-making. It is challenging both intellectually and emotionally but, arguably, 'an unexamined reason is no reason at all'.[46] As Woods[47] argues, in considering ethical dilemmas, it is necessary to adopt a reflexive and deliberative approach to the morally relevant features that ought to be taken into account. Of course, it would be impractical to subject every morally significant action to a process of deliberation. This is required only when there is a challenge to our personal or collective 'customs' or when our 'moral habits'[48] leave us ill-equipped to deal with a new situation. Moral habits can be improved through 'moral' education. [49] Reflective deliberation enables the individual to map the moral domain, establish the 'givens' of moral action and provide skills that help to make them habitually sensitive to the interests of others. This is a process that can be carried out individually, or collectively, on an ongoing basis to improve moral understanding. The validity of this approach can be assessed by:

---

41   See e.g. the debate during the progress of the Human Fertilisation and Embryology Bill 2008: Rees-Mogg, W., 'Human Fertilisation and Embryology Bill: whatever happened to the 'yuk' factor?', *The* Times, 24 March 2008.

42   See e.g. Douglas, M., *Purity and Danger: an analysis of the concepts of pollution and taboo*, London, Routledge, 1991.

43   See the discussion in Nussbaum, M., 'Danger to Human Dignity: the Revival of Disgust and Shame in the Law': http://chronicle.com/free/v50/i48/48b00601.htm.

44   Mason and Laurie, *supra*, n. 33.

45   Ibid., at p. 10.

46   See Pattinson, S.D., *Medical Law and Ethics*, London, Sweet and Maxwell, 2006 at p. 3.

47   See e.g. Woods, S., *Death's Dominion: Ethics at the End of Life*, Berkshire, Open University Press: McGraw-Hill Education, 2007.

48   See ibid., Chapter 1 for a fuller account of this concept.

49   Ibid.

... the robustness of our arguments but also to the way in which this new understanding coheres with the rest of moral knowledge, can be incorporated into our moral practices, and accommodated by our social institutions. The judgment that leads us to accept a new understanding of a moral practice does not follow from an abstract moral theory, but from our knowledge of harm and suffering and how to respond to it, it is the practices which give substance to our moral concepts and not the reverse.[50]

Where this reflective deliberation requires relevant sources of information, in my experience, health professionals in the paediatric setting struggle to find accessible material. They often want to consider legal and ethical issues that concern them in a way that appreciates the realities of the context in which they work. I hope that my experience in the NHS adds to this perspective.

I also want to indicate how I think any assertion of rights should be evaluated. I share the belief that the best decision-making in non-routine cases involves as many relevant people as possible each providing their own expertise, experience and ethical standpoint. In the clinical setting, contentious or otherwise difficult decisions should not be made only by the senior doctor in charge even though this satisfies legal requirements. This would be too restricted. To imply that one individual has the breadth of knowledge and experience to be able to consider all relevant factors in making difficult ethical decisions would be arrogance. It could also be emotionally burdensome for that individual. Team decision-making, involving the patient and family as much as possible should be routine where ethical or legal challenges are presented. This will usually mean that problems can be resolved at the local level.

The following provides an outline of the remaining chapters. Where these are more relevant for health professionals than for lawyers, this will be indicated.

Chapter 2: The Law and Children's Autonomy

Chapter 2 offers an account of children's interests, the part autonomy plays in these, and how the law can progress the autonomous interests of children. The chapter will address the particular issues raised by mature minors. It sets out the current legal position with respect to the boundaries of decision-making for competent children noting some recent developments under the HRA. As it does so, it will begin to raise some of the concerns expressed about judicial decisions, recent statutory developments and aspects of clinical practice. A particular feature here will be the noting of the cautious approach taken in assessing children's competence and how this might be further challenged under the HRA. The ability of a child to make very significant decisions such as refusing life-saving interventions will be explored in relation to this point.

---

50   Ibid. at p. 2.

Chapter 3: Parental Responsibility and Medical Decision-making

Where children are not legally competent, parents act as their proxy decision-makers. Whether younger children still possess any right to autonomy and, if so, the extent of its scope, are questions that will be explored in this chapter. The fact that those with parental responsibility must act in a child's best interests is a well-established legal principle. The chapter will discuss the circumstances in which parents may determine these without judicial intervention or authorization. In practice, opinions as to what constitutes best interests will coincide with the health care team. The resolution of disagreements between parents and health professionals will be addressed in some detail given the prevalence of these and the consequent concern amongst the professions. The chapter will provide an overview of the current legal position, set out how challenges to this might be presented and how parental responsibility should be exercised. Also, in the light of the various reports on the organ retention scandals[51] that took place throughout the UK, the key role parents now have in the decision-making process regarding the use of human material of their deceased children will be presented.

Chapter 4: Confidentiality and Children

The inherent tension between the interests of individuals and those of others is particularly apparent in the case of children. There is potential conflict between empowering children by treating them as autonomous individuals who have rights of confidentiality, and the need to protect them from harm. Where the line should be drawn between respecting rights to confidentiality and disclosure is one of the questions this chapter will address. The chapter will set out the common law duty of confidence as well as statutory provisions affecting confidentiality towards children. There is a real desire on the part of health professionals to respect duties of confidentiality when dealing with minors. However, difficult dilemmas often arise in relation to parents wishing to be involved in the health care decisions affecting their child when this may not always be appropriate. Health professionals may also be presented with suspected child abuse and this creates a great deal of anxiety. They can be reassured by suggestions as to the approach that should be adopted. Legal and ethical guidance, as well as appropriate processes, provide the means by which decisions can be made. The section dealing with permitted disclosures will be of assistance here. This also highlights a forthcoming case which may re-draw the scope of a doctor's duty of confidentiality with respect to third parties. A general discussion of the legal and ethical obligations with respect

---

51   The Bristol Inquiry, *supra*, n. 14 and *The Royal Liverpool Children's Inquiry Report*, HC 12-11, 2001, (the 'Alder Hey Report'). Of course, organ retention also involved adult human material but it was the removal and storage of children's tissues and organs that proved to be the most emotive.

to confidentiality is provided as the context for this discussion and necessitates a discussion of key adult cases. The chapter as a whole highlights the particular issues that arise for those dealing with children in the healthcare setting.

Chapter 5: Genetic Testing and Counselling: the Paradigm Case for Family Medicine?

Genetic testing and counselling provide key examples of when it may be legitimate to interfere with individuals' autonomy, including that of children, in the interests of others. Not only may disclosure of confidential information protect children from harm but it may also serve the interests of others in some circumstances. The third party perspective with respect to disclosure of genetic information is introduced because it has a particular resonance in relation to child and family services. The chapter discusses whether the particular issues raised by genetic information may be legitimately addressed by treating the family as 'the patient'. On the one hand genetic information may be seen in the same way as any other health information and dealt with accordingly. Alternatively, it may be viewed as a particular case and provide a useful example of when it might be acceptable to override individual autonomy. The chapter provides a theoretical framework that may be used to justify such an interference with autonomy. An assessment is made as to whether traditional legal approaches to disclosure are sufficient for this task.

Chapter 6: Negligence and Complaints

The prospect of a negligence action or a complaint being mounted against them fills most health professionals with horror. While the purpose of the chapter is not to provide a definitive guide to negligence actions, it will attempt to give a reasonably detailed overview. It will do this by setting out the elements that need to be established for a successful action in negligence focusing on the issues that have particular relevance for the paediatric health practitioner. The section on breach is especially pertinent in this regard. Inevitably, a discussion of key cases involving adults will be necessary to establish general principles of law before noting their application to children. While the chapter is more technical than the others, good clinical practice is not just about adopting professionally accepted standards and being competent to avoid litigation and complaints. It also entails ethical considerations. The need for informed consent is germane to this point. The proposed reforms to the compensation system will also be addressed together with an assessment of how the HRA has had an impact on the area.

Chapter 7: Children in Research

Whilst the legal principles governing this area will be addressed in the preceding chapters, this topic is worth highlighting as a stand-alone chapter because of its complex and controversial nature. The area is governed by myriad laws and ethical guidance. Given their inherent vulnerability as a research participant, there is a great deal of concern from many quarters that children are only used appropriately. This chapter will consider the extent to which children should be allowed to decide whether to participate in research, whether there should be an expectation that children *should* be engaged as research participants and if it is ever permissible to override their autonomy in the interests of others.

Chapter 8: Children's Participation and Foundation Trusts: Some New Opportunities?

This chapter addresses the right of children to be involved in policy formulation. The topic would not normally be included in a medical law and ethics book but I believe that it is legitimate to do so because it is another means by which children can be empowered in the health care setting. Children's wider, other-regarding decision-making enhances their competence and aids the citizenship agenda more generally. This supports the ideas propounded in the previous chapter. Such engagement is becoming increasingly possible. This is as a result of policy changes, some new NHS structures and evolving legal frameworks. These developments are long overdue and represent some recognition of children's participatory rights as advocated under the UNCRC. However, it will be proposed that more needs to be done not least because of the remaining wide 'deficit' in relation to children's participation. This chapter will set out how young people can be engaged in relevant processes and the benefits this will bring.

Chapter 9: Concluding Remarks

Here, there will be a summary of the key points arising from the preceding chapters together with suggestions as to how medical law and ethics can take forward the issue of children's empowerment and protection. It will argue that any hostility to the human rights approach that is advocated throughout the book is misplaced. A human rights approach is ideally placed to ensure everyone's interests are given sufficient recognition and that children's welfare is not sacrificed as a result of any balancing exercise. That is not to suggest that other theories, or more pragmatic approaches, have no place in ethical debate in the health care setting. What is required is a framework for discussion that ensures a level of rigour in decision-making, rendering it more justifiable by giving children's interests predominance where appropriate.

Chapter 2
The Law and Children's Autonomy

Introduction

It is imperative that the law adheres to a strong notion of children's right to autonomy. That is not to say that children's rights to have their decisions fulfilled should be unfettered. However, a presumption of autonomy will help to redress the current imbalance in the way mature children in particular are dealt with when decisions are made in the health care setting. When competent, children have the right to more than mere consultation about their views. Strong statements of this legal principle are essential in the light of increasing recognition of children's rights and persuasive empirical evidence that children are more capable of making decisions than is generally thought to be the case: they can understand the implications of what they are deciding.[1] The ability of a child to make very significant decisions such as refusing life-saving interventions will be explored in relation to this point. Unfortunately, practice remains inconsistent and incoherent with conservative assessments of children's ability to be involved in decisions about their medical treatment remaining the norm.[2] Of course, problems only arise

---

1   See e.g. Chesney, M., Lindeke, L., Johnson, L., Jukkala A. and Lynch, S., 'Comparison of child and parent satisfaction ratings of ambulatory pediatric subspecialty care' (2005) 19(4) *Journal of Pediatric Health Care* 221–9, Alderson, P., 'In the genes or in the stars?' (1992) 18(3) *Journal of Medical Ethics* at 119–124, Alderson, P., *Children's Consent to Surgery*, Buckingham, OUP, 1993, Eiser, C., 'Changes in understanding of illness as the child grows' (1985) 60 *Archives of Disease in Childhood* 489–492, Fielding, D. and Duff, A., 'Compliance with treatment protocol: interventions for children with chronic illness' (1999) 80 *Archives of Disease in Childhood* 196–200, Alderson, P. and Montgomery, J., 'What about me?' (1996) *Health Service Journal* April 22–24, Hammond, L., *Children's Decisions in Health Care and Research*, London, Institute of Education, 1993, Brook, G., 'Children's competency to consent: a framework for practice' (2000) 12(5) *Paediatric Nursing* 31; Curtis, K., Liabo, K., Roberts, H. and Barker, M., 'Consulted but not heard: a qualitative study of young people's views of their local health service' (2004) 7(2) *Health Expectations* 149–156 and Sutcliffe, A., Alderson, P. and Curtis, K., *Children as Partners in Their Diabetes Care*, London, SSRU, Institute of Education, University of London, 2004: http://eppi.ioe.ac.uk/ssru_docs/DiabetesReportFinal.pdf, Elliott, E. and Watson, A., 'But the doctors aren't your mum', (1997) 30 *Health Matters* 8–9.

2   Alderson, P. and Montgomery, J., *Health Care Choices: Making Decisions with Children*, London, IPPR, 1996, discovered this to be the case based on a 1993 research project generally and more recent evidence suggests this is still so: BMA working party on children's consent, http://www.bma.org.uk/ap.nsf/Content/consenttk2. This seems

when there is disagreement about the course of action to be adopted. There is anecdotal and other evidence that where parents and health professionals agree with a child who does not wish to receive even life-saving treatment, the child's decision is allowed to stand.[3] It is only when there is no such concurrence that the courts will have to decide whose opinion should prevail. It is likely that, in some cases, treatment goes ahead against a competent child's wishes because of the current attitude of the judiciary. It will be suggested here why such acquiescence should be opposed.

This chapter will first explore a realistic version of autonomy that can recognize the position of children before addressing whether they have a *right* to have this respected. It will then explore the current legal status of mature minors' decision-making to establish whether the law has fulfilled its potential in recognizing their autonomous interests.

The Nature of Autonomy

Rights are important because they enable claims by persons to be treated as dignified subjects of respect on the ground of desert rather than relying on the whim of others to act benevolently.[4] One theory of human rights requires the treatment of persons as equals and entails respect for an individual's autonomy

---

to be the case even in specialist children's settings: see Healthcare Commission's *State of Healthcare*, 2007 at p. 71 and personal communication from Dr J. Wales, Consultant Paediatrician, Sheffield Children's NHS Foundation Trust.

3   Contact with a range of health professionals across the UK over the last 20 years indicates that there is significant anecdotal evidence that some mature minors are allowed to refuse life-saving treatment in agreement with their parents and the medical team treating them. See also 'Tributes paid as Joanne, 19, dies after refusing double transplant', *Northern Echo*, 5 March 2007, which publicizes how Joanne Vincent was allowed to refuse a life-saving heart-lung transplant at the age of 12 years because she wished to enjoy the time she had left with her family. A similar scenario has been described in de Bruxelles, S., 'Girl wins fight to turn down transplant', *The Times*, 11 November, 2008 about a 13 year-old-girl, Hannah Jones. These cases are supported by the comments in Jackson, E., *Medical Law: Texts, Cases and Materials*, Oxford, Oxford University Press, 2006 at p. 247. Of course, this type of agreement means that the matter does not need judicial resolution but may give a more balanced picture of actual practice. Great Ormond Street Hospital has a policy of not proceeding with transplantation without the agreement of the potential child recipient even where they are as young as ten-years-old: 'Will I still love my mum?', Channel 4, 3 August 2005 and 'Do we need the child's consent?', *The Times*, 27 July 2005. However, as the discussion below will demonstrate, the autonomy of the mature minor is not always this protected. What is needed is *consistent* protection where the necessary conditions for autonomy are present.

4   Feinberg, J., 'Duties, Rights and Claims', (1966) 3(2) *American Philosophical Quarterly* 1 at p. 8.

or rather their capacity for it.[5] Autonomy has become the predominant concept in the biomedical context now prevailing over notions of paternalism, particularly in health care.[6] The concept is often presented as being self-evident in its meaning but can carry different emphases.[7] For example:

> As Kant argued, moral autonomy is a combination of freedom and responsibility; it is a submission to laws that one has made for oneself. The autonomous man, insofar as he is autonomous, is not subject to the will of another.[8]

Dworkin[9] believes that attempts to define such a complex concept as autonomy would undermine its usefulness and prefers instead to characterize the notion. A satisfactory theory of autonomy for him is one that can fulfil several criteria. The theory should be logically consistent, an empirical possibility and be capable of explaining why the state of autonomy has been seen as a desirable state of affairs that is, possessing value conditions. In addition, it must be ideologically neutral in that it holds some value for different ideological perspectives and have normative relevance in that it makes philosophical uses of the concept intelligible. Finally, the notion should be in general accord with judgments that are made about autonomy such as those of an empirical nature that suggest its promotion in adults is best served by allowing increasing levels of autonomy in children. In developing his theory, Dworkin recognizes that issues such as the justification for political institutions, how non-political institutions of a society affects its members' values and ideas of equal respect have to be taken into account. It should already be becoming clear that any proposal about an individual's self-determination is going to be constrained by these influences.

In sum, Dworkin[10] conceives autonomy as a second-order capacity of persons to reflect critically upon their first-order preferences and the ability to accept or attempt to change these in light of higher-order preferences and values:

---

5 Freeman, M., *The Rights and Wrongs of Children* (London: Pinter, 1983) at p. 54.

6 See, e.g. Laurie, G.T., *Genetic Privacy: A Challenge to Medico-legal Norms*, Cambridge, Cambridge University Press, 2004 at p. 194. Beauchamp, T.L. and Childress, C.F., *Principles of Biomedical Ethics*, (5th ed.), Oxford, Oxford University Press, 2001 at p. 177.

7 Dworkin, G., *The Theory and Practice of Autonomy*, Cambridge, Cambridge University Press, 1988 at p. 6 where he lists the broad range of meanings attributed to autonomy.

8 Wolff, R.B., *In Defense of Anarchism*, New York, Harper & Row, 1970 at p. 14 cited in Dworkin, ibid., at p. 5. Kant speaks to persons being rational in the decisions that they make but this is not what the law in England and Wales requires for competence: see e.g. *Re T (adult: refusal of medical treatment)* (1993) Fam. 95, *per* Lord Donaldson at 102.

9 *Supra*, n. 7 at pp. 7–9.

10 Ibid., at p. 20.

By exercising such a capacity, persons define their nature, give meaning and coherence to their lives, and take responsibility for the kind of person they are.[11]

He sees these higher-order preferences and values arising as a result of the crucial feature of persons to be able to reflect upon and adopt attitudes toward their first-order preferences.[12] So, for example, a person might identify with the influences that motivate them at a first-order preference level and be happy to assimilate these into their sense of self. Equally, there may be resentment that they are motivated in certain ways and, upon reflection, seek to be influenced in different ways.

Dworkin's account of autonomy requires procedural independence, a state that promotes and improves reflective and critical faculties, but no particular substantive content. He notes how all moral theories have some idea of treating others as equal in certain ways to oneself, that actions require moral justification and that what we do must reflect the preferences of those who are affected by what we do. In addition, these theories accept that some element of choice exists under conditions of procedural independence so that, for example, each person is seen as the best judge of their own interests.[13] He believes that inherent in these common assumptions is a shared conception that a person consists of their life-plans and that by pursuing autonomy, the person gives meaning to their life. This will not be the same for everyone so autonomy cannot have substantive content. In their ability to define themselves, all deserve moral respect although this may be subject to a threshold.[14] Determining where this threshold should lie is the challenge in paediatric medical decision-making.

Dworkin's theory of autonomy is consistent with other important values including our attachment to others, a willingness to grant authority to the state to create the sort of society in which we wish to live and the sort of citizen we wish to be.[15] Here we have a version of autonomy that realistically sees the individual in their wider social context. To give autonomy undue pre-eminence would, for Dworkin, be 'intellectually imperialistic'.[16] For him, other concepts are both important and fundamental. His version of autonomy addresses some of the concern expressed, *inter alia*, by communitarian thinkers: that an undue focus on maximizing individual autonomy plays down the significance of the person as situated in a social and relational context.[17] Taylor's view, for example, is that

---

11   Ibid.
12   Ibid., at p. 15.
13   Ibid., at pp. 30–2.
14   Ibid., at p. 31.
15   Ibid., at p. 21–8.
16   Ibid., at p. 32.
17   See e.g. Mulhall, S. and Swift, A., *Liberals and Communitarians*, (2nd ed.), Oxford, Blackwell, 1997.

'some limits on self-determination are required to preserve the social conditions which enable self-determination'.[18] Perhaps the single most important extrinsic factor for autonomy is *relational*, in that the extent to which one can expect one's own autonomy to be respected is relative to the right and freedom of others to act autonomously. This implies that an individual's autonomy is enhanced by and dependent on others in that they may provide essential information or may manipulate the environment to that person's advantage or otherwise. Dworkin's approach to autonomy is helpful in the medical setting where it may be necessary to consider how the autonomous interests of individuals may have an impact on others.

It was claimed earlier that there should be a presumption of autonomy with respect to children to help address the lack of recognition that their autonomy tends to receive. What is the basis of this proposal?

Do Children Have a Right to Autonomy?

International instruments promoting children's rights put forward the view that part of a good upbringing involves encouraging children to develop a capacity for self-determination.[19] The United Nations Convention on the Rights of the Child 1989 (UNCRC) avers that children have human rights and attempts to disaggregate these from the rights of families and the state by ensuring they are seen as independent actors who should be given every opportunity to influence decisions. This position accords with the children's liberationists' view, which argues that children do have rights and are able to take greater responsibility for their lives than is traditionally the case. Whilst this is important for children's own sakes, developed societies do need children who, on achieving maturity, are equipped to implement skills of citizenship given the tasks they are expected to carry out as adults. This includes voting responsibly and engaging with the criminal justice system as jurors as well as being able to make important decisions about their own lives. Children need to be provided with opportunities to develop into autonomous adults by their parents and society more widely. This view does not necessarily entail that children have a right to *autonomy* and it may be disputed that the UNCRC rights are truly 'rights' at all: rights can be seen as merely claims to further children's needs.[20] They may be seen merely as rights to participate. Nevertheless, the wide ratification of the UNCRC suggests that states accept the idea that children possess rights that should be recognized and the language of rights is a useful rhetorical

---

18   Kymlicka, W., *Contemporary Political* Philosophy, Oxford, Oxford University Press, 2002 citing Taylor, C., 'Shared and Divergent Values', in Watts, R. and Brown, D. (eds), *Options for a New Canada*, Toronto, University of Toronto Press, 1991 at p. 216.

19   See, e.g. Articles 12, 13 and 14 of the United Nations Convention on the Rights of the Child.

20   See, for example, Feinberg, *supra*, n. 4.

device to ensure these claims are acknowledged and, all things being equal, met.[21] The use of rights discourse is also important because language can be seen as an important instrument of social change:[22] the more we talk about children's rights, the more society will attend to their interests in an appropriate manner along the lines suggested here.

There is a distinct lack of consensus about how to identify children's rights, how to balance these where they are in conflict with each other and where they diverge from the rights of others. It is important that the exercise to establish moral and legal principles is undertaken, not only to inform health professionals in the way they engage with children, but to give the law added credibility.

Feinberg[23] provides an example of the view that rights-holders need the ability to choose whether to exercise the right in question. A key objection to the idea of children having rights is their inability to implement such a choice where they lack capacity. An interest theory of rights can accommodate the idea that children have rights notwithstanding their lack of adult capacities. Such a theory, advocated amongst others by MacCormick,[24] holds that a person has rights where their interests are protected by

> ... (legal or moral) normative constraints on the acts or activities of other people with respect to the object of one's interest.[25]

Philosophical objections to the language of rights generally have been raised by commentators such as O'Neill. She argues, *inter alia*, that children are dependent on adults for the enforcement of any right, so she prefers the concept of the 'obligations' owed to them by others.[26] This would address some of the concerns raised about the lack of attention to the caring relationship between the child and

---

21   Ibid., at p.153.

22   Whorf, B.L., Language, thought and reality, (edited by Carroll, J.), Cambridge, Mass., MIT Press, 1956 at p. 252. Whorf was the most prominent, modern proponent of the idea that patterns of the language we use affects the configuration of our thought and thus our culture: our view of the world is determined by language. 'Weak determinism' whereby the influence of language on thought is recognized, remains persuasive: see, for example, Schlesinger, I.M., 'The wax and wane of Whorfian views' in *The Influence of Language on Culture and Thought*, Cooper, R.L. and Spolsky, B., (eds), New York, Mouton de Gruyter, 1991 at pp. 19–29.

23   Feinberg, *supra*, n. 4.

24   MacCormick, N., *Legal Right and Social Democracy: Essays in Legal and Political Theory*, Oxford, Clarendon Press, 1982.

25   Ibid.

26   O'Neill, O., 'Children's Rights and Children's Lives' in Alston, P., Parker, S. and Seymour, J., (eds) *Children Rights and the Law*, Oxford, Clarendon Press, 1992 at pp. 38–9.

its parents.[27] That said, we must be mindful of the fact that children's and parents' interests are not necessarily synonymous despite this apparent assumption within the Children Act 1989.[28] The Act does not even require parents to consult children aged over 12 years about major decisions in their lives, unlike their Scottish counterparts.[29] For MacCormick, enforcement is a separate issue that does not preclude the establishment of rights. In any event, the creation of the Children's Commissioners[30] in the UK has provided an opportunity to promote and protect children's rights. MacCormick's simple proposition that a moral right is 'a good of such importance that it would be wrong to deny it to or withhold it from any member of C (a given class)'[31] is helpful in its support for notions of children's rights, but determining which interests may become moral rights that then may be translated into legal rights is still challenging.

One way in which interests may become rights is Eekelaar's idea that a community should behave towards children as if they have rights (as is demanded by the UNCRC) and this will then define the rights children should have.[32] Eekelaar suggests a hierarchy of basic, developmental and autonomy interests.[33] The mechanism he proposed initially was to employ an adult's 'imaginative leap' to decide what children might have wanted retrospectively once they reach maturity. To avoid any distortion of children's interests by adult perceptions, he proposed that these should be only 'those benefits which the subject himself or herself might plausibly claim in themselves.'[34] From the child's perspective, an autonomy interest means

> ... the freedom to choose his own lifestyle and to enter social relations according to his own inclinations uncontrolled by the authority of the adult world, whether parents or institutions.[35]

---

27   See Bridgeman, J., *Parental Responsibility, Young Children and Healthcare Law*, Cambridge, Cambridge University Press, 2007 *passim* for an account of the importance of the parental perspective on a child's best interests.

28   Fortin, J., *Children's Rights and the Developing Law*, (2nd ed.) London, Butterworths, 2003 at p. 8.

29   See s. 6 Children (Scotland) Act 1995.

30   E.g. the English Children's Commissioner was established by the Children Act 2004. The Commissioner's capacity to promote children's rights is curtailed by, *inter alia*, resource constraints: see 11 MILLION Annual Report 2006–7.

31   MacCormick, *supra*, n. 24 at p. 160.

32   Eekelaar, J., *Regulating Divorce*, Oxford, Clarendon Press, 1991 at p. 103.

33   Eekelaar, J., 'The Emergence of Children's Rights' (1982) 6 *Oxford Journal of Legal Studies* 161 at pp. 170–71.

34   Ibid.

35   Ibid.

Such an interest includes 'that most dangerous but most precious of rights, the right to make [ones] own mistakes.'[36] Eekelaar subsequently developed this into a more sophisticated model to ensure children's interests in choice are promoted: a theory of 'dynamic self-determinism'.[37] This is intended to

> ... bring a child to the threshold of adulthood with the maximum opportunities to form and pursue life-goals which reflect as closely as possible an autonomous choice.[38]

This type of approach does not allow the child to make all decisions but that their wishes are a significant factor to be taken into account. Other classifications have been proposed[39] but, in practice, the balance to be struck between the child's need for protection vis-à-vis the importance of promoting their capacity for self-determination[40] will always be a consideration. Account must always be taken of the physical and mental differences between children and adults but these are not always accurately assessed.[41]

Feinberg[42] presents an important justification of the right to intervene in the lives of children for the sake of the child's future autonomy, their 'right to an open future':[43] where a child's decision or behaviour is such that it threatens his or her own future autonomy it represents sufficient grounds for intervention. Feinberg emphasizes that such measures can be regarded as means to hold the child's right in trust until such a time as the child reaches maturity and has the competence to exercise such a right. His concerns are with decisions that threaten the child's future autonomy in substantive ways, for example, by threatening future health; mental ability; affecting reproductive choice and so on.

In the light of Feinberg's disquiet, such measures seem proportionate. However, this kind of argument with regard to children is, in principle, problematic for liberals. This approach inevitably relies upon stipulating a demarcation between adult and child, since there is no fixed correlation between age and capacity for autonomy (particularly if one also takes context into account: for example, the child who is an experienced patient), but rather a loose, contingent relationship.

---

36   Ibid. at p. 182.

37   Eekelaar, J., 'The Interests of the Child and the Child's Wishes: The Role of Dynamic Self-Determinism' (1994) 8 *International Journal of Law and the Family* 42 at p. 53.

38   Ibid.

39   For a summary of some of these see Fortin, *supra* at n. 28.

40   See Freeman, *supra*, n. 5, Chapter 2 for an outline of what may constitute a child's right to autonomy.

41   Competency not always accurately assessed: see nn. 54–67 *infra* in particular.

42   See the discussion of Feinberg, J., 'The Child's Right to an Open Future' in *Freedom and Fulfilment*, Princeton, Princeton University Press, 1992 at pp.76–98 in Chapter 3 for his proposals for protecting children so that they may enjoy an 'open future'.

43   Ibid.

There is, therefore, an inevitable Sorites[44] problem, which must be addressed. This is not merely a philosophical puzzle but an issue that strikes at the heart of the consent and children debate. Great care must be taken in the desire to protect the child from making apparently unwise decisions, that their right to autonomy is not inappropriately undermined. Intervening in decisions made by adults or children can be justified if this will better promote their or others' interests, such as their longer-term autonomy. This is entirely consistent with the version of autonomy presented here. However, this can, and should, be problematic in some cases. If we take the case of the chronically ill child who is refusing life-saving treatment, can we be sure that overriding their wish is in their interests?

Freeman appeals to Rawl's hypothetical social contract to determine the parameters of the liberal paternalism to which he subscribes, which allows for interference in the decisions of mature adolescents.[45] This contract, he considers, comes closest to expressing the idea of treating persons as equals with respect to their capacity for autonomy. The formulation of this social contract consists of the selection of principles of justice in the 'original position'[46] behind a 'veil of ignorance'.[47] Put simply, Rawls believes equal liberty and opportunity with an arrangement of social and economic inequalities that would benefit the least advantaged would be chosen.[48] Using this premise as a basis, Freeman argues that the question that should be asked with respect to children is:

> … what sorts of action or conduct would we wish, as children, to be shielded against on the assumption that we would want to mature to a rationally autonomous adulthood and be capable of deciding on our own system of ends as free and rational beings?[49]

This proposal has considerable force but is less persuasive where children have been enduring long periods of discomfort or pain or where they hold mature, established beliefs which lead them to refuse certain types of intervention.

The support here is for children to be prepared for future citizenship as autonomous adults from a young age by giving them increasing responsibilities but at an appropriate rate. As Freeman[50] states, children need to be brought

---

44 Sorites or the 'heap' problem: the classical philosophical problem of judging when one thing has achieved the transition into another when the transition involves small incremental changes. So at what point does the developing child reach the point at which they deserve the respect due to the adult with full capacity? The law of England and Wales gave a clear answer, at least until the decision in *Gillick v West Norfolk and Wisbech Area Health Authority* [1986] AC 112 discussed *infra* n. 106 *ff*.

45 Freeman, *supra*, n. 5 at p. 57.

46 Rawls, *A Theory of Justice*, London, Oxford University Press, 1971 at p. 17.

47 Ibid., at p. 136.

48 Ibid., at p. 302.

49 Freeman, *supra*, n. 5 at p. 57.

50 Freeman, *supra*, n. 5.

... to a capacity where they are able to take full responsibility as free, rational agents for their own system of ends.[51]

At the same time, account must be taken of the empirical evidence that illustrates that children have significant abilities to make complex decisions at a much younger age than is often thought. It is to this evidence that the discussion now turns.

If a minor is assessed to be competent, their autonomous interests have the potential to restrict the scope of parental responsibility. The extent of this will depend upon the view of children's competence in relation to making decisions about medical treatment. There is strong empirical evidence that children are more capable of making decisions than is generally thought to be the case: they can understand the implications of what they are deciding.[52] Notwithstanding the emphasis on understanding the implications of a decision by the judiciary in cases concerning the mature minor's legal competence to consent,[53] in practice, using age[54] and traditional ideas about general intelligence alone continues, even in institutions that pride themselves in their focus on the individual child.[55] This approach is a weak measure of a child's capacity to have sufficient understanding and de-emphasizes the importance of the social component of cognitive development and the impact of contextual factors.[56] Established[57] and contemporary[58] research highlights how young children can process and interpret the demands of their world, in particular their social world, at a very early age. Also, psychometric

---

51   Ibid., at p. 57.

52   *Supra*, n. 1.

53   See e.g. *Gillick*, *supra*, n. 44, discussed infra n. 99 *ff.*

54   As suggested by s. 1 (3) (a) Children Act 1989.

55   *Supra*, n. 2.

56   See Chapman, M., *Constructive Evolution: Origins and Development of Piaget's Thought*, Cambridge, Cambridge University Press, 1988, in which he provides a more accurate assessment of Piaget's evolving theories on child development rather than as a key proponent of 'stage' theories as he is more usually presented.

57   Mandler, J.M., 'A new perspective on cognitive development in infancy', (1990) 78 *American Scientist* 236–43.

58   Woodward, A.L., Sommerville, J.A. and Guajardo, J.J., 'How infants make sense of intentional action' in Malle, B., Moses, L. and Baldwin, D., (eds) *Intentions and Intentionality: Foundations of Social Cognition*, Cambridge MA, MIT Press, 2001, pp. 149–69; Meltzoff, A.N., 'Origins of mind, cognition and communication' (1999) 32(4) *Journal of Communication Disorders* 251–69; Pinker, S., *The Blank Slate: The Modern Denial of Human Nature*, London, Penguin Books, 2002. This is not a particularly contentious view in the field of child psychology: personal communication from Dr B.E.E. Johnson, Principal Psychologist, Dyslexia Action.

measuring tools now measure intelligence as a multifactorial construct addressing broad and specific abilities.[59] Other disciplines echo these developments:

> Competence is more than a skill, it is a way of relating and can be understood more clearly when each child's inner qualities are seen within a network of relationships and cultural influences.[60]

These 'inner qualities' may include those gained from the experience of having a chronic illness or disability and should be taken into account.[61] Indeed, there is evidence that relevant experience of illness, disability and treatment is a more indicative factor in assessing competency than age.[62] In order to recognize children's autonomy to the optimum extent possible, we must avoid arbitrary cut-off points where possible and make assessments about their ability to make decisions on a case-by-case basis where there is disagreement. There is a claim that:

> [t]he search for a single test of competency is a search for a Holy Grail ... In practice, judgements of competency go beyond semantics or straightforward applications of legal rules; such judgements reflect social considerations and societal biases as much as they reflect matters of law and medicine.[63]

Be that as it may, there are sophisticated tools that can measure, for example, cognitive social maturity.[64] These can introduce a welcome element of objectivity into any assessment of whether a child can satisfy a requirement to be able, not only to understand information, but to weigh it up when reaching a decision.

The belief here is that:

> (Children) finally pass to the level of autonomy when they recognise that rules are alterable, that they can be criticized and should be accepted or rejected on a basis of reciprocity and fairness. The emergence of rational reflection about

---

59   Deary, I.J., Looking down on human intelligence: from psychophysics to the brain, Oxford, Oxford University Press, 2000, passim.

60   Alderson, *supra*, n. 1 at p. 123.

61   Eiser, *supra*, n. 1, Fielding and Duff, *supra*, n. 1 and Alderson and Montgomery, *supra*, n. 2.

62   Hammond, *supra*, n. 1.

63   Roth, L.H., Meisel, A. and Lidz, C.W., 'Tests of competence to consent to treatment', (1977) 134 *American Journal of Psychiatry* 279–84.

64   Levers-Landis, C.E., Greenley, R.N., Burant, C. and Borawski, E., 'Cognitive Social Maturity, Life Change Events, and Health Risk Behaviors among Adolescents: Development of a Structural Equation Model', (2006) 13(2) *Journal of Clinical Psychology in Medical Settings* 111–20.

rules ... central to the Kantian conception of autonomy, is the main feature of the final level of moral development.[65]

Such a conception of autonomy assists those who attempt to evaluate the status of children. Familiarity in working with children and developing communication skills[66] with younger patients in particular will facilitate recognition of whether the child truly possesses this level of reflective thinking: assessing children's competence may have as much to do with assessors' competences and assumptions as with anything related to the individual children themselves.

To what extent does the law address adequately such notions of children's autonomy?

Legal Competence to Consent: Children Aged 16 to 18 Years

In English law an adult patient who has no mental incapacity has an 'absolute right'[67] to choose whether to consent to medical treatment, to refuse it or whether to choose one rather than another of the treatments being offered. The courts have reiterated this right and refused to interfere with the decisions of competent adults,[68] thereby demonstrating a clear commitment to patient autonomy, which consent is seen to protect.[69] However, the determination of whether children have the capacity to consent to, and refuse, treatment gives rise to considerable contention.[70]

The law treats anyone below the age of 18 as a child and refers to them as 'minors' to reflect the fact that they have yet to reach the age of majority.

---

65   Peters, R.S., 'Freedom and the Development of the Free Man', in *Education and the Development of Reason*, Dearden, R.F., (ed.), London, Routledge and Kegan, 1972 at p. 130 cited in Dworkin, *supra*, n. 7.

66   See e.g. Kinnersley P., Butler C., 'Context bound communication skills training: development of a new method', (2002) 36 *Medical Education* 377–83.

67   *Re T (adult: refusal of medical treatment)* [1993] Fam 95, per Lord Donaldson at 102.

68   Apart from the period in which pregnant women, who were near full-term gestation and refused a clinically indicated Caesarian section, had their refusal overridden: see e.g. *Re S (adult: refusal of treatment)* [1992] 4 All ER 671. This position has now been rectified: see *St George's Healthcare NHS Trust v S* [1999] Fam 26.

69   See, e.g. *Re B (adult: refusal of medical treatment)* [2002] 2 FCR 1 per Dame Butler-Sloss at para. 20 and *Re MB (adult: medical treatment)* [1997] 2 FCR 541 although consent has been seen more as a device to protect doctors from legal claims than as a means to protect autonomy: see e.g. *Re W (a minor) (medical treatment)* [1993] Fam 64, discussed *infra* at nn. 118–22.

70   Decisions about the medical treatment of younger children, who have not yet achieved legal competence, are made by those with parental responsibility, (s. 3(1) Children Act 1989), and the exercise of this is addressed in Chapter 3.

Competent 16 to 18-year-olds can consent to treatment under section 8(1) of the Family Law Reform Act 1969 (FLRA).[71] The capacity of anyone over 16 is now determined under the Mental Capacity Act 2005 (MCA)[72] which largely enshrines the common law approach. The MCA applies to the capacity to make decisions in general, not just medical decisions but the focus here is on the Act's impact on medical decision-making. There remains a tension with respect to the refusal of treatment until the age of majority is achieved which will be discussed below.[73]

There is a rebuttable presumption of capacity under the MCA,[74] which is determined with respect to the decision to be made[75] so that a more serious and/ or complex decision will require a higher level of competence.[76] There is also a requirement to take all practicable steps to help the individual make that decision[77] which may be significant.[78] Under section 3(1), the patient must be able to understand the information relevant to the decision, to retain that information and to use or weigh that information as part of the process of making the decision. This encapsulates the adult test of capacity in *Re C*.[79] There is also a requirement that the individual must be able to communicate their decision by some means.[80] Only being able to retain the information for a short time or expressing ambivalence about the decision being made[81] will not necessarily mean the patient is incompetent[82]

---

71 Subsequent case law has made it clear that this children's right to consent to treatment does not extend to refusal: see *Re W, supra,* n. 69.

72 S. 2(5).

73 *Infra,* nn. 93–9.

74 S. 1(2).

75 Ss. 1(3), 1 (4) and 3(1) in particular.

76 As in *Re T supra,* n. 67 at 113 and *Re MB, supra* n. 69 at 437 per Butler-Sloss LJ. This is also discussed in Pattinson, S.D., *Medical Law and Ethics,* London, Sweet and Maxwell, 2006 at pp. 137–9.

77 S. 1(3).

78 There are onerous requirements contained in Part 2, Chapter 3 of the Code of Practice in some detail as to what might be expected including appropriate settings and the use of aids.

79 *Re C (adult: refusal of medical treatment)* [1994] 1 All ER 819 confirmed in *Re MB, supra,* n. 77 at 437 and *Re B, supra,* n. 69, per Dame Butler-Sloss at para. 33. The ability to understand does not require the level of actual understanding as seems to have been suggested in *Re C* at 823 and discussed by Pattinson, *supra,* n. 76 at p. 135 which could depend on the information given by a doctor: note the discussion in *Re L (medical treatment: Gillick competency)* [1998] 2 FLR 810 where adequate information was not provided to the mature minor discussed *infra,* nn. 132–5. For consent to be valid, there will need to be an actual understanding of the broad nature of the proposed intervention subject to the caveat noted at *Chatterton v Gerson* [1981] 1 QB 432 at 443.

80 This had been suggested in *Re F (mental patient: sterilization)* [1990] 2 AC 1 at 63 and 75 as a necessary component and also noted in *R (Burke) v GMC* [2004] EWHC 1879 at para. 10.

81 *Re B, supra.,* n. 69, per Dame Butler-Sloss at paras. 9, 34, 35, 40, 41 and 92.

82 S. 3(3).

but they will need to understand the implications of deciding one way or another or not at all.[83] Additionally, a person is not to be assumed to lack capacity merely because of their age or appearance[84] or because others believe they have made an unwise decision.[85] This captures the common law approach: there are a number of cases which emphasize that it does not matter whether the reasons for making a particular decision are irrational[86] unless this arises from a mental disorder where reality for the patient is clearly distorted.[87] This may be a somewhat startling conclusion given that in *Re C* itself, the patient suffered from, *inter alia*, the delusion that he was a renowned doctor as a result of his paranoid schizophrenia but was deemed to be competent to refuse an apparently life-saving amputation. The common law position with respect to mature minors differs markedly to the attitude to adults.[88] Where incompetence is established, all those dealing with the individual must act in their best interests[89] and the Court of Protection may make appropriate provisions where necessary.[90]

For individuals aged 16 to 18 years, the MCA does make some key distinctions. They cannot make advance directives to refuse treatment, unlike their adult counterparts,[91] nor can they appoint a Lasting Power of Attorney to manage their affairs in the event they become incompetent.[92] There may be some confusion regarding the consent of 16 and 17-year-olds now that the MCA is in force. Section 8(1) of the FLRA states that the consent of a minor who has attained the age of 16 to any medical, surgical or dental treatment shall be as effective as it would be if they were of full age.[93] However, section 8(3) provides that this section does not make ineffective any consent that would have been effective if this section had not been enacted. This may mean that the effect of judicial decisions when interpreting these provisions needs to be taken into account. Case law has made

---

83   S. 3(4).

84   S. 2(3).

85   S. 1(4).

86   See e.g. *Re T, supra.*, n. 67 at 102 per Lord Donaldson, *Re MB, supra*, n. 69 at 432 and 436–7 per Butler-Sloss LJ and *Re W* [2002] EWHC 901.

87   *Re MB, supra*, n. 69 at 437 per Butler-Sloss L.J. and *NHS Trust v Ms T* [2004] EWHC 1279 at paras 61 and 63.

88   See e.g. *Re E (a minor) (wardship: medical treatment)* [1993] 1 FLR 386 discussed *infra* nn. 125–31.

89   S. 4 and the Code of Practice.

90   See e.g. ss. 15–20 and 35–6 with regard to issuing declarations, the appointment of Deputies and Independent Mental Capacity Advocates respectively.

91   Ss. 24–6.

92   Ss. 9–13.

93   The limiting of the child's consent to medical, surgical or dental treatment may mean that non-therapeutic treatment, such as organ donation, is not included so that a child of this age would need to demonstrate '*Gillick* competence' (discussed *infra* at nn. 104–224) to consent to any procedure not deemed to be treatment given s. 8(3) FLRA preserves the common law on the consent of children.

it clear that section 8(1) of the FLRA provides 16 and 17-year-olds with a right to consent to treatment but no corollary right to refuse treatment.[94] Thus, the consent of those with parental responsibility and the consent of the courts will suffice to protect the doctor if the child refuses treatment. On the other hand, the *Re C*[95] adult test of competence, which is given statutory force in the MCA, generally applies to consent and refusal of any medical procedure. Given that both Acts are currently on the statute book there may be uncertainty about refusals of treatment and consents to treatment by 16 and 17-year-olds which is not personally therapeutic. Notwithstanding the usual effect of principles of statutory interpretation,[96] there is a view that the common law will still be used for this age group.[97] This is because the courts' inherent jurisdiction over minors may continue until the age of 18 although it should be remembered that *parens patriae* jurisdiction did not survive earlier legislative reforms with respect to incapacitated adults.[98] If applications under the courts' inherent jurisdiction with respect to 16 and 17-year-olds remain possible, these are likely to be more flexible than the MCA system, though the latter is likely to be used as a guide.[99] The better view would be that the MCA prevails and that refusals of treatment by 16 and 17-year-olds should be approached in the empowering spirit of the MCA.

The following section illustrates how the prospects for the under 16s to be given the chance to be fully involved in decision-making are more circumscribed.

Legal Competence to Consent: Children Aged Under 16

Where children are deemed to be legally incompetent, those with parental responsibility have the capacity to consent to medical treatment on behalf of a child and this must be exercised in the child's best interests.[100] This is discussed in more detail in Chapter 3 which addresses the position of younger children with respect to medical decision-making. Suffice to say here, parental consent will not be sufficient in cases of non-therapeutic sterilizations,[101] abortion,[102] or donation of non-regenerative tissue[103] in which cases court authorization must be sought.

---

94 *Re W, supra*, n. 69. The inability of *all* children to refuse treatment is discussed in more detail below.

95 *Re C, supra*, n. 79.

96 I.e. the later statute will take precedence on the basis of Parliamentary sovereignty.

97 See Bartlett, P., *Blackstone's Guide to the Mental Capacity* Act, Oxford, Oxford University Press, 2005 at pp. 94–5.

98 See the discussion in *Re F, supra*, n. 80 at 26 *per* Neill L.J.

99 *Ibid.*

100 *Gillick, supra*, n. 44 at 127.

101 *Re B* [1997] 2 All ER 206 at 214 per Lord Templeman.

102 *Re P (a minor)* (1982) 8 LGR 301.

103 *Re F, supra*, n. 80 at 390 per Lord Donaldson MR.

Such authorization will also be necessary where parents refuse to consent to life-saving procedures and may be advisable wherever there is any uncertainty or disagreement about a particular intervention.[104] A reasonable level of force may be used to ensure that the treatment is given to an objecting child.[105] Much, of course, will turn on the interpretation of 'reasonable'. Could it entail shackling a young person to an operating table in order to administer anaesthesia? Would forcible sedation be acceptable? Many paediatric health professionals would not proceed on either basis or at all unless the intervention was sufficiently compelling. Life-saving interventions would render chemical or physical restraint as being reasonable and therefore lawful.

Gillick v West Norfolk and Wisbech Area Health Authority[106] was hailed as an important case in the development of respect for children's autonomy.[107] Mrs Gillick challenged DoH guidelines which set out the conditions for adolescents to seek confidential advice on contraception. Although there was no suggestion one of her daughters might avail herself of such a service, Mrs Gillick wished to establish the right of parents to be informed if their child sought such advice. The case was pursued to the House of Lords where she lost by the barest majority although, in the courts overall, she received more judicial support than the Department of Health. The case more broadly established the right of children under 16 to consent to medical interventions provided they have 'sufficient understanding and intelligence to enable him or her to understand fully what is proposed'.[108] It was also suggested that there should be an understanding of the 'moral and family' issues involved,[109] but this aspect has not been given any emphasis[110] and would demand more of a child than an adult. The child only needs a level of maturity sufficient to address a particular issue,[111] so even very young children may be able to make decisions that are of a lesser order and, indeed, should do so wherever possible.[112] Should a health professional wrongly assess a child as incompetent adult cases suggest that damages may be awarded.[113] However, the courts may be more sympathetic to cases concerning children, provided a decision was made in good faith.

---

104   See the discussion about parental disagreement in Chapter 3.

105   *Re C (detention: medical treatment)* [1997] 2 FLR 180.

106   *Gillick, supra*, n. 44.

107   See e.g. Bridge, C., 'Religious Beliefs and Teenage Refusal of Medical Treatment', (1999) 62(4) *Modern Law Review* 585–94 at p. 585.

108   *Gillick, supra*, n. 44, per Lord Lord Scarman at 189.

109   Ibid.

110   See e.g. DoH, *Seeking Consent: Working with Children*, 2001 and BMA, *Consent, Rights and Choices in Healthcare for Children and Young People*, 2001 where this is not mentioned.

111   *Re R (a minor) (wardship: consent to medical treatment)* [1991] 4 All ER 177.

112   See e.g. the discussion in Chapter 3.

113   See e.g. *St George's, supra*, n.68.

It was clear that Gillick prevented parents from vetoing a child's consent to medical treatment,[114] but, furthermore, nothing in the judgment prevented the conclusion that the termination of the parental right also extended to a child's decision to refuse medical treatment. However, subsequent cases concerning mature minors have marginalized the protection that *Gillick* offers to the protection of the autonomy of mature minors.

Re R[115] concerned a 15-year-old girl with a troubled history who manifested psychiatric disturbance including physically aggressive behaviour and suicidal thoughts. At one time, she had been deemed 'sectionable' under the Mental Health Act 1983 (MHA). However, by the time the case reached the Court of Appeal she did not meet the criteria allowing the mental health legislation to be used and the psychiatrist involved in her case considered that she was *Gillick* competent. The judges disagreed, on the basis that such competence imported the notion of stability as part of the ability to make a rational judgment. This is in direct contrast to the attitude adopted to adults where the latter's decisions are apparently to be respected no matter how irrational they appear to others unless it concerns an issue of competence.[116] Lord Donaldson took the view that consent was like 'a key which unlocks the door'[117] so that, in the family situation, parents and children could unlock the door to treatment. Parents are also in a position to override a child's veto on the advice of doctors as indeed could the court exercising its wardship jurisdiction.

In *Re W*,[118] a 16-year-old girl, also with a disturbed background, was anorexic and likely to refuse all treatment. As we have seen, section 8(1) of the FLRA gives the authority to consent as though they were of majority to 16 and 17 year olds. Nevertheless, the local authority sought to treat her without consent under section 100(3) of the Children Act 1989. The Court of Appeal acknowledged that proper weight must be given to objections made by minors but if their welfare is threatened by a serious and imminent risk of grave and irreversible mental or physical harm, the court and any person with parental responsibility could authorise treatment.[119] This time, Lord Donaldson preferred the analogy of consent acting as a legal 'flakjacket' to avoid any threat of an action for battery.[120] The Court took the view that W's experience and condition affected her ability to make real choices hence that she was not *Gillick* competent. Lord Donaldson was explicit that he did not

---

114   See *Re P (a minor)* [1986] 1 FLR 272 where a 15-year-old schoolgirl was allowed to consent to an abortion against her parents' wishes after demonstrating that she understood the implications of her decision.

115   *Re R, supra*, n. 111.

116   See e.g. *Re T, supra*, n. 67.

117   Ibid., at 184. However, Lord Donaldson rejected this analogy in *Re W, supra*, n. 69 at 78 because keys can also lock doors.

118   *Re W, supra,* n. 69.

119   Ibid., at 88 and 94 per Balcombe and Nolan LLJ respectively.

120   Ibid., at 72.

want to use mental health legislation, to avoid stigmatizing the young woman,[121] even though anorexia is generally perceived to be a mental disorder.[122]

The *full* impact of the Children Act 1989 was considered in *South Glamorgan County Council v W and B*.[123] This was important given the Act was supposed to enshrine the concept of Gillick competence in that children of sufficient understanding to make an informed decision may refuse to submit to medical or psychiatric assessment for the purposes of interim care or supervision order proceedings.[124] The 15-year-old girl in this case led a reclusive life, exhibiting domineering and controlling behaviour which succeeded as a result of the threats of self-harm that she made. There was a long history of various professionals' involvement, all seemingly reluctant to resort to using measures available under the MHA, perhaps because of the level of coercion that would be required. There was a considerable delay before action was taken by the local authority because the girl was deemed to be *Gillick* competent, despite her mental disturbance, and there appeared to be an apparent right of veto available to her under the Children Act 1989. In addition, wardship proceedings were now only available to private individuals. Any decision to uphold the child's autonomy would have resulted in further mental deterioration, so the court decided that its *parens patriae* jurisdiction survived the Act allowing it to overrule minors and/or parental decisions. It is surprising that the court was able to reach such a conclusion in the light of these express and unambiguous statutory provisions when it has been held that prerogative powers cannot undermine these.[125] The subsequent decision in *Re K, W and H (Minors) (Medical Treatment)*[126] confirmed that only where all parties holding the power to consent to treatment refused, would a veto arise necessitating application for a specific issue order under the Children Act 1989.[127]

The courts have been particularly willing to overrule what they perceive to be unwise decisions on behalf of intelligent minors with no mental disorder who refuse medically appropriate treatment on the basis of long-held, deep religious beliefs. In such cases, the courts have sought to find reasons to deem the minor incompetent rather than honestly acknowledging that although the minor is capable of achieving capacity, the decision will be overridden if it is seemingly imprudent. Two cases concerning Jehovah's Witness children aptly demonstrate how little respect the common law offers for the seemingly injudicious decisions of otherwise competent minors. Furthermore, these two decisions show that the law requires nothing to be done to facilitate the under 16s understanding of the

---

121 Ibid., at 76.

122 See e.g. *South West Hertfordshire HA v B* [1994] 2 FCR 1051.

123 [1993] 1 FLR 574.

124 Ss. 38(6), 43(8) and 44(7).

125 *A-G v De Keyser's Royal Hotel Ltd.* [1920] AC 508; *Richards v Richards* [1984] AC 174.

126 [1993] 1 FLR 854.

127 S. 10(9).

information relevant to the proposed medical treatment.[128] Indeed, it appears that the common law does not even require capacity-assessors to ensure that the minor is fully and accurately informed.

In *Re E*, [129] a devout 15-year-old Jehovah's Witness suffering from leukaemia refused a blood transfusion, which was necessary to save his life. After acknowledging his 'intelligence', his 'calm discussion of the implications' of his decision and, crucially, his 'awareness that he may die as a result' of the refusal,[130] Ward J oddly considered him to be too young to understand the implications of refusing a blood transfusion, hence he was deemed to lack competence.[131] It was presumed that E's beliefs might diminish as he got older and that he lacked understanding of the pain he had yet to suffer, in particular the increasing breathlessness that would ensue.[132] However, it was noted that neither the doctors caring for E nor the courts had explained to E the breathlessness that he might experience,[133] thus preventing the very opportunity for understanding. Further, to expect the young man to grasp fully the process of dying sets the competency test at too high a standard: would not such a level of understanding defeat many adults? Is a diminution of his religious values likely given his beliefs were long-held, well-articulated and he enjoyed a close relationship with his family? Such an attenuation was possible but a weak ground upon which to predicate the court's ultimate decision. When he reached his 18th birthday, E refused further blood transfusions and died believing he had committed an ungodly act.[134] The approach taken here was paternalistic and, given the torment he might have encountered when blood transfusions were administered against his will, unnecessary.[135]

Re L[136] considered a refusal of life-saving treatment by a 14-year-old Jehovah's Witness girl, whom the court felt had serious commitment and maturity.[137] L had an advance medical directive, drafted only two months earlier, refusing blood and blood products. Despite finding L to be mature,[138] Sir Stephen Brown decided that she was 'not "Gillick competent" in the context of all the necessary details

---

128 *Cf.* s. 1(3) of the MCA and accompanying Code of Practice requirements with respect to the over 16s.

129 *Re E*, *supra*, n. 88; *cf. Re S (a minor) (medical treatment)* [1993] 2 FLR 1065 where the minor's introduction to her faith was more recent and, arguably, she suffered defects in reasoning and control as a result of her illness and mother's influence.

130 *Re E*, Ibid., at 391.

131 Ibid.

132 Ibid.

133 Ibid.

134 Pattinson, *supra*, n. 76 at p. 162.

135 *Cf.* Lowe, N. and Juss, S., 'Medical Treatment – Pragmatism and the Search for Principle', (1993) 56 *Modern Law Review* 865–72 at pp. 871–2 who argue that paternalism is justified where a child's decision would cause irreparable harm.

136 *Re L*, *supra*, n. 79.

137 Ibid., at 811.

138 Ibid.

which would be appropriate for her to be able to form a view about.'[139] However, similar to E, she had not been given all the information about the death that she would suffer if she continued to refuse blood transfusions. Given this, it was clearly impossible for L to understand fully the risks involved. These decisions demonstrate the courts willingness to interfere with what they believe to be unwise medical decisions on behalf of otherwise competent minors under 16. In both decisions the minor concerned displayed at least the potential to understand the information relevant to the decision and the implications of their decision, therefore ostensibly achieving the *Gillick* standard. However, in order to interfere with these arguably imprudent decisions, the courts sought to portray the children as lacking in sufficient understanding. However, it seems that any lack of understanding on the children's behalf, was based on a (deliberate?) failure to ensure that they were fully informed, as opposed to any intrinsic lack of ability by the children to understand the relevant information.

In *Re M*,[140] a 15-year-old girl's refusal of a heart transplant was overridden without expressly commenting on her capacity status. Nevertheless, it seems Johnson J did consider her to satisfy the *Gillick* criteria because he thought that she could potentially have given a valid consent.[141] Interestingly, the court went to significant lengths to hear M's wishes. Crucially she said: 'I don't want to die, but I would rather die than have the transplant and have somebody else's heart, I would rather die with 15 years of my own heart.'[142] Nevertheless, the court overruled her wishes. This appears questionable when one considers that M's statement can be contrasted to that voiced by the adult patient in *Re C*[143] which laid down the common law standard for capacity for adults.[144] In *Re C* the question was whether the adult patient's schizophrenia rendered him incompetent to refuse a life-saving leg amputation.[145] Although there were doubts about C's competence to refuse the amputation, the court placed crucial emphasis on the fact that C said he would rather die with two feet than live with one.[146] The court concluded that his understanding of the view that he might die without treatment demonstrated his capacity that required him to be able to take in and retain the information, to believe it and to weigh that information balancing risks and needs.[147] Is M's statement that she would 'rather die than have the transplant'[148] not a similar indication of her clear

---

139   Ibid., at 813.

140   *Re M (a child) (refusal of medical treatment)* [1999] 2 FLR 1097.

141   Ibid., at 1097.

142   Ibid., at 1100.

143   *Re C, supra*, n. 79.

144   Ibid.

145   Ibid., at 819: there was an 85% chance of death if the amputation, due to gangrene, was not performed. Despite this high risk he actually went on to survive.

146   Ibid., at 821.

147   Ibid., at 822–4.

148   *Re M, supra*, n. 140 at 1100.

grasp of the fact that she would die without treatment? Did this not demonstrate her ability to absorb and retain the information, to believe it and to weigh that information balancing risks and needs?[149] Was M's ambivalence not similar to that of Ms B when she expressed relief at not having the ventilation switched off?[150] The court accepted her interpretation that her relief was at not having to say sad farewells rather than relief at still being alive.[151] Ambivalence is only relevant if it genuinely strikes at the root of the mental capacity of the patient.[152]

Some may emphasize the fact that M expressed that she was glad that she had had the transplant after the event.[153] However, it might be argued this anecdotal evidence cannot serve as a basis for future decision-making. Would we have physicians and the courts overrule all decisions that they believe the patient might come to regret? If respect for individual medical choice is to be consistent, it must be based on principle. Respect for autonomy is widely accepted to be the fundamental principle underpinning decision-making, thus autonomy should be respected wherever autonomy is possible. This principled approach should not be usurped on the basis of subjective judgments of the patient's possible future feelings. Such an *ad hoc* approach would not promote consistency or clarity. For all those who might subsequently express gratitude that their decision was ignored, there may be many others who feel angry and violated.[154]

In *Re MB*,[155] the adult patient who refused to consent to a Caesarean section later expressed satisfaction that her own decision had been disregarded and a healthy child had been delivered. Nevertheless, the Court of Appeal held that however desirable it might be for the mother to be delivered of a live and healthy baby, the mother's *ex post facto* satisfaction was not a strictly relevant consideration. The Court decided that even if the pregnant woman might later regret the outcome,

---

149 Ibid. M showed a clear understanding of the implications of living with a transplanted heart such as constant medication, checkups and depression. She also said that she did not want to die. However, when she had to choose between death and heart transplant she preferred death. Many sick people may say in abstract that they do not want to die but when they have to weigh death against the prospect of life-long invasive medical treatment they may think that death, although not an attractive option in abstract, is a preferable option than treatment. Are we to presume that the outcome would have been different in *Re C* if he had prefaced his statement that he would rather die with two legs than live with one with an abstract view that he did not want to die? Such a statement would not interfere with the level of understanding the court required in *Re C*, thus, there would appear to be no legal basis to override his decision even if he had expressed such an abstract wish not to die.

150 *Ms. B*, *supra*, n. 69 at paras. 40–1.

151 Ibid., at para. 92.

152 Ibid., at para. 35.

153 Personal communication from an anonymous reviewer for *Medical Law Review.*

154 Which may explain why a court declaration was sought about the lawfulness or otherwise of the forced Caesarean section in St George's, *supra*, n. 68 notwithstanding the delivery of a healthy infant with whom the mother had eventually bonded (at 35).

155 *Re MB*, *supra*, n. 69.

the respect owed to her was more important than a protection of the woman from her own potential reactions to the consequences of her autonomous decision.[156] Savulescu argues that the fact that a patient whose wishes had been disregarded later adjusts to the situation created by the disregard of his/her original desire does not mean that the autonomous decision expressed at the time was wrong and coercion therefore justified: rather it merely shows that perceptions can change and that the human person is able to adjust to changing circumstances.[157] Furthermore, Michalowski contends that even though it might seem easy to hold that the patient's gratitude of having a healthy baby retrospectively justified any disregard of the competent woman's wishes, competence to make health care decisions presupposes that the patient is in a position to determine what is in her best interests and that she will have to accept and be able to live with the consequences of her decision.[158]

The decisions concerning children's refusal of treatment demonstrate that when it comes to children, the courts are more concerned with what the patient *should* want than what they *do* want, possibly reflecting their determination of what public policy requires. As Devereux et al. say this shows:

> ... the Catch 22 by which patients whose competence is in doubt will be found rational if they accept the doctor's proposal but incompetent if they reject professional advice.[159]

This attitude affords little, if any, weight to the child's autonomy and their right to be wrong.[160] When discussing Lord Donaldson's approach to refusals of treatment by mature minors in the post-*Gillick* rulings, Kennedy has rightly said:

> His failure to accept that the power to refuse is no more than the obverse of the power to consent and that they are simply twin aspects of the single right to self-determination borders on the perverse.[161]

---

156   Ibid., at 554.

157   Savulescu, J., 'The Trouble with Do-Gooders: the Example of Suicide' (1997) 23 *JME* 108 at 111.

158   Sabine Michalowski, 'Court-authorised caesarean sections, the end of a trend?' (1999) *The Modern Law Review* 62, 115 at 119.

159   Devereaux, J.A., Jones, D.P.H. and Dickenson, D.L., 'Can children withhold consent to treatment?', (1993) 306 *British Medical Journal* 1459–61.

160   Brazier, M. and Bridge, C., 'Coercion or caring: Analysing adolescent autonomy' (1996) 16 *Legal Studies* 84 at p. 88. An alternative view of the case see further discussion in the text accompanying n. 189*ff* especially.

161   Kennedy, I., 'Consent to Treatment: The Capable Person' in Dyer, C. (ed.), *Doctors, Patients and the Law*, Oxford, Blackwell, 1992, 44–71 at pp. 60–1.

This view is presented more forcefully by Harris:

> ... the idea that a child (or anyone) might competently consent to a treatment but not be competent to refuse it is a palpable nonsense.[162]

Re R[163] in particular has been criticized[164] for its lack of articulation as to why minority justifies overriding a decision of a *Gillick* competent child and because the discussion of fluctuating competence was confused. While *Re R* and *Re W*[165] may be criticized for their reasoning, the outcomes are more justifiable: academic comment has pointed out that the conditions of these minors were not unique to age. They suffered from the defects of reasoning and control[166] thus leading to an inability to make a proper choice of treatment. These adolescents would have failed the application of the adult *Re C*[167] test. This test could be just as valid for their age group, but age allowed courts to avoid the use of mental health legislation because they did not want to 'stigmatize' the adolescent. This very avoidance actually perpetuates stigmatization by viewing the label of mental illness in a negative way. The use of such terminology as 'flakjackets' and 'keyholders' is also unfortunate because it gives the impression of the law focusing on the need to protect the medical profession rather than the rights of individuals. However, closer examination of the text in *Re W* does reveal *some* commitment to giving consideration to the preferences of the minor,[168] but these are very circumscribed.

The fundamental factor in autonomous decision-making, the ability to make a choice, would extend the notion of *Gillick* competence by taking into account more than the ability to understand[169] and include the elements of the adult capacity test, particularly the ability to weigh information.[170] For some, this choice will involve choosing not to live with a particular condition because they believe that their state is worse than death.[171] The concern is that those assessing a child's ability to understand the implications of a decision will be resolved, to a lesser or greater extent, by whether others, such as the doctors in *Re W*, approve of the outcome

---

162   Harris, J., 'Consent and End-of-Life decisions', (2003) 29 *Journal of Medical Ethics* 10 at p. 12.

163   *Re R, supra*, n. 111.

164   Brazier and Bridge, *supra*, n. 160. *Cf.*, Mason, J.K. and Laurie, G.T., *Law and Medical Ethics*, (7th ed.), Oxford, Oxford University Press, 2006 at pp. 369–70 who are more supportive of the decision.

165   *Re W, supra*, n. 69.

166   Discussed *infra*, at n. 181.

167   *Re C, supra*, n. 79.

168   More recently, in *Bro Morgannwg NHS Trust v 'P' and others* [2003] EWHC 2327 (Fam) (*Re P*), Johnson J was prepared to acknowledge that there may be cases where older children would be permitted to refuse treatment.

169   Brazier and Bridge, *supra*, n. 160 at p. 90.

170   S. 3(1)(c) MCA.

171   See e.g. *Re B, supra*, n. 69 at para. 94.

of the decision should the child determine it for themselves.[172] This approach was firmly rejected by the Law Commission[173] which preferred a 'functional' test of competence that requires an ability to act on the information and using it to make a decision. This position was enshrined in the common law test of adult competence,[174] now codified in the MCA.[175]

Of course, both mature minors and adults may be unable to make decisions because of mental disturbance. In those cases, it might be legitimate to dispense with consent requirements and treat them using mental health legislation with all the protection this provides.[176] The judges need to be very circumspect when considering supposed stigmatization in an era in which society is encouraged to be more accepting of mental illness.[177] The failure to use mental health legislation appropriately could breach Article 5 of the European Convention of Human Rights (ECHR), the right not to be deprived of liberty and security of the person except in accordance with a procedure prescribed by law and with various safeguards. This is even more likely to be the case if there is any element of compulsion unless provided by law. Case law under the MHA illustrates how the HRA adds a further protection to existing barriers to compulsory treatment in cases where patients resist it.[178] This represents only a partial solution to the dilemmas which may be presented by the adolescent for, in many instances, other unhelpful factors may be undermining the ability to make a proper choice such as undue influence[179] and lack of adequate information.[180]

The adult case of *Re T*[181] discussed one version of the idea of fully autonomous choice but it fails to arrive at an explicit analysis of what this might be. Suggestions have been made that this is an aspiration and, in reality, only maximally autonomous choice is possible.[182] Four types of defect are identified as undermining respect for particular choices: control, reasoning, information and stability. Defects in control will include mental disability, addictions and undue influence but only in so far as

---

172   Brazier and Bridge, *supra*, n. 160 at p. 90.

173   Law Com Report No. 231, *Mental Incapacity*, London, HMSO, 1995, para. 2.52.

174   *Re C, supra*, n. 79.

175   S. 3 and note the presumption of capacity set out in s. 2.

176   Such as a second opinion, a time-limited application and opportunity for independent review.

177   See e.g. DoH, *Action on stigma: promoting mental health, ending discrimination at work*, 2006.

178   See, e.g. *R (on the application of PS) v G (RMO) and W (SOAD)* [2003] EWHC 2335 (Fam) regarding unnecessary compulsory treatment and *Keenan v UK* (2001) EHRR 38 with respect to unreasonable physical force.

179   As in *Re T, supra*, n. 67.

180   As in *Re E, supra*, n. 88 and *Re L, op. cit.*, n. 79.

181   *Re T, supra*, n. 67.

182   Brazier and Bridge, *supra*, n. 160 discussing Harris, J., *The Value of Life*, London, Routledge, 1985 at pp. 195–205.

it affects the ability to make particular decisions. Manifestly irrational decisions may be *prima facie* evidence of constituting a defect in reasoning but deeply held religious beliefs will not, *necessarily*, form part of this category.[183] Clearly, the individual must be in possession of sufficient information to make a proper choice. It is argued here that there must be a rigorous assessment of their competence and that account must be taken of their experience.[184] In *Re R*, fluctuating competence was more than a defect in stability: it involved a defect in reasoning that had less to do with her age than her mental state. An explicit recognition of this would have been helpful.

Brazier and Bridge[185] have proposed that society should accept the notion of evolving autonomy. This view accords with the conceptions of autonomy here and is supported by empirical evidence. Such an approach makes far more sense than imposing arbitrary age limits with respect to capacity. The approach adopted in the MCA,[186] where there is a presumption of capacity allowing for the right to self-determination is suggested as equally relevant for the maturing minor. Such a presumption would, of course, be rebuttable. In *some* cases it might even be appropriate to allow mature minors to refuse life-saving treatment even if this conflicts with society's interest in preserving life.[187] It is not being argued that there should be general unfettered decision-making by those under 16, only that they are given the opportunity to maximize their potential for capacity, and thus autonomy, where that potential is present as is the case for those over 16.

So the post-*Gillick* rulings may be seen as inconsistent in not allowing competent children to consent to and refuse treatment[188] but an alternative view of the case is that it was about preventing Mrs Gillick from depriving her children of access to confidential medical advice and treatment rather than giving children strong rights to determine their medical treatment.[189] Here, the preference is for the former interpretation. *Gillick* has provided a precedent for furthering children's interests and should have been used to expand the parameters of what they may be permitted to do. More recent case law suggests this interpretation has some force, subject to certain caveats.[190] A legitimate proposition could be that consenting to treatment requires, as a matter of law, an understanding of all the consequences of not having any treatment in which case children should be able to consent to

---

183 *Cf.* Lord Donaldson in *Re T, supra*, n. 67 following *Sidaway v Board of Governors of the Bethlehem Royal Hospital and the Maudsley Hospital* [1985] AC 871 on this point.

184 See e.g. nn. 1 and 52–64.

185 Brazier and Bridge, *supra*, n. 160 at pp. 10.

186 S. 1(2) echoing the common law position in *Re T, supra*, n. 67.

187 See e.g. *supra*, n. 241 and nn. 276–80 *infra*.

188 Bainham, A., 'The Judge and the Competent Minor', (1992) 108 *Law Quarterly Review* 194–200.

189 Lowe and Juss, *supra*, n. 135.

190 Discussed *infra* at nn. 219–233.

and refuse any intervention.[191] The requirement that the *Gillick* competent minor 'understand fully' what is proposed[192] suggests that there is little, if anything, that a *Gillick* competent minor will not understand with regard to the particular treatment. [193] Given this, it follows that the level of understanding that will have been attained by a *Gillick* competent minor is not materially different to the level of understanding attained by an adult who has met the requirements of the adult standard for capacity laid down in the MCA. That is, the achievement of capacity for both groups, in essence, depends on the ability to retain and understand the relevant information and the implications of deciding one way or another or not deciding at all.[194]

Hope has been expressed that the Human Rights Act 1998 (HRA) might address some of the perceived shortcomings manifested by the courts when they make decisions about children's autonomy.[195] Has it realized its potential?

The Influence of the Human Rights Act 1998

The HRA, by largely incorporating the provisions of the ECHR, provides an opportunity to challenge traditional notions of children's ability to make decisions.[196] Article 8(1), which requires respect for private and family life, would be at the centre of any claim now made by the mature minor who believes they should not have their refusal of treatment overridden by the court and/or their parents. Article 3, which includes the right not to be subject to inhuman and degrading treatment, the right not to be deprived of liberty and security of person under Article 5 and the right not to be discriminated against in the enjoyment of other Convention rights under Article 14 may also be engaged. The right to freedom of thought,

---

191   Including those that are life-prolonging. This has particular force where the child has suffered from a long-term, debilitating condition: e.g. *supra*, n. 241 and nn. 276–80 *infra*.

192   *Gillick, supra*, n. 44 *per* Lord Scarman at 189.

193   None of their Lordships expressly addressed the capacity to refuse treatment in *Gillick*. Thus, it is at least arguable that their Lordships envisaged that the *Gillick* competent child's right to consent to treatment entailed a concomitant right to refuse it. However, as we have seen, subsequent case law foreclosed this possibility, see *Re R, supra*, n. 111 and *Re W, supra*, n. 69 *per* Lord Donaldson at 84.

194   One commentator argues that much more is required of a child to achieve *Gillick* capacity than is required of an adult under the *Re C (supra*, n. 79) test: see Pattinson, *supra*, n. 76 at p. 160. From this perspective, children who are deemed to be *Gillick* competent may possess a greater ability to understand the information relevant to the decision and, crucially the implications of deciding one way or another or not deciding at all, than an adult who meets the *Re C* test.

195   Hagger, L., 'Some implications of the Human Rights Act 1998 for the medical treatment of children' (2003) 6 *Medical Law International* 25–51.

196   Ibid.

conscience and religion under Article 9 will be relevant in cases where a child's parents or the child are refusing an intervention on the grounds of their beliefs.[197] Article 5 of the European Convention on Human Rights and Biomedicine (Oviedo Convention),[198] that requires free and informed consent to medical interventions, can be used to interpret ECHR provisions[199] and professional guidelines make their own demands.[200]

Currently, a failure to assess competence accurately is unlikely to constitute a breach of Article 3. However, it could if this is then followed by very significant medical intervention. Generally, *necessary* therapeutical treatment given without consent would not constitute inhuman and degrading treatment.[201] Conversely then, the imposition of an unnecessary intervention without appropriate consultation with the child and/or without sufficient risk information, could infringe Article 3. This is even more likely to be the case if there is any element of compulsion and case law suggests that the HRA has strengthened the protection for potentially unwilling patients subject to compulsory treatment.[202] Of course, the practical reality is that parents and/or doctors are unlikely to force young people to accept treatment but there is a need to be alert to different levels of coercion.

It should only be possible to interfere with the right not to be deprived of liberty and security of person contained in Article 5 in accordance with a procedure prescribed by law and with various safeguards. As noted earlier, this is pertinent given the criticism that the failure to use mental health legislation appropriately with adolescents means they are not provided with its protection. Although interference with this right may be justified in relevant circumstances, where the mature minor is concerned this must mean a clear articulation of the balancing process when considering whether to override their wishes in their perceived best interests. This will inevitably improve decision-making which has the effect of respecting the dignity of the person involved.[203] However, in this particular context, the case law is not promising. In *Nielsen v Denmark*,[204] it was decided that a 12-year-old child had not been deprived of his liberty when compulsorily detained for over five months in a psychiatric hospital at his mother's request without any independent

---

197 Discussed in more detail in Chapter 3.

198 Council of Europe's Convention on Human Rights and Biomedicine, Oviedo, 1997.

199 E.g. *Glass v UK* (2004) 39 EHRR 15 para. 58.

200 See e.g. GMC, *Good Medical Practice*, 2006, para. 36, GMC, *Seeking Patients' Consent: the Ethical Considerations*, 1998 and GMC, *0–18 years: guidance for doctors*, 2007, paras. 22–41.

201 *Herczegfalvy v Austria* (1992) 15 EHRR 437.

202 See, e.g. *R (on the application of PS) v G (RMO) and W (SOAD)* [2003] EWHC 2335 (Fam) regarding unnecessary compulsory treatment and *Keenan v UK* (2001) EHRR 38 with respect to unreasonable physical force.

203 Feldman, D., *Civil Liberties and Human Rights in England and Wales*, Oxford, Oxford University Press, 2002 at p. 131.

204 Eur. Ct. HR, Series A, No. 144, Judgment of 28 November, 1988.

review of his detention on the basis of his medical condition: the child's liberty was necessarily restricted by properly exercised parental authority.

The right to freedom of thought, conscience and religion under Article 9 is discussed in Chapter 3 with respect to younger children. Suffice to say here that this is not an absolute right so that it is possible to interfere with a child's, or their parents', refusal of a medical intervention on the basis of their beliefs.

The right not to be discriminated against in the enjoyment of other Convention rights under Article 14 carries no express public interest exceptions and imposes a positive obligation on states as to the way in which the enjoyment of these rights is secured.[205] Article 14 requires another of the Convention Articles to be engaged though not necessarily breached.[206] Where there is a breach of a substantive right, the European Court's tendency is not to examine Article 14 because it would serve no useful purpose.[207] Where it does receive scrutiny, the approach will be to establish whether there is differential treatment or outcome, an acceptable ground for this and whether the resulting difference is justifiable.[208] In formulating a claim about the lack of recognition of competency in the mature minor, age discrimination would seem to be the inevitable focus of any Article 14 discussions.

Article 8(1) is particularly important because it can support a child's autonomous interests in making decisions for themselves and others. The flexibility of the HRA is demonstrated well by Article 8(2) which allows consideration of other interests that may interfere legitimately with any Article 8(1) rights. This means that parental and societal concerns about protecting a child can receive adequate attention for example. This last point should be subject to the caveat that assumptions should not be made about society's views on allowing competent children to refuse life-saving treatment where they suffer from a long-term, debilitating condition. Article 8(1) has been given a relatively broad reading including 'attacks on his physical or mental integrity or his moral or intellectual freedom'.[209] In addition, the Commission of the Council of Europe[210] declared:

> The scope of the right to respect for private life is such that it secures to the individual a sphere within which he can freely pursue the development and fulfilment of his personality. [211]

---

205   *Belgian Linguistic* case, Series B, No. 3 (1967), 24 June 1965, 305–6.

206   Ibid.

207   See e.g. *Dudgeon v United Kingdom*, Series A, No. 45 (1981).

208   Feldman, *supra*, n. 202 at pp. 144–6.

209   J. Velu, 'The European Convention on Human Rights and Right to Respect for Private Life, the Home and Communications' in A. H. Robertson (ed.), *Privacy and Human Rights* (Manchester, Manchester University Press, 1973) 12–128 at p. 92.

210   Now the Court of First Instance.

211   *Andre Deklerek v Belgium*. Application No. 8307/78 DR21, 116.

More recently, in *Botta v Italy*,[212] the Court wrote:

> Private life, in the Court's view, includes a person's physical and psychological integrity; the guarantee afforded by Article 8 of the Convention is primarily intended to ensure the development, without outside interference, of the personality of each individual in his relations with other human beings ... [213]

As the Strasbourg court said in *Pretty v United Kingdom*:[214]

> ... the concept of 'private life' is a broad term not susceptible to exhaustive definition. It covers the physical and psychological integrity of a person. It can sometimes embrace aspects of an individual's physical and social identity ...
> [215]

The Court added:

> The very essence of the Convention is respect for human dignity and human freedom.[216]

Article 8(1) also enshrines the right to make autonomous decisions about medical treatment.[217] There is some domestic case law acknowledging that children have recognizable rights under Article 8(1)[218] but no cases that *robustly* challenge traditional notions of the mature minor's competence by allowing a refusal of life-saving treatment. It has been argued that the courts need to adopt a different approach when addressing children's best interests so that their rights are considered in *all* relevant cases and not just when they mount a legal claim.[219] When, on the rare occasion children's interests are given due attention (usually under Article 8), they should be analysed thoroughly so that the extent of the rights enjoyed by all parties is clear and balanced accordingly. Within family law, for example, it is inadequate to assume the fulfillment of Children Act 1989 requirements implicitly meets the requirements of the ECHR. However, the judiciary has begun to suggest a stance towards the mature minor's autonomy that is more aligned to the liberal interpretation of *Gillick*.

---

212   *Botta v Italy* (1998) 26 EHRR 241.
213   Ibid., at para. 32.
214   (2002) 35 EHRR 1.
215   At para. 61.
216   At para. 65.
217   *NHS Trust A v M, NHS Trust B v H* [2001] Fam. 348, *per* Dame Butler-Sloss at 361.
218   For support see Fortin, J., 'Accommodating children's rights in a post Human Rights Act era' (2006) 69(3) *Modern Law Review* 299–326.
219   Fortin, *supra*, n. 28.

The approach adopted by Munby J. in *Re Roddy*,[220] where he argued that minors should be able to enjoy the general autonomy rights being developed by the Strasbourg courts[221] provided they have the capacity to do so, is noteworthy. This would ensure a full consideration of what the interests may be and how they are to be prioritized. In *Mabon v Mabon et al.*,[222] Thorpe L.J. commented that, in measuring the sufficiency of a child's understanding, account should be taken of the greater appreciation of their autonomy and consequential right to participate in the decision-making processes that fundamentally affect their family life. [223] However, so far there is limited evidence that this view of children's autonomy has filtered into domestic decisions regarding medical decision-making to any significant extent.

In *R. (Axon) v Secretary of State for Health (Family Planning Association intervening)*,[224] *Gillick* was essentially revisited in the light of Mrs Axon's right to family life under Article 8(1) of the HRA[225] in that she wished to be informed if either of her daughters, then aged 12 and 15, sought an abortion. This case is discussed in more detail in Chapter 4 which specifically addresses confidentiality issues. Citing Articles 16(1) and 12(1) of the United Nations Convention on the Rights of the Child 1989 and the judgment of Thorpe L.J. in *Mabon v Mabon*,[226] Silber J. indicated that the international instruments illustrate:

> ... that the right of young people to make decisions about their own lives by themselves at the expense of the views of their parents has now become an increasingly important and accepted feature of family life.[227]

With respect to Mrs Axon's argument based on Article 8(1) of the ECHR in particular, Silber J concluded that:

> ... any right to family life on the part of a parent dwindles as their child gets older and is able to understand the consequence of different choices and then to

---

220   *Re Roddy (a child) (identification: restrictions on Publication)* [2004] 2 FLR 949.

221   Ibid., at 961–2 where he discusses *Niemetz v Germany* (1993) 16 EHRR 97, para. 29, *Botta, supra*, n. 202, *Bensaid v UK* (2001) 33 EHRR 10 and *Pretty, supra*, n. 204, para. 61 which notes that Article 8 ECHR includes the right to personal development.

222   *Mabon v Mabon et al.*[2005] 3 WLR 460.

223   Ibid., at 462 and 466–7.

224   *R (Axon) v Secretary of State for Health (Family Planning Association intervening)* [2006] EWHC 37 (Admin).

225   In relation to Guidance for Doctors and other Health Professionals on the Provision of Advice and Treatment to Young People under 16 on Contraception, Sexual and Reproductive Health (29 July 2004), Gateway Reference No 3382. Relevant parts of the Guidance are set out at [2006] EWHC 37 (Admin), at paras. 22 to 24.

226   *Mabon, supra*, n. 222.

227   *Axon, supra*, n. 224, para. 80.

make decisions relating to them…. [The child's] autonomy must undermine any Article 8 rights of a parent to family life'[228]

On the face of it, Silber J.'s judgment recognizes the importance of providing legal protection for the autonomy of mature minors. However, it remains to be seen whether this approach to the protection of minors' autonomy will apply outside the ambit of issues associated with teenage pregnancy,[229] confidentiality issues more generally and family law proceedings where life or health-threatening conditions are not at stake. In the latter cases, it is likely recognition of the child's autonomy will be strictly circumscribed so that more challenging issues will continue to be addressed paternalistically. This cynicism has some foundation given that these cases, which purportedly protect child autonomy, also have a strong focus on child welfare. Indeed, Thorpe L.J. in *Mabon*[230] *says:*

> In testing the sufficiency of a child's understanding I would not say that welfare has no place. If direct participation would pose an obvious risk of harm to the child arising out of the nature of the continuing proceedings and, if the child is incapable of comprehending that risk, then the judge is entitled to find that sufficient understanding has not been demonstrated.'[231]

In addition, Silber J.'s judgment in *Axon*[232] suggests that the *Fraser* guidelines for assessing competence[233] require a very high level of understanding of the decision to be made, and that the decision is in the child's best interests if it is made without parental knowledge or consent. There needs to be further evidence that these factors will not be used to undermine children's autonomy.

More recently, in *Re P*,[234] Johnson J. was prepared to acknowledge that there might be cases where older children would be permitted to refuse to receive blood products. Further cases decided along these lines would give an unequivocal message and encourage a further cultural shift in attitudes. However, it is still

---

228   Ibid., para. 129–30.
229   The reduction of which is high on the political agenda: see, for example, Department of Health: Teenage pregnancy next steps: guidance for local authorities and primary care trusts on effective delivery of local strategy, 20 July 2006.
230   Mabon, *supra*, n. 222, at para. 29.
231   Ibid., at para. [29].
232   *Axon, supra,* n. 224.
233   Laid down in *Gillick, supra*, n. 44. As Lord Fraser explained, '[s]ocial customs change, and the law ought to, and does in fact, have regard to such changes when they are of major importance' and, explaining current perceptions of the parent/child relationship, he said that 'most wise parents relax their control gradually as the child develops and encourage him or her to become increasingly independent' and 'the degree of parental control actually exercised over a particular child does in practice vary considerably according to his understanding and intelligence', at 171F and 171D-F respectively.
234   *Re P, supra,* n. 167.

unlikely a child under 16 would be accorded similar levels of respect for their beliefs. The proposal here is that the use of a human rights framework can recognize children's right to autonomy within their social context: such an approach can establish the parameters of autonomy to the extent that this is possible. This does not need to undermine their relationships with others or deny any need for protection. Respecting children's self-determination does not mean we are expressing indifference rather than concern or that we are abandoning them to an unhappy fate. It is according them the same rights enjoyed by competent adults where there is evidence they are similarly capable. This evidence may be derived from a process that assists their decision-making to the extent offered by the MCA's Code of Practice to the over 16s which includes formal, expert assessment.[235] The HRA can balance competing claims when a potential interference with a child's rights is under consideration.[236] This can be done on a non-confrontational basis and will ensure all relevant interests are adequately addressed.

A Further Critique of the Current Legal Position

Not all competent people will be similarly capable and all incompetent people similarly incapable. However, the notion of a threshold for competence sorts people into two basic ability groups. Furthermore, a threshold is meaningless unless all those above the threshold are treated as equally competent and those below it as equally incompetent. English law effectively lays down the same capacity threshold for adults and minors, leading to a situation where minors above the threshold possess an equal ability with respect to capacity[237] as their adult counterparts who also reach the threshold. Nevertheless, the courts have refused to accord equal weight to the interests of capacitated minors. By confining a child's rights to consent only, the courts have created a situation where they afford very little respect to the autonomy of a minor whose level of understanding is such that paramount importance would be attached to their autonomy if an adult. This position engenders inconsistency in the protection of legal interests without adequate justification. The suspicion is that the concept of competence is being distorted in order to protect children's welfare. An honest acknowledgement that decisions made by children under the age of majority that are viewed as harmful by society will not be countenanced would be more coherent. Such a position is not one that would be seen as acceptable here unless there is a very careful

---

235   MCA, Code of Practice, Chapter 3. Such tests could include those noted *supra*, n. 64.

236   As is the case when considering autonomy interests under Article 8(1) vis-à-vis those contained in Article 8(2): see, for example, the discussion in *Axon, supra*, n. 224.

237   Determined as an ability to retain and understand the relevant information and the implications of deciding one way or another or not deciding at all.

examination of whether a decision is as damaging as it may appear. Is a decision to refuse life-saving interventions always so detrimental to the individual?

Under the common law a competent minor is a very different concept to a competent adult. The decision of an adult who has the ability to retain and understand the information relevant to a decision and the implications of deciding one way or another or not deciding at all, will be respected despite its apparent irrationality.[238] However, the decisions of minors who possess an equal ability must be outwardly rational if they are to be respected.[239] Expecting there to be some measure of 'rational reflection'[240] as part of the weighing up of information to reach a decision may be reasonable. However, requiring the decision to be rational from the perspective of the capacity-assessor is a step too far. In the medical context, where the rejection of a particular treatment will result in avoidable continued ill health or death, it seems that the courts will only accept as rational a decision that promotes life or health. From this perspective, rationality will generally require assent to medical opinion. The upshot of this unequivocal emphasis on rationality is that prolonging minors' lives appears to trump the protection of their autonomy.

Wicks has argued that to treat all young people under 18 as incompetent with respect to refusal of treatment is unacceptable because:

> ... it involves an assumption in favour of treatment; it destroys any possibility of a competent minor making an autonomous choice (the power to say yes is not a power to choose) and it prioritizes the legal protection of the medical profession over the rights of the vulnerable patient.[241]

This proposal has particular force in the case of the experienced child patient who is suffering from a chronic condition where the treatment may offer a limited prospect of success and/or the treatment itself is very distressing. Some jurisdictions do allow mature minors to refuse treatment within prescribed parameters. For example, in the Netherlands, children between 12 and 16 must normally have their parents' consent before they may request euthanasia. However, in 'exceptional' cases such as those involving serious and incurable disease or intolerable and unrelenting suffering, a doctor may agree to such a child's request even without parental request. Requests by children aged 16–17 do not require parental consent

---

238   See e.g. *Re T, supra*, n. 67 *per* Lord Donaldson at 102.

239   As the discussion in this chapter demonstrates, the courts will override minors' decisions where they consider them to be unwise, let alone irrational: see *Re M, supra*, n. 140, *Re E, supra*, n. 88 and *Re L, supra*, n. 79

240   See Peters, *supra*, n. 65.

241   Wicks, E., *Human Rights and Healthcare*, Oxford, Hart Publishing, 2007 at p. 114.

although parents should be involved in decision making.[242] Forcible treatment, which may involve restraint or even detention, needs strong justification. The reality for practitioners is that without the co-operation of the mature minor, many procedures will be impossible to administer without force.[243]

The prolonging of life or health, in a manner that is against a patient's will, might be justified on the basis of paternalistic beneficence. However, paternalism has fallen out of favour.[244] Paternalism is contrary to the ethical underpinnings of the principle of respect for autonomy.[245] The courts now place great emphasis on the concept of autonomy and have de-emphasized the concept of paternalistic beneficence with regard to adults who have the capacity to make their own decisions.[246] The case law concerning mature minors discussed here indicates that, with respect to minors, the English courts foster dependency rather than promote their autonomy, even where the necessary conditions for autonomy are present. The law should consistently respect patient autonomy whenever it is achievable, irrespective of age, confining the principle of paternalistic beneficence to those cases where the fundamental requirements for autonomy are lacking. This would provide consistency within the law and offer increased rigour given the empirical evidence of children's abilities. The common law fails to achieve this and far from promoting consistency in the law, the MCA exaggerates this inconsistency without adequate justification by not including the under 16s within its remit.

We have seen that sometimes the reason children are not allowed to refuse treatment appears to be because they lack an understanding of the implications of their decision although this may be because they are not given sufficient

---

242 http://www.family.org.au/Journals/2004/dutch.htm.

The US state of Virginia has now passed a law (VA Code No 63.2-100 (2007)) allowing parents of a child at least 14-years-old with a life-threatening condition to refuse medically recommended treatment where the parents and child made the decision jointly, the child is sufficiently mature to have an informed opinion on the treatment, other treatments have been considered and they believe in good faith that their choice is in the child's best interests: Mercurio, M.R., 'An Adolescent's Refusal of Treatment: Implications of the Abraham Cheerix Case', (2007) 120(6) *Pediatrics* 1357–1358.

243 *Supra*, n. 3.

244 Laurie, *supra*, n. 6 at p. 198.

245 As interpreted by English law. It might be argued that a standard of autonomy based on an objective set of ideals linked to rationality is, in effect, a manifestation of paternalism. In medical decision-making, a paternalistic approach involves making a decision which accords with others' views of the subject's best interests. For a discussion of paternalism see, for example, Dworkin, *supra*, n. 7, Chapter 8. In the same way it might be argued that, in the medical context, to be rational and, therefore, autonomous, in the sense of according with objective ideals, any decision must be in one's best interests.

246 See e.g. *Re T, supra*, n. 67 *per* Lord Donaldson at 102, *St George's Healthcare NHS Trust v S; R v Collins and others; ex parte S* [1999] Fam. 26 *per* Judge LJ at 63 and *Re B, supra*, n. 69.

information to do so.[247] In such cases, the courts have sought to find reasons to deem the minor incompetent rather than honestly acknowledging that although the minor is, in fact, capable of achieving capacity, the decision will be overridden if it is seemingly unwise. On other occasions, the reason is more explicitly, and honestly, made about the law seeking to protect the welfare of children in which case it is logical to allow children to consent to treatment doctors have decided is good for them, but not to refuse.[248]

One analysis is that the current legal position, which differentiates adult and child autonomy, justifies the notion of concurrent consents[249] because even though the child can consent, the child's abilities are not such as to extinguish totally the parents' or the courts' role of protection where a child refuses treatment. This position accords with Feinberg's [250] qualms about extending full rights to self-determination to children. A mature minor's right to have their autonomy respected brings with it a right to make informed decisions and be provided with the same opportunities as those over 16 to maximize their capacity. There are powerful arguments to this effect in the case of those young people who have a unique perspective on their quality of life as affected by a long-term illness.[251] In other cases, such a position may be less palatable. Where there is clear evidence the young person lacks capacity as a result of mental illness, this should be acknowledged and appropriate use of mental health legislation instigated to ensure they are provided with the safeguards this brings. The presumption of capacity could also be rebutted where the young person thinks that they are competent but the parents disagree and may be correct in their assumptions. This would provide the opportunity for parents to exercise their responsibilities appropriately in those cases. Consider the case of anorexic young people: they would claim they are competent but their body dysmorphia would suggest otherwise or where their child has joined a cult and the suspicion is that 'brainwashing' may have taken place. Even where there is a very strong commitment to optimize the autonomy of adolescents, it will be hard to resist the idea that

> ... [w]here a choice has irreversible consequences the temptation to take some account of defects in stability is nigh on irresistible.[252]

---

247   As in *Re E, supra*, n. 88.

248   As in *Re M, supra*, n. 140.

249   See *Re R, supra*, n. 111 and *Re W, supra*, n.114.

250   Feinberg, *supra*, n. 4.

251   Rosenbaum, P., 'Children's quality of life: separating the person from the disorder', (2008) 93(2) *Archives of Disease in Childhood* 100–101. See also Morrow, A.M., Quine, S., Loughlin, E.V.O. and Craig, J.C., 'Different priorities: a comparison of parents' and health professionals' perceptions of quality of life in quadriplegic cerebral palsy', (2008) 93 *Archives of Disease in Childhood* 119–25 which highlights how parents and health professionals need to communicate well to ensure the latter have a better understanding of a child's emotional and social well-being.

252   Brazier and Bridge, *supra*, n. 160 at p. 93.

The Way Forward

It was noted that practice remains inconsistent and incoherent with conservative assessments of children's ability to be involved in decisions about their medical treatment remaining the norm.[253] Can the law be of any assistance now? It is worth noting that the Scottish jurisdiction may admit the possibility of competent children refusing even life-saving treatment. While yet to be the subject of litigation, interpretation of the Age of Legal Capacity (Scotland) Act 1991, despite it offering a presumptive and evidential test of competence in common with the jurisdiction of England and Wales, may yield a different result to that in the rest of the UK. Similarly, the Act is silent on the issue of refusing consent but does not mention the parental power of consent. It has been argued that this means competent 16-year-olds cannot have their decisions overridden in line with the Scottish Law Commission's position on this prior to the 1991 enactment.[254] Further, it has been proposed that such a child may be permitted to consent to non-therapeutic procedures such as organ donation because the Act does not define the relevant interventions, which would also support the idea that they should be able to refuse those seen as beneficial.[255] As far as under 16-year-olds are concerned, section 2(4) of the Act is the equivalent to a *Gillick* competent child, and this could also be interpreted robustly so that such a child could not have its decision overruled. For example, in *Houston, Applicant*[256] Sheriff McGowan thought it

> … illogical that on the one hand a person under the age of sixteen should be granted the power to decide upon medical treatment for himself but his parents have the right to override his decision. I am inclined to the view that the minor's decision is paramount and cannot be overridden.[257]

We saw how the UNCRC confirms that children have human rights although they are limited by capacity and the cultural context.[258] The Convention underpins the UK's legal framework but some of its key Articles are not fully reflected in law, policy and practice.[259] The lack of enforcement measures that undermines

---

253   *Supra*, n. 2.

254   Elliston, S., 'If You Know What's Good for You: Refusal of Consent to Medical Treatment by Children' in McLean, S.M., (ed.) *Contemporary Issues in Law, Medicine and Ethics*, Aldershot, Dartmouth, 1997.

255   Ibid.

256   (1996) SCLR 943.

257   Ibid., at 945. This has been accepted as the legal position by the General Medical Council, *0–18 years: Guidance for doctors* 2007.

258   See e.g. Feinberg, *supra*, n. 4 at pp. 76–98.

259   James, A. and James, A.L., *Constructing Childhood: Theory, Policy and Social Practice*, Basingstoke, Palgrave: Macmillan, 2004 and the *UK Commissioner's Report to the UN Committee on the Rights of the Child*, 2008 which expresses disappointment at the continuing lack of progress made on children's rights in the UK.

the effect of the UNCRC may be counteracted to some extent by the HRA.[260] Notwithstanding the Convention's focus on human rights rather than children's rights *per se*, it has had an impact on important children's issues throughout Europe[261] and domestic case law acknowledges that children have recognizable rights under its auspices.[262] However, as suggested earlier, there have been few cases that *strongly* challenge traditional notions of the mature minor's competence by allowing them to refuse treatment[263] which would give an unequivocal message and encourage a further cultural shift in attitudes although policy and professional documents have demonstrated a more enlightened approach.[264] The encouraging reflections in *Re P*,[265] suggesting that there might be cases where older children would be permitted to refuse life-saving treatment should now be built upon in relevant cases.

We have also seen that the indications under the common law are that mature minors' decisions are particularly susceptible to being overridden because they are unwise or because the child has not attained sufficient understanding. Thus, in terms of protection for personal medical autonomy, such children would gain a great deal if the capacity-maximizing principles in sub-sections 1 (3) and 1 (4) of the MCA, applied to them. It would seem that what is required under section 1 (3) of the MCA is an individualized plan of communication which takes into account the particular individual's circumstances and incorporates assessment and re-assessment. Mature minors would stand to derive the same benefit from such an individualized method of communication: it would maximize their capacity to make autonomous decisions about medical treatment. During Hansard debate, references were made to the fact that only those over 16 would come within the ambit of the MCA.[266] However, the issue of whether this curtailed ambit in fact represented evidence of ability and was therefore appropriate was not considered.

The vast majority of minors will have the potential to exercise fully autonomous choice in the future, which may not be the case with respect to many of those to whom the Act is currently addressed. Children, given the opportunity, can develop their independent decision-making skills on the journey to becoming fully

---

260   Fortin, *supra*, n. 28, Chapter 2.

261   Ibid.

262   Ibid and Fortin, *supra*, n. 218.

263   Although see *Re P, supra*, n. 167.

264   DoH consent forms and accompanying documentation: www.doh.gov.uk/ publications and the Royal College of Paediatrics and Child Health (2000) *Advocating for Children*.

265   *Re P, supra*, n. 167.

266   See, e.g. Hansard debate, Mental Capacity Bill, 2nd sitting, 19th October 2004, Mr Burstow at Column 52. Ironically, Hansard debate of the Bill contains significant discussion of children's ability to make decisions on behalf of others, particularly parents and siblings, under a Lasting Power of Attorney, see, for example, 2nd sitting, 19th October 2004, Mr Boswell at Column 54 and 5th sitting, 26th October 2004, Mr Lammy at columns 143–4 and 164, but no discussion of children's ability to make their own decisions.

autonomous individuals.[267] Many of those who fall within the remit of the Act will never attain such a position notwithstanding the extensive measures they must be given to assist them to make particular decisions.[268] International instruments promoting children's rights put forward the view that part of a good upbringing involves children being encouraged to develop a capacity for self-determination.[269] However, the limitations imposed on mature minors' medical decision-making under the common law and statute thwart the development of capacity essential for autonomy. Children are still developing their decisional capacity so it is important that their capacity is harnessed and encouraged. Children need to gain experience of decision-making to practice their skills on the road to reaching 'a capacity where they are able to take full responsibility as free, rational agents for their own system of ends'.[270] As Lord Donaldson noted in *Re* W:

> Adolescence is a period of progressive transition from childhood to adulthood and as experience of life is acquired and intelligence and understanding grow, so will the scope of the decision-making which should be left to the minor, for it is only by making decisions and experiencing the consequences that decision-making skills will be acquired...... [G]ood parenting involves giving minors as much rope as they can handle without an unacceptable risk that they will hang themselves.[271]

Simply allowing minors to consent to medical treatment arguably does little to enable them to acquire such decision-making skills.[272] Giving them 'as much rope as they can handle' should involve taking all practicable steps to facilitate autonomous decision-making where this is a possibility. With respect to non-lifesaving treatment, allowing competent minors to make an independent decision whether to choose whether to 'consent to treatment, to refuse it or to choose one rather than another of the treatments being offered'[273] would go much further in helping mature minors to develop the decision-making skills Lord Donaldson had

---

267   Carnegie United Kingdom Trust (2002) *Measuring the Magic? Evaluating and Researching Young People's Participation in Public Decision-making* at p. 2 and Yates, M. and Jouniss, J., (eds) *Roots of Civic Identity: International Perspectives on Community Service and Activism in Youth*, Cambridge: Cambridge University Press, 1998 *passim.*

268   S. 1(3) and 1(4) MCA.

269   See, e.g. Articles 12, 13 and 14 of the UNCRC.

270   See Freeman, *supra*, n. 5 at p. 57. *Cf. Gillick* per Lord Templeman who stated that there may be many things a young person needs to practice but sexual intercourse is not one of them.

271   *Re W, supra*, n. 69 *per* Lord Donaldson at 81. See also Silber J.'s remarks in *Axon, supra*, n. 224 at para. 129.

272   As is currently the position under English common law: see e.g. *Gillick, supra*, n. 44 and the limitation of this decision in *Re W, supra*, n. 69, *per* Lord Donaldson at 84.

273   The 'absolute right' afforded to competent adults see *Re T, supra*, n. 67, *per* Lord Donaldson at 102.

in mind. Engaging children in all types of decision-making to the extent of their capacity recognizes their autonomous interests and the process itself enhances their competence to participate. Meaningful involvement increases:

> ... confidence, self-belief, knowledge, understanding and changed attitudes, skills and education attainment.[274]

Given these abilities and the international trajectory of children's autonomous interests, there appears to be no justification for the failure of the MCA to afford minors the same assistance to make medical decisions as adults whose capacity is questionable.[275] This is not to suggest that minors' medical decision-making should always be unrestrained but merely that, like for those over 16, all practicable steps should also be taken to help them to make autonomous medical decisions when they are potentially capacitated.

It is less easy to view the refusal of life-saving treatment on behalf of minors as part of a trajectory to adulthood decision-making. Not respecting a child's decision to refuse treatment does not necessarily render the decision-making experience nugatory: they are experiencing the fact that none of us always gets the outcome we desire and part of growing up is learning to be patient.[276] When they reach 18, they will be able to refuse treatment for any reason or no reason at all. However, the earlier comments made about children who, as 'expert patients', should perhaps be allowed to refuse even life-saving treatment because of their unique perspective on their condition is relevant here. It is worth re-iterating that this argument has particular force where a treatment is distressing and/or has a limited prospect of success. Children suffering from cancer who come out of remission know only too well how unpleasant further treatment will be and it is not always possible to ameliorate their symptoms. Palliative medicine has made huge advances in pain management but this is not always readily available.[277] Consider a paediatric version of the case of *Re B*[278] where a child believes that to survive by long-term ventilation is a fate worse than death. Do we really want these children to be prevented from having the dignified and peaceful passing they may desire until they reach the age of 18?[279] As we know, the young man in *Re E*, [280] acknowledged as mature, did not even experience this when he was finally able

---

274   Carnegie, *supra*, n. 267 and emphasized by Koller, D., '"Making a Difference": Youth Participation in Education and Health Care' presentation at the University of Sheffield, Centre for the Study of Childhood and Youth: 'Childhood and Youth: Choice and Participation' International Conference, 2006.
275   S. 1(3) and 1(4) MCA.
276   Thanks are owed here to Derek Morgan for usefully elucidating this point.
277   *Supra*, n. 3.
278   *Supra*, n. 69.
279   *Supra*, n. 3.
280   *Re E, supra*, n. 88.

to refuse transfusions on attaining the age of 18: he died believing he was defiled in the eyes of his religion. Adherence to the strong notions of children's autonomy expressed here and supported by empirical evidence would have avoided the anguish he must have suffered when blood transfusions were administered against his will. The court's countervailing position that his beliefs might diminish as he got older and that he lacked understanding of what it is like to die are weak grounds upon which to base the overriding of E's wishes, particularly when he was not offered sufficient information to help his understanding. In the light of his long-held, well-articulated views, were these not exactly the circumstances that should have received the approach suggested in *Re P*[281]whereby older children might be permitted to refuse treatment?

There will, of course, be cases where mature minors' wishes or decisions cannot be respected because the necessary conditions for autonomy are lacking. The lack of such necessary conditions, however, applies equally to adults and this does not debar them from benefiting from the provisions of the MCA. The possible lack of capacity in the under 16s should not, therefore, preclude them. Nor is it acceptable for the common law to adopt a less than robust position when considering mature minors' decision-making powers. The case law indicates that the lack of such conditions is more readily, but not necessarily more justifiably, presumed with regard to mature minors. Indeed, there is significant evidence that mature minors are eminently capable of achieving the capacity to make autonomous decisions about medical treatment. In the absence of other evidence, it can only be assumed that the legislature excluded this group from these provisions in order to preserve the paternalistic approach which doctors and the courts traditionally adopt towards its members. With all these points in mind, the concluding chapter will suggest a more appropriate approach in the way we treat competent children.

Conclusion

The legislature has missed an opportunity to enhance the protection for the autonomy of mature minors who are under 16 by not including them within the remit of the MCA. The MCA and its accompanying Code of Practice impose significant burdens on practitioners to maximize the autonomy of those over 16.[282] Given the Code's comprehensive provisions, it might be that nothing further would be required to assist mature minors under 16 to make their own decisions, to which those with experience of working with them can easily attest.[283] In the light of the increasing empirical evidence that minors possess the potential to achieve the requisite level

---

281   *Re P, supra*, n. 167.

282   Note the new GMC, 2007, *supra*, n. 200, which adopts an empowering approach to doctors' dealings with children and young people including capacity-maximizing provisions in the section on communication: paras 14–21.

283   *Supra*, n. 3.

of understanding to make their own medical decisions,[284] 16 is an arbitrary cut-off point which draws stark and unnecessary distinctions between those who are nearing that birthday and those who have just attained it. Provisions could be aimed at mature minors that focus on their capacity to understand and weigh up information, based on the most recent evidence about cognitive development and decision-making capabilities, which are at the heart of medical decision-making. There should not necessarily be unconstrained decision-making by those under 16, but they should be given the opportunity to maximize their potential for capacity where that potential is present. In the absence of a legislative change of heart, the only hope for the younger age group is that the judiciary is emboldened in their approach to mature children's decision-making. They should insist on the same robust approach to the under 16s as is offered by the legislature to those over 16 by using a human rights framework and the approach of the MCA as a guide. Such a proposal has particular force in the case of children who have long-term experience of a chronic condition and no longer wish to be subjected to unpleasant interventions that may only be postponing an unavoidable early death.

The potential for possible legal challenges under the HRA and the demands of the clinical governance agenda in ensuring standards of health care are of a high quality must mean that clinical practice is examined to ensure this is so. This should include an assessment of ethical approaches that are commonly employed and should be carried out at both a local and national level. By adopting an ethical framework for decision-making, interventions that are geared to individual patients should ensure the highest possible standards. NHS Trusts are fully accountable for what happens in their organizations and need to ensure appropriate mechanisms are in place for a review of practice. Where particular issues arise, such as those outlined here, one approach might involve a framework of broad principles against which different disciplines may examine their own practice in light of particular patient groups' needs. Royal Colleges, the professional bodies and the Department of Health all have a role in providing suitable guidance. Children should not be treated as 'little adults'. They have their own particular needs and conditions that may require very different interventions to those of adult patients. The political and legal context demands that communication with patients and families is adequately addressed and that child patients in particular are accorded the respect for their autonomy to which they are entitled as human beings.

---

284   See e.g. *supra*, n. 1 and 56*ff.*

Chapter 3
Parental Responsibility and Children's Health Care Treatment*

Introduction

As proxy decision-makers for children, those with parental responsibility[1] have the capacity to consent to medical treatment on behalf of a child.[2] Where more than one person has parental responsibility the consent of one will usually be sufficient.[3] However, there are some procedures that should not be carried out where parents disagree, unless specific judicial approval has been given.[4] The courts will resolve any dispute, based on an assessment of what is in the welfare of the child taking a wide-ranging number of factors into account.

The fact that parents should act in a child's best interests[5] in relation to medical treatment is a well-established legal principle. Although it is arguable that all that a parent is required by the law to do is act in a way which is not against a child's best interests.[6] Following that principle would give parents authority to consent to certain non-therapeutic interventions on their children.[7]

A central argument in this chapter is that responsible parenting also involves taking the child's views into account. International legal instruments suggest that even very young children should be involved in the decision-making process to an optimal extent.[8] All children, whatever their age and circumstances, can provide

---

* A version of this chapter appears in a forthcoming book: *Parental Responsibility* published by Hart Publishing, Oxford, UK.

1 S. 3(1) Children Act 1989.

2 See e.g. *Re Z* [1997] Fam 1 at 26.

3 S. 2(7).

4 Sterilization, change of surname, male circumcision and immunization would constitute such procedures; see, for example, *Re C (a child) (immunization: parental rights)* [2003] 2 FLR 1095, paras. 15–17.

5 *Gillick v West Norfolk and Wisbech Area Health Authority* [1986] AC 112 at 127.

6 See *S v S* [1972] AC 24 where it was considered that to allow paternity testing against the mother's wishes would not be against the child's interests and was justifiable in the general public interest discussed *infra* at n. 27.

7 Pattinson, S.D., *Medical Law and Ethics*, London, Sweet and Maxwell, 2006 at p. 165.

8 See, e.g. Articles 12 and 13 of the United Nations Convention on the Rights of the Child 1989.

valuable perceptions that can improve their clinical care.[9] Even young children are more competent than is traditionally perceived,[10] particularly where they have experience of a long-term illness.[11] With appropriate techniques, children as young as four can make helpful comments about their experiences of health services[12] and like to be involved in this way.[13] Where they have an opinion, it may not be given in an expected way. They need to be empowered through creative means and allowed originality in their views. The General Medical Council (GMC) has also stated that children should be able to influence what happens to them as much as possible,[14] even though the ultimate decision about medical treatment may be taken by those with parental responsibility, or, in the event of a conflict, by the court.[15] However, that represents good practice and the law does not *require* parents to involve their children in making decisions.

---

9   See e.g. Chesney, M., Lindeke, L., Johnson, L., Jukkala A. and Lynch, S., 'Comparison of child and parent satisfaction ratings of ambulatory pediatric subspecialty care' (2005) 19(4) *Journal of Pediatric Health Care* 221–9, Alderson, P., 'In the genes or in the stars?' (1992) 18(3) *Journal of Medical Ethics* at 119–24, Alderson, P., *Children's Consent to Surgery*, Buckingham, OUP, 1993, Eizer, C., 'Changes in understanding of illness as the child grows' (1985) 60 *Archives of Disease in Childhood* 489–92, Fielding, D. and Duff, A., 'Compliance with treatment protocol: interventions for children with chronic illness' (1999) 80 *Archives of Disease in Childhood* 196–200, Alderson, P. and Montgomery, J., 'What about me?' (1996) *Health Service Journal*. April 22–4, Hammond, L., *Children's Decisions in Health Care and Research*, London, Institute of Education, 1993, Brook, G., 'Children's competency to consent: a framework for practice' (2000) 12(5) *Paediatric Nursing* 31; Curtis, K., Liabo, K., Roberts, H. and Barker, M., 'Consulted but not heard: a qualitative study of young people's views of their local health service' (2004) 7(2) *Health Expectations* 149–56 and Sutcliffe, A., Alderson, P. and Curtis, K., *Children as Partners in Their Diabetes Care*, London, SSRU, Institute of Education, University of London, 2004: http://eppi.ioe.ac.uk/ssru_docs/DiabetesReportFinal.pdf, Elliott, E. and Watson, A., 'But the doctors aren't your mum' (1997) 30 *Health Matters* 8–9.

10   See e.g. Woodward, A.L., Sommerville, J.A. and Guajardo, J.J., 'How infants make sense of intentional action' in Malle, B., Moses, L. and Baldwin, D., (eds) *Intentions and Intentionality: Foundations of Social Cognition*, Cambridge MA, MIT Press, 2001 at pp.149–69; Meltzoff, A.N., 'Origins of mind, cognition and communication' (1999) 32(4) *Journal of Communication Disorders* 251–69; Pinker, S., *The Blank Slate: The Modern Denial of Human Nature*, London, Penguin Books, 2002 and Deary, I.J., *Looking down on human intelligence: from psychophysics to the brain*, Oxford, Oxford University Press, 2000 *passim*.

11   Eizer, *supra*, n. 9, Fielding and Duff, *supra*, n. 9, Alderson and Montgomery, *supra*, n. 9 and Bluebond-Langner, M., *The Private Worlds of Dying Children*, Princeton, Princeton University Press, 1978 *passim*.

12   Curtis et al., *supra*, n. 9.

13   Elliott and Watson, *supra*, n. 9.

14   GMC, *0–18 years: guidance for doctors*, 2007.

15   See e.g. *R v Portsmouth NHS Trust ex p. Glass* [1999] 2 FLR 905.

This chapter will provide an overview of the scope of parental responsibility in relation to the medical treatment of younger children and how that should be exercised. Part of this will question the extent to which children should be involved in decision-making and whether it is legitimate to consider parental and family interests as part of this process. The first section will address the minimum legal standards that are imposed on persons with parental responsibility with respect to the health of the children who are in their care.

What Does Parental Responsibility Require?

The law imposes obligations on those with parental responsibility in the context of medical care for their children. Not seeking appropriate medical treatment can amount to a criminal offence or lead to care proceedings.[16] In seeking medically necessary treatment those with parental responsibility should act in their child's best interests.[17] A justification for this is that it can be seen as a reasonable presumption of the child's wishes. It may also be possible to act merely not against their interests. This latter point will be explored further below. In *Gillick*,[18] Lord Scarman stated that 'parental rights must be exercised in accordance with the welfare principle and can be challenged, even overridden, if it is not.'[19] Of course, it is only if the matter is brought before the court that the parent's decision will be challenged as being contrary to a child's welfare. Where agreement cannot be reached between parents, carers and health professionals, it will be necessary to seek a court authorization from the High Court under its inherent jurisdiction or for a specific issue order under section 8 of the Children Act 1989 (CA) to determine the appropriate way forward.[20] The court will make its order based on what it determines is in the welfare of the child. The courts have adopted a broad reading

---

16   See e.g. s. 1 (1) and (2) of the Children and Young Person's Act 1933. From the doctor's perspective, in the case of more routine treatment, consent should be obtained from parents. Where this is not feasible, the defence of necessity would justify an emergency intervention. However, it would be wise to seek consent from parents or court authorization if time permits. If not, they may intervene even where parents object (*Re O* [1993] 2 FLR 149). Anyone caring for a child may do 'what is reasonable in all the circumstances of the case for the purpose of safeguarding or promoting the child's welfare' under section 3(5) CA and this appears to allow consent to be given for medical treatment (suggested in *B v B* [1992] FLR 327). It is unlikely that this provision would extend to major interventions that are not emergencies or where there is parental objection.

17   *Gillick*, *supra*, n. 5.

18   Ibid.

19   Ibid., at 184.

20   Judicial sanction is a legal requirement where a child is a ward of court when important steps are being considered: see e.g. *Re J (a minor) (medical treatment)* [1992] 2 FLR 165.

of best interests, which encompass medical, emotional and other welfare factors,[21] including the psychological and social benefits to the child.[22] The court must have regard to the wishes and feelings of the child concerned as far as they can be ascertained according to their age and understanding.[23] The views of the parents will also be taken into account as part of the assessment of a child's welfare. The nature of judicial reasoning often means that, rather than seeing parents as having a fundamental interest in their children's welfare, their interests are seen as in conflict with those of their child. However, not only do parents possess unique, detailed knowledge of their child, they also have high levels of empathy, and a stake in the child's well-being.[24]

Recently, the courts have been enthusiastic about adopting a balance sheet approach whereby a list is drawn up of benefits and burdens of proposed courses of action and following the approach which has the greatest overall benefit.[25] That notwithstanding, relying on an application of the welfare principle can be seen as unpredictable, lacking in substance, susceptible to bias, and can mean a child's interests are insufficiently acknowledged.[26] In *Re W (contact: joining child as party*,[27] it was stated that a child had a right to a relationship with his father whether he wanted it or not. As James[28] notes:

> This uniquely judicial construction of the concept of the child's right, which does not embrace the right of the child *not* to have contact with his father, demonstrates not only the readiness of the courts to deny children's ability to behave and decide responsibly and to set aside their wishes and feelings, it also demonstrates the power of the language of welfare and how it can be used to deny children's agency.[29]

In James' view, any changes that appear to have taken place in the family law context in terms of 'children's right to participate in decisions that affect their

---

21   *Re A (male sterilization)* [2000] 1 FLR 549 *per* Dame Butler-Sloss P at 555.

22   *Re Y* [1997] 2 WLR 556 at 562.

23   S. 1(3) (a).

24   See the discussion with respect to *An NHS Trust v MB* [2006] 2 FCR 319 discussed *infra*, nn. 83–6.

25   See e.g. *Wyatt and another v Portsmouth Hospital NHS Trust and another* [2005] EWCA Civ 1181.

26   Reece, R., 'The Paramountcy Principle: Consensus of Construct?', (1996) 49 *Current Legal Problems* 267 at p. 303.

27   [2001] EWCA Civ 1830.

28   James, A., 'Responsibility, Children and Childhood', in Bridgeman, J., Keating, H. and Lind, C., (eds) *Responsibility, Law and the Family*, Aldershot, Ashgate, 2008.

29   Ibid., at p. 153.

future, are more rhetorical than real'[30] and, further, that this approach is embedded in welfare professionals' practice.[31]

There is doubt over whether a parent can consent to a non-therapeutic procedure. Clearly, medically necessary therapeutic interventions are likely to be viewed as being in the child's best interests, and this could include so-called 'cosmetic' procedures where these can be justified on the basis of emotional well-being. This could range from relatively simple 'ear-pinning' to the rather more significant limb-lengthening treatment for those suffering from restricted growth. Limb-lengthening may be viewed as necessary by parents who are only too aware of the adversity that may be faced by their child with substantially diminished stature.[32]

Overall, the law allows considerable discretion in the way parents make medical decisions for their children. They must seek essential medical attention and provide sufficient care to ensure their child develops. Apart from that, it is only where there is a disagreement between parents, or between parents and health professionals, about a proposed medical intervention that a court will be required to determine what is in the best interests of the child. Only then is the child given a *certain* opportunity to have their needs and wishes addressed. Examples of the latitude given to parents by the law will now follow.

What Does Parental Responsibility Allow?

Although the courts have said that parents should act in their child's best interests,[33] they have also stated that medical interventions may be permissible provided they are not against the child's best interests.[34] Changing the best interests' criterion to a 'not against the child's best interests' test could be criticized. It could be seen as a dilution of the welfare principle.[35] However, it could render non-therapeutic interventions lawful provided they do not cause significant harm.

One example of where parents may consent to a non-therapeutic intervention can be found in ritual circumcision where there is no clinical need for the operation.[36] Male circumcision is, increasingly, a matter of debate. The current British Medical Association (BMA) guidance[37] suggests that both parents should consent, that

---

30   Ibid., at p. 154.

31   Ibid., at p. 155.

32   *Cf.* Shakespeare, T.W., *Disability Rights and Wrongs*, London, Routledge, 2006, for an exposition of the need for society to accommodate the disabled rather than the latter feeling the need to conform to societal norms.

33   Gillick, *supra.*, n. 5 at 184.

34   *S v S* [1972] AC 24 discussed *supra* n. 6.

35   Fox, M. and McHale, J., 'In Whose Best Interests?', (1997) 60 *MLR* 700–709.

36   See Hutson, J.M., 'Circumcision: A Surgeon's Perspective' (2003) 30 *Journal of Medical Ethics* 238–240 who discusses the possible protective effects of circumcision and their alternatives.

37   BMA, The Law and Ethics of Male Circumcision: Guidance for Doctors, 2006.

competent children should decide for themselves and that even if incompetent, children's views should be considered. So-called 'female circumcision' is prohibited under the Female Genital Mutilation Act 2003, but male circumcision is generally available for religious purposes as well as those situations where it is medically advisable. Despite some evidence that it does provide protective effects from certain diseases,[38] a number of surgeons nevertheless consider it to be unnecessary, if not positively harmful. Given the level of concern that the procedure is difficult to reverse, possibly medically unnecessary and performed on a child who cannot consent, it seems unlikely the matter is settled. Is this religious concession to minority groups coherent when other procedures are forbidden, despite being regarded as acceptable in some cultures? While so-called 'female circumcision' is abhorrent to most and is not physically equivalent to the male procedure, the degree of physical intrusion is only a question of degree. There are of course differences. As traditionally carried out, female genital mutilation is a more painful procedure (even if carried out under anaesthetic), carries higher risks of complications and reduces sexual pleasure, than male circumcision.[39] Further, while the majority of women who have had female genital mutilation as minors may wish they had not had it when they grow up and feel strongly about this, only a minority of circumcised males seem to regret having had the procedure if the media coverage of these topics is any indication.[40] Despite these differences further cogent ethical arguments are required to justify male circumcision on children.[41] There does seem to be a legal anomaly in that the court will allow parents to arrange a procedure as harmful as circumcision and yet prohibit such procedures as tattooing for those under 18 even with parental consent. The courts may be reluctant to pursue this line of thought given the cultural significance of male circumcision under Jewish and Muslim traditions. Further, there are practical considerations. Even surgeons who are uncomfortable with carrying out an intervention that is not clinically indicated will carry out circumcision because they fear the effects of parents taking their male children to unskilled practitioners, with the attendant dangers of significant harm and even death.[42] Nevertheless,

---

38   See, for example, Minniberg, D.T., 'Circumcision' and Rickwood, A.K.M., 'British Attitudes to Circumcision in Paediatric Urology' in O'Donnell, B. and Koff, S.A., (eds), *Pediatric Urology*, Oxford, Butterworth Heineman, 1997 and personal communication from Mr J. Roberts, paediatric surgeon at Sheffield Children's NHS Foundation Trust. See also Baker, D., 'The unkindest cut of all?', *The Times*, 24 March 2008 for a discussion about the advantages and disadvantage of the procedure.

39   http://www.who.int/reproductive-health/fgm/index.html.

40   See e.g. http://news.bbc.co.uk/1/hi/health/medical_notes/241221.stm.

41   Fox, M. and Thomson, M., 'Short Changed? The Law and Ethics of Male Circumcision', (2005) 13 *International Journal of Children's Rights* 161–81 at 170.

42   Personal communication from Mr J. Roberts, *supra*, n. 38 and 'Hunt for Nigerian 'medic' over circumcision death' *The Sunday Times*, August 24, 2003. See also GMC, *Personal beliefs and Medical Practice*, 2008 which expands on guidance in GMC, *Good Medical Practice*, 2006 about when doctors are asked to help with lawful procedures about

judicial attitudes may change if cases arise in the UK, which parallel those in the US where adult males have sought restorative surgery and/or instigated legal actions for battery.[43] Additional difficulties arise where there is also disagreement between parents about whether the surgery should be carried out and in these cases it will be necessary to seek a court authorization. The circumcision cases have provided some interesting examples of how disagreements between parents might be resolved more generally.

Re J[44] demonstrates that where there is parental agreement circumcision is lawful, but in this case a divorced Muslim father wanted his five-year-old son circumcised against the nominally Christian mother's wishes. The child lived with the mother but had regular contact with the father. Both households were essentially non-religious and the boy attended a secular school, although the father gave him some instruction in Islamic matters. In his application for a specific issue order under section 8 of the Children Act 1989, the father argued that circumcision was essential for the child's religious and personal identity and must be part of his upbringing. He also invoked his right under Article 9 of the European Convention on Human Rights (ECHR) to freedom of religious expression. Conversely, the mother indicated that he was not being raised as a Muslim nor would he associate with Muslims sufficiently to justify a non-medically indicated intervention that carried significant psychological and some small physical risks.

The judge agreed that the procedure was part of upbringing for the purposes of section 1 of the Children Act A 1989 and required the consent of both parents, or court approval. In determining whether the mother's wishes should be overruled, Wall J considered that this would not be in the boy's best interests under section 1(3) using the checklist and, *inter alia*, GMC guidelines[45] to assist him. The advantage of helping the boy identify with his father and confirm him as a Muslim was outweighed by the pain of the operation, which he agreed carried significant psychological risks, and the opposition of a mother engaged in a hostile contact battle with the father. The child would also be an exception amongst his secular peers and could decide when old enough to be circumcised whereas a reversal would be more challenging.[46]

---

which they have a conscientious objection such as circumcision: they must refer patients to another doctor. They must not be obstructed from accessing services or be left with nowhere to turn.

43   See Edge, P.W., 'Male circumcision after the Human Rights Act 1998' (2000) 5(3) *Journal of Civil Liberties* 320–37 for a useful discussion about male circumcision from a legal and ethical perspective and Hinchley, G., and Patrick, K., 'Is infant male circumcision an abuse of the rights of the child?' (2007) 335 *BMJ* 1180–1.

44   *Re J (specific issues orders: muslim upbringing and circumcision)* [1999] 2 FLR 678 at 690.

45   GMC, Guidance for Doctors Who are Asked to Circumcise Male Children, 1997.

46   As confirmed by Goodwin, W.E., 'Uncircumcision: a technique for plastic reconstruction of a prepuce after circumcision' (1990) 144 *Journal of Urology* 1203–5 and personal communication from Mr J. Roberts *supra* n. 33.

In *Re S (specific issue order: religion: circumcision)*[47] the court took the view that a girl aged ten and her eight-year-old brother should continue to be exposed to the Muslim and Jain faiths as they had been during their parents' marriage. However, the decision to circumcise the boy should be taken by him upon achieving *Gillick* competence. This had become an issue because each religion took a different view of the intervention: for the Jain faith circumcision is seen as mutilation and unacceptable violence, as do many doctors and some of those who have been subjected to the procedure.[48] It may be argued that this case turns very much on its own facts. In situations where the religious and cultural views might be different, the court may adopt an alternative stance. As the discussion in *Re J* demonstrates, the welfare of a child is taken in an overall sense where religious and cultural aspects of a child's upbringing are only some of the factors considered. Although Article 9 provides a right to manifest religion and might be seen as strengthening the religious 'hand', this did not help these particular parents.

There are other medical procedures can only be lawfully performed if there has been judicial approval, even where all those with parental responsibility are in agreement. These include medical treatment or surgery performed on a child primarily for another person. *Re Y*[49] concerned an incapacitated adult but the application of the best interest principle involves the same considerations whatever the age of the individual. Here, the court was willing to authorize a bone marrow donation from the *incapax* to her sister even though this was not in her medical best interests on the basis that the procedure was in her *social* best interests. If the donation did not take place, the sister was likely to die and the distress of their mother could mean that she would be unable to maintain contact with her other daughter. Connell J. cautioned that the case was not to be viewed as a precedent[50] but similar reasoning could be used in other cases.[51] As suggested earlier, social and other interests may be as important as medical best interests in the impact on emotional well-being. However, it is suggested that only where the indirect benefit to the child from a third party's gain is very clear that the emotional benefit should

---

47   [2004] EWHC 1282.

48   Personal communication from Mr J. Roberts above n. 38 and www.cirp.org/news/ABCnews.

49   *Re Y, supra*, n. 22.

50   Ibid., at 116.

51   Feenan, D., 'A good harvest? *Re Y (mental incapacity)*: bone marrow transplants' (1997) 9 *CFLQ* 305. An interesting example of where third party interests may be in play was provided by the case of Katy Thorpe. Her mother proposed that she have a hysterectomy because she was severely learning disabled and would not be able to cope with menstruation nor would she ever have a family. Opinions expressed in the media were divided: see e.g. Gibb, F., 'Should the Court of Appeal allow Katy Thorpe's womb to be removed?', *The Times*, 18 October 2007. This has not been pursued in the courts after her local hospital refused to treat her in this way. It would have been useful to explore the extent to which the family's interests were a legitimate consideration given the mother's extensive carer responsibilities for her daughter.

be seen as justifying the medical procedure on the child. Where non-regenerative human material is concerned, the courts are likely to more circumspect about any such authorization.[52]

What Does the Responsible Parent Do?

Parents will usually support treatment to keep the child alive on the basis of medical opinion and will generally act in accordance with the best scientific information in the interests of their child's health. An example of this would be participation in immunization programmes. However, religious and/or cultural views about specific interventions can cause parents to opt out of accepted medical practice. In some cases this can even threaten the child's life. Parents may disagree with doctors' views of what is in the child's best interests and either demand treatment against the prevailing clinical opinion or, less commonly, refuse to consent to treatment. Such tensions are particularly vivid where life-sustaining treatment is concerned. If such disagreement cannot be resolved locally, a court will be asked to determine the appropriate way forward.[53] How do the courts approach these highly emotive cases?

Traditionally, the courts have taken parental views of the quality of a child's life into account when determining best interests but have not allowed these to be the sole determinants of such issues. The case of *Re T (wardship: medical treatment)*[54] has been seen as an aberrant decision[55] or, conversely, as more progressive than most:[56] aberrant if viewed as a reversion to the idea of the natural rights of parents, progressive because it took into account the important aspect of the caring relationship.[57] Here, in view of the mother's perception that a liver transplant was not in the child's best interests, contrary to those of the health team involved, the

---

52   See e.g. Article 20 of the influential European Convention on Human Rights and Biomedicine, which prohibits the donation of non-regenerative organs and tissue from an incapacitated person and Lord Donaldson's ambiguous remarks about organ donation from mature minors in *Re W (a minor) (medical treatment)* [1993] Fam 64 at 78–9 and 83–4, with a recommendation to seek authorization from the court.

53   Authorization will be sought from the High Court under its inherent jurisdiction or for a specific issue order under s. 8 of the Children Act 1989 remembering that doctors will not be compelled to act against their clinical judgment: *Re C (a minor) (medical treatment)* [1998] 1 FLR 384 discussed *infra* at n. 88.

54   [1997] 1 WLR 242.

55   Bainham, A., 'Do Babies Have Rights?' (1997) 56 *Cambridge Law Journal* 48–50 and Michalowski, S., 'Is it in the Best Interests of a Child to have a Life-saving Transplantation?' *Re T (wardship: medical treatment)* (1997) 9 *Child and Family Law Quarterly* 179–89.

56   Bridgeman, J., *Parental Responsibility, Young Children and Healthcare Law*, Cambridge, Cambridge University Press, 2007 at pp. 137–42.

57   The ethic of care is explored in Chapter 5.

court decided not to overrule her wishes. This was understandable given the level of post-operative care that would be required of her.[58] The sacrifices required would have been very significant because the parents lived abroad.[59] If she was less than fully supportive such care would, undoubtedly, have been compromised. In addition, the mother's view was within the band of reasonable decisions a sensible person could take, that is, she was making an informed, educated decision, rather than merely a religious one.[60] Further, the child had already undergone an unsuccessful operation that had caused pain and distress. Nevertheless, some commentators have regarded this decision as a regressive step because, *inter alia*, the interests of the child and the mother were not fully articulated.[61] Great care needs to be taken when considering the views of parents.[62] There may be occasions when parents do not have a child's interests truly at heart and it cannot be assumed that the interests of parents and children are exactly aligned.[63] However, this mother was not seen as anything less than a loving parent,[64] Recognition of the caring relationships is to be welcomed, although there is a need to be clear about how they should be valued and acknowledged.[65] Nor should it be forgotten that there is the option of finding a foster carer/adoptive carer if the parent no longer wishes to carry out the parental role[66] as has become necessary in the *Wyatt*[67] case discussed below.[68]

In some cases parents of extremely ill children have insisted on inappropriate (so-called 'futile') medical treatment for children. No doubt, in such cases, it is extremely difficult for parents to relinquish the child to its fate. There will always be a need to have sensitive discussions with families. Decisions subsequent to *Re T*[69] have adopted an approach that focuses on the child's best interests, rather than appearing to conflate these with those of the parents. The traditional approach adopted a presumption in favour of prolonging life while weighing up the pain and suffering involved in further treatment against the quality of life that would result from by it.[70] Treatment would only be withheld or withdrawn if, from the

---

58   *Supra*, n. 54 at 251.

59   *Supra*, n. 54, n. 48 at 252.

60   *Supra*, n. 54, n. 48 at 250.

61   See the discussion in Bainham and Michalowski, *supra*, n. 55.

62   Bainham, *supra*, n. 55.

63   Michalowski, *supra.*, n. 55.

64   *Supra*, n. 54 at 246.

65   Fox and McHale, *supra*, n. 35.

66   Bainham, *op. cit.*, n. 50.

67   *Portsmouth NHS Trust v Wyatt and Wyatt, Southampton NHS Trust Intervening* [2004] EWHC 2247 and Wyatt and another, *supra*, n. 24.

68   Templeton, S.K., 'Carers sought for baby Charlotte as parents part', *The Times*, 15 October, 2006.

69   *Re T, supra*, n. 54.

70   *Re J (wardship: medical treatment)* [1991] 2 WLR 140 drawing on *Re B (a minor) (wardship: medical treatment)* [1981] 1 WLR 1421.

child's perspective, the child's life would be intolerable.[71] More recently, the 'intolerability' point was addressed in the *Wyatt* case, where Hedley J. was explicit that this was not an additional test to best interests but part of the process for determining what these might be[72] with the test sometimes providing a 'valuable guide in the search for best interests in this type of case.'[73]

In *R v Portsmouth Hospitals NHS Trust ex parte Glass*,[74] Lord Woolf MR[75] established important principles of law in such cases. These principles require the courts to take into account 'the natural concerns and the responsibilities' of parents.[76] However, the parents' views will be overruled where they are seen to be in conflict with the best interests of the child. In this case, the mother disagreed with the medical team that her severely disabled 12-year-old son, with a limited life span, should be given no more than palliative care. Following a respiratory tract infection the doctors prescribed diamorphine to make him comfortable but this has the effect of further depressing lung function. To make matters worse, they placed a 'Do Not Attempt Resuscitation' order on his medical notes without discussing this with his mother. The family forcibly intervened to resuscitate the child and took him home where he was successfully treated by the family doctor. At this point the Trust wrote to the family stating that they could no longer offer life-prolonging treatment to David and that future care should be offered at a nearby hospital.

As her relationship with the team had deteriorated to such an extent, Mrs Glass sought a declaration from the court as to the intervention her son could expect on further admittance to the hospital. The Court of Appeal declined to give such an anticipatory authorization because it would unduly restrict the doctors involved. The ideal is for doctors and parents to agree in a climate of consultation and full information but where this is no longer possible, the court should only be called upon to adjudicate on actual facts as they occur at the time. At that point, the court would determine the best interests of the child.

The *Glass* case was then brought before the European Court of Human Rights,[77] that held that the administration of diamorphine against the mother's wishes had breached the right to respect for private and family life under Article 8 of the ECHR in relation to his right to physical integrity.[78] They were particularly critical of the Trust's failure to seek an earlier authorization from the High Court or otherwise defuse the situation.[79] In many ways this case has proved to be a salutary

---

71   *Re J* ibid., at 147–9 *per* Taylor L.J.
72   *Portsmouth NHS Trust v Wyatt, supra,* n. 67 at para. 24.
73   *Wyatt and another, supra,* n. 24 at paras 75–6, 87 and 91 *per* Wall LJ.
74   [1999] 2 FLR 905.
75   As he then was.
76   *Supra* n. 74 at 911.
77   *Glass v UK* [2004] 39 EHRR 15.
78   Ibid.. para. 70.
79   Ibid., para. 79.

lesson for the health and legal professions alike not least because, as one of the judges noted in the European Court, 'maternal instinct has had more weight than medical opinion'.[80] Despite the prognosis David had survived for more than six years following these events. Notwithstanding the important recognition of David Glass' individual rights, and also of the right that his parents' consent be sought, the decision does little to improve overall decision-making in these cases of very dependent children. The obligation of doctors to consult with David Glass' family was made clear but the concern remains that if the parents do not agree with the doctors and a court order is sought then undue judicial deference to medical opinion means that the doctors' views will carry much the greater weight in the court room. In particular, there is a concern that the medical perception of quality of life will rule the day. The suspicion is that quality of life is seen very much from the able-bodied perspective. In fact, the views of the disabled person themselves should be a major determining factor.[81] Where this is not possible, those caring for them on a day-to-day basis, should they be relatives, carers or health professionals, should have a central say in determining these matters.[82] Of course doctors understand better than most the most suitable clinical approach to the prevention, cure or relief of disorders. However, it is the patient and/or their carers who understand their temperament, experience of other medical interventions and other important factors.

More recently, *An NHS Trust v MB*[83] provides an unusual example of where the courts have recognized the parents' views as to the quality of their child's life, notwithstanding the profound disability of spinal muscular atrophy. At the time of referral to the court, MB was artificially ventilated, had very limited movement but was said to be cognitively aware by the parents. The extent of this was uncertain, as was the amount of pain the child experienced.[84] Uncertainty of this order makes decision-making in accordance with the best interests principle very challenging. The mother's view was that it was not in the child's interests to have ventilation removed and her opinion was supported by the court. This was despite the fact that there were opposing opinions from no fewer than 14 consultants. This would accord with Jonas'[85] view that where levels of pain or the extent of an infant's higher-order interests such as autonomy cannot be established, parental views about treatment should prevail notwithstanding any resource implications. Parents have strong claims in decisions for infants because they usually have their best

---

80   (2004) 39 EHRR 15, 364 (Separate Opinion of Judge Casadevall).

81   This was the concern of the Disability Rights Commission expressed in *R (on the application of Burke) v GMC* [2005] QB 424.

82   Asch, A., 'Distracted by Disability' (1998) 7 *Cambridge Quarterly of Healthcare Ethics* 77–87.

83   *An NHS Trust v MB*, *supra*, n. 31.

84   Jonas, M., 'The baby MB case: medical decision making in the context of uncertain infant suffering', (2007) 33 *Journal of Medical Ethics* 541–4.

85   Ibid.

interests at heart. These decisions also have a profound and enduring impact on them so their views should be taken seriously: '[t]hey rejoice when their child flourishes and grieve when her welfare deteriorates.[86] Where a parent disagrees, more weight should be given to the opinions of the primary care giver.

The Religious and/or Cultural Dimension

Religious and/or cultural views are often at the heart of disputes between doctors and parents.[87] In *Re C (a minor) (medical treatment)*,[88] Orthodox Jewish parents argued that their 16-month-old daughter, who suffered from muscular atrophy, should continue to be ventilated. This was contrary to medical opinion, which considered such intervention to be futile because ventilation would only prolong the child's life by a few days. The parents' faith dictated that all efforts should be made to preserve life, but the court preferred the doctors' views. The courts have generally demonstrated an unwillingness to order doctors to carry out medical intervention which parents seek but which the doctors believe to be medically inappropriate. Where parental views include adherence to religious and/or sub-cultural views, it may be easier to be dismissive of these as being less than rational in the light of clinical judgment.

A dramatic example of this may be seen in *Re C (HIV test)*.[89] A local authority applied for a specific issue order[90] permitting an HIV test to be carried out on two children, to ensure the children received the optimal medical care. The parents opposed the application. The local authority relied on medical opinion that estimated the children were at 25 per cent risk of having HIV. The mother, who was HIV positive, breast-fed the baby against medical advice and was generally sceptical about the testing for, and treatment of, HIV. She preferred to rely on complementary medicine. She and the father argued that should a test prove positive, subsequent treatment would be more toxic than beneficial and that such sero-positive status would stigmatize the child. The parents challenged the application as an affront to their parental autonomy. Medical opinion considered the children to be at risk without the test. If they developed an illness, a doctor treating them would have to cater for the possibility that they did have the virus and over-aggressive treatment might be adopted when they were, in fact, uninfected. Alternatively, should they be affected by the virus, and were treated in the future by a doctor unaware of this, under-treatment might be advocated in ignorance.

---

86   Ibid., at p. 546.

87   See Macaskill, M., 'Parents of ill vegan girl may face police', *The Sunday Times*, 8 June 2008 for an interesting example of parental beliefs in a particular diet proving to be severely detrimental to their daughter's health.

88   *Supra*, n. 53.

89   [1999] 2 FLR 1004.

90   S. 8 Children Act 1989.

The level of intrusion involved in the tests was minimal and the court was not persuaded by the views of the parents preferring to concentrate on the welfare and the rights of the child as provided by section 1(1) of the Children Act 1989.

Further examples of the religious context arise in relation to Jehovah's Witness families. Currently, the courts usually support the doctor's view as to what is in the child's best interests although the parents' genuinely held beliefs that they are acting in the child's best interests are acknowledged.[91] This means that there have been a number of cases where doctors have been authorized to give children a blood transfusion, despite their religious objections of their Jehovah's Witness parents and, sometimes, the child.[92] The approach of the courts could be challenged under the HRA, focusing on the rights under Articles 8(1) and 9(1), neither of which are absolute rights.[93] Given the courts' commitment to the sanctity of life and best interest considerations with respect to children, the ability to derogate under Article 8(2) or 9(2)[94] would be relied upon to protect the child. The courts will not allow parents to make martyrs of their children in the name of religion[95] and they have had little appetite to permit mature minors to refuse life-saving treatment.[96] So any attempt to use these Articles to further a child's right to manifest their religion would seem doomed to failure. More recently, in *Re P*,[97] Johnson J. was prepared to acknowledge that there might be cases where older children would be permitted to refuse to receive blood products.

There are examples of good practice where NHS Trusts engage in constructive dialogue with the Jehovah's Witness community through their hospital liaison committees, which have resulted in useful guidance for health professionals dealing with children from these families.[98] This guidance contains consent forms for parents to sign whereby parents are relieved of their agonising decision-making. There is an acknowledgement that they would never agree to the use of certain blood products but equally recognize that the medical team may decide it is in the child's best interests to do so. This proves acceptable to the Jehovah's Witness community who then do not ostracize a family whose child does receive blood products. The reaction of the religious community has been a key influence on parents in this situation.

---

91   See the discussion in Bridgeman, *supra*, n. 56 at pp. 143–9.

92   See e.g. *Re R (a minor) (blood transfusion)* [1993] 2 FLR 757, *Re S (a minor) (medical treatment)* [1993] 2 FLR 1065 and *Re O (a minor) (medical treatment)*, *supra*, n. 16.

93   See *R (Williamson) v Secretary of State for Education and Employment and Others* [2005] 2 FLR 374 where it was held that religious beliefs did not justify allowing corporal punishment.

94   Which, *inter alia*, provide for the protection of the rights and freedoms of others.

95   *Re E* [1993] 1 FLR 386.

96   Ibid.

97   *Bro Morgannwg NHS Trust v* 'P' and others [2003] EWHC 2327 (Fam).

98   Personal communication from Mr J. Reid, Director of Clinical Operations, Sheffield Children's NHS Foundation Trust.

Apart from the decisions in *Re T*[99] (which, arguably, turned on its own particular facts and was subject to widespread criticism),[100] and *An NHS Trust v MB*,[101] the courts generally support medical opinion[102] and thus far the HRA has failed to challenge this approach to any significant degree.[103] However, the HRA does provide a much stronger means whereby families may challenge any perceived lack of involvement in the health care decision-making process under Article 8(1).[104] This means that more account should be taken of the parental perspective both in practice and in future judicial decision-making.

Taking Account of the Child's Views

In Chapter 2 it was noted that an important aspect of the responsibilities of parents is to ensure their children achieve competent adulthood. Children need to gain experience of decision-making to practice their skills on the road to reaching 'a capacity where they are able to take full responsibility as free, rational agents for their own system of ends'.[105] Responsible parents should give weight to the child's views given the empirical evidence that children are capable of making significant decisions at very young ages.[106] The proposal here is that a rights-based approach where the focus is on the individual child, at least initially, can help to challenge the lack of attention paid to children generally[107] and emphasize their need to be involved in decision-making. The plea for specific legislation, with a code of practice, dealing with all aspects of children's healthcare decision-making should be supported. Any departure from the code of practice should require justification

---

99   *Supra*, n. 54.

100   See e.g. *supra*, n. 35.

101   *Supra*, n. 31.

102   See *NHS Trust v (1) A (A Child) (Represented by an Officer of CAFCASS as Child's Guardian) (2) Mrs A (3) Mr A* [2007] EWHC 1696 (Fam) for a recent example where the court agreed with the medical team that the 50 per cent prospect of a full, normal life with painful treatment for a seven-month-old child against certain death before eighteen months without treatment outweighed all other considerations notwithstanding the parents' faith that God would cure the child and their concern about further suffering.

103   See e.g. *Re L* [2004] EWHC 2713 and *Wyatt v Portsmouth NHS Trust, supra*, n. 24. *Cf.* An *NHS Trust v MB, supra*, n. 31.

104   See e.g. *Glass, supra*, n. 77.

105   See Freeman, M., *The Rights and Wrongs of Children*, London, Pinter, 1983 at p. 57.

106   See the discussion in Chapter 2 and *supra*, nn. 9–13.

107   James, A. and James, A.L., *Constructing Childhood: Theory, Policy and Social Practice*, Basingstoke, Palgrave: Macmillan, 2004 passim. See also UK's Children Commissioners' Report to the UN Committee on the Rights of the Child, 2008 on the continuing disappointing level of progress made on children's issues.

through formal procedures.[108] As also suggested in Chapter 2, the Mental Capacity Act 2005 (MCA) could have made improved decision-making with children under 16 along these lines if they had been included within its remit.[109] In the absence of empowering measures, it is even more important that the courts adopt a robust approach to the need to hear young children's views. The use of rights language is having a positive influence on the way in which public bodies deal with more vulnerable members of society[110] and judicial pronouncements that acknowledge younger children's rights to be heard would help further to foster a culture in which this becomes commonplace.

Notwithstanding these observations, the natural tendency of parents is to try and maintain a strong influence on the behaviour of their children not least to protect them from harm. The desire to safeguard children does not diminish as they approach adulthood. However, parents do not fulfil their duties if they do not gradually relinquish their proxy decision-making role so that their maturing offspring are given opportunities to make their own decisions, thus developing their skills to become competent adults.

It would be remiss in a chapter such as this to neglect the sense of parental responsibility that remains with parents following a child's death. A moment's reflection reveals the extent to which this may be seen as an inevitable fact. If evidence is needed, one only has to consider the scandals revealed by the Bristol and Alder Hey inquiries[111] and the consequences for affected families.

Parental Responsibility Following a Child's Death

The Inquiry set up to investigate the paediatric cardiac service at Bristol Royal Infirmary[112] revealed that organ and tissue retention post-mortem was common practice across the UK. It was used for a wide range of (sometimes valuable) purposes including audit, medical education and research but was often not used at all and was simply stored. It became apparent that the largest collection of hearts for example, was at the Royal Liverpool Children's Hospital. This led to a further Inquiry and the subsequent Alder Hey Report[113] underlined the fact that

---

108   Alderson, P. and Montgomery, J., *Health Care Choices: Making Decisions with Children*, London, IPPR, 1996.

109   See also guidance to this effect in DoH consent forms and accompanying documentation: www.doh.gov.uk/publications.Dec. 2001.

110   British Institute for Human Rights, *The Human Rights Act: Changing Lives*, 2007: this report shows how the language and ideas of the HRA are being used to change the approach taken in dealing with more vulnerable members of society for example.

111   The Report of the Public Inquiry into Children's Heart Surgery at the Bristol Royal Infirmary 1984–95: Learning from Bristol (Cmnd 5207 (1)) 2001 and The Royal Liverpool Children's Inquiry Report, HC 12–11, 2001, (the 'Alder Hey Report').

112   Ibid.

113   The 'Alder Hey Report', *supra*, n. 111.

the practice was pervasive and longstanding.[114] Removal of children's organs and tissues was often done without the consent or even knowledge of parents. This was thought to be acceptable practice at the time. This is perhaps unsurprising given that the law concerning the removal of body parts was complex and unclear. However, the subsequent reaction of families after the revelations is an indication that the removal was ethically unsound. There was an assumption that whether a relative was 'complete' or not would not be of concern to families, that discussing removal of the material would add to their distress and that progressing science should be an overarching objective.

For those cases not subject to the rigours of the Anatomy Act 1984, control of the body rested with those who are in lawful possession of the body at the time of death. This will often be the hospital where post-mortems may be carried out. Relying on the provisions of the Human Tissue Act 1961,[115] hospitals assumed they could remove organs and tissue for research and education purposes if no family member objected. Where removal was discussed with families, they often did not understand to what they were consenting or that they could object. Where post-mortems were carried out under the Coroners Act 1988 for inquest purposes,[116] relatives' authorization for removal of organs and tissue was more clearly required following the procedure.[117] In practice, pathologists were allowed to use the material as they saw fit.

When the extent of the retention was revealed, not surprisingly, there was a public outcry. It was not that parents did not recognize the need for such material but that their consent was not obtained for its use.[118] It was thought this indicated a lack of respect for them and their deceased relative. There was resentment

---

114   *Cf.* McLean, S.A.M., (Chairperson), Independent Review Group on Retention of Organs at Post-mortem Report, 2001 in Scotland discussed infra at n. 122–5.

115   Especially s. 1(2) provides that the hospital may authorize removal and retention of body parts if after ' … such reasonable enquiry as may be practicable, there is no reason to believe: (a) that the deceased had expressed an objection to his body being so used after his death … or (b) that the surviving spouse or any surviving relative objects to his body being so dealt with.'

116   Under s. 8(1) a coroner may order a post-mortem if he is informed that the body of the deceased is lying within his district and there is reasonable cause to suspect that the deceased ' … (a) died a violent or unnatural death; (b) has died a sudden death of which the cause is unknown; or (c) has died in prison or such a place or in such circumstances as to require an inquest under any other Act.' Harris, J., 'Law and Regulation of Retained Organs: the Ethical Issues', (2002) 22 *Legal Studies* 527 and Brazier, M., 'Retained Organs: Ethics and Humanity', (2002) 22 *Legal Studies* 550.

117   Brazier, M. and Cave, E., *Medicine, Patients and the Law*, (4th ed.) London, Penguin Books, 2007 at p. 474.

118   Brazier, M., *Medicine, Patients and the Law*, (3rd ed.) London, Penguin Books, 2003 at p. 470 and personal communications from affected families and teams of NHS staff, who were involved in supporting them through the scandal at Sheffield Children's NHS Foundation Trust.

about the lack of control over the disposal of their remains. This sometimes had a religious basis. It is imperative for the Jewish and Muslim faith for example, to bury the body intact. Even where this was not an issue, the feeling for many families was that they could not lay their loved one to rest if they were incomplete. In some paediatric cases, the body may well have been a 'shell' given the amount of organs and tissues removed. Above all, the reaction of families clearly indicates the close connection they continue to feel with the deceased. This is particularly the case where a child has been lost. Parents continue to feel responsible. They feel that an appropriate burial is the last thing they can do for their child. Many felt this was denied to them as a result of this practice. The removal of body parts interfered with families' image of their loved one who was still a person to them, not merely a useful object.[119]

Subsequent to the following debate, [120] the Human Tissue Act 2004 has now been enacted in an attempt to deal with the shortcomings of its predecessor. In particular, the position of parents' rights with respect to the use of their child's remains has been addressed. Section 2 provides that where a child is competent, they can make an advance decision concerning their consent to the removal and use of their human material. Such a decision must be respected. If the child was incompetent, the person with parental responsibility can consent for the child, apart from the use of the body for anatomical examination: this requires consent from the child. Where the child has died leaving no one with parental responsibility, someone in a 'qualifying relationship' can consent to the removal, storage and use of the material.[121] It should be noted that the Scottish Report on Retained Organs at Post-mortem[122] recommended that the term 'authorization' should be used in this context[123] rather than consent. This proposal is persuasive because intrinsic to the notion of consent given by proxies is that this is done on the basis of acting in the particular child's best interests. This cannot be relevant to a post-mortem examination.

The Report took the view that the use of the word 'authorization' rather than 'consent' strengthens the role of parents in decision-making about the way in which their children should be dealt with and clarifies the scope of the (legally valid) decision-making powers which they have in respect of such children in these circumstances.[124] Further, a valid consent is generally expected to follow the provision of information. Authorization is not constrained by this requirement and this meets the concerns of those parents who do not wish to receive information

---

119   BMA, *Medical Ethics Today*, London, BMJ, 2004 at p. 417.

120   E.g. Chief Medical Officer, The Removal, Retention and Use of Human Organs and Tissue from Post Mortem Examination, 2001 and Department of Health (DoH), Human Bodies, Human Choices, 2002.

121   S. 2(7). The hierarchy of qualifying relationships are set out at s. 27(4).

122   *Supra*, n. 114.

123   Ibid., paras. 6, 28, 47 and 59–72 for example.

124   Ibid., at Section 1, para. 17.

about post-mortem examination and/or the subsequent removal and retention of organs or tissue, but who do not object to this.[125]

Paediatric health professionals often see the family as the 'patient'.[126] The familial and social context has to be acknowledged as playing a role in caring for the child. To do so is the preferred holistic approach. Nowhere is the care offered to families more evident than when a child reaches the end of their life. There are many eloquent testaments about the support families receive.[127] They speak of the time taken in helping them to reach decisions about treatments that were right for them. In the sad event that a child dies, the families often continue to receive support through bereavement counselling.[128] Health professionals sometimes accompany parents when they visit their child in the mortuary because they want to help the relatives. They also wish to spend time with the child with whom they have often formed a relationship. The new legislative provisions mean that a similar level of care must be taken when examination of the child's human material can offer some benefit. When this is properly explained to families, they are usually only too willing to assist. This underlying wish to help is confirmed by the statements made by affected parents during the Bristol Inquiry.[129] Their complaints centred on the lack of respect shown to them and their relative. They thought their loved one was treated with contempt: as a mere convenience. As Mrs Susan Francombe, mother of Rebecca, said:

> I know I felt if another baby could be helped by the retention and, if that was the reason, then we would have said yes; but the fact that they were kept without our knowledge came as a very, very big shock.[130]

125　Ibid. Notwithstanding these arguments, this is not a view shared by their counterparts in England and Northern Ireland for example (see Brazier, M., 'Retained organs: Ethics and Humanity', (2002) 22(4) *Legal Studies* 550–69 at p. 556), does not represent English law and is ' … of academic rather than practical significance.' Mason, J.K. and Laurie, G.T., *Law and Medical Ethics*, (7th ed.), Oxford, Oxford University Press, 2006 at p. 494. The latter view is supported by the DoH, *supra* n. 120 at p. 52. However, if language is seen as an important instrument of social change as suggested at n. 22 in Chapter 2, the use of the term authorization has relevance with respect to parental decision-making more generally. This is beyond the focus here and does not, in any case, detract from the more general observations about children and consent that are made throughout this book.

126　Personal communication from a range of health professionals throughout my NHS experience.

127　E.g. personal communication from Sabine Vanacker and David Kelly, the parents of Isabel who suffered from Tay-Sachs disease and was treated at Sheffield Children's NHS Foundation Trust. Their experience of support from the hospital was recorded and presented at the Value of Life, the Value of Death ETHOX Annual Conference, Sheffield, 21 May 2008.

128　This may also be true in cases involving the loss of an adult patient of course.

129　*Supra*, n. 111.

130　The Bristol Royal Inquiry Interim Report, 2000, at para. 27.

Conclusion

The law requires those with parental responsibility to act in a child's best interests[131] in relation to medical treatment but the parameters of this may yet need extension. We know that 'cosmetic' procedures and even non-therapeutic interventions may be legitimate in certain circumstances.[132] It is also clear that parents will have to support medically necessary treatment where that is underpinned by clinical evidence regardless of their own values, where there is a reasonably significant medical benefit. The boundaries of determining best interests becomes more contentious when establishing whether a child's experience of life justifies significant medical interventions and the extent to which they should be involved in the decision-making process. This chapter has attempted to support the idea that those caring for child patients have a unique perspective on how this should be conducted and that the child's views should be given greater predominance than has hitherto been the case. The law has a crucial role to progress this agenda.

---

131   Or at least not against their interests: *supra*, n. 34*ff.*
132   *Supra*, n. 36ff.

Chapter 4
Confidentiality and Children

Introduction

As we have seen in the preceding chapters, concepts such as autonomy, dignity and privacy have as much relevance for children as they do for adults. In many ways, it is easier to demonstrate a clear commitment to children's autonomous interests by recognizing that their private information should be kept confidential than by allowing them to make medical decisions whether to have treatment or not. However, these interests may have to be restricted to protect children when they lack competence. As with competent adults, there may also be a need to override children's autonomy in the interests of others. The emphasis on individual's rights with respect to confidence is not easily achieved in the modern medical setting and may even be seen as outdated and unhelpful, particularly in relation to the need to develop medical services.[1] We all hope to benefit from these advances so we all bear a responsibility to share information, albeit within limited parameters,[2] otherwise there is a risk progress will be unduly restricted.

The ability to consider third party interests under the law means that the duty of confidentiality cannot be said to be absolute. It can be necessary, in some circumstances, to release information in the patient's and others' interests. The intrinsic tension between the interests of individuals and those of others is particularly apparent in the case of children. There is potential conflict between empowering children by treating them as autonomous individuals who have rights of confidentiality, and the need to protect them from harm. This will become evident in the discussion about when it may be legitimate to disclose information confided by the mature child patient or where there is a suspicion of child abuse. Where the line should be drawn between respecting rights to confidentiality and disclosure is one of the questions this will address. Not only may disclosure protect children from harm but it may also serve the interests of others in some circumstances. The particular issues raised by genetic information are addressed in the following chapter as an example of where it might be more appropriate to treat the family as 'the patient'.

---

1   Rubinstein, H., 'If I Am Only for Myself, What Am I? A Communitarian Look at the Privacy Stalemate', (1999) 25 *American Journal of Law and Medicine* 203–32 at p. 227, cited in Herring, J., *Medical Law and Ethics*, Oxford, Oxford University Press, 2006, 1999 at p. 192.

2   See the discussion in Chapters 5 and 7 which notes the importance of other-regarding perspectives.

The long-established[3] principle, that information passed from a patient to their doctor should be kept confidential, is seen as sacrosanct. This is also true of other health professionals and continues to be widely supported by the law, international instruments, professional and Department of Health (DoH) guidance.[4] A rationale for this is that a doctor cannot effectively treat a patient unless there is a full sharing of information which might not be forthcoming if there are worries that it is not kept private.[5] This could also affect the public's willingness to trust health professionals more generally. There are different ideas about the nature of the wrong done by a breach of confidence. To share personal information with others without authorisation may be seen simply as a breach of a promise or fidelity,[6] and this can be seen as a wrong in itself. Alternatively, there is the view that respect for autonomy requires that people should lead their lives as they choose, which is not possible if privately shared information is divulged. The right to control private information may be seen as a core aspect of individuals' sense of self and identity.[7] This is as true for children as it is for adults. The right to respect for private and family life under Article 8(1) of the European Convention of Human Rights (ECHR) supports this view. It emphasizes notions such as privacy, dignity and autonomy.[8] This strengthens the position for the individual. However, interference with this right is permissible under Article 8(2), broadly in the interests of other

---

3   Hippocratic Oath: 'Whatsoever things I see or hear concerning the life of men, in my attendance on the sick or even apart therefrom, which ought not to be voiced abroad, I will keep silence thereon, counting such things to be sacred secrets.'

4   See, for example, the World Medical Association's International Code of Medical Ethics (the latest version was adopted by WMA 58th General Assembly, Copenhagen, Denmark October 2007) that requires the duty of confidentiality to extend beyond death as does the GMC, *Confidentiality: Protecting and Providing Information*, 2004 at para. 30 and DoH, *Confidentiality Code of Practice*, 2003 at p. 29.

5   British Medical Association (BMA), *Medical Ethics Today*, London, BMJ, 2004 at p. 165.

6   Beauchamp, T.L. and Childress, J.F., *Principles of Biomedical Ethics*, (5th ed.), Oxford, Oxford University Press, 2001, pp. 307–10.

7   O'Brien, J. and Chantler, C., 'Confidentiality and the Duty of Care' (2003) 23 *Journal of Medical Ethics* 36–40. See Mason, J.K. and Laurie, G.T., *Law and Medical Ethics*, (7th ed.), Oxford, Oxford University Press, 2006, at p. 177, where the preference for the concept of informational privacy is discussed. This is thought to better protect individuals' private sphere not least because it does not demand a relationship between the relevant parties. It would also allow better ongoing control of personal information.

8   See e.g. *Campbell v MGN* [2004] UKHL 22, where these concepts are discussed. *Mosley v News Group Newspapers Ltd* [2008] EWHC 1777 (QB), established that individuals have a reasonable expectation of privacy with respect to sexual activities carried out between consenting adults on private property, regardless of their conventionality or otherwise and exemplary damages are not available for an infringement of privacy.

individuals and in the public interest. With this in mind, UK law continues to develop under the Article's influence.[9]

The balance between an individual and the rights of others is under constant review.[10] This chapter will explore how legal and ethical requirements manage this inherent tension as well as noting a forthcoming case that may re-draw the scope of a doctor's duty of confidentiality with respect to third parties. A general discussion of the legal and ethical obligations with respect to confidentiality is provided as the context for this discussion and necessitates a discussion of key adult cases. The chapter as a whole highlights the particular issues that arise for those dealing with children in the healthcare setting.

Forms of Consent

Generally, the obtaining of consent for particular disclosure from patients, where this is possible, will ensure legal, ethical and professional compliance with the common law duty of confidence. A valid consent to disclosure of information acts as a waiver to the legal duty of confidence.[11] It is the parameters and nature of the consent that may be called into question.[12] Consent may be either 'express', or 'implied'. Express consent in the form of the written or spoken word or by equivalent conduct such as nodding assent, will be the most straightforward form of consent. A classic example of implied consent is where a patient holds out their arm for an injection. Where a patient expressly consents to one intervention that necessarily involves another procedure, consent to the following procedure will also be implied. While the practice of modern medicine necessitates the sharing of personal information with the healthcare team and consent to such use will be implied,[13] many people will only realize this is the case upon reflection.[14] As it is, where patients do realize and object to the sharing of specific information, this must be respected.[15] Still less will they realize that administrators such as medical records' clerks and even inspectorate bodies such as the Healthcare Commission

---

9   See e.g. *Re W (children) (identification: restriction on publication)* [2005] EWHC 1564 (Fam).

10   See e.g. *Campbell, supra*, n. 8.

11   E.g. Sch. 3 of the Data Protection Act 1998 (DPA), *C v C* [1946] 1 All ER 562 and *Z v Finland* (1998) 25 EHRR 371, para. 112, with respect to statute, the common law and Art. 8(1), respectively. In the case of the DPA, the consent will, generally, need to be explicit.

12   It is likely the same requirements regarding consent to treatment apply to consent to the disclosure of confidential information i.e. the need for capacity, to be broadly aware of what is being consented to and to be acting voluntarily (see Chapter 2).

13   BMA, *supra*, n. 5 at pp. 177 and 180.

14   See Herring, J., *Medical Law and Ethics*, Oxford, Oxford University Press, 2006 at pp. 193–4 for a sample of surveys about the public perception (sometimes misguided) of how health information is used within the NHS.

15   *Birmingham CC v O* [1983] 1 All ER 497.

can also have access to their files. The *Caldicott Report*[16] identified approximately 150 individuals who can have access to a patient's health information in a single episode. In addition, the promotion of electronic health records by the DoH[17] makes the protection of confidential information more difficult and is often attacked by the medical profession.[18]

However, there are concerns about a perceived over-reliance on implied consent, where there is an assumption the patient will be aware of the uses made of their personal information.[19] What of the use of health data for research, teaching and audit? Obtaining consent for certain types of research, particularly projects relying on historical data, may be impracticable if not impossible. Routine teaching, clinical and other audits may also involve disproportionate effort if individual consents are required. It may be more accurate to see the use of personal health data for these purposes as involving imputed consent.[20] The DoH's view is that implied consent covers the use of personal information for clinical audit, monitoring public health and research.[21] The General Medical Council (GMC) states that express consent should be obtained for even the sharing of information amongst the healthcare team.[22] For these reasons, many Trusts will present an information sheet which sets out that information to be shared for a range of purposes including teaching and audit to ensure high standards of care. In the paediatric setting, this should be in a format that is accessible to children. The patient can indicate their consent for some or all of these purposes in accordance with guidance.[23] The better information sheets will remind patients that all Trust employees have a confidentiality clause

---

16   NHS Executive, *Caldicott Report on the Review of Patient-identifiable Information*, 1997. There is presumed consent for the essential sharing of information with others in the healthcare system: see Information Commissioner, *Use and Disclosure of Health Data: Guidance on the Application of the Data Protection Act 1998*, 2002.

17   DoH, *NHS National Plan*, 2000.

18   See e.g. Hawkes, N., 'Four out of five doctors believe patient database will be at risk,' *The Times*, 31 December 2007.

19   See e.g. the Royal College of General Practitioners, *Confidentiality*, 2000 at p. 1.

20   See Pattinson, S.D., *Medical Law and Ethics*, London, Sweet and Maxwell, 2006 at p. 191 on this point and pp. 199–202 for an analysis of *Source* on these and other aspects of the duty of confidence. See *R v Department of Health ex p. Source Informatics* [2000] 1 All ER 786 discussed *infra*, at nn. 29–30 and 107–16.

21   DoH, *The Protection and Use of Patient Information* 1996; *cf.* BMA, *supra*, n. 5 at pp. 177 and 180, where it distinguishes clinical audit, essential for ensuring the quality of patient care, requiring only implied consent from other formers of audit, research and teaching for which express consent should be obtained.

22   GMC, *supra*, n. 4 at para. 10 and concurs with the BMA, ibid. that express consent should also be obtained where identifying information is to be used for research, epidemiology, financial audit or administration: para. 16.

23   See e.g. GMC, *supra*, n. 4 at paras. 13 and 14 in relation to clinical audit. This is the case at Sheffield Children's NHS Foundation Trust.

as part of their employment contract and that the obligation extends to volunteers[24] and to contractors to the NHS.[25] Another key impetus for such initiatives has been the Data Protection Act 1998 (DPA) which highlighted everyone's obligations to safeguard information to an unprecedented extent and is discussed below. The Information Commissioner, who has overall responsibility for ensuring compliance with the DPA, takes the view that there is implied consent for the processing of data for essential health services from patients who refer themselves for and accept care.[26] This will include the administration of records and clinical audit but not clinical research. NHS health authorities and Trusts must have a 'Caldicott Guardian' who acts as a steward of the system.[27] In the hospital setting this is often part of the role of the Medical Director.

Given the criticisms that the implied consent model is too artificial,[28] an alternative approach would be to argue that the sharing of information, where there are legitimate reasons for this within the NHS system, is justifiable in the public interest because it enables organizations to function at an optimal level. Legal support for this position is found to a limited extent in *R v Department of Health ex p. Source Informatics.*[29] Simon Brown LJ. stated *obiter*:

> ... it is clear on the information before us that for certain limited purposes patient information is used in identifiable rather than anonymized form. As the Department of Health states, 'thorough research and management depend in part upon the possibility of others checking that anonymized and aggregated information does correspond to the real world, by audit procedures which must inevitably involve checking identifiable cases.' For present purposes, I say no more than that, provided, as I understand to be the case, the use of such identifiable data is very strictly controlled, there appears no reason to doubt that this is acceptable ... [30]

Thus, the use of patient identifiable information can be legitimate for NHS purposes such as research and management. He did not specify whether this was because there is a public interest justification or because there was no breach of confidence.

---

24   DoH, *supra*, n. 4 at p. 16.

25   DoH, *Confidentiality and Disclosure of Information: General Medical Services, Personal Medical Services and Alternative Provider Medical Services Code of Practice*, 2004.

26   Information Commisioner's Office, *supra*, n. 16.

27   *Caldicott Report*, *supra*, n. 16.

28   Beyleveld, D. and Histed, E., 'Case Commentary: Anonymisation is Not Exoneration', (1999) 4 *Medical Law International* 69–80 at 75–6.

29   *Source Informatics*, *supra*, n. 20 and discussed *infra* at nn. 107–16. This can only be claimed as limited support because the reasoning is the case is controversial (see e.g. Beyleveld, D. and Histed, E., 'Betrayal of Confidence in the Court of Appeal', (2000) 4 *Medical Law International*, 277–311) and because of subsequent common law developments e.g. *Campbell*, *supra*, n. 8.

30   *Source Informatics*, *supra*, n. 20 at 444.

Confidentiality and Children

Statutory Obligations and Permissions

The Data Protection Act 1998 (DPA) is the most significant statute that protects confidential information[31] and there are a number of others that permit or require the disclosure of confidential information about adult and child patients. A doctor must give information to the Home Office about any drug addict being treated[32] and to the Chief Medical Officer about terminations of pregnancies.[33] Specified notifiable diseases must be reported to the relevant authorities[34] as well as certain sexually transmitted diseases.[35] The Government has resisted attempts to include HIV/AIDS as a notifiable disease mainly because it is has a low risk of transmission with responsible behaviour. Such reporting might also discourage affected patients from seeking treatment. The Public Disclosure Act 1998 is notable because it was enacted to encourage people to raise concerns about malpractice in the workplace relating to negligence, breach of contract, administrative law, miscarriage of justice and danger to health and safety or the environment. It applies whether or not the information is confidential provided any disclosure is made in good faith. Thus, the 'whistleblower' will be protected from sanction where they breach a confidence

---

31   Others include the Computer Misuse Act 1990 which creates an offence of 'hacking' into a database to retrieve confidential information: *R v Bow Street Metropolitan Stipendiary Magistrate ex p. Government of the USA* [2000] 2 AC 216 illustrates that authorization to only certain parts of a database means that accessing others will be an offence. S. 33 of the Human Fertilisation and Embryology Act 1990 imposes non-disclosure obligations on past and current members of the Human Fertilization and Embryology Authority.

32   Misuses of Drugs (Notification of Supply to Addicts) Regulations 1973, S.I. 1973/799.

33   Abortion Regulations 1991, S.I. 1992/499 require the NHS number, date of birth and full post code only.

34   Public Health (Control of Disease) Act 1984 lists cholera, plague, relapsing fever, smallpox and typhus. Following a consultation in 2007, the DoH plans to update the powers in Part II of the Act for preventing and controlling the spread of disease, extending them to cover radioactive or chemical contamination. It is thought these powers provide flexible and proportionate safety measures to ensure that where an individual refuses to take action voluntarily to protect the public from infection or contamination, they can be required to do so to safeguard public health. http://www.dh.gov.uk/en/Aboutus/MinistersandDepartmentLeaders/ChiefMedicalOfficer/ProgressOnPolicy/ProgressBrowsableDocument/DH_5014411.

35   See e.g. NHS (Venereal Diseases) Regulations 1974, SI 1974/29 which prohibits, *inter alia*, a health professional from disclosing information about the patient's attendance at a genitourinary clinic without consent, even to their GP; NHS Trusts and Primary Care Trusts (Sexually Transmitted Diseases) Directions 2000. Nor can a doctor disclose information about a patient's attendance at a fertility clinic without consent, even to their GP, under the Human Fertilisation and Embryology Act 1990 as amended by the Human Fertilisation Embryology (Disclosure of Information) Act 1992.

provided they raise their concerns using their line management hierarchy before 'going public'.

The DPA was implemented to give effect to the European Directive on Personal Data 1995[36] whose aim is to protect the fundamental rights and freedoms of individuals, particularly their right to privacy, and the free flow of all types of personal data between Member States.[37] Detailed information on this Act may be found for any number of medical law sources.[38] For our purposes here, it should be noted that children come within its remit and that adequate consent from patients that their data may be used for particular purposes should satisfy DPA requirements. It is necessary to alert patients as to what these might be, perhaps by using an information sheet as suggested earlier. The purpose of the Act is to regulate the processing of personal data belonging to data subjects by data controllers.[39] It covers any activity in relation to all types of personal data, including health records, and both individuals and organizations may constitute data controllers. The First Data Protection Principle[40] requires, *inter alia*, that personal data should be processed lawfully. Common law interpretation of what constitutes legitimate disclosure will assist in determining whether the processing of certain data may proceed without consent.[41] The HRA will also be influential because privacy rights have been given a wide reading and may mean that protection offered by the DPA will have to be robust.[42]

The common law will also be applicable where the DPA does not apply. An example of the latter includes personal information disclosed to a health professional that is not recorded. Another example would be where medical information is recorded in handwriting by someone who is not treating the patient, and is not held in a relevant storing system.[43] While the dense nature of the Act presented challenges to those falling within its remit, the level of detailed provisions gave the issue of confidentiality an unprecedented focus in the NHS.

---

36   EC Directive 95/46/EC.

37   Art. 1. See Beyleveld, D., 'The Duty to Provide Information to the Data Subject: Articles 10 and 11 of Directive 95/46/EC', in Beyleveld, D., Townend, D., Rouillé-Mirza, S. and Wright, J., (eds), *The Data Protection Directive and Medical Research Across Europe*, Aldershot, Ashgate, 2004 for criticisms that the Act's implementation is inadequate.

38   See e.g. Mason, J.K. and Laurie, G.T., *Law and Medical Ethics*, (7th ed.), Oxford, Oxford University Press, 2006, Chapter 8.

39   S. 1(1).

40   In that the First Data Protection Principle in Sch. 1, Part 1 of the DPA requires, *inter alia*, that personal data should be processed lawfully.

41   See e.g. Sch. 3 conditions.

42   S. 3 of the HRA requires that all legislation to be interpreted, as far as possible, so as to give effect to Convention rights which, of course, includes the privacy rights under Article 8(1), which could include personal data.

43   As pointed out by Pattinson, *supra*, n. 20 at pp. 188–9, s. 68(2) requires that a health record is one that has been made by, or on behalf of, a health professional in connection with the care of that individual.

The Common Law

There is a general duty of confidence owed to children (a similar duty is owed to incapacitated adults) with respect to certain types of information that includes medical information.[44] In the case of incompetent children where those with parental responsibility are acting as proxy decision-makers,[45] it will often be necessary to disclose personal information about their child in order to gain the best possible treatment. This ensures that they are acting in the best interests of the child.[46] This argument is less compelling if the child has achieved competence.[47]

Children over 16 are governed by the requirements of the Mental Capacity Act 2005 (MCA) and will be presumed to be competent and thus subject to the same common law and statutory principles as adults with respect to confidentiality.[48] The under 16s who satisfy the *Gillick*[49] test of competence[50] have the right to have their private information kept secret. The Data Protection (Subject Access Modification) (Health) Order 2000 emphasizes this position. It states that competent children can prevent their records being disclosed to parents where they understand the implications of an application for such access. As we saw in Chapter 2, in *R (Axon) v Secretary of State for Health (Family Planning Association intervening)*,[51] *Gillick* was essentially revisited in the light of Mrs Axon's right to family life under Article 8(1) of the Human Rights Act (HRA).[52] The influence of the HRA

---

44   *Venables v MGN* [2001] Fam 430 at 469 per Butler-Sloss L.J. *Re C (a minor) (Wardship: medical treatment)(No 2)* [1989] 2 All ER 791 notes the specific duty in relation to health professionals and *Re Z* [1997] Fam 1 at 25 per Ward L.J. suggests that a parent may owe such a duty to their child. These cases do not articulate the basis on which the duty is founded.

45   S 3(1) of the Children Act 1989 and *Re Z* ibid., at 26.

46   *Gillick v West Norfolk and Wisbech Area Health Authority* [1986] AC 112 at 127.

47   See Pattinson, *supra*, n. 20 at pp.182–3 where he points out that, in applying a capacity test to children under 16 to decide if they are owed a duty of confidence, DoH guidelines (DoH, 1996, *supra*, n. 21) are legally suspect because this is more restrictive than case law suggests: the issue of capacity is only relevant with respect to possible disclosure and this guidance means that incapacitated adults are owed no duty at all.

48   See further the Code of Practice, Chapter 16, MCA 2005 and *Torbay Borough Council v News Group Newspapers* [2003] EWHC 2927 where an almost 17-year-old girl had her right to decide whether to disclose information about her teenage pregnancy to the press upheld.

49   *Supra* n. 46.

50   Broadly based on intelligence and ability to understand the implications of a decision (*Gillick*, *supra*, n. 46 at 189 *per* Lord Scarman).

51   *R (Axon) v Secretary of State for Health (Family Planning Association intervening)* [2006] EWHC 37 (Admin).

52   In relation to *Guidance for Doctors and other Health Professionals on the Provision of Advice and Treatment to Young People under 16 on Contraception, Sexual and Reproductive Health*, 2004, Gateway Reference No 3382. Relevant parts of the Guidance are set out at [2006] EWHC 37 (Admin), at paras. 22–4.

with respect to private life under Article 8(1) is discussed below. Here, Mrs Axon wished to be informed if either of her daughters, aged 12 and 15, sought an abortion notwithstanding the indications of the 2004 DoH Guidance on the matter.

Mrs Axon sought a declaration that the 2004 Guidance is unlawful because, *inter alia*, it misrepresented the House of Lords' decision in *Gillick* and did not satisfy the state's positive obligation to give practical and effective protection to the claimant's rights under Article 8(1). She also sought a declaration that health professionals are under no obligation to keep confidential advice and treatment that they provide with regard to contraception, sexually transmitted infections and abortion. Parents should be informed unless this might jeopardize the child's physical or mental health so would not be in their best interests.

Silber J. concluded that the Guidance did not misrepresent the law, and that the approach in *Gillick* applied to *all* forms of medical advice and treatment, including, therefore, abortion advice and treatment.[53] He stated that the Fraser guidelines[54] were legal pre-conditions[55] that should be strictly observed. These include the stringent test for capacity set out by Lord Scarman in *Gillick* that requires the child to understand *all* aspects of the advice. [56] He acknowledged the child's right to confidence in medical matters. He was not persuaded that the public interest that confidences should be preserved and protected was outweighed, as counsel had argued, by a:

> ... significant public interest in promoting family life that means that the courts should not sanction secrecy on important aspects of a child's life such as sexual matters.[57]

While the public interest point is legitimate, it had to be considered in the context of the *Gillick* case, evidence in the particular facts of the case, the fact that the child concerned may not want the parent to be informed, the risk of not obtaining advice and the consequences of that risk.

Silber J. was unable to agree with Mrs Axon's proposals because this inevitably meant that *Gillick* was wrongly decided. The key features of the majority opinions in *Gillick* were that, in certain circumstances, the medical profession need not notify a parent. In addition, he noted that the likely foreseeable consequences of

---

53 Silber J. acknowledged that this required separate consideration because it 'involves invasive and irreversible surgical procedure with potentially serious risks, consequential and side effects', 'raises potentially difficult non medical issues such as moral, ethical, religious and cultural issues', and has consequences with which the person must live for the rest of her life: at para. 83.

54 Laid down in *Gillick*, *supra*, n. 46.

55 *Axon*, *supra*, n. 51 at paras. 110 and 111.

56 *Axon*, *supra*, n. 51 at para. 154.

57 *Axon*, *supra*, n. 51 at para. 44. Citing in support a dictum of Lord Goff of Chieveley in *Attorney General v Guardian Newspapers Ltd (No 2)* [1990] 1 AC 109, 282.

making the declaration sought would deter young people from seeking advice and/or treatment. This would be 'very undesirable and far reaching' for children's health.[58] Also, a child would not be able to predict whether their doctor would pass on the information or not.

Citing Articles 16(1) and 12(1) of the United Nations Convention on the Rights of the Child 1989 and the judgment of Thorpe LJ. in *Mabon v Mabon*,[59] Silber J. indicated that the international instruments illustrate:

> ... that the right of young people to make decisions about their own lives by themselves at the expense of the views of their parents has now become an increasingly important and accepted feature of family life.[60]

He concluded:

> In the light of this change in the landscape of family matters, in which rights of children are becoming increasingly important, it would be ironic and indeed not acceptable now to retreat from the approach adopted in the *Gillick* case ... and to impose additional new duties on medical professionals to disclose information to parents of their younger patients.'[61]

With respect to Mrs Axon's argument based on Article 8(1) of the ECHR in particular, Silber J. concluded that:

> ... any right to family life on the part of a parent dwindles as their child gets older and is able to understand the consequence of different choices and then to make decisions relating to them ... . [The child's] autonomy must undermine any Article 8 rights of a parent to family life'[62]

In his view:

> ... parents do not have Article 8 rights to be notified of any advice of a medical professional after the young person is able to look after himself or herself and make his or her own decision.[63]

In his Lordship's view, there was nothing in the Guidance that interferes with a parent's Article 8 rights[64] because advice and/or treatment must be in the child's

---

58   *Axon, supra*, n. 51 at para. 73.
59   *Mabon v Mabon* et al. [2005] 3 WLR 460 at paras. 26 and 32.
60   *Axon, supra*, n. 51 at para. 80.
61   Ibid.
62   *Axon, supra*, n. 51 at para. 129–130.
63   Ibid.
64   *Axon, supra*, n. 51 at para. 134.

best interests. Even if the Guidance did interfere with these rights, Silber J. held that this could be justified under Article 8(2). The Governmental objective of reducing unwanted pregnancies and the incidence of sexually transmitted diseases, contained in the DoH Guidance, is sufficiently important to justify constraining the Article 8 rights of parents. He considered that the Fraser guidelines were rationally connected to that objective and impaired freedom no more than necessary to achieve the aim.[65]

The *Axon* decision could be interpreted as indicating that the focus in mature minors' decision-making should be on their autonomy not their welfare. This would mean that their decisions should be respected, even if the consequences are unpalatable.[66] Silber J.'s remarks in the case may represent the beginnings of a reversal from what has been perceived as a retreat from *Gillick* in subsequent Court of Appeal decisions on children's capacity to refuse consent to medical treatment.[67] Silber J.'s judgment appears to recognize the importance of providing legal protection for the autonomy of mature minors. However, the suggestion that the Fraser guidelines[68] require a very high level of understanding of the decision to be made and that it is in the child's best interests if it is made without parental knowledge or consent,[69] means there remains a strong focus on child welfare that could be used to undermine children's autonomy.[70]

The recent guidance from the GMC[71] is welcome in that it emphasizes the importance of treating children and young people with the same respect accorded to adults. In formulating the guidance, the GMC canvassed the opinions of children. There was surprise about the extent of the concern regarding not being listened to by doctors, being spoken to over their heads and not having an expectation that divulged information would be kept confidential.[72] Of course, as will be seen, it may be necessary to breach a confidence for the child's protection but this must not be done lightly and possibly after consultation with a suitably experienced colleague, a named or designated doctor for child protection or a Caldicott Guardian.[73] Doctors and their staff must give no indication that they would be unwilling to see a child under 16 on their own and some GPs have had notices in their surgeries to this effect. The guidance broadly follows the legal position. It emphasizes the need

65   *Axon, supra*, n. 51 at paras. 150–152.

66   R. Taylor, 'Reversing the retreat from *Gillick? R (Axon) v Secretary of State for Health*' [2007] *CFLQ* 81.

67   Ibid.

68   Laid down in *Gillick, supra*, n. 46 and referred to by Silber J.

69   *Axon, supra*, n. 51 at para. 154.

70   See the discussion in Chapter 2.

71   GMC, *0–18 years: guidance for doctors*, 2007 which is in addition to GMC, *Good Medical Practice*, 2006 at para. 37 and GMC, 2004, *supra*, n. 4.

72   Anthony, S., 'Child Care Matters: the GMC's new guidance on roles and responsibilities towards treating young people is relevant to all doctors', (2006) 16(1) *Medical Protection Society Casebook* 7.

73   GMC, 2007, *supra*, n. 71 at para. 60.

for anonymized or minimal disclosure where the patient is identifiable, informing the patient as to the possible use of information at the outset[74] and obtaining their consent where possible. All of these steps will demonstrate respect for children and young people[75]

Legal Liability

Common Law

Legal liability lies under common and statute law. Causes of action under the common law can arise in contract, tort and from an equitable obligation to respect confidential information. An action for breach of contract is available where there is an express or implied duty of confidence. This is the case with respect to NHS employment contracts. An action in contract is more straightforward than an action in tort because of the significant hurdles the claimant in the latter case will need to overcome.[76] An action in the tort of negligence is theoretically available where the duty of care imports an obligation of confidence, so a patient could bring a negligence claim against a health professional who has disclosed information or who has taken insufficient steps to ensure its security.[77] However, domestic courts have generally been reluctant to award a level of damages that would justify taking a court action. This is because compensation is only generally available for financial or physical losses. Injured feelings suffered as a result of a disclosure are unlikely to qualify as a relevant loss. If false information was disclosed that led to others thinking less of the patient, a defamation action might assist. However, doctors have a defence of 'qualified privilege' if they reasonably believed the statement made was true and the person to whom it was communicated had a legitimate interest in the information.[78]

The most advantageous claim for a patient, aggrieved about a disclosure, is to rely on the equitable obligation to respect confidential information. The nature of this obligation was discussed in *A-G v Guardian Newspapers Ltd (No 2)*[79] that affirmed the public interest in preserving confidences where they were imparted in circumstances that suggested the information was confidential. Thus the information required a necessary quality of confidence, the relationship between the parties was such that an obligation of confidence was imported and there was

---

74   See e.g. Wilson, K. and James, A. (eds), *The Child Protection Handbook: the practitioner's guide to safeguarding children,* (3rd ed.), Philadelphia, Baillière Tindall Elsevier, 2007 at p. 396.

75   GMC, 2007, *supra*, n. 71 at paras. 43–4.

76   See Chapter 6.

77   *Swinney v Chief Constable of the Northumbria Police* [1996] 3 All ER 449.

78   Brazier, M., *Medicine, Patients and the Law*, London, Penguin, 2003 at p. 70.

79   [1990] AC 109.

an unauthorized use of the material. The first two elements are unlikely to present difficulties in the medical setting.[80]

These potential causes of action do not currently survive death. This is because breach of confidentiality gives rise to a potential personal action. However, patients may be concerned about possible posthumous disclosure. This explains the fact that some ethical guidance states that the duty of confidence does extend this far.[81] This position has now been supported in *Lewis v Secretary of State for Health*,[82] which established that some information is so sensitive that it required a high degree of confidentiality that would endure for many years after the death of the individual concerned. On the facts in the instant case, it was decided that the relevant information could be disclosed to the Redfern Inquiry that was established to determine whether the organs of employees in UK nuclear facilities contained a radionuclide presence. The public interest in the disclosure of the material sought outweighed the public interest in maintaining the confidentiality of medical records.

The Influence of the Human Rights Act 1998

The long heralded tort of breach of privacy has yet to materialize fully but seems very possible under the developing jurisprudence of Article 8(1) of the ECHR.[83] The HRA makes provision for challenges against public authorities for alleged breaches of the ECHR under sections 6–8. Section 3 of the Act provides that, wherever possible, primary and subordinate legislation must be interpreted in a way which is compatible with 'Convention rights' as set out in the Act. The HRA is also relevant where private parties are involved in cases of potentially unlawful disclosure. The courts, as public bodies under section 6, must interpret all forms of law in accordance with the ECHR. Article 8(1) protect notions of dignity and autonomy[84] and the Strasbourg courts have adopted a pragmatic approach to the health systems of member states to ensure the public will not refrain from sharing essential information so that they receive the treatment they need and, in cases of transmissible conditions, do not affect the wider community. As we saw in Chapter 2, interference with Article 8(1) may be justified on the grounds of one of

---

80　If confirmation is needed, several cases have affirmed the obligation applies as between health professional and patient: see, e.g. *Hunter v Mann* [1974] QB 767, *W v Edgell* [1990] 1 All ER 835 and, more recently, *Campbell, supra*, n. 8.

81　*Supra*, n. 4.

82　[2008] EWHC 2196 (QB).

83　Notwithstanding the rejection of this in *Wainwright v Home Office* [2003] 3 WLR 1137.

84　*Pretty v United Kingdom* (2002) 35 EHRR 1 at paras 61 and 65 and *R (on application of A, B, X, & Y) v East Sussex County Council (No. 2)* [2003] EWHC 167 (Admin).

the factors listed in Article 8(2) so any disclosure of confidential information must be 'necessary in a democratic society' in the interests of:

> ... national security, public safety or the economic well-being of the country, for the prevention of disorder or crime, for the protection of health or morals, or for the protection of the rights and freedoms of others.

At first sight these appear to be very broad exceptions but the 'necessary' requirement means that there must be a vivid public need and Strasbourg jurisprudence has emphasized the need for proportionality so that the least restrictive protection of any countervailing interest is employed. Before establishing how children's interests in having their private information kept confidential is addressed, the following adult cases establish some important principles.

In *Z v Finland*[85] the applicant challenged the Swedish authorities' right to retrieve, *inter alia*, medical data while pursuing a criminal investigation under Article 8(1). She was particularly concerned because of the likely disclosure of her HIV status. The European Court of Human Rights stressed that the protection of personal data is of fundamental importance to a person's enjoyment of their right to respect for private and family life as guaranteed by Article 8(1). Respecting the confidentiality of health data is a vital principle in the legal systems of all the Contracting Parties. It is crucial also to preserve a patient's confidence in the medical profession and in the health services in general.[86] Domestic law must therefore afford appropriate safeguards to prevent any such communication or disclosure of personal health data as may be consistent with these guarantees.

The disclosure of the applicant's identity and medical condition in the Court of Appeal's judgment was held to represent a breach of Article 8(1). The other complaints, concerning the giving of other medical evidence and the use of other medical records, were dismissed on the basis that this interference with Article 8(1) pursued a legitimate aim under Article 8(2), that is, the importance of pursuing criminal proceedings. However, the Court emphasized that this must not be an *ex post facto* assessment of the actual impact of the evidence. The use of the data satisfied the 'necessary in a democratic society' requirement despite the recognition that a person's HIV status required particularly careful consideration. The Court accepted that the interests of a patient and the community as a whole in protecting the confidentiality of medical data might be outweighed by certain interests. These included the investigation and prosecution of crime, and in the publicity of court proceedings, where such interests are shown to be of even greater importance. Throughout its deliberations, the Court stated that it should not substitute its views for those of the national authorities as to the relevance of evidence used in the judicial proceedings. It recognized that a margin of appreciation should be left to competent national authorities in striking a fair balance: here, between the interest

---

85   *Z v Finland*, *supra*, n. 11.
86   Ibid., at paras. 95–6.

of publicity of court proceedings on the one hand, and the confidentiality of such data on the other. The scope of this margin will depend on such factors as the nature and seriousness of the interests at stake and the gravity of the interference.

A similar balancing approach was evident in *MS v Sweden*,[87] MS had been diagnosed with spondylolisthesis at the age of 14. Sixteeen years later, she slipped at work and injured her back. In 1991, she made a claim for compensation under Sweden's Industrial Injury Insurance Act. Medical evidence was sought by the Social Insurance Office (SIO) and was provided by the clinic that had treated her during that period. This included information about an abortion in 1985 that she had requested because of her back complaint. The consent of MS had not been sought to the release of the information nor was it required under Swedish legislation where the SIO requested information from a medical practitioner.

MS appealed to the European Court arguing that the submission of her medical records to the SIO constituted an unjustified interference with her Article 8(1) rights. The Court reiterated that the protection of personal data, particularly medical data, is of fundamental importance to a person's enjoyment of Article 8 protections. The Court held that there had been an interference with MS's Article 8(1) right but went on to find that this was justified under Article 8(2). The interference was in accordance with the law of Sweden under which consent to disclosure in these circumstances was not required. It had a legitimate aim of protecting the economic well-being of the country by permitting the allocation of public funds to deserving claimants. It was also necessary in a democratic society, since the information was needed properly to assess the claim and the clinic could have incurred civil or criminal liability if it had failed to provide the information on request. It can be seen from these cases that the right to private life under Article 8(1) is very broad: a pre-existing confidential relationship is no longer required. Any interference with the right will only be justified where it is necessary to protect an interest contained in Article 8(2).[88]

Campbell v MGN [89] provides an exposition of the current law in the UK. Although the case did not involve disclosure by a health professional, it clearly has relevance for the healthcare setting. The press had a great deal of interest in the antics of the 'super model' Naomi Campbell and photographs of her leaving

---

87   (1998) 45 BMLR 1.

88   More recently, see *Odièvre v France* (2004) 38 EHRR 43 for an illustration of how the European Court of Human Rights addresses the balance between parental anonymity and a child's desire to know its origins. It was held that French legislation permitting anonymous births did not breach Art. 8(1). This was because the margin of appreciation (afforded to Member States allowing the flexible interpretation of ECHR requirements in the local setting), sanctioned its approach to the mother's rights under Art. 8(2). See also *Mikulic v Croatia* [2002] 1 FCR 720 where the applicant attempted to establish paternity of her putative father. It was held that paternity proceedings came within the scope of 'private life under Art.8', which could sometimes include aspects of an individual's physical and social identity as well as physical and psychological integrity.

89   *Campbell, supra*, n. 8.

Narcotics Anonymous were published in the *Daily Mirror* together with an article describing her addiction to drugs and subsequent treatment. She sued for breach of confidence finally succeeding in the House of Lords with an award of £2,500 in damages and a further £1,000 in aggravated damages. The judges failed to concur on the basis of the award given[90] but all agreed that an improper disclosure of confidential information would receive legal protection whether that was through tort, equity or some unclassified right.

The House explored the nature of the duty of confidence recognizing that dignity and autonomy require the legal protection of confidential information.[91] This requires a consideration as to whether it falls within the remit of Article 8(1) and then whether interference with the right is justified on the basis of Article 8(2), here, in the public interest. Although Ms Campbell had placed the facts of her drug addiction into the public domain, the majority took the view that this did not mean the details of her treatment should not be protected.[92] Having satisfied the House that the publication was a breach of Article 8(1), whether this was justified under Article 8(2) was decided by balancing her right to respect for private life with the Article 10 right to freedom of expression. Here, the relative lack of public interest in the facts meant the publication was an unjustified breach of the right to private life.

There are four criteria that now need to be satisfied for a successful action where it is alleged the equitable obligation to respect confidential information has been breached. First, the relevant information is of a personal, private or intimate nature,[93] as perceived by the person to whom the information relates and who had a reasonable expectation that it would be protected.[94] It might reasonably be assumed that medical information would always qualify but it would seem that more trivial complaints might not[95] although the law is not clear on this point.[96]

---

90   For example, Lords Hope and Hoffman mentioned a new common law right to protect private information, while Baroness Hale discussed the matter in terms of the equitable duty of confidence and Lord Nicholls talked about the tort of misuse of private information.

91   *Campbell, supra*, n. 8 at para. 53 *per* Lord Hoffman.

92   *Cf. Mosley v News Group Newspapers Ltd, supra*, n. 8, where the sexual antics of the claimant with several prostitutes were very evidently in the public domain given the extensive coverage in the media, including Internet postings.

93   *Campbell supra*, n. 8.

94   Ibid., at para. 21 per Lord Nicholls.

95   Ibid., at para. 157 per Lady Hale which suggests that release of information about minor ailments may be justifiable on the ground of public interest such as freedom of the press. It may be easier to justify a disclosure on the basis that the balance, in such cases, lies with freedom of expression.

96   *Cf. Ashworth Hospital Authority v MGN* [2001] 2 All ER 991 where the subjective element in confidentiality was noted so that if the individual thought information was sensitive, that would suffice notwithstanding the views of others. The DoH, 2003, *supra*, n. 4 at p. 7 seems equivocal in that it sees a duty of confidence arising where a disclosure takes

Second, the person receiving the information knows, or ought to know, that the information is to be regarded as confidential.[97] Medical information would easily satisfy this requirement even to the extent of exchanges in a group therapy session where there is more than one recipient of the information.[98] Should anyone discover such information, they will be similarly obliged.[99] The third requirement is that the revelation must have been to the detriment of the individual concerned. Alternatively, if they are not specifically affected, there must have been harm to the public interest perhaps by the diminution of trust in doctors.[100] Finally, an unauthorized person must have seen it rather than the public at large.[101]

The scope of medical confidentiality under Article 8(1) was more recently raised in *Sayers v Smithkline Beecham plc.*[102] The courts found, *inter alia*, that disclosure of confidential information in expert reports used by claimants in MMR/ MR vaccine litigation would not breach Article 8(1) if the data were appropriately anonymized. Further, even if it did, this would be a legitimate interference because defendants need access to the relevant material in the interests of justice. It would also be for the protection of health if the proceedings would allay concern about the effects of the vaccine. There may be further interesting developments given the European Court of Human Right's ruling that a case on medical confidentiality and its relationship with the right to life under Article 2 is admissible.[103] The case highlights the conflict of interests arising from the duty of confidentiality where infectious diseases are concerned. It also raises the interesting question whether, in the light of increased life expectancy for HIV patients undergoing retroviral treatment, infection with HIV constitutes such an immediate threat to life that Article 2 is engaged. This is discussed below.[104]

As far as children specifically are concerned, *Murray v Express Newspapers plc and another*[105] is of note. The claimant was the one-year-old offspring of a well-known author who had been photographed with a long-range lens without

---

place in circumstances where it is reasonable to expect that the information will be held in confidence. The BMA, *supra,* n. 5 at p. 167 suggests that even information about a patient visiting a doctor should be seen as confidential information. The GMC, 2004, *supra,* n. 4 at p. 1 guidance proposes that all information given to doctors should be kept private.

97   *Campbell, supra,* n. 8 at para. 14 per Lord Nicholls.

98   *Venables v MGN, supra,* n. 44.

99   *Attorney-General v Guardian Newspapers Ltd, supra,* n. 57, at 281 per Lord Goff.

100   Ibid., and *Ashworth, supra,* n. 96. The need for patients to trust their doctor is emphasized in professional guidance including the Royal College of Paediatrics and Child Health (RCPCH), *Good Medical Practice in Paediatrics and Child Health: Duties and Responsibilities of Paediatricians,* 2002 at para. 19.

101   *Supra,* n. 44 at 260.

102   [2007] EWHC 1346 (QB).

103   *Ayse Colak and others v Germany (Admissibility Decision)* 8 January 2008.

104   See discussion *infra* at n. 157–8.

105   [2008] EWCA Civ 446.

consent for the purpose of publishing the picture in the media. While the child could be seen in some detail, nothing untoward was evident in the photograph. *Inter alia*, a claim was brought on the basis that this constituted a breach of his Article 8(1) privacy rights. Although the court recognized that a child had a reasonable expectation of privacy, this was seen as only the first step. The second involved the balancing of these rights with the publisher's right to freedom of expression under Article 10 of the Convention. In the court of first instance, it was held that activities in a public place did not attract a reasonable expectation of privacy and the claim was struck out. On appeal, the view was expressed that more account needed to be taken of the fact that the claimant was a child with his own right to respect for his privacy distinct from that of his parents. A child may attract a different approach to his reasonable expectation of privacy. Accordingly the claimant's parents were permitted to proceed to trial on the child's behalf to consider the point.

Ownership and Anonymization of Health Information

The ownership and anonymization of health information is relevant for adults and children. The criminal law has some significance in this area because although information cannot be stolen,[106] the paper on which it is written, an X-ray or computer disk, could be taken. *R v Department of Health ex p. Source Informatics*[107] raised an important issue in the healthcare setting. The question was whether patients 'own' their medical information so that if an unauthorized disclosure takes place they can bring a property claim. The Court of Appeal rejected the basic tenet of the claim holding that the ownership lies with the relevant NHS organisation so that it can control the access to the information. However, it does not have an unfettered discretion as to what it can do with it.[108] It was also an important decision in that it addressed whether the release of confidential information in an anonymized form would constitute a breach of confidentiality.

Source Informatics established a scheme whereby GPs and pharmacists would be paid to provide information about the amount and name prescribed drugs together with the doctor's name although that of the patient would be removed. This information was then sold on to pharmaceutical companies. The DoH issued guidelines stating that notwithstanding the information was in an anonymized form, its use without the patient's consent would constitute a breach of confidentiality. This was not the position of the Court of Appeal when the DoH's approach was challenged by Source Informatics. The touchstone in determining the scope of the duty of good faith towards the confider was whether the individual in receipt of

---

106   *Oxford v Moss* (1978) 68 Cr App R 183.
107   *Source Informatics, supra,* n. 20.
108   *R v Mid-Glamorgan FHSA ex p. Martin* [[1995] 1 All ER 356.

the information would be troubled by the release of the information.[109] So here it was deemed that there was no breach of the duty of good faith in the absence of identifying information because there was no harm or invasion of privacy. This element of the reasoning is controversial. It was assumed that the public would not object to such use but evidence is mixed[110] and even where they may not object in general, they may to particular uses. The good faith requirement may not represent the law given Lord Hoffman's remarks in *Campbell v MGN*[111] where he stated that the protection of human dignity and autonomy of the person to whom the information related should be the focus when considering any potential breach of confidence.

The *Source Informatics* decision is important because it held that the release of confidential information in an effectively anonymized form was not a breach of confidentiality provided it has been lawfully obtained. This challenges the idea that informational autonomy and privacy rights are not necessarily extinguished just because information is in a non-identifiable form.[112] What is clear is that there was a shift in approach from the protection of confidential information to addressing whether it was being fairly used or whether those concerned were acting in good faith. This may even mean that the burden on the user of private information to justify its use could be transferred to the patient: they may have to demonstrate that it was used in bad faith. Professional guidance[113] and case law[114] continues to emphasize the importance of protecting confidential information. If anonymized data is found to fall within the remit of privacy rights under Article 8(1) in *Campbell*,[115] this may mean that justifying its disclosure could be more strictly circumscribed given the requirement under Article 8(2) that any interference with the right must be necessary and proportionate. DoH guidelines[116] require the anonymization of patient information, if it is to be disclosed, where possible. For these guidelines, disclosure will have to be justifiable as will any lack of anonymization.

An inappropriate disclosure of information will give rise to potential legal liability but there is a limited range of remedies available under the common law.[117] It may be possible to obtain an injunction prohibiting a disclosure but knowledge

---

109   *Source Informatics, supra,* n. 20 at para. 31 per Simon Brown L.J.

110   See Herring, *supra,* n. 14 at p. 162.

111   [2004] UKHL 22 at para. 51.

112   Pattinson, *supra.*, n. 20 at pp. 199–205.

113   Laurie, G., *Genetic Privacy: A Challenge to Medico-legal Norms*, Cambridge, Cambridge University Press, 2004 at p. 228.

114   See, for example, *Campbell, supra.*, n. 8 at para. 51 per Lord Hoffman, where he stressed that the right to privacy and autonomy underpins the law on the protection of confidential information.

115   Ibid.

116   DoH, *The Protection and Use of Patient Information*, 2004.

117   This could be subject to a challenge under the HRA: see Herring, *supra*, n. 14 at p. 186.

about a possible divulgence of relevant information more usually arises after the event. Damages are a possibility but English courts have been reluctant to award monetary compensation where there has been no financial loss. The lack of legal cases concerned with breaches of confidentiality is not necessarily an indication that the public are happy with the way their private information is handled in the healthcare setting. There is perhaps a grudging acceptance that a range of professionals in the hospital setting will have access to the information but concern about GP receptionists revealing sensitive information while on the telephone in front of other patients are legion. The lack of adequate financial remedies and the fact that legal proceedings are costly, long and stressful, means that aggrieved patients are more likely to complain to professional bodies and individual Trusts. Disciplinary proceedings may follow. The NHS has its own guidelines indicating its commitment to fair, lawful and transparent processing of information[118] and individual organizations could hold their own internal proceedings for a breach of the employment contract. These offer a reasonably robust alternative.[119] Trusts that provide health services to children need to demonstrate a clear commitment to respecting children's right to confidentiality.

Supplementing the requirements that exist under the law are the guidelines provided by professional bodies and the DoH. They do have a certain status in that the courts may refer to them when determining whether a health professional has maintained appropriate standards in relation to confidential information.[120] Whatever the basis of a legal action with respect to a breach of the duty of confidence, such as negligence, equity or human rights, following up-to-date guidelines is likely to be in accordance with law and ethics given the advice received in their compilation. In many instances the guidance goes beyond the requirements of the law that is important because health professionals are likely to be more familiar with these. They may be used as evidence in confidentiality cases[121] and those brought under negligence when determining appropriate standards in relation to the duty of confidence,[122] including those relating to children.[123]

A range of professional and statutory bodies has provided guidance on the law and ethics of various aspects of healthcare in accessible formats.[124] As an example of the latter, the General Medical Council's guidance in particular is consistently

---

118   DoH, 2003, at p. 4, *supra*, n. 4.

119   My confidence in this view comes from my experience of running disciplinary panels in NHS organizations and their effect on those involved.

120   See, for example, *W v Edgell* [1990] 1 All ER 835.

121   Ibid.

122   See the discussion in Chapter 6 on the role of guidelines in determining appropriate standards of care.

123   See e.g. GMC, 2007, *supra*, n. 71 which is in addition to GMC, *Good Medical Practice*, 2006 at para. 37 and GMC, 2004, *supra*, n. 4.

124   See, for example, the GMC, 2004, *supra*, n. 4 and 2007, *supra*, n. 71, BMA, *supra*, n. 3, Nursing and Midwifery Council (NMC), *Code of Professional Conduct*, 2002 and DoH, 2003, *supra*, n. 4.

of a high standard and this is no less the case with its new guidance on dealing with children.[125] All guidelines emphasize that confidential information should only be used for the purposes for which it was given. It should only be disclosed with consent unless required by law or can be justified on the public interest. The GMC guidance underlines that sufficient information must be given to a patient to help them decide whether they will give express consent to a disclosure including the reasons, the amount of information, to whom it will be given and any implications.[126] The public interest point will usually arise where the individual concerned or another is at risk of death or serious harm.[127] Possible harms to the patient and the doctor-patient relationship must be weighed with the benefits of disclosure. Many of the concerns about a breach of trust could be avoided by setting the parameters of the relationship at the outset. It should be made clear that confidences will be respected unless certain specified circumstances arise. Trust is then less likely to be damaged if disclosure becomes necessary and/or the patient will be more careful about what they divulge.

There have been allusions to the need for consent for disclosure of health data to others throughout this chapter and the discussion now turns to where it may be acceptable to dispense with this requirement more specifically in the healthcare environment.

Legitimate Disclosure

Health professionals are particularly taxed by suggestions that it might be legitimate to impart confidential information to others who are not health professionals in certain circumstances. This is despite the fact that detailed guidance from professional bodies sets out when this might be appropriate, such as those concerned with child protection.[128] The BMA considers that all patients are owed a duty of confidence but that it is justifiable to disclose confidential information to those with a legitimate interest in an incompetent patient's care provided this is strictly circumscribed.[129] Of course, where others may be adversely affected, it may also be legitimate to disclose private information to protect them. The following discussion again establishes some general legal principles drawn from adult cases before addressing how these may be applied in those involving children.

---

125   GMC, 2007, *supra*, n. 71.

126   Ibid. at para. 16.

127   Ibid. at p. 22 and NMC, *supra*, n. 124 at paras 5.1 and 5.3.

128   RCPCH, *Responsibilities of Doctors in Child Protection Cases with Regard to Confidentiality*, 2004, Foreword.

129   BMA, *supra*, n. 5 at p. 178 with which the GMC concurs where it is 'essential' to do so: GMC, *supra*, n. 4 at para. 28.

A Threat of Serious Harm to Others

Violence

That a risk of serious harm to another justifies the disclosure of confidential information in the public interest is not contentious. Where there may be differences of opinion is how serious the harm must be to defend the release of the information. The GMC requires there to be a serious risk of death or serious harm,[130] whereas the British Psychological Society notes only a 'risk of harm'.[131] The BMA would include psychological harm and the risk of assault and traffic accidents.[132] While the DoH guidelines provide some obvious examples of what will constitute serious harm including rape, kidnapping and child abuse, they also state that national security and crimes causing substantial financial gains or loss would be included.[133] The financial perspective may initially seem a step too far but serious fraud in the NHS may have an impact on resources available for others. Notwithstanding these suggestions as to what may be considered serious harm, the health professional will be left to make a judgment in individual circumstances about appropriate disclosure. They may wish to seek the advice of colleagues,[134] a Clinical Ethics Committee, their professional body and/or the medical defence unions. They may feel sufficiently robust to make the decision alone but should ensure they discuss this with the patient first where possible.[135] They should be prepared to justify their stance where they decide not to disclose information where their patient is the victim of abuse.[136] It may be that a doctor considers that an adult, competent patient suffering abuse should seek appropriate intervention. Such an option is not available where the victim is a child however.[137] The few legal parameters provided by case law may assist in such decision-making.

The leading case on justifiable disclosure of confidential information in the public interest with respect to public safety is *W v Edgell*[138] where W had been convicted of the manslaughter of five people and of wounding two others. He was ordered to be detained indefinitely in a secure hospital and could only be released by order of the Home Secretary if he was considered to be no longer a danger to the public. W sought a review of his case with a view to a transfer to a regional secure unit. His legal representatives secured a report from an independent consultant

---

130   Ibid. at para. 22.
131   British Psychological Society, *Guidelines on Confidentiality and Record Keeping*, 2002 at p. 4.
132   BMA, *supra*, n. 5 at p. 190.
133   DoH, 2003 at para. 33, *supra*, n. 4.
134   As suggested by the GMC, 2004 at para. 29, *supra*, n. 4.
135   DoH, 2003 at para. 32, *supra*, n. 4.
136   GMC, 2004 at para. 29, *supra*, n. 4.
137   Discussed *infra* at nn. 168*ff.*
138   [1990] 1 All ER 835.

psychiatrist that was unfavourable so the application for transfer was aborted. However, W was due for a routine review of his detention and the psychiatrist became aware that his report would not be included in the patient's notes. He feared that decisions would be taken on inadequate information with consequent danger to the public. He therefore sent a copy to the medical director of the hospital and a further copy reached the Home Office. W brought an action in contract and equity alleging breach of a duty of confidence.

In considering the breadth of the duty, the trial judge, Scott J, referred to the GMC's then guidelines, para. 79 of the 'Blue Book':

> Rarely, cases may arise in which disclosure in the public interest may be justified, for example, a situation in which the failure to disclose appropriate information would expose the patient, or someone else, to a risk of death or serious harm.[139]

He decided that a doctor in similar circumstances also had a duty to the public requiring him to disclose such information to the proper authorities, independent of the patient's instructions.

The Court of Appeal supported the judge at first instance but was slightly more reserved. In particular, Bingham L.J. considered that W's confidentiality was still covered to the extent that the psychiatrist was not at liberty to sell this information to a newspaper nor could he publish it in a learned journal, his memoirs or gossip about it with friends unless W's identity was concealed.[140] Rather than conceiving of the private interest competing with the public interest, there was an emphasis on the public interest in maintaining professional duties of confidence. Thus, any balancing of interests would only be carried out in circumstances of unusual difficulty. Moreover, section 76 of the Mental Health Act 1983 showed a clear Parliamentary intention that a restricted patient should receive such confidential advice. Only the most compelling circumstances would justify a doctor acting contrary to the patient's perceived interests in the absence of consent. Nevertheless, the facts of the case were found to be sufficiently convincing.

It would seem that a legitimate use of the public interest defence means that the threat of serious harm to others must be a distinct possibility, the disclosure is made only to those necessary in order to protect the public[141] and where the level of detail is restricted to the minimum necessary ideally in an anonymized form.[142] Pattinson suggests that a reasonable belief approach would avoid the need for complete deference to medical opinion and objective proof that a risk exists before action can be taken.[143] There is an additional requirement that the confider must be

---

139   Ibid., at 843.

140   At para. 419.

141   Kennedy, I. and Grubb, A., *Medical Law*, (3rd ed.) London, Butterworths, 2000, 1100–101.

142   GMC, 2004 at para. 1, *supra*, n. 4.

143   Pattinson, *supra*, n. 20 at p. 193.

informed about the intended disclosure where possible[144] and this will provide an opportunity for the matter to be aired before the court. A legitimate disclosure is thus one where the threat of serious harm to others must be a significant possibility.

A disclosure should be made where a health professional has a concern about a colleague generally putting patients at risk.[145] The release of the information must only be made to those with a legitimate interest in knowing. This could be the public at large in some circumstances. Disclosure to certain bodies, which have a responsibility to ensure the public are protected from professional misconduct, will also be valid. In *Woolgar v Chief Constable of Sussex Police,*[146] a registered nurse was arrested following the death of a patient in her care. The police informed the local authority's registration and inspection unit that there was insufficient evidence to effect a criminal prosecution. The unit was concerned about other allegations about the nurse and referred the matter to the regulatory body for nursing which requested relevant information from the police. The nurse sought an injunction to restrain disclosure but the case was dismissed. The Court of Appeal adopted the approach taken in *MS v Sweden*[147] and dismissed the appeal on the basis that, although there was a public interest in ensuring the free flow of information in criminal investigations so that confidential information should not be used for a collateral purpose, there was also a public interest in protecting public health and safety.[148]

Where a patient reveals an intention to seriously harm or even kill, the health professional fails to alert the relevant authorities and the harm is actually carried out, *Palmer v Tees Health Authority*[149] suggests that they will only be potentially liable if there was an identifiable individual in the threat.

HIV

We have seen that it is necessary for health professionals to disclose information about certain communicable diseases.[150] Disclosure about a colleague's medical condition may be legitimate even when the colleague is a patient. However, there should not be an assumption that a health professional colleague with HIV should

---

144   *Woolgar v Chief Constable of the Sussex Police* [1999] 3 All ER 604.

145   RCPCH, 2002 at paras. 26–8, *supra*, n. 100 and GMC, 2006 at paras 43–5, *supra.*, n. 71.

146   *Supra*, n. 144.

147   (1998) 45 BMLR 1.

148   See, also, *R (A) v Chief Constable of C* [2001] 1 WLR 461 where the court was of the view that confidential information about unproven allegations of inappropriate behaviour with children was legitimately disclosed to another public body.

149   [1999] Lloyd's Rep Med 359.

150   *Supra*, nn. 34–5.

be reported given the very low transmission rate of the condition to patients,[151] unless they are engaged in the type of surgery where a cut could lead to infecting a patient.[152] Whether to inform a partner of a patient who has contracted HIV and refuses to impart the information themselves can trouble health professionals. The fact that it may be possible to prevent infection and that the risks are potentially lethal may well justify a breach of confidence along normal common law principles bearing in mind the need to encourage individuals to come forward for testing without fear that information about this will be disclosed. The GMC allows such disclosure though falling short of deeming this to be an obligation and requires the patient to be informed this has or will be done.[153] There is an arguable case that the state has a duty to inform others of such a serious risk under Article 2 of the HRA (the right to life) and Article 3 (the right not to be subject to inhuman or degrading treatment).[154] Above all, it is a criminal offence to engage in unprotected sexual relations where someone knows they are infected with HIV.[155] This fact should reassure health professionals that it is legitimate to disclose this information to the partner and/or to the police[156] where the patient will not.

In light of the preceding points, the case of *Ayse Colak and others v Germany*[157] may prove to be illuminating. Complaints were made pursuant to Articles 2 and 6 (the right to a fair trial) of the ECHR. This concerned the failure of a family physician to inform a patient that her partner had AIDS, the alleged failure of the state to provide clear guidelines for the medical profession to follow in such situations and the approach of the domestic courts in civil proceedings issued against the physician. It was argued, *inter alia*, that the failure to inform prevented the taking of protective measures against the HIV infection from which she now suffered. The domestic court took the view that there would only have been an obligation to disclose if this was the only possibility of preventing an infection but this was not the case. The applicant's companion had been consistently advised to take necessary precautions against such infection and the doctor could reasonably believe the advice would be followed. The appeal court considered that the physician had overestimated his duty of confidence but that he had not disregarded medical standards in a blindfold way. Thus, his behaviour did not constitute a gross error as required by German law.

---

151   DoH, *HIV Infected Health Care Workers: A Consultation Paper on Management and Patient Notification*, 2002 para. 2.2 which reports only two cases. Evidence indicates that transmission is far more likely from a patient to a health professional: see Mason and Laurie at p. 391, *supra*, at n. 7.

152   DoH, *The National Health Service Litigation Authority: Framework Document*, 2002, Chapter 8.

153   GMC, *supra.*, n. 4 at paras 23 and 25.

154   *Osman v UK* [2000] 29 EHRR 245.

155   *R v Dica* [2004] EWCA Crim 1231.

156   Brazier, *supra*, n. 78 at p. 71.

157   *(Admissibility Decision) supra*, n. 104.

The first applicant complained before the Strasbourg court that the discontinuance of criminal proceedings against the physician and the failure of the domestic courts to accept the causal link between the physician's error in treatment and her HIV infection breached her right to life under Article 2. The Article was also engaged on the basis that her companion's behaviour amounted to attempted murder. She also invoked Article 6(1) in connection with her argument that the civil courts had misconstrued the meaning of 'gross error in treatment'.[158] All aspects of her claim were considered to be significant enough to merit a full examination by the European Court and were therefore declared to be admissible. The full consideration of this case will be very important in establishing the scope of medical confidentiality and the extent to which the state will be expected to protect life under Article 2.

As we have seen, many of the leading cases on confidentiality involve discussion about the public interest in preserving press freedom under Article 10 of the ECHR. Whether not allowing the disclosure of a health worker's HIV status is a legitimate interference with the right has been considered in *X v Y*[159] and *H (A Healthcare Worker) v Associated Newspapers Ltd and N (A Health Authority)*.[160] Any interference must be justified on the basis of significant harm.[161]

In X v Y,[162] which pre-dated the HRA, a health authority employee disclosed to a tabloid newspaper confidential information about two general practitioners who had been diagnosed as HIV positive and continued to practise medicine. The health authority sought an injunction restraining publication of the doctors' names. The newspaper argued that the patients, and the public, had a right to the information. Rose J. in the High Court took the view that the publication of the names of two general practitioners would not be in the public interest because the risk of transmission of the virus to patients was negligible after appropriate counselling about safe practice. In addition, such disclosure would discourage others from being tested. The judge granted the injunction and stated:

> In the long run, preservation of confidentiality is the only way of securing public health; otherwise doctors will be discredited as a source of education, for future individual patients will not come forward if doctors are going to squeal on them. Consequently, confidentiality is vital to secure public as well as private health,

---

158   The second and third applicants' (the children of the union) claims that their right to private and family life under Article 8(1) had been infringed were dismissed on the basis that they had not exhausted domestic remedies pursuant to Article 35(1) and (4) of the Convention since they had not participated in the civil proceedings.

159   [1988] 2 All ER 649.

160   [2002] 210 (CA).

161   See *Ashworth*, *supra*, n. 96, where administrative difficulties and use of resources would not constitute a justifiable interference.

162   [1988] 2 All ER 649.

for unless those infected come forward they cannot be counselled and self-treatment does not provide the best care ... .[163]

In *H (A Healthcare Worker) v Associated Newspapers Ltd and N (A Health Authority),*[164] a health professional sought an injunction to prevent the health authority from contacting his patients after he tested positive for HIV given the very low risk of transmission to patients. They planned to offer the patients an HIV test. H also sought an injunction against the *Daily Mail* to prevent them from publishing any details of the matter that would identify him, his speciality or the health authority. The court of first instance agreed only that his identity should be withheld from publication. On appeal, H argued that the disclosure of information about the speciality and the authority would be sufficient to identify him. The Court of Appeal partially agreed but held that there was a legitimate interest in a debate on the risk of HIV so the speciality could be named. The Court was also concerned that patients might discover the news via the media rather than being contacted by the Authority with an offer of counselling.

Re W[165] is interesting because it illustrates further the extent of the right to confidentiality that is accorded to children. *Re W* upheld a local authority application for an injunction restraining the publication by the local newspaper of the identity of a defendant and her victim in a criminal trial and the fact that they had the HIV virus. This was in order to protect the privacy of their children who had not been involved in the trial but had been the subject of care proceedings. The mother of the two children concerned was charged with knowingly infecting one of the children's fathers and there had been some abuse and harassment by the local, tightly-knit community once knowledge of her status had come to light. The worry was that there could be an outcry at the local nursery attended by one of the children and that the residential placements of the children could also be jeopardized if such publicity was allowed. In addition, there could be longer-term adverse effects as a result of the 'stigma' of the condition given the widespread ignorance as to its implications. These arguments were thought to be speculative and not sufficiently compelling by the newspaper proprietor. In balancing the children's Article 8(1) rights with the freedom of the press under Article 10, the court decided that the granting of the injunction against publication was necessary and proportionate to protect the children from a likelihood of harm.

A different result occurred in *Re S.*[166] The case did not concern HIV status but it demonstrates how a court might be less willing to protect a child's interest in not having their identity divulged. Here, the House of Lords had to consider whether the anonymity of a dead child and the mother accused of murder should be restrained merely to protect the identity of the surviving child who was not

---

163   [1988] 2 All ER 649 at 653.
164   [2002] 210 (CA).
165   *Re W, supra,* n. 9.
166   *Re S (a child) (identification: restriction on publication)* [2004] 4 All ER 683.

directly involved in the trial. Approving the approach taken in *Campbell*,[167] it was noted that neither Articles 8 nor 10 had precedence over the other. Where there is conflict between the two, an intense focus on the comparative importance of the specific rights being claimed in the individual case is necessary. In addition, the justification for any interference with each right must be taken into account and the proportionality test must be applied to both. There was considerable emphasis on the fundamental importance of the freedom of the press to report on the progress of a criminal trial without restraint. On these particular facts, allowing such reporting would have an impact on the child's development but this was indirect so insufficient to outweigh Article 10.

The following section includes a discussion of an aspect of serious harm that has particular relevance for the health professional working with children.

Child Protection

The need to protect children from abuse is a very clear example of where it is legitimate, and essential, to share information with others. This is widely accepted but it is necessary to build up trust amongst other relevant professionals such as social workers and the police that information will be guarded to the same standard. Using *Caldicott* guidelines,[168] that establish protocols for the sharing of information, is helpful in this regard.

With 150 children still dying as a result of maltreatment each year, approximately 400,000 considered at risk because of potential abuse, neglect or lack of supervision and about 40,000 with active child-protection plans in place, it is hardly surprising the Royal College of Paediatrics and Child Health (RCPCH) has issued the first evidence-based guidance on detecting child abuse.[169] The College sees child abuse as a significant public health problem and has collaborated with GPs, dentists, radiologists, forensic physicians and other medical colleagues to provide training manuals and leaflets as well as the substantive guidance. It estimates that one in seven British paediatricians have been subject to a formal complaint about child protection that in the worst cases could lead to them being struck off the medical register. As a result, there is now a shortage of qualified doctors prepared to act as witnesses that US doctors have had to provide opinions in some cases in the UK.[170]

There are strong moral and professional obligations on health professionals to refer any concerns they may have about the potential abuse of a child to a relevant

---

167   *Campbell, supra*, n. 8.

168   Caldicott, *supra*, n. 16.

169   RCPCH, *The Physical Signs of Child Sexual Abuse: An Evidence-based Review and Guidance for Best Practice*, 2008; Rose, D., 'Doctors "must be alert to signs of child abuse"' *The Times*, 19 March 2008. The National Institute for Health and Clinical Excellence is also to produce similar guidance in 2009.

170   Rose, ibid.

person or organization.[171] Those working with children and young people should have the knowledge and skills to identify abuse and neglect. They need to be aware of policies, procedures and organisations that work to protect children and promote their welfare, as well as the use of frameworks for assessing children and young people's needs. They also need to be conscious of the work of Local Safeguarding Children's Boards and Child Protection Committees.[172] Doctors should fully participate in child protection procedures and ensure policies are in place to ensure the appropriate sharing of information amongst agencies.[173]All doctors need to be alert to the possibility of abuse and/or neglect, not just those directly dealing with children. Even where doctors only see adult patients, knowledge may still come to light that a child is at risk.[174] Any decision not to disclose concerns must be justified, recorded and made after consultation.[175] From the legal perspective, such a disclosure could be justified under the doctrine of necessity[176] and under Article 8 of the ECHR. The infringement of the suspected abuser's rights would be valid under Article 8(2) that is, in the interests of protecting the child and the public interest in justice. There are detailed provisions in the latest guidance from the DoH following the death of Victoria Climbié at the hands of her carers as to appropriate procedures to follow[177] but it should be noted that there must not be over-reliance on information-sharing as a solution. Appropriate action must also be forthcoming.[178]

Any health professional reluctant to pass on concerns to external colleagues should be reminded about the potential implications. It has almost become trite in the healthcare setting, but health professionals are often asked during child protection training (which is mandatory for anyone dealing with children on a clinical basis) to whom would they prefer to justify their position: the Information Commissioner about inappropriate release of information or a court where a child has been avoidably injured or killed? Unfortunately, there continues to be evidence, anecdotal and otherwise, that doctors are failing to act promptly where

---

171   See e.g. RCPCH, 2004, *supra*, n. 128, *passim* for a useful, clear synthesis of the legal and ethical obligations with respect to child protection. See also GMC, *supra*, n. 4 at para. 29, that refers to the obligations with respect to *any* patient and notes that a decision not to disclose should be made after consultation with an experienced colleague. The doctor will need to be prepared to justify such a decision.

172   GMC, 2007, para. 71, *supra*, n. 58. It is expected that those working with children should be aware of a range of sources to help them identify abuse such as the National Society for the Prevention of Cruelty to Children, *CORE-INFO: Thermal injuries on children*, 2006.

173   Ibid., at paras 62 and 63.

174   Ibid., at para. 5 and Anthony, *supra*, n. 72.

175   GMC, 2007, *supra*, n. 71 at para. 61.

176   *Re M* [1990] 1 All ER 205 at 213.

177   Chief Secretary to the Treasury, *Every Child Matters*, Cm 5860, HMSO: London, 2003.

178   RCPCH and Rose, *supra*, n. 169.

children were subjected to emotional and/or physical abuse either because of a lack of awareness or they fear 'putting their head above the parapet'.[179] That said, the courts have established criteria to consider when deciding whether to order the disclosure of reports containing parental statements to the police in cases of alleged child abuse or not, in the interests of encouraging frank exchange.[180] A claimant in legal proceedings may request the disclosure of all relevant information but this may not be granted if a court decides that there is a public interest in keeping some information secret. In *D v NSPCC*[181] the court refused to allow the identity of an individual who had accused the plaintiff of child abuse to be released because it would discourage others from reporting similar concerns. As it is, advice on all of these matters may be sought from the doctor with overall responsibility for the provision of child protection measures within each relevant organization who will be very familiar with current requirements.

A doctor may decide to place a suspected victim of abuse on to at-risk register[182] in the hope that this will alert relevant bodies such as social services departments of the local authority to offer extra support to a family. The idea is that further incidents will be avoided. Sadly, the lack of resources available can mean that many children on these registers do not even receive a visit. Alternatively, communication amongst the helping agencies can be so poor that other violent events have inevitably followed.[183] Health professionals are only too aware of misdiagnoses, the distress these cause and the resulting disincentive for parents to seek help they need.[184] They can also worry that, in the event their concern about a child was misplaced, there may be a claim against them for defamation. The fact that recognized bodies do not have to name informants in defamation actions is

---

179   RCPCH and Rose, *supra*, n. 169. See also Williams, C., 'Bearing Good Witness: The Reluctant Experts' [2008] *Fam Law* 153–8 for a useful perspective on the controversy surrounding child abuse cases where it was alleged expert opinion led to miscarriages of justice.

180   *Re C (a minor) (care proceedings: disclosure)* [1997] Fam 76.

181   [1978] AC 171.

182   The RCPCH, 2004, *supra*, n. 128 provides guidance on this matter.

183   As highlighted by a number of notorious reports into the abuse and/or neglect of children: see e.g. *Keeping Children Safe: The Government's Response to the Victoria Climbié Inquiry Report and Joint Chief Inspectors' Report Safeguarding* Children, Cm 5861, Crown Copyright, 2003.

184   Wheeler D.M. and Hobbs, C.J., 'Mistakes in Diagnosing Non-Accidental Injury: 10 Years' Experience', (1988) 296 *BMJ* 1233; Bishop, N., Sprigg, A. and Dalton, A., 'Unexplained fractures in infancy: looking for fragile bones', (2007) 92 *Archives of Diseases in Childhood* 251–6.

See *R v Harrow LBC, ex p. D* [1978] AC 171 and *R v Hampshire CC, ex p. H* [1999] 2 FLR 359 for examples of the distress caused to parents.

reassuring.[185] However, public interest and child considerations,[186] may still affect such decisions. The sensitive communications amongst agencies during child care proceedings will attract qualified privilege in defamation cases with respect to disclosure, provided these are made in good faith and with the objective of acting in the child's best interests.[187]

Of course, child protection is likely to involve the police at any stage of investigation but health professionals may wish to consider their obligations to assist other enquiries.

Assisting Police Enquiries and Legal Proceedings

There is no general obligation on health professionals to share confidential information when requested to do so by the police[188] unless there is a need to identify a driver alleged to have committed a motoring offence[189] and they must disclose proactively any suspicion someone has been involved with terrorist activities.[190] They may disclose confidential information about a possible crime provided they have the consent of the patient or the disclosure is justifiable in the public interest.[191] The DoH has provided some useful guidance about the types of crime where health professionals may wish to consider using this provision.[192] The offence must be sufficiently serious. It would include causing death by dangerous driving, where the prevention or detection of the crime would be impaired without the disclosure, where it will only be used with respect to the alleged criminal and will be destroyed after use. Provided health professionals have a lawful excuse not to answer police enquiries, such as guarding confidential information, they will not have committed an offence unless they give false or misleading information.[193]

As we saw earlier, *D v NSPCC*[194] illustrates how a claimant in legal proceedings may request the disclosure of all relevant information but this may not be granted if a court decides that there is a public interest in keeping some information secret. That case involved Crown immunity which applies to bodies acting in the public interest, but similar balancing would be likely in cases where the courts have to consider whether breaching confidentiality is justified in the interests of

---

185   *D v National Society for the Prevention of Cruelty to Children* [1978] AC 171.

186   See *Interbrew SA v Financial Times Ltd* [2002] 1 Lloyd's Rep 542 although this is a non-medical case.

187   *W v Westminster City Council and others* [2005] 1FCR 39.

188   *Sykes v DPP* [1962] A.C. 528 at 564 per Lord Denning.

189   S. 172 Road Traffic Act 1988.

190   Ss. 19 and 20 Terrorism Act 2000.

191   S. 115 Crime and Disorder Act 1998.

192   DoH, 1996, *supra*, n. 21.

193   *Rice v Connelly* [1966] 2 All E.R. 649.

194   *Supra*, n. 185.

assisting a legal action. Disclosure rules may present particular difficulties for police surgeons who may record information during an examination but do not have specific consent for its release.

Where a court orders a health professional to disclose confidential information, to refuse to do so would be a contempt of court. Of course, it is open to the health professional to persuade the court that the refusal is justifiable. In *AB v Glasgow and West of Scotland Blood Transfusion Service*[195] a Scottish court accepted that to name the donor of infected blood would discourage blood donation more generally. Conversely, a health professional may offer information in the interests of criminal justice and this is likely to be viewed sympathetically.[196]

Medical Research

Other ethical issues that arise in relation to medical research with children are discussed in Chapter 7. The focus here is on confidentiality. Section 33(1) and (2) of the DPA requires that disclosure of personal data for research purposes can only be carried out without consent where no measure or decision relating to a particular individual is based on it. Its use must be unlikely to cause substantial damage or distress to the data subject. This could arise where a data subject objects to the research in question. It is argued that 'medical research' should be narrowly interpreted and seen as strictly necessary before anonymization and use of the information is seen as acceptable without notifying patients.[197] The research community was concerned that their work would be significantly impeded by the DPA.[198] This led the Secretary of State, using Section 60(1) of the Health and Social Care Act 2001, to enact regulations dispensing with the consent requirement for the use of identifiable patient information where it is seen as necessary or expedient in the interest of improving patient care or is otherwise in the public interest.[199]

---

195   (1989) 15 BMLR 91 (Scottish Court of Session) (Outer House).

196   As in *R v Crozier* (1990) 12 Cr. App. R. (S) 206 where a psychiatrist instructed by a defendant in an attempted murder case released his report to the prosecution after sentencing and additional orders were imposed under the Mental Health Act 1983. The disclosure was held to be justified because there is a public interest in ensuring appropriate sentences were imposed in criminal cases.

197   See the discussion in Pattinson, *supra.*, n. 20 at pp. 199–202.

198   Notably the Cancer Registries: see http://www.bmj.com/cgi/content/full/322/7285/549 and http://www.bmj.com/cgi/content/full/322/7285/549L. See also M. Henderson, 'Life-saving research is blocked by overzealous data privacy', *The Times*, 18 January 2006 and Hagger, L., Woods, S. and Barrow, B., 'Autonomy and Audit-Striking the Balance', (2004) 6 *Medical Law International* 105–16. Many of the concerns have proved to be ungrounded but some researchers have abandoned their plans for using patient data for research purposes for fear of contravening the DPA: see Mason and Laurie, *supra*, at n. 7, at p. 27.

199   This relaxation of the consent requirements is in accord with DoH, 2004, para. 34, *supra*, n. 4, which suggests that disclosure to a researcher may be legitimate where

Although the term 'section 60' is still used as short-hand, the section has been repealed and replaced by section 251 of the National Health Service Act 2006.[200] The provision permits the temporary setting aside of the common law duty of confidentiality for the use of medical records for specific purposes. It does not set aside the requirements of the DPA.[201] The appropriate use of medical records to support direct patient care would not be considered a breach of confidentiality.[202] It cannot be assumed that anonymization is always possible merely by not mentioning names. Some conditions are so rare in children and adults that individuals can be identified from these alone.[203] Acceptable purposes are preventative medicine, medical diagnosis, medical research, the provision of care and treatment and the management of health and social care services. Informing individuals about their physical/mental health or condition, the diagnosis of their condition or their care or treatment would also be acceptable objectives. The primary purpose cannot be to *determine* the care and treatment of specific patients. This exemption is only applicable where there is no immediate practicable way of gaining patient consent or switching to using anonymized data. It must be in the interests of patients or serve a wider public good.

Although there is a potential for over-reliance on the public health justification for disclosure, the Secretary of State must consult with the Patient Information Advisory Group (PIAG) before issuing regulations.[204] The PIAG comprises expert and lay members and has responsibility for overseeing arrangements made under any regulations. Regulations will be issued where there are no practicable alternatives and anonymized data is not an option, not merely issued to ease access to medical data.[205] It may be that a project will not require the issuing of a regulation and approval from PIAG will suffice. If PIAG give a 'class support' rating, the project may proceed once approval is complete and any conditions are satisfied. Class support may permit the processing of patient identifiable information without consent for one or more of the following reasons: to obtain anonymized data from individual patient records to support medical purposes; to look at patient-identifiable information in order to select patients who are to be

---

to seek consent would involve disproportionate effort and the risk of harm to a patient is negligible and unlikely.

200   http:/www.ggd.org.uk/images/File/NHS_Act_2006_summary.pdf.

201   Use and Disclosure of Health Data: Guidance on the Application of the Data Protection Act 1998, Office of the Information Commissioner, http://www.dataprotection.gov.uk/dpr/dpdoc.nsf.

202   See the DoH, 2003, *supra*, n. 4 for details concerning appropriate use of medical records to support direct patient care.

203   See the opposing arguments about whether publication of such information is justifiable in the public interest in Oberklaid, F., 'Consent to publication-no absolutes', (2008)337 *BMJ* 608 and Newson, A.J. and Sheather, J., 'The view of the BMJ's Ethic Committee', (2008) 337 *BMJ* 610–11.

204   Established under s. 61.

205   DoH, PIAG *Annual Report*, 2005–6, 2007.

invited to participate in medical research or to contact patients to obtain consent for their information or human material to be used; to use geographical information from records for analysis; to validate data obtained from more than one source and to process patient identifiable information for the purpose of auditing, monitoring and analysing patient care and treatment.

If the application requires 'specific support', then appropriate regulations will need to be drafted and submitted to Parliament. This may take some time and there is no guarantee that Parliament will adopt the Regulations as presented. The Health Service (Control of Patient Information) Regulations 2002[206] were the first to be made under section 60(1) of the Health and Social Care Act 2001 and allow patients suffering from neoplasia to have their data placed on to Cancer Registries without their consent or anonymization. In all cases approval to dispense with consent requirements will still entail that the information in question is protected to the maximum extent possible along the lines required by the DPA.

These developments notwithstanding, there is widespread belief that the law hinders research.[207] Although education about a robust approach to the law should go some way in addressing these concerns, the fact remains that significant amounts of paperwork are needed to provide evidence of legal compliance and to gain essential research ethics approval.[208] Many Trusts have specific research governance support for these tasks that can assist. What is encouraging is that some organizations have involved patients and service users in discussions about the collection of data even with respect to areas that are difficult and sensitive.[209] In one case, this included children aged 14 to 18 years on the basis that this group were likely to be *Gillick* competent and able to make their own decisions about what happened to their personal data as live patients. The Confidential Enquiry into Maternal and Child Health and the National Children's Bureau undertook two consultation events with regard to the ethical issues and sensitivities involved in Child Death Review.[210] Three case studies were used as a source for discussion. This was done on the advice of the National Advisory Committee for Enquiries into Child Health and because PIAG had made this a condition for approval. The children and young people in the focus groups thought that the project was useful and that the potential benefits outweighed the difficulties involved in collecting such sensitive information. In addition, they thought that the work of the Enquiry should receive greater publicity and young people should have more opportunities to engage with it.

---

206   S.I. 2002/1438.

207   Peto, J., 'Data Protection, Informed Consent and Research' (2004) 328 *BMJ* 1029.

208   *Cf.* Mason and Laurie, *supra*, n. 7 at p. 257.

209   PIAG *Annual Report*, *supra*, n. 205 at p. i.

210   Ibid., at p. 25 and www.cemach.org.uk/child_health_enquiry1.htm. See also the discussion about children's effective participation in policy-making in Chapter 8.

Access to Health Information

It is very important that health professionals keep good records of their patients' health care to ensure optimal treatment. These notes are likely to be read by a number of health professionals who need to understand the record. Additionally, patients (and others), have rights of access to it so intelligible, detailed and appropriate notes will encourage patients to trust that the medical team are being open with them. While such transparency should reassure patients, conversely the medical jargon could give rise to or exacerbate existing anxiety. The not unreasonable expectation that communicating with patients should include explanations would reduce this risk.

Children with capacity have the same legal rights as adults to access their own health records and can allow or prevent access by others, including their parents, unless the exceptions outlined above apply.[211] The DPA provides notable rights of access to personal information.[212] Individual rights of access to policy and management information arise under the Freedom of Information Act 2000. In terms of the DPA, the right of access includes the right to know what information is being used, for what purposes, to whom it will be disclosed and the requirement for the information to be in an intelligible form. This means that explanations of terms may need to be forthcoming.[213] After seeing the information, a patient has the right to ask the data controller to amend any inaccuracies[214] and desist from processing the data further where this will cause substantial and unwarranted distress to the patient or another.[215] Information held for research, historical or statistical purposes is exempt unless it is used to support decisions with respect to particular individuals or processing will, or is likely to, cause substantial damage or distress to any data subject.[216] Health professionals can also refuse access to patients where they can confirm that disclosure will cause serious harm to the physical or mental condition of the patient or another,[217] or it would reveal information about a third party without their consent for disclosure unless it is reasonable to do so.[218] The likely instances where a third party claims the right of access to data will be where someone with parental responsibility wishes to see their child's medical records or where someone is lawfully representing an incompetent adult. In the latter case,

---

211   See e.g. The Data Protection (Subject Access Modification) (Health) Order 2000.
212   Ss. 7 and 8.
213   S. 8(2).
214   S. 14.
215   S. 10.
216   S. 33(1)(4).
217   See *ex p Martin, supra*, n. 108, which notes that medical records were owned by health authorities and doctors but that this is not absolute.
218   S. 7(4). Third party rights was the concern of the authorities refusing to allow access in *MG v UK* [2002] 3 FCR 413 which confirms that such rights are part of Art. 8(1).

the representative will not have access to information previously imparted on the basis that it would not be disclosed.

The Access to Health Records Act 1990 is still relevant for rights of access to information about deceased patients on the part of the executors of their estate or a family member with a potential legal claim arising from the death. The Access to Medical Reports Act 1988 governs the preparation of medical reports for employment and insurance purposes. In such a case, patients may see the report, prevent its release and/or add comments where they disagree with its content.[219] An application may be made to court to ensure compliance.[220] Doctors may refuse access if they believe it would have an adverse impact on the patient's physical or mental health or would harm the interests of an informant.[221] Additionally, the Supreme Court Act 1981 allows the discovery of documents, including health records, during legal proceedings but any information likely to cause harm to a patient must be shown only to their medical or legal adviser.[222] The statutory exception provisions are broadly supported by the common law.[223]

Conclusion

On the one hand we have an apparent shift from a discussion about the duty of confidence to the fair use of private information in legal cases and DoH guidance. This can be seen as necessary to ensure the NHS works at an optimal level. On the other hand, we have the DPA and other legal cases that, under the influence of the HRA, emphasize the importance of the duty to protect autonomy, privacy and dignity together with professional guidance which demand exacting standards. This tension is likely to remain. The need to share personal information in the modern healthcare setting must be recognized but health professionals need to ensure this is strictly circumscribed if they are to ensure the public trust the professional relationship. Given the evidence[224] that children do not believe their confidences will be kept secret, their health advisers should be at pains to emphasize that this will be the case unless there are compelling reasons to disclose them. The scope of the duty of confidentiality continues to be subject to review and development. Rights are being extended to younger children. Whatever the duty may be in relation to adults, the law has made it clear that this duty must also be accorded to mature minors.[225] This is encouraging and must remain a clear principle to follow.

---

219   S. 5.
220   S. 8.
221   S. 7.
222   S. 33(2).
223   *Ex p. Martin, supra*, n. 108.
224   Anthony, *supra*, n. 72.
225   *Axon, supra*, n. 51.

Chapter 5

Genetic Testing and Counselling:
The Paradigm Case for Family Medicine?

Introduction

Genetic testing and counselling provide key examples of when it may be legitimate to interfere with individuals' autonomy, including that of children, in the interests of others. This can arise where a patient is reluctant to share their genetic information with other family members. This chapter discusses the nature of genetic information, how it may be seen as a special case, and provides an ethical justification for overriding an individual's wish not to disclose information to others. This is followed by an example of where this position has been advocated, suggestions for a 'family model' to be adopted in relation to genetic testing and counselling and how this may be underpinned by the law.

The paediatric setting has strong associations with centres for genetic screening and counselling. These are seen very much as family services and ideally located alongside other children's services. The detection of foetal abnormality and/or the birth of a child with a known genetic condition will usually drive parents to seek such assistance before they embark on another pregnancy. To help them, geneticists may require information from other family members who may not give permission for this to be shared. Whether accessing and revealing the information is justifiable is a point of contention. As knowledge about genetic disorders increases, the debate about whether such personal information should be disclosed to wider family members gains force.[1] Health professionals, with their focus on the individual patient, understandably feel uncomfortable that confidentiality might be breached in this way. However, this may be a paradigm case of where it is entirely appropriate to see the family as the patient. Discussions about individual patients in this chapter apply equally to competent child patients. Proxies will make decisions about disclosure for younger children but this should also be considered in the light of what follows.

---

1   This has been a topic at the Sheffield Children's NHS Foundation Trust's Clinical Ethics Forum because of its responsibility for genetic services and nationally because most clinical ethics groups belong to the national organization ETHOX, which shares ethical issues for debate in a periodic newsletter.

The traditional approach of English law is that there are no duties to benefit others[2] but the idea that a less individualistic approach be adopted is gaining ground in the international arena,[3] in practice[4] and in academic comment.[5] Genetic information may be seen as different to other health information because testing on other family members is necessary and gaining a valid consent is problematic when results may not be determinative. Additionally, some conditions have a late manifestation and any results may have legal and social implications[6] including the significance for other family members. One consequence that may arise is the results of tests making it apparent that paternity is not established in relation to the ostensible father which requires very careful management.[7] Of course, other medical tests also carry significance for family members[8] and some would argue that a genetic predisposition to a condition is no different to a predisposition as

---

2   Montgomery, J., *Healthcare Law*, (2nd ed.), Oxford, Oxford University Press, 2002 at p. 277.

3   Article 29 Data Protection Working Group, *Working Document on Genetic Data*, 2004, pp. 8–9 where it argues that genetic data has a family dimension and should be shared to the extent that is has implications for them but notes that it will be necessary to develop mechanisms for dealing with potential conflicts as they arise with respect to the different claims of family members. See Mason, J.K. and Laurie, G.T., *Law and Medical Ethics*, (7th ed.), Oxford, Oxford University Press, 2006, at p. 276 where they note that a purposive approach to Icelandic data protection legislation has been adopted by their Supreme Court to allow a daughter to have access to certain data about her deceased father.

4   *Supra*, n. 1.

5   See, for example, Skene, L., 'Genetic Secrets and the Family: A Response to Bell and Bennett', (2001) 9(2) *Medical Law Review* 162–9 who prefers a family approach and Ball, D. and Bennett, B., 'Genetic Secrets and the Family', (2001) 9(2) *Medical Law Review* 130–61. See also the discussion about the duty of confidentiality of a doctor towards a patient potentially continuing after the patient's death in the broader public interest in *Lewis v Secretary of State for Health* [2008] EWHC 2196 (QB) noted in Chapter 4.

6   Knowledge about an individual's genetic make-up could adversely affect their ability to obtain reasonably priced insurance cover, a mortgage or employment for example. There is currently a moratorium undertaken by the Association of British Insurers on the request for genetic information until 2014 (Budworth, D., 'Insurers Postpone Genetic Testing', *The Times*, 14 June, 2008). See also the discussion in Mason and Laurie, *supra.*, n. 3 at pp. 236–40 on the inadequacy of the Disability Discrimination Act 1995 to deal with discrimination on the ground of genetic background and the need for more focused legislation: s. 1(1) states that 'a person has a disability for the purposes of this Act if he has a physical or mental impairment which has a substantial and long-term adverse effect on his ability to carry out normal day-to-day activities'; even when read in conjunction with Sch. 1 for interpretive purposes, a person must be symptomatic which precludes those with only a genetic predisposition to a condition. A MORI poll suggests that 80 per cent of the public support the moratorium presumably preferring that any risk is carried by all (MORI 2001, para. 7.2) who presumably prefer that the risk is carried by all.

7   *Supra,* n. 1.

8   Mason and Laurie, *supra*, n. 3 at p. 207.

a result of other causes.[9] Is there no essential difference between genetic threats and those from infection, contagion or other physical harms? As Herring notes,[10] what is different in relation to genetic testing are the potential claims that could be made by relatives. It should not be forgotten that such information allows people to prepare psychologically and in practical ways for the onset of conditions. It may affect their reproductive choices.

We need to bear in mind that the routine sharing of information with a wide range of NHS staff commonly occurs without leaking it to the outside world.[11] The Government may need information about the likely incidence of genetic disease as it does with other conditions in order to ascertain the provision of screening and treatment services for example. The focus here is whether genetic information possesses particular qualities that indicate that a different approach should be adopted when considering whether to disclose it to other blood relatives.

The Nature of Genetic Information

Genetic information can be categorized into familial information where a mutation is in the family and where a particular person has tested positive for the mutation. One view is that a person's own genetic status is personal information and should generally be kept confidential in the same way as information concerning the patient's clinical or surgical history. Whether the person chooses to disclose his or her own genetic status to family members, or even chooses not to know it at all, is a matter for that person alone. Genetic conditions generally have a family history. Although a mutation may arise spontaneously, that is the exception. This means that it will often not come as a surprise for blood relatives to learn of the existence of a particular mutation in the family. Genetic disease is transmitted through reproduction so there is a predisposition for the relevant condition to be shared by family members who are biologically related. This is by no means automatic because the condition's manifestation will depend on a range of factors. Nevertheless, genetic information about an individual may reveal information about their relatives which is 'specific' in that the person has or will develop a genetic disease or 'predictive' in that the person has an unspecified risk of developing the disease.[12] Other specific factors associated uniquely with genetic information contribute to its 'shared' character: it may have to be supplemented by information obtained from relatives in order to make it meaningful. This is because in relation

---

9   Gostin, L. and Hodge, J., 'Genetic privacy and the law: an end to genetic exceptionalism', (1999) 40 *Jurimentrics* 21 cited in Herring, J., *Medical Law and Ethics*, Oxford, Oxford University Press, 2006 at p. 178.

10   Herring, ibid.

11   See the discussion in Chapter 4.

12   L. Skene, 'Patients' Rights or Family Responsibilities? Two Approaches to Genetic Testing' (1998) 6 *Medical Law Review* 1–41 at p.10.

to many genetic conditions there is currently no direct test for the gene and a marker or linkage test is necessary.[13] The accuracy and usefulness of such tests are improved by larger sample pools. Linkage tests are now less frequently used but, even where a direct gene test is available, it is important to confirm the mutation in at least one other affected family member.[14] This is particularly so where, as is commonly the case for genetic disorders, there is more than one form of genetic mutation which causes the disorder. In addition, multiple genes may cause the disorder so the starting point for genetic testing is

> ... to identify the mutation responsible for the disorder in an affected family member, who may be a symptomatic individual or a carrier. Testing relatives is a much simpler process as the family's specific mutation is now known and a specific test can be developed to identify it.[15]

To validate a diagnosis, clinical practice usually requires inter-generational familial information to establish a family pedigree even where relatives are not tested.[16]

Can the law's traditional approach to the disclosure of medical information be applied to genetic information in the light of these unique features? Even if it can, should the individual's interest in having their genetic information protected (including that of children), be de-emphasized to take into account the relational aspects of genetic information? The inherent shared nature of such information may justify different ethical and legal rules because both an individual patient and their genetic relatives have interests in it although the latter's interest in not knowing genetic information may also need to be respected.

Disclosure of Genetic Information: Legal and Ethical Perspectives

The disclosure of genetic information is as yet untested in the courts. Should a case arise regarding a potential breach of confidentiality in relation to genetic information, the traditional approach will justify disclosure.[17] There may be some limited contexts in which a doctor's disclosure of genetic information to a patient's relative may prevent or reduce a serious or imminent threat to their life or

---

13   Ibid., at p. 5.

14   Ibid.

15   Bell and Bennett, *supra*, n. 5 at p. 131, quoting the National Health and Medical Research Council, *Ethical Aspects of Human Genetic Testing: An Information Paper*, Australian Government Publishing Service, 2000.

16   Skene, *supra*, n. 12.

17   Gilbar, R., 'Medical Confidentiality Within the Family: the Doctor's Duty Reconsidered' (2004) 18(2) *International Journal of Law Policy and the Family* 195–213 at p. 197.

health. Existing law would probably allow disclosure in such circumstances.[18] The judiciary is used to balancing the interests and needs of both individual patients and third parties. However, genetic information is more usually predictive than determinative of whether a particular disease will occur so that the requirement for a high risk of significant harm to justify a disclosure will not be satisfied. If law cannot accommodate the particular features of genetic information in the way it affects others, should a different approach be adopted for the purposes of confidentiality? Given its essential 'familial' nature, perhaps there should no longer be a presumption that an individual's interest in the confidential status of that information must be respected. The following discussion presents arguments that may legitimize a shift away from the focus on the individual.

I noted in Chapter 2 that communitarians in particular have an antipathy to those moral theories that they perceive to have an undue focus on the individual. On the face of it, their claims have a specious appeal. Critics of liberalism are disturbed by the negative vision of humanity that it implies.[19] It is argued,[20] at its extreme, that liberalism presents a very negative view of society as a colony of individuals engaged in competitive negotiations with other equally independent individuals, attempting to agree the set of compromises that will secure the best sort of life for themselves. In this version of society the only shared ideal is merely the set of compromises. Communitarians object to the liberal view of the self as too abstract, artificially removed and isolated from the community from which it takes its identity and purpose. The charge is that liberal thought has been too influenced by a Kantian view of the self which emphasizes the self's power of rational deliberation and its isolation from any context in its consideration of what is good. These features are clearly recognizable in John Rawls' thought experiment, where he imagines a group of citizens reflecting upon the principles of justice behind a 'veil of ignorance' where they are 'unencumbered' by knowledge of their actual role, talents, and handicaps.[21] Rawls summarizes his view as the claim that 'the self is prior to the ends which are affirmed by it'.[22]

The liberal position is that the self both defines and constrains those ends. By leading a life from the inside according to beliefs about value that may be challenged, we can lead the good life. The role of the state is to protect the capacity of individuals to judge for themselves the worth of different conceptions of the good life and to provide a fair distribution of rights and resources to enable its citizens to pursue this. Communitarians maintain that it is what is already known, what is shared, which

---

18   See the discussion on disclosure in the preceding chapter.

19   Mulhall, S. and Swift, A., *Liberals and Communitarians*, (2nd ed.), Oxford, Blackwell, 1997.

20   See e.g. Woods, S., *Death's Dominion: Ethics at the End of Life*, Berkshire, Open University Press: McGraw-Hill Education, 2007 at p. 92.

21   Rawls, J., *A Theory of Justice*, London, Oxford University Press, 1971.

22   Ibid., at p. 560.

helps both to define and place limits on how the good is defined.[23] As Mulhall and Swift[24] comment, criticisms of the liberal position do not

> ... entail that individual autonomy should be altogether scrapped or entirely downgraded as a human good. It is rather designed to question the absoluteness of the priority and the universality of the scope that liberals are prone to assign to that good; it serves to suggest that both the priority and the scope should be modified or restricted.[25]

Kymlicka[26] also highlights how, in contrast to Marxist notions of community that require a complete overhaul of political systems, current communitarianism holds that community already exists with its shared social practices and understandings as well as cultural traditions: community needs to be respected and protected hence the charge that these approaches are inherently conservative and do not foster reflexivity and internal criticism. Kymlicka comments:

> No matter how deeply implicated we find ourselves in a social practice, we feel capable of questioning whether the practice is a valuable one ... [27]

Here is not the place to provide an exhaustive account of communitarian ethics and its conception about the self and its ends. This has been more than adequately done elsewhere.[28] For our purposes here, I want to focus on how communitarians see the individual in their social and relational context.[29] An important observation to make at this point is that the version of autonomy propounded by some liberals does take account of notions such as Taylor's social thesis.[30] However, there is a key difference in that the latter rejects the idea of a neutral state which does not justify its actions on the basis of the intrinsic superiority or inferiority of conceptions of the good life nor deliberately attempts to influence people's judgments about the value of these conceptions. For him, such a state cannot protect adequately the social environment necessary for self-determination. In addition, self-determination needs to be circumscribed to ensure the social conditions that enable self-determination

---

23   MacIntyre, A., *After Virtue: A Study in Moral Theory*, London, Duckworth, 1981.

24   Mulhall and Swift, *supra*, n. 19.

25   Ibid., at p. 163.

26   For a useful outline of contemporary communitarianism. See Kymlicka, W., *Contemporary Political Philosophy* (2nd ed.), Oxford, Oxford University Press, 2002, Chapter 6.

27   See Kymlicka, ibid., at p. 226.

28   Ibid.

29   See e.g. Mulhall and Swift, *supra.*, n. 19.

30   Taylor, C., *Philosophy and the Human Sciences: Philosophical Papers*, vol. ii, Cambridge, Cambridge University Press, 1985 at pp. 190–1 and the discussion of Gerald Dworkin's theory of autonomy in Chapter 2.

are preserved.[31] His 'social thesis' is 'perfectionist' to the extent that the capacity to choose a conception of the good life can only be exercised within a community that advances a politics of the common good. In comparison to the 'neutral' view of the good assumed by liberals, communitarians are said to be perfectionist to the extent that certain ways of life are said to constitute the good (perfection) and should be promoted by the state and its various institutions. The communitarian position that, like religious and other ancient philosophical beliefs, takes the view that the good life for human beings can be captured in terms of an over-arching framework of values that gives both meaning and purpose to life. Doubts about the intentions and abilities of governments apart, do we not share enough with others around us that a well-meaning perfectionist government could, by drawing on their wisdom and experience, arrive at a reasonable set of beliefs about its citizen's good?[32]

The liberal interpretation of the common good is the result of a process of combining preferences, all of which count equally but are not evaluated by the state. In contrast, the communitarian conception of the common good is constituted of a substantive conception of the good life that defines the community's *modus operandi*. In this version, the common good provides public standards by which preferences are evaluated. Further, it is maintained that only communitarian politics of the common good can ensure valuable forms of life contained in cultural structures remain viable[33] and that, in reality, individual judgments require the sharing of experiences and collective deliberation and evaluation:

> [S]elf-fulfillment and even the working out of personal identity and a sense of orientation in the world depend upon a communal enterprise. This shared process is the civic life, and its root is involvement with others: other generations, other sorts of persons whose differences are significant because they contribute to the whole upon which our particular sense of self depends. This mutual interdependency is the foundational notion of citizenship … [34]

Again, liberals do not necessarily reject such collective enterprises but merely that the state is the forum in which they should take place.[35]

There is also an argument that individual choices require a secure cultural context assured by a stable and legitimate political context.[36] The liberals' position that this is attained through shared principles of justice is insufficient according to the communitarian view that believes that there needs to be a shared 'way of

---

31   Taylor, *supra*, n. 30.

32   See Kymlicka, *supra*, n. 26 at p. 216.

33   Raz, J., *The Morality of Freedom*, Oxford, Oxford University Press, 1986 at p. 162.

34   Kymlicka, *supra*, n. 26 at p. 249 citing Sullivan, W., *Reconstructing Public Philosophy*, Berkeley, University of California Press, 1982 at p. 158.

35   See e.g. Rawls, *supra*, n. 21 at pp. 328–9.

36   Kymlicka, *supra*, n. 26 at p. 252.

life'.[37] Helping fellow citizens then becomes more likely because this shared way of life is strengthened, as is the individual's own position. However, a major flaw of this proposition is defining shared ends that can serve as the basis for a politic of the common good which would be legitimate for all groups in society. The supposed shared ends found in historical practices were invariably based on excluding various groups within society[38] such as beggars, 'lunatics', women and children. Kymlicka suggests that a possible explanation of why it is possible to feel a special sense of obligation to our fellow citizens is the modern appeal of nationhood, hence a sense of belonging to a single political community.[39] The terminology involved in this concept emphasizes that this community belongs to the people irrespective of class, gender, physical or intellectual ability and so on.[40] Nationalism may exist independently from strictly liberal or communitarian ideologies although it is likely to embrace elements of both.

The debate between liberal individualism and communitarianism has engendered a desire to transcend the opposition between the positions and to integrate the demands of liberal justice and community membership.[41] Citizenship has materialized as a useful, supplementary concept that can mediate between these two stances given that it embraces liberal ideas of individual rights and membership of communities.

Post-war notions of citizenship suggested that everyone should be treated as a full and equal member of society with the full panoply of political, civil and social rights.[42] More recently there has been a call for this rather passive 'right to have rights'[43] to be supplemented, if not replaced, by the active exercise of citizenship responsibilities and virtues. These include the need to participate in debate, rendering political decision-making more legitimate with the increased opportunities for everyone to have their views heard and considered. The experience can be empowering and is likely to lead to greater unity and solidarity as a result of enhanced mutual understanding and empathy. This 'civic friendship',[44] whereby community members do not merely act for their own personal benefit may extend to the wish to help others in other ways. Whether politically active or not, responsible citizenship requires personal responsibility and mutual obligation. Only focusing on the self denies our inherently social nature. Individuals require society to lead a truly human life.[45] Modern democracies require more than institutional checks and balances to temper the over-enthusiastic pursuit of self-

---

37   Ibid., at p. 257.
38   Ibid., at p. 259.
39   Ibid., at p. 261.
40   Ibid., at p. 262.
41   Ibid., at p. 284.
42   Ibid., at pp. 287–93.
43   Ibid., at p. 288.
44   Ibid., at p. 291.
45   Ibid., at p. 296.

interest: some level of civic virtue, such as a willingness to participate, and public spiritedness is required. States cannot meet all the needs and demands of their citizenry without some restraint and co-operation. Taking health as an example, citizens must behave responsibly so as not to exhaust the finite resources available for health care. [46]

Does being a child alter one's moral obligations? Having such an expectation, even of children, should be construed as part of the initiation into good citizenship. Children should grow up socialized into a world in which the society in which they thrive has legitimate expectations in return. This is of course an unpopular and admittedly difficult argument to make in the light of the Bristol and Alder Hey scandals[47] and the subsequent collapse in the trust in health professionals that has ensued. A society can only begin to insist upon such expectations where it has gained and is proved worthy of the trust of its citizens.[48] This is emphatically not to say that a citizen may not grow up to criticize and ultimately reject the values of their own culture.

Civic friendship can gain support from aspects of care theory. Gilligan's[49] proposal that women's mode of moral reasoning differs from that of men in that it centres on responsibility and relationships, has been extremely significant and has been characterized as an ethic of care.[50] She contrasts this with an 'ethic of justice', whereby the conception of morality as fairness means that moral development requires an understanding of rights and rules. While there is some doubt that as to whether this different 'voice' actually exists and, further, whether there is a significant correlation with gender, this feminist position has been very influential.[51] Any perceived differences may not indicate different thought processes, but consideration that women focus on preserving social relations rather than issues of justice and rights,[52] possibly due to gender role. That apart, controversy remains about whether this perspective should be extended beyond private relationships and into the realm of public affairs.[53]

For Gilligan, the essence of the differences between an ethic of care as opposed to an ethic of justice approach, lies in three main areas: the importance of developing moral dispositions, such as the ability to perceive people's needs accurately and imaginatively respond to them; seeking resolution of problems

---

46   Ibid., at p. 285.

47   The Report of the Public Inquiry into Children's Heart Surgery at the Bristol Royal Infirmary 1984–95 (Cm 5207(1)) and http://www.rlcinquiry.org.uk/.

48   O'Neill, O., *Autonomy and Trust in Bioethics*, Cambridge, Cambridge University Press, 2002.

49   Gilligan, C., *In a Different Voice: Psychological Theory and Women's Development*, Cambridge, Mass., Harvard University Press, 1982 at p. 238.

50   *Cf.* Sevenhuijsen, S., *Citizenship and the Ethics of Care: Feminist Considerations on Justice, Morality and Politics*, London, Routledge, 1998.

51   Kymlicka, *supra*, n. 26 at p. 400.

52   Ibid.

53   Ibid., at p. 400.

on a case-by-case basis, and attending to responsibilities and relationships. An ethic of justice gives apparent predominance to learning moral principles, solving problems by seeking principles that have universal applicability and attending to rights and justice. Kymlicka[54] contends that the latter also requires the same moral sensitivities even if insufficient attention has been given to it perhaps because justice develops out of a sense of care initially learned within the family. This is where it is possible, in the ideal case, for children to learn about fairness by understanding the role of kindness and sensitivity to the aims and interests of others. Further, he argues that by expecting imagination, character and actions to respond appropriately to complex situations, suggests that moral principles are not only unnecessary but possibly counter-productive in a way that does not withstand scrutiny: moral principles are essential to determine which features of a situation are morally relevant because this may not always be immediately apparent. They are also required to help decide how to resolve any conflict between various demands that may arise and invite reflection.

Kymlicka[55] then turns his attention to what he sees as the nub of the ethic of care proposal: that we need principles of responsibilities and relationships. A key component of this is the idea that preserving relationships is more important than aims of universality or impartiality. Such a position could easily lead to a lack of consideration for those who fall outside the ambit of significant others but Gilligan proposes that we are all responsible to everyone because we 'are connected to them by virtue of being another person'.[56] As Kymlicka points out, this idea of shared humanity does rather suggest a principle of universality, evident in other theories.[57] To the charge of care theorists who maintain that justice theories neglect individual characteristics, he argues that this criticism cannot be maintained. The common humanity of the ethic of care position gives rise to general, abstract and repeatable characteristics. In addition, justice theories do have to attend to the particular: utilitarianism needs an awareness of preferences, and Rawls' original position requires a consideration of the identities, aims and attachments of others as of equal concern to our own.[58]

The other distinction between justice and care reasoning offered by Gilligan is that the former relies on respecting rights-claims as expressing concerns for others whereas the latter does this by accepting responsibilities. For her, rights can be protected merely by leaving others alone, and rights-based duties to others consist of reciprocal non-interference, while accepting responsibility for others requires some positive concern for them and, as such, is a less selfish and individualistic

---

54   Ibid., at p. 401–4.
55   Ibid., at p. 404.
56   Gilligan, *supra*, n. 49 at p. 57.
57   Kymlicka, *supra*, n. 26 at p. 406.
58   Ibid.

focus.[59] Kymlycka[60] points out that even libertarian theories of rights do not deny there are positive duties concerning the welfare of others although they may not accept these are legally enforceable. Rights impose responsibilities on others, which is the language of some proponents of the ethic of care.

For Kymlicka,[61] the exact points of disagreement between the two theories is unclear, although care theorists seem to emphasize subjective hurt rather than objective unfairness as grounding moral claims. Justice theorists believe that this means that all of an individual's interests would require the attention of others, which would be unduly burdensome for them, and there needs to be some personal responsibility for *some* of these. A feminist ethic of care counters the first objection by the notion of a 'self-inclusive' conception of care that allows women in particular to care for themselves as well as others.[62] The justice perspective allows a legitimate expectation as a matter of fairness that others attend to some of an individual's interests even if it limits the pursuit of others' good, but not all. In addition, to attend to subjective hurts could lead to the perpetuation of unjust states of affairs where these are based on unfair and selfish expectations. Claims of justice are founded on rightful expectation. So the debate between the two positions is not about rights and responsibilities, because the latter is central to the justice ethic.

For care theorists, the conflict between autonomy and responsibility for others must be decided in the context of the particular caring relationship without the use of an abstract rule. Kymlicka[63] disagrees with this position believing predictable limits on moral responsibilities are required where interactions between competent adults are concerned. He advocates that attention to subjective hurts has more resonance when considering dependent others such as children but that this should nevertheless diminish as dependency subsides. If justice theories become associated with interactions with autonomous adults and care theories in our relations with dependants, the danger is that caring for the latter could fall to those with the relevant proclivities leading to potential exploitation. This suggests to Kymlicka that certain practices of care should be seen as an obligation of citizenship that will require a breaking down of traditional divisions between the public and private spheres of life.

The preceding discussion, which highlights some of the ethical bases for proposing that we all have obligations to others, is particularly compelling where family members are concerned. It can at least be construed that there could reasonably be an expectation to share genetic information. To expect this sharing of genetic information with family members is to presume willingness to do what any reasonable, moral person should be prepared to do given the only (unlikely?)

---

59   See e.g. Gilligan, *supra*, n. 49 at pp. 22, 136 and 147.
60   Kymlicka, *supra*, n. 26 at p. 409.
61   Ibid., at p. 411–13.
62   Gilligan, *supra*, n. 49 at p. 149.
63   Kymlicka, *supra*, n. 26 at pp. 415–20.

risk that they might be ostracized by their relatives. Not to do so because of family tensions, where motivation might include spite, is an unconvincing justifications.

Where should the balance lie when a patient continues to withhold their permission for disclosure of their personal genetic information to relevant family members? Assuming all efforts have been made to present a suitably persuasive case, should their wishes be disregarded? Using the other-regarding arguments in the genetics context, the starting point that individuals who are the source of information of a medical nature are entitled to have that information kept secret, is undermined. This would be especially true where close relatives are concerned. Nevertheless, each case should be determined on its merits subject to the demands of current legal and ethical guidance. Any assessment will require a detailed analysis of the factors suggested as relevant throughout this chapter. The Australian Anti-Cancer Council of Victoria Report[64] (Australian Report) provides an example of where a communitarian perspective is recognized as a legitimate position to adopt. This is relatively unusual where health care ethics is under debate.

Australian Anti-Cancer Council of Victoria Report

Ball and Bennett[65] usefully discuss the Australian Report and its reduced emphasis on the individual. In relation to the confidentiality of information about genetic cancer, the Australian Report observes the strong presumption in favour of confidentiality, so that such information may be disclosed, even to family members, albeit in special circumstances. However, it considers that it is important to remember that the 'flipside' of doctors' obligations is that patients have ethical responsibilities. The duty of confidentiality presupposes that patients are 'undertaking responsibility for improving their health or at least managing their illness'.[66] Just as the broader social context in which the doctor-patient relationship is situated places limits on the doctor's obligation of confidentiality, so patients:

> ... need to appreciate that the communal context of their medical interaction may involve them in considering more than just what will contribute to their own health.[67]

Of the broader relationship between the individual and the community, the Report recognizes the importance of confidentiality, privacy and consent in

---

64   Anti-Cancer Council of Victoria, Cancer Genetics Ethics Committee, *Ethics and Familial Cancers: Including Guidelines on Ethical Aspects of Risk Assessment, Genetic Testing and Genetic Registers*, 1997.

65   Ball and Bennett, *supra*, n. 5.

66   Ibid., n. 5 at p. 38.

67   Ibid.

medical practice, but is less disposed to a focus on individual rights. It prefers an emphasis on wider responsibility and communal concern.[68]

Using this communitarian approach, a range of medical institutions and personnel, acting as representatives of the wider community, would act as custodians of genetic material (which has personal and social significance), rather than the individual 'owning' it *per se*. In relation to familial cancer susceptibility, the Council's position is that patients do not necessarily have the right to block disclosure of medical information when this may identify them and/or their genetic status. Patients are at risk as members of families and usually seek out a genetic test because of a shared family history of disease.[69] The propensity for developing cancer where the familial adenomatous polyposis (FAP) gene mutation is involved, which invariably leads to the cancer, creates a stronger case for disclosure. The Report notes the range of relatives who may be potentially uncovered by a consultation, who may be unaware of it and may not wish to know about any complex information that comes to light about their genetic risk of cancer and especially the results of gene tests. In addition, tests will become possible which had not been recognized or possible at the time that a sample was taken.

In common with many ethical guidelines on legitimate disclosure,[70] the Council suggests that non-consensual disclosure should only be made after attempts have been made to persuade the patient voluntarily to disclose the information to relevant family members. It may be possible to advise relations of their cancer susceptibility without identifying the original patient. However, if objections to disclosure persist and non-identification is not possible, this would not constitute a legitimate reason for the information not to be used.[71] Other Australian bodies are more cautious about discarding the current presumption of confidentiality, principally because non-consensual disclosure is allowed in very limited circumstances only by law and ethics.

Laurie[72] has argued that a relative who is aware of their genetic risk, perhaps through their family history, but does not want to be informed of the details, should have those wishes respected. They may not wish to know of these risks where there is no effective treatment or preventative measures they can take to avoid contracting the condition for example. This right 'not to know' can be

---

68 Australian Report, *supra*, n. 64 at p. 38–41.

69 Whether the expectations we can reasonably anticipate of each other would justify mandatory screening is a question beyond the scope of this book but one that is worth considering in light of the preceding discussion.

70 See Human Genetics Commission, *Inside Information: Balancing Interests in the Use of Personal Genetic Data* 2002, para. 3,68 discussed *infra* at n. 76.

71 Australian Report, *supra*, n. 64 at p. 57–8.

72 Laurie, G.T., 'The Most Personal Information of All: An Appraisal of Genetic Privacy in the Shadow of the Human Genome Project', (1996) 10 *International Journal of Law, Policy and the Family* 74 at p. 91.

derived from the concept of privacy. In this context, the wishes of the individual can help to define the scope of the privacy interest. The expression of a wish not to know is meaningful because such relatives are likely to be aware of the nature of the disease from which they are at risk. To seek to inform them of genetic information would be an affront to their dignity and an invasion of their privacy. Some individuals will prefer to have this knowledge so that they can plan their affairs accordingly. All are likely to suffer varying degrees of distress.[73] The Australian Report acknowledges this and states that one relevant factor in deciding whether or not to disclose is the nature of the genetic condition. Where the risk is high, as with FAP, there is a risk of considerable harm that can be prevented by a disclosure and an individual's wishes are unknown, Laurie argues that in these circumstances 'arguably, privacy should be invaded to prevent the harm'.[74] As the Australian Report states,[75] there should be a 'strong presumption' that blood relatives will appreciate the opportunity to ascertain their risk. The original patient or other family member is the best person to approach blood relations but if family involvement is not possible the doctor may have to initiate contact. Predicting who would or would not choose to know will be challenging and, where possible, it may be better to establish with the relevant family member whether they would like to be made aware of any results or not.[76]

In the UK, the British Medical Association's guidance[77] may be influential. Not only does that body view the family as the patient in these circumstances but it provides some useful factors that might be determinative when deciding whether to disclose genetic information. These include the severity of the disorder, the predictability of the test and whether there is an effective action the family member can take for protection from or amelioration of the risk. It would also be necessary to consider the consequences of withholding the information, the reasons for refusing to share the information and whether it is possible to identify the relatives without the patient's help. The UK Human Genetic Commission's guidance further suggests that an attempt must have been made to persuade the patient to consent to the disclosure. Here, the benefit to those at risk must be so considerable as to outweigh any distress caused to the patient by the disclosure. The information should be anonymized where possible, and restricted to the least detail necessary to communicate the risk.[78]

---

73   See Mason and Laurie, *supra*, n. 3, Chapter 7 for a thorough exploration of the medical, legal and ethical implications of genetic information and at pp. 219–20 on the psychological effects of having such knowledge in particular.

74   Laurie, *supra*, n. 72.

75   Australian Report, *supra*, n. 64 at p. 44.

76   *Supra*, n. 1.

77   British Medical Association, *Medical Ethics Today*, London, BMJ, 2004 at pp. 315–17. See also Mason and Laurie, *supra*, n. 3 at p. 225 on this point.

78   Human Genetics Commission, *supra*, n. 70.

Skene[79] has noted that a number of international instruments have recognized that divulging genetic information to family members may be different from disclosure to other third parties, and that this has generally been reflected in any legislation or recommendations. She notes the onerous legal requirements in the 'legal/rights/privacy' model, based on autonomy and self-determination,[80] for validating the family history from medical records, access to tissue samples and the control of personal information. The individual alone must decide the people who will know the existence of the genetic mutation.[81] She also considers the duty to warn relatives. In limited circumstances, the common law in some jurisdictions in the United States based on the rule in *Tarasoff v Regents of the University of California*[82] might impose a duty on doctors to warn relatives. However, the model genetic privacy statutes enacted in some US states appear to override the effect of any such common law requirement by prohibiting disclosure without the consent of the person concerned. Whether the patient has a legal duty to warn his or her blood relatives is another question, which is not addressed in the statutes and which has not been judicially considered.[83] Skene then proposes a useful approach in the way genetic information is conceived.

A Way Forward?

Skene discusses a medical (now called a 'family') model[84] as illustrated by the Australian guidelines to deal with the genetic context. She sees this approach as rejecting a consideration of rights, focusing instead on the care of patients and their families, and envisages a proactive role for doctors in this process.[85] This is justified on the basis of her experience with doctors involved in genetic testing and counselling.[86] She highlights doctors' views that conditions such as FAP may affect all blood relatives, and that families should be encouraged to share information in their common interest. The practice at some clinics is to give people diagnosed with FAP printed material about the condition and its implications in order to show to their relatives. The clinic encourages the relatives to come to the clinic which holds familial files. In considering whether a pregnant woman can have a genetic test for Huntington Disease (HD) on her fetus in *utero* without her

---

79   Skene, *supra*, n. 12.

80   Ibid., at p. 32.

81   Ibid., n. 12 at pp. 20–21.

82   551P. 2d 334 (1976).

83   Skene, *supra*, n. 12 at p. 21.

84   Skene, *supra*, n. 5. She prefers 'family' to 'communitarian' which implies duties to the wider community, rather than to blood relatives.

85   Skene, *supra*, n. 12 at p. 2.

86   Ibid., at pp. 1–2. Having also spent a large part of my professional life with doctors listening to the medical viewpoint on these issues, I can support her perspective.

husband's consent, she notes that this would be allowed in some clinics[87] although this would not conform to widespread clinical practice elsewhere. In the clinic concerned, their view is that the role of a clinician or a counsellor is to inform and support both parties. Thus clinicians and counsellors focus on situations that they face in day-to-day practice as the starting point in developing guidelines on how they should behave; they do not start with legal principles. An alternative approach to the constraints of the law, which traditionally has not allowed consideration of third parties' interests, is to start with what the professionals do and what rules they think are needed to achieve the best result for the family. The current Australian, English and Welsh law is that doctors have duties towards patients. It could, however, be that doctors and counsellors undertaking genetic testing and counselling have duties towards families as well.[88]

Under the family model, people would not have a 'right' to control their genetic information and the use of their tissue taken for genetic testing, and 'doctors will have a special role in providing and imparting genetic information that may appear contrary to their traditional obligation to maintain patient confidentiality'.[89] Generally, the medical model envisages a very different role for the doctor where they care for more than an individual patient.[90] Thus, the doctor may sometimes obtain genetic information about the inquirer's relatives without first seeking the patient's consent to validate the family history from medical records. Access to tissue samples should be available to all family members who might benefit from such access. Patients would not have an invariable right to block disclosure of genetic information because it is familial information. Skene observes that a doctor who follows the Council's guidelines is probably in compliance with the existing common law, which recognizes that it may be lawful to breach confidentiality where there is a serious risk of harm to others. As far as the duty to warn relatives is concerned, Skene considers that the argument that doctors owe third parties a duty of care in limited circumstances is unlikely to be successful in the context of genetics notwithstanding some developments in this direction in the US.[91] However, in the UK we need to be alert to developments in *Ayse Colak and others v Germany*[92] which may yet extend doctors' duties to warn.

Should there be a duty to warn in the context of genetics? Laurie[93] notes several potential difficulties with such a concept. It can be difficult to predict the likelihood of harm to relatives from multi-factorial genetic conditions. It is necessary to

---

87   Supported by guidelines of the Huntington Disease Association and the World Federation of Neurology.

88   Skene, *supra*, n. 5 at p. 2.

89   Skene, *supra*, n. 12 at p. 24.

90   Ibid., at pp. 26–30.

91   (1996) 291 N.J. Super. 619.

92   *(Admissibility Decision)* 8 January 2008 discussed in Chapter 4 that may lead to stronger duties for doctors to warn relatives about a patient's HIV status.

93   Laurie, *supra*, n. 72.

consider the kind of harm that will justify the imposition of such a duty. Some relatives will only be affected by knowledge of their carrier status, rather than more directly. If the only risk of harm is to any future children, the question must be asked whether this is sufficient to defend a duty of disclosure obligation. Also pertinent to this proposition is the health professional's knowledge of the risk of harm the patient might pose to the third party. However, one person does not pose a risk to another in the context of genetics merely because they are a relative. The risk is finding out that they are carriers. In addition, it is necessary to consider whether harm can be averted by the disclosure given the very limited number of conditions for which there is a cure.[94] It is still possible to argue in favour of disclosure in the absence of a cure because information could provide relatives with the opportunity to change their lifestyle and minimize their risk of the disease occurring. However, the multifactorial nature of many genetic diseases means that test results may have limited predictive capability, thus limiting the benefits of disclosure.[95] Nevertheless, affected individuals might want to take advantage of monitoring and surgery where this is required. Reproductive decisions are also relevant. There may not be a cure for the affected relative but they may not wish to have children if they would be at risk of inheriting the condition. Pre-implantation diagnosis may assist in avoiding such a dilemma, but not all genetic conditions can be detected in this way at least as yet. A further factor to be considered is any potential for discrimination notwithstanding the current moratorium on this at least by the insurance industry.[96]

The preceding discussion highlights the range of issues to be considered in relation to the disclosure of genetic information to blood relatives where consent from a patient is not forthcoming. Bell and Bennett have proposed that the common law approach is adequate to deal with issues of disclosure so that this should only take place where arguments are sufficiently compelling.[97] This is disputed by Skene.[98] She highlights the shortcomings of the common law. An example may be found in the requirement that there should be 'real risk of consequent danger to the public'.[99] The courts have also emphasized that disclosure should be to a responsible authority.[100] These constraints suggest that the public interest basis for disclosure has not, thus far, been contemplated for a situation such as disclosure to a family member of genetic information. This is because such a condition will rarely, if ever, present an immediately life-threatening risk, and also because such disclosure would ultimately have to be disclosed to the family member rather than a responsible authority. If the relative is not a patient of the doctor's,

---

94   Ibid., n. 72 at pp. 82–3.
95   Ibid., at p. 86.
96   Mason and Laurie, *supra*, n. 3.
97   Bell and Bennett, *supra*, n. 5 at p. 15.
98   Skene, *supra*, n. 5.
99   *W v Edgell* [1990] 1 CH 359, *per* Bingham L.J. at 424.
100   Ibid.

it may be disclosed to that relative's treating doctor. However, Skene[101] finds it difficult to imagine a situation in which a genetic risk would satisfy traditional legal requirements. She uses FAP as an example of where she sees non-authorized disclosure as most justified. Here, the risk is serious, as it is a potentially lethal condition and the diagnosis is certain. There is an effective intervention, in that monitoring and surgery is available, if required. However, the risk could not be described as imminent. For these reasons she does not believe the common law exception is sufficient.

Skene notes that the medical model might require new laws.[102] She considers three alternative approaches: to legislate, to do nothing and allow the law to develop case by case as issues come before the courts, or to attempt to regulate by contract. Her preference is for either an express or implied contractual provision to the effect that the patient agrees to share genetic information with, *inter alia*, family members.[103] This is a contentious requirement given that an obligation to warn is not normally required, but one that could be ethically justified along the lines discussed by the Australian Report. It should be established with the patient at the outset, prior to any testing, that such information will be disclosed appropriately. The decision to proceed with the testing on this basis then rests with the patient. This approach could seem unduly harsh to some health professionals, but establishing early parameters avoids more intense difficulties should it be decided at a later date that disclosure to relatives must take place and be justified at that point. Any arguments that a quasi-contractual approach could be overly simplistic may be more legitimate. There may be reasons other than family dysfunction that motivate the patient to withhold consent for disclosure.

The Human Rights Act 1998 (HRA) with its incorporation of the European Convention on Human Rights (ECHR), offers an alternative to any contractual proposal. The use of the HRA provides a mechanism for the balancing of everyone's interests along the lines discussed in the preceding chapter. In sum, there must be a fair balance between the protection of the rights and freedoms of the individual and the interests of the community as a whole. Where there is any interference with an individual's rights, it must be lawful and proportionate. There is a right to have genetic information kept private under Article 8(1) of the ECHR[104] but this may be circumscribed by Article 8(2) in the interests of other individuals' interests and those of wider society. The potential for serious risk of harm to another could qualify as a legitimate interference with Article 8(1) in the context of genetic information. The ECHR is a living instrument that has demonstrated its ability to develop with changing social mores.[105] If ever this

---

101   Skene, *supra*, n. 5 at p. 4.

102   Skene, *supra*, n. 12.

103   Ibid., at pp. 35–7.

104   *A London Borough Council v Mr & Mrs N* [2005] EWHC 1676.

105   See e.g. the developing jurisprudence concerning autonomy discussed in Chapter 2.

facility was needed, it is in response to the changing face of genetic information. The world of genetics is new territory and needs different solutions because genetic information may be seen as belonging to relatives. Such data might also be important for public health objectives if the Government needs to determine its provisions for screening and treatment. Any attempts to avoid falling within the HRA's remit by turning to private testing providers, the internet or engage doctors under private contractual arrangements for example, should be resisted. Alternative providers should either be seen as performing a public function so falling within the Act's ambit[106] or there should be increased regulation so that they are expected to adhere to the same ethical standards. Some clinical specialities do have systems whereby the parameters of the relationship between patients and health professionals are set out before any intervention takes place.[107] Nevertheless, this has not become commonplace. However, this should be encouraged to make everyone's responsibilities in the professional relationship clear. This will, *inter alia*, enhance trust because the patient will understand that relevant information may be disclosed to others in specified circumstances rather than discovering this without any warning when they may have assumed their genetic information, as with their other medical information, would be kept private.

Conclusion

While the UK lacks specific legislation dealing with the control and use of genetic information, the ethical position is currently clear with respect to children under 16. There should be no pre-symptomatic testing for late onset disorders for which there are no clinical treatments.[108] This approach protects the child's privacy interests and avoids any potential for the child to be treated differently in the light of any knowledge. As more genetic knowledge becomes available about other conditions, there will need to be multi-disciplinary team working with children and families to support them as they consider risk factors and their implications for their future health and well-being.[109]

There is understandable concern that leaving decision-making about the release of genetic information to the individual patient could lead to harm to blood relatives where consent to such disclosure is not forthcoming. Underpinning

---

106   See the discussion in *YL v Birmingham City Council and others (Secretary of State for Constitutional Affairs intervening)* [2008] 1 AC 95.

107   This would be the practice of some Child and Adolescent Mental Health Services' teams at Sheffield Children's NHS Foundation Trust.

108   See e.g. HGC, *supra*, n. 70. This position is echoed elsewhere, notably in the US Genetic Privacy Act 1995.

109   Patenaude, A.F., 'Pediatric Psychology Training and Genetics: What will Twenty-First Century Pediatric Psychologists Need to Know?' (2003) 28(1) *Journal of Pediatric Psychology* 135–45.

this present approach however is the desire to uphold an individual's right to autonomy. However, this atomized view of autonomy is not one that is accepted here. The context of genetic information is one that compels a consideration of the relational aspects of autonomy. It is because we operate in a social context that most individuals do share information from genetic tests with other family members in most cases.[110] Where they do not, the common law will require further interpretation by the HRA to ensure that disclosure may be permitted against an individual's wishes even where there is no risk of immediate, serious harm as it is traditionally conceived. Further, any interpretation should take account of a familial concept of medical information. While this would require a major departure from the presumptions of existing law, it is one that is justified in the legitimate interests of both the wider family and society where public health measures made need to be taken.

---

110   Personal communication from Dr O. Quarrell, Consultant Clinical Geneticist, Sheffield Children's NHS Foundation Trust and member of the Huntington Disease Association.

Chapter 6
Negligence and Complaints

Introduction

The purpose of this chapter is not to provide a definitive account of the tort of negligence. It will provide an overview of the tort's requirements. Inevitably, this will require a discussion of key cases involving adults but the principles also apply to children. Where appropriate, attention will be drawn to issues that have particular relevance for the paediatric health practitioner. In particular, the paediatric health professional needs to be alert to the need to reach appropriate standards of care. This will be discussed in the section on breach of the duty of care. Appropriate practice should not just be about adopting professionally accepted standards to avoid litigation and complaints, but should also involve consideration of the ethical dimension of their practice. This is especially relevant when considering the requirement that patients should give informed consent. The chapter will also demonstrate that tort actions can be a poor means of vindicating patients' rights given the focus on doctors' duties, although there are signs this is beginning to change.[1] This may be due in part to the influence of the HRA[2] but professional guidance has also encouraged patient-centred care. Health professionals should be reassured that if they adopt appropriate practice, including vigilant record keeping, although they may not avoid claims being made against them, they should be able to withstand many legal challenges not least because of the undoubted sympathy of the courts towards the difficult environment in which they work.

The chapter will also attempt to highlight the main flaws of the tort system. It is there, *inter alia*, to hold people to account for their actions, deterring poor practice[3] and to compensate victims of such poor practice. This may not be attributable to one individual but be the result of systems' failures.[4] In addition, not all incidents result in identifiable loss to a patient so improving practice will have to rely on alternative

---

1   See the discussion of *Chester v Afshar* [2005] 1 AC 134 at para. 9.

2   Lord Irvine of Craig, 'The Patient, the Doctor, their Lawyers and the Judge: Rights and Duties', (1999) 7 *Medical Law Review* 255 at p. 267 where he noted that the incorporation of the European Convention of Human Rights was likely to de-emphasize the importance of professional standards in favour of patients' rights.

3   Although the fact that the employing organization is financially responsible for any awards means that this role for torts is somewhat undermined.

4   The Report of the Public Inquiry into Children's Heart Surgery at the Bristol Royal Infirmary 1984–95: Learning from Bristol (the 'Bristol Inquiry') (Cmnd 5207 (1)) 2001 at para. 13.8.

reporting systems.[5] Although damage to an individual must be addressed, we must be mindful that this is in the context of finite resources. Individual patients should receive adequate sums for their injuries but not at such a high level that the system is overwhelmed with claims. We want health professionals to be more careful in the way they deal with patients including good communication, checking and record-keeping, to help maintain trust in the doctor-patient relationship, but not to the point, for example, that they start to behave defensively to avoid litigation[6] by the inappropriate referral by GPs to hospital consultants, the over-use of diagnostic tests[7] or by the avoidance of any innovative practice. Eyes are often cast across the Atlantic when concerns such as these are raised but it is unlikely that the US experience will be duplicated here as that jurisdiction has a very different system and other factors can account for some oft-cited domestic examples.[8]

The Medical Malpractice Context

Notwithstanding general satisfaction with health care services[9] medical mishaps seize the headlines, distorting perceptions and predisposing health professionals to fear the possibility of a negligence action against them. It is facile to suggest that the increased number of claims represents a more litigious society eager to make easy money. Studies suggest aggrieved patients are motivated as much by a need to have a thorough investigation of what went wrong and receive an apology.[10] Part

---

5   Such as referral to the General Medical Council, NHS organizations' own internal complaints procedures and the National Patient Safety Agency's National Reporting and Learning System which collects reports of adverse incidents and near misses across England and Wales (http://www.npsa.nhs.uk).

6   Jones, M. and Morris, A., 'Defensive Medicine: Myths and Facts', (1989) 5 *Journal of the Medical Defence Union* 40.

7   Although this could result in better patient care because patients will be reassured and unsuspected conditions may be discovered: see Jones, M., *Medical Negligence*, London, Sweet and Maxwell, 1996 at pp. 6–7.

8   See Deakin, S., Johnston, A. and Markesinis, B., *Tort Law*, (5th ed.) Oxford, Clarendon Press, 2003 at pp. 324–5 and 214–60 for a useful comparison of the UK and US approaches.

9   Healthcare Commission, *The Annual Health Check, 2006–2007: a national overview of the performance of NHS trusts in England*, October 2007.

10   See, for example, Department of Health (DoH), *Making Amends: A Consultation Paper Setting Out Proposals for Reforming the Approach to Clinical Negligence in the NHS*, (2003) at p. 75. The *Making Amends* consultation document was a response to some of the recommendations of the 'Bristol Inquiry' (op. cit., n. 4) calling for, *inter alia*, greater openness about adverse events and an exploration of alternatives to the torts system including wholly or partially insurance-funded health care or a state compensation system such as no-fault compensation.

of the rise[11] in claims is represented by the category of claimant who alleges that negligence occurred before treatment has even commenced because there was a failure to disclose the risks of the intervention. Health professionals do not want to harm their patients and adverse events are usually a result of inadvertent behaviour though conduct can be cavalier. Even notorious scandals in the NHS, such as that that took place at the Bristol Royal Infirmary, where inappropriate treatment was carried out on children, was as a result of over-optimism rather than any deliberate intent.[12] Health professionals can see complaints as an attack on their professional integrity, potentially making them defensive and appearing dismissive, thus exacerbating a patient's sense that they are not being taken seriously.[13] The idea of having to defend their practice in court creates significant levels of anxiety[14] and this is as true in the paediatric setting as anywhere else. Fear of litigation may mean that health professionals are less likely to be honest about mistakes.

The fact is that only a small proportion of potential claims from the victims of medical negligence bring an action for damages. Of those that do bring a claim, over three quarters of these fail[15] with relatively few cases actually reaching the hearing stage in the court. This may be of small comfort to health professionals undergoing scrutiny. The huge costs involved will deter those who cannot get legal aid and, given the restrictions on access to this,[16] this will be the majority of potential claimants. Of course the 'no win, no fee' arrangements, much touted on daytime television, may help certain categories of claimant.[17] In order to reflect

---

11   See Morris, A., 'Spiralling or Stabilizing? The Compensation Culture and Our Propensity to Claim Damages for Personal Injury', (2007) 70(3) *Modern Law Review* 349–78 where she suggests that compensation claims for personal injury generally have actually stabilized rather than continue to increase as suggested by the media and at p. 360 where she notes that, with respect to clinical negligence in particular, a higher number of claims might be expected given the high number of avoidable adverse events.

12   The 'Bristol Inquiry', *supra*, n. 4 at p. 2. The recent landmark decision in *Telles v South West Strategic HA* [2008] EWHC 292 (QB) allowing a successful claim against the Infirmary for brain damage suffered as a result of the heart surgery 20 years ago, is likely to lead to further actions: 'Brain-damaged woman is first successful case in Bristol baby scandal', *The Times*, 14 March 2008.

13   Interestingly, some surveys suggest that children are a slightly under-represented source of complaints: see e.g. Medical Protection Society, 'Child Complaints', (2008) 16(2) *Casebook* 11–14.

14   *Making Amends*, *supra*, n. 10, indicates that 38 per cent of doctors facing a medical negligence action suffer from clinical depression and the fear of litigation combined with press vilification is suggested as being major causes of job dissatisfaction, at pp. 43–4. See, also, Tallis, R., *Hippocratic Oaths: Medicine and Its Discontents*, London, Atlantic Books, 2004.

15   National Audit Office, *Handling Clinical Negligence Claims in England*, HC 403, Session 2000–2001, 3 May 2001.

16   Brazier, M., *Medicine, Patients and the Law* (3rd ed.), London, Penguin Books, 2003 at pp. 175–6.

17   As provided by the Courts and Legal Services Act 1990.

the risk to lawyers who may carry out work without reward if the case fails, they receive a greater proportion of the damages. Although this is a detriment to the claimant, it does not carry the risk of them losing money. This system does not appear to have led to a flood of extra litigation despite early concerns.[18] Crucially, in cases involving children, there is likely to be assistance with legal aid because their means are assessed separately from their parents.[19] All cases must of course be meritorious to qualify though there is a view that the system fails to filter out weak cases. This has significant implications for the NHS as a whole with legal costs for medical litigation amounting to £579.3 million in 2006–2007.[20] This does not take account of the £33.9 million paid out for non-clinical negligence claims. Another criticism is that the failed party normally pays the other side's costs which are not available if funded by legal aid. This may encourage health bodies to settle cases they might have won had they gone to court. As it is, many cases are settled through negotiation with each side being aware of the likelihood of success on the basis of judicial decisions. This reduces costs to the NHS and avoids setting precedents as well as adverse publicity. The involvement of the NHS Litigation Authority[21] means that claims are addressed at a corporate level in the most cost-

---

18   See Morris, *supra*, at n. 11 where she suggests that compensation claims for personal injury generally have actually stabilized rather than continue to increase as suggested by the media.

19   S. 7 of the Access to Justice Act 1999.

20   http://www.nhsla.com/home.htm but note the need for a balanced consideration of all the figures available which suggest that the so-called compensation culture may not have reality as its foundation and some meritorious claims may not be brought because individuals do not wish to drain NHS resources in Herring, J., *Medical Law and Ethics*, Oxford, Oxford University Press, 2006 at pp. 64–6.

21   The health professional's costs, if sued on an individual basis, will be borne by their employer if the sum is less than £10,000 or by the NHS Litigation Authority (established under s. 21 (3)) of the NHS and Community Care Act 1990 for sums over that amount through the Clinical Negligence Scheme for Trusts (CNST) to which NHS providing and commissioning organizations subscribe as provided by the NHS (Clinical Negligence Scheme) Regulations 1996/251 under s. 21 of the NHS and Community Care Act 1990. As a risk management measure, trusts can reduce the premiums they pay to the Scheme by achieving certain standards including quality of health care provision. A failure to achieve the most basic Level One standard would mean the trust would be required to develop an action plan to address any shortfalls. The work of the Healthcare Commission in ensuring compliance with certain quality standards and the National Patient Safety Agency that allows, *inter alia*, the anonymous reporting of concerns supports the containment of risks within the system. Where concerns are expressed about individual health professionals, these may be referred to the National Clinical Assessment Authority for advice short of formal reference to a professional body.

efficient way.[22] This can lead to a health professional feeling aggrieved when this happens because they may prefer to clear their name.[23]

Lord Woolf introduced important reforms to the pre-hearing stages.[24] This gave judges enhanced powers to manage cases to encourage greater transparency and use of alternative dispute resolution in the hope of early settlement, avoidance of delay and the misuse of expert evidence by having a single expert with responsibilities to the court. Lower claims may use so-called 'fast-track' procedures that should mean the matter is concluded in a relatively shorter time frame. These improvements notwithstanding, the oft-cited dissatisfaction with the current system from practitioners,[25] the public and academic commentators, remains. There are calls for a complete overhaul of the system.[26] The perception is that it is largely lawyers who benefit from the torts system. The delays and costs[27] to those involved causes unnecessary stress and perhaps harms the doctor-patient relationship. Alternative approaches will be discussed below.[28]

Other Forms of Liability

It is worth noting that although a claimant has the choice of suing individual health professionals for alleged negligence, they may also sue the employing organization under the doctrine of vicarious liability whereby employers are liable for the tortious acts of their employees who are acting in the course of their employment.[29] In the latter case, the employer can then pursue their employee for

---

22   The establishment of this body does seem to have improved efficiency: see *Making Amends*, *supra*, n. 10, particularly pp. 11–12.

23   Montgomery, J., *Healthcare Law*, Oxford, Oxford University Press, 2003 at p. 200.

24   Civil Procedure Rules 1998/3132 enacted under the Civil Procedure Act 1997. From 6 April 2008, there are much stronger requirements to consider the use of alternative dispute resolution to confine legal costs and a failure to do so may be considered by the court (http://www.justice.gov.uk/civil/procrules_fin/index.htm#updates).

25   British Medical Association (BMA) Mediation, clinical negligence claims and the medical profession, 2001.

26   See e.g. Brazier, *supra*, n. 16, at Chapter 10 where she examines the case for a no-fault compensation scheme rejected by the Royal Commission on Compensation for Personal Injury (the Pearson Commission) Cmnd 7054–1, 1978.

27   National Audit Office, *Handling Clinical Negligence Claims in England* 2001 which highlights how the average length of time taken to settle a case worth more than £20,000 was five years for the year 1999–2000 although since the adoption of fast-track procedures for smaller claims these have been dealt with more quickly. The Report also shows how costs can often exceed the compensation actually received by the victim.

28   *Infra*, nn. 214–27.

29   See *Godden v Kent and Medway SHA* [2004] EWHC 1629 for an example of how the doctrine may be expanding in that it was stated that a health authority could be held

any damages paid out. Not only is there a commitment from the NHS not to do this[30] but, in any event, the health professional's costs, if sued on an individual basis, will be borne by their employer or by the NHS Litigation Authority. GPs are responsible for their own costs as they are self-employed and must arrange cover through the medical insurance industry,[31] as should any NHS staff offering private care. Any treatment carried out in the private sector at the behest of the NHS *may* not remain the latter's responsibility in the event of negligence occurring, though this point is not settled.[32]

A claimant may also sue the providing organization directly for primary liability for, for example, not providing sufficient numbers of adequately trained staff.[33] It is thus essential that health professionals are appropriately trained to deal with children in the paediatric setting. An employer may also be primarily liable if appropriate systems are not in place to check that equipment is working properly and it causes damage, unless this is clearly the responsibility of an employee; staff must also be kept appraised of medical developments.[34] In the last case, there is an obligation on health professionals to keep reasonably abreast of advances in their area.[35] In a case of primary liability, it is likely that the *Bolam* standard will be inappropriate so that a hospital may claim that it acted in accordance with practices elsewhere[36] but it is open to a judge to deem that these are unreasonable standards.[37] Witting[38] has argued that courts should adjust the standard of care to take account of resource constraints in the NHS, as occurs in judicial review cases. This would reduce the standard of care in many cases, thus making it harder for claimants to establish a breach of duty. In his view, a more flexible standard of care would reflect the reality of the situations in which health professionals work. A shortage of resources inevitably leads to more accidents and mistakes that are the result of systemic rather than individual failings. Traditional negligence principles that require something to be done properly or not at all, is not appropriate. Most people would rather be offered some sort of intervention rather than none at all.

---

vicariously liable for the acts of a GP who had indecently assaulted and possibly negligently treated his patients.

30   NHS Executive: NHS indemnity arrangements for handling clinical negligence claims against NHS staff HSG (96)48 (1996).

31   Ibid.

32   *A (A Child) v Ministry of Defence* [2004] EWCA Civ 641 at para. 55.

33   *Godden v Kent and Medway SHA* [2004] EWHC 1629.

34   *Blyth v Bloomsbury HA* [1993] 4 Med LR 151.

35   *Gascoine v Ian Sheridan & Co* [1994] Med LR 437.

36   *Knight and others v Home Office and another* [1990] 3 All ER 237 at 243 where the court allowed for a lack of resources should be taken into account when determining the appropriate standard of care.

37   *Bull v Devon AHA* [1993] 4 Med LR 117, where the system for summoning assistance between two sites caused an unacceptable delay.

38   Witting, C., 'National Health Service Rationing: Implications for the Standard of Care in Negligence' (2001) 21(3) *Oxford Journal of Legal Studies* 443–71.

Clearly, some people will be left with physical injury for which they may have no redress but Witting believes this to be just: if Government rationing is responsible for mistakes, they, not health professionals, should take the responsibility at the ballot box.[39]

Both an individual health professional and an organization may be found to be negligent. Liability for the former will be determined on the basis of the extent to which the harm could have been avoided in the way in which the work was being carried out. If the system was a major contributing factor, and it often is,[40] the organization is likely to pay most of the damages.[41] Of course, the financial liability will be carried by the organization even if the individual was wholly at fault but, where they were not, it is of great significance to the health professional that fault is attributed appropriately. Where more than one health professional is responsible for harm to a patient, apportionment allows the whole sum to be recovered from just one so that the defendant will have to pursue the other for their share. This will be determined on the degree of responsibility attributed.[42] The NHS indemnity scheme means that NHS staff will not be individually liable so apportionment is only likely to be relevant for GPs or where treatment has been provided in conjunction with a private provider.

Theoretically, a range of additional actions is available to an aggrieved patient. For example, in extreme cases, criminal charges may be brought but these are relatively rare, hence the focus here on negligence.[43] Actions in contract may also be available to an aggrieved private patient but a contractual breach will be difficult to establish provided the health professional has used reasonable endeavours.[44] Professional disciplinary proceedings through employing organizations[45]and

---

39   *Garcia v St Mary's NHS Trust* [2006] EWHC 2314 (QB) seems to follow the modified standard of care approach though not to the extent proposed by Witting, ibid.

40   DoH, *An Organisation with a Memory*, 2000.

41   *Jones v Manchester Corporation* [1952] 2 All ER 125.

42   Civil Liability (Contribution) Act 1978.

43   In addition to a battery action discussed in Chapter 2, gross negligence manslaughter is the most likely criminal charge as in *R v Adomoko* [1995] 1 AC 171 where an anaesthetist failed to notice an endotracheal tube feeding oxygen to his patient had become disconnected for some four minutes. The charge may result in a conviction even where there is no proof that harm was intended or foreseen; some argue that a criminal negligence prosecution should only be brought where a doctor 'deliberately and culpably took a risk with their patients' and that gross incompetence should be dealt with in other ways such as disciplinary proceedings: see, for example, Mason, J.K. and Laurie, G.T., *Law and Medical Ethics* (7th ed.), Oxford, Oxford University Press, 2006 at pp. 344–77. Prosecutions appear to be on the increase with only four between 1970–90 but 17 between 1990–99 (Ferner, R.E., 'Medication errors that have led to manslaughter charges' (2000) 321(7270) *BMJ* 1212–16).

44   *Thake v Maurice* [1986]1 All ER 497.

45   DoH Health Service Litigation Authority (Functions) (England and Wales) Directions 2005: NHS Trusts will be responsible for disciplinary investigations and proceedings involving members of their staff.

bodies such as the General Medical Council (GMC)[46] for doctors may also be used as well as or instead of legal actions. They will not necessarily provide monetary redress for victims unless a Chief Executive of a Trust decides to make an *ex gratia* payment as a gesture of goodwill. The same is true of other NHS complaints procedures. The Healthcare Commission currently oversees internal complaints' procedures though individual trusts are expected to investigate and respond to the complainant.[47]

To gain a more complete picture of weaknesses in health care practice, we cannot merely rely on law reports as we have seen, for many matters are settled out of court. A number of bodies report on failures with the NHS and they highlight a number of disturbing features which undermines the public's confidence in those caring for them: for example, the Chief Medical Officer (CMO) has noted that 10 per cent of hospital admissions lead to an adverse event, [48] half of which were preventable if ordinary standards of care were used.[49] The National Audit Office has also reported on thousands of incidents or near misses and deaths in NHS hospitals.[50] Add to this fact that levels of reporting are probably an underestimate of

---

46   The GMC in particular has improved its practices following widespread public dissatisfaction with the regulation of the medical profession in the wake of scandals such as Shipman but their powers are undermined in the light of the CMO's proposals and those contained in the Health and Social Care Act 2008 following the White Paper, DoH, *Trust, Assurance and Safety: The Regulation of Health Professionals*, 2007. The hope is that the reform of professional regulation will enhance public and professional confidence in the system of professional regulation and strengthen clinical governance as part of the Government's response to the Shipman Inquiry: the investigating function of the GMC will be separated from the adjudication function; the civil standard of proof will apply to all health care regulators; a duty of collaboration will be established between health organizations to share information; a 'responsible officer' in each Trust will act as a central contact for doctors when concern is raised about their practice; the Care Quality Commission will be a new integrated regulator for health and adult social care bringing together existing health and social care regulators into one regulatory body, with tough new powers to ensure safe and high quality services.

47   It should be noted that some of these responsibilities are due to be withdrawn from the Commission in due course. A consultation process has taken place with the intention of establishing a more local approach with the Healthcare Commission monitoring the adequacy of complaints resolution, the standard of complaints handling and how the professions can learn from the complaints; appeals against the local resolution process will go directly to the Ombudsman: DoH, *Making Experiences Count: the proposed new arrangements for handling health and social care complaints – response to consultation*, 2008.

48   *Making Amends, supra*, n. 10 at p. 8.

49   Vincent, C., Neale, G. and Woloshynowych, M., 'Adverse events in British hospitals: preliminary retrospective record review', (2001) 322 *BMJ* 517–19.

50   National Audit Office, *A Safer Place for Patients: Learning to Improve Patient Safety*, 2005: 974,000 incidents/near misses with over 2,000 people dying from medical mistakes.

actual events[51] and other figures showing less than satisfactory patient experience[52] and we can see even more clearly that reported legal cases truly are only the tip of the iceberg of dissatisfaction with health care.

The Law of Negligence

For a successful action in negligence it must be established that the health professional concerned owed the claimant a duty of care, that this was breached, that there was a causal connection between the breach and the damage and that damage was not too remote.

The Duty of Care

There is an inherent imbalance of power in the doctor-patient relationship. Patients will feel vulnerable as a result of their condition and because they have to place their trust in someone who has greater levels of knowledge and expertise than they. This is even more the case where children are patients. It has been proposed[53] that a fiduciary relationship would best capture the true nature of the relationship and how it should be. This would adopt a description and recognition of the relationship that places emphasis on the need to protect but, at the same time, empower patients by upholding their rights. However, this has not been forthcoming from the English judiciary. Here, the preference has been for the one-dimensional notion of the duty of care owed by doctors towards their patients.

Once a medical intervention is commenced,[54] it is easily established that a duty of care is owed by the health professional to the patient.[55] Questions about duty of care become problematic if the health professional wishes to assist an individual in a public setting. Another instance of where questions may be raised is whether a duty is owed to those close to the patient in some circumstances.[56] Any

---

51   A study in a US teaching hospital has shown that most doctors agree that reporting errors is vital for patient safety but do not practice what they believe: Medical Protection Society, 'Doctors would like to report errors, but don't', (2008) 16(2) *Casebook* 5. This appears to be mirrored in the UK: 'Don't tell the boss about it', *The Times Public Agenda*, 27 May 2008.

52   See, for example, Healthcare Commission, *Patient Survey Report*, 2004: only 76 per cent of patients understood their GP's answer to their questions.

53   Kennedy, I.M., 'The Fiduciary Relationship – Doctors and Patients', in Birks, P. (ed.), *Wrongs and Remedies in the Twenty First Century*, Oxford, Clarendon Press, 1996.

54   This must be the case to protect health professionals from the legal consequences from incidents over which they have no control.

55   A duty of care is owed to patients merely attending an accident and emergency department (*Barnett v Chelsea and Kensington HMC* [1968] 1 All ER 1068).

56   *Goodwill v BPAS* [1996] 2 All ER 161 illustrates how the courts may be willing to imply an undertaking to assist claimants in that it noted that a duty may be owed to a

doubt as to whether a duty of care is owed will be determined by the modern test established in *Caparo Industries v Dickman*[57]which asks whether it was reasonably foreseeable that the defendant's actions would cause the victim harm, whether there is a sufficiently close relationship or proximity between the defendant and the patient and whether it is fair, just and reasonable, that is, any public policy reasons, not to impose a duty of care.[58] These sometimes overlapping elements will be applied on a case-by-case basis so that any development of a duty of care will be on an incremental basis.

The proximity of relationship perhaps gives rise to the most discussion often also involving the concept of foreseeabilty. There is no duty to act in English law so failing to assist at an accident will carry no legal liability,[59] unless a GP fails to help an identifiable patient of theirs.[60] It may infringe professional good practice[61] not least because such an action could bring the profession into disrepute. Most major moral theories recognize positive duties to act[62] however, and, anecdotally, few health professionals would not come to someone's aid provided they feel competent to do so. With this in mind, even health professionals who undertake no private practice would be advised to maintain insurance cover for such events because it is not provided under the NHS indemnity scheme. Should the health professional decide to intervene, thus assuming responsibility, a duty will be established.[63] It has been suggested that their liability would be limited to the extent they made any condition worse rather than for failing to offer a particular treatment.[64]

Some categories of harm make it difficult for claimants to establish a duty of care. In the medical setting, psychiatric injury presents particular problems because of the tendency to find insufficient proximity between the parties and because of the trend to take a restrictive approach to such claims on the basis

---

patient's current sexual partner when giving advice but not those in the future who will not be within the doctor's contemplation.

57   [1990] 2 AC 605.

58   *Palmer v Tees HA* [1999] Lloyd's Rep Med 359 illustrates that the courts will not impose a duty of care to the general public on the NHS organization where they have released a known, dangerous patient into the community who then harmed a member of the public; it would not be just and reasonable to expect such an organization to detain any outpatient who might pose a risk to others.

59   *F v West Berkshire HA* [1989] 2 All ER 545 at 567.

60   NHS (General Medical Services) Regulations 1992 (SI 1992/635).

61   GMC, *Good Medical Practice*, 2006 at para. 11 and Nursing and Midwifery Council, *Code of Professional Conduct*, 2002, para. 8.5.

62   See Pattinson, S.D., *Medical Law and Ethics*, London, Sweet and Maxwell, 2006 at pp. 67–8 on this point.

63   *Barrett v Ministry of Defence* [1995] 3 All ER 87.

64   *Powell v Boldaz* [1997] 39 BMLR 35 and *Capital and Counties v Hampshire CC* [1997] Q.B. 1035.

of legal policy considerations. Although the categories are not finally settled,[65] the law divides victims of psychological harm into 'primary' and 'secondary' victims who may be adults or children. The former include those who are directly involved as participants in the traumatic event.[66] Any victim of psychiatric harm who cannot be classified as primary will be a secondary victim, such as where a relative witnesses negligent treatment to a child or hears about a traumatic event affecting their child. Both types of victim will need to suffer from a recognized psychiatric disorder, so only grief and distress that gives rise to 'pathological grief disorder'[67] will form the basis of a claim.

Once found to be suffering from a recognized psychiatric condition, primary victims only then need to show that physical or psychiatric harm was reasonably foreseeable.[68] Secondary victims have additional proximity and foreseeability criteria to satisfy as held in *Alcock v Chief Constable of South Yorkshire Police*.[69] Claimants will have to show that they have experienced a single, shocking event that would have caused psychiatric injury to a person of reasonable fortitude; that they have sufficiently close ties of love and affection to the primary victim, such as parents and children; that they were present at the traumatic event or its immediate aftermath and that they directly perceived the traumatic event or its immediate aftermath with their own, unaided senses. It will not be possible to satisfy a single, shocking event where there is only a gradual realization that there may have been negligent treatment of a loved one.[70] However, the traumatic event need not be of short duration.[71] This approach can operate harshly and there have been calls for reform[72] though these are yet to materialize.

---

65   See, for example, *W v Essex CC* [2001] 2 AC 592 at 601.

66   I.e. those within the range of foreseeable physical injury (*White v Chief Constable of South Yorkshire Police* [1999] 2 AC 455), those with a contractual claim for work-related stress as identifiable individual employees suffering from foreseeable psychiatric harm (*Hartman v South Essex Mental Health* [2005] EWCA Civ 6) and those made to feel responsible for harm inflicted on another (*Salter v UB Frozen and Chilled Foods*) (2003) S.L.T. 1011.

67   As in *North Glamorgan NHS Trust v Walters* [2002] EWCA Civ 1792 where a mother recovered for a pathological grief reaction after a negligent failure to diagnose her 10-month-old son's liver condition followed by his death 36 hours later in her arms when life-support treatment was withdrawn.

68   *White v Chief Constable of South Yorkshire Police* [1999] 2 AC 455.

69   [1992] 1 AC 310.

70   *Sion v Hampstead HA* [2002] EWCA Civ 1792.

71   See *North Glamorgan NHS Trust v Walters supra* n. 67, para. 34, where the long 'drawn-out experience' of the negligent treatment of the child constituted the requirement for one shocking event.

72   Law Commission, *Report on Liability for Psychiatric Illness*, No. 249, London, HMSO, 1998.

Although the concept of the duty of care has been, and will no doubt continue to be, used as a mechanism for restricting liability (often for policy reasons),[73] this can no longer be assumed to be the case given the influence of the Strasbourg courts.[74] The law has developed in relation to local authorities in particular and this is especially evident where children are involved. In *D v East Berkshire Community Health NHS Trust et al.*,[75] the House of Lords decided that children are owed a duty of care by local authorities when they are investigating child abuse and making decisions as to whether or not to take a child into care. The decision in *Phelps v Hillingdon Borough Council*[76] established far-reaching consequences in that the local authority was found to be vicariously liable for the negligence of educational psychologists who failed to diagnose learning difficulties such as dyslexia.

The Breach of the Duty

Once the duty of care is established the next step is to ask whether that duty has been breached. To determine this, the court would usually ask whether the defendant has behaved as a reasonable person would in those particular circumstances.[77] The

---

73   There has been a judicial reluctance to find that public bodies owe a duty of care not least because of the resources implications of diverting public funds into private law actions, the fact that claims often involve pure economic loss and omissions to act which present problems for tort law and whether public law is a more appropriate mechanism given the existence of statutory powers: see e.g. the discussion in Steele, J., *Tort Law: Text, Cases and Materials*, Oxford, Oxford University Press, 2007 at pp. 399–429.

74   The *Osman v UK* (2000) 29 EHRR 245 case stated that the denial of a duty of care breached the Article 6 right to have determinations of one's civil rights and obligations made by an independent tribunal. Although its flawed reasoning in the case was recognized in *Z v UK* (2002) 34 E.H.R.R. 97 at 100–101 in particular, domestic courts must now be more circumspect when determining whether a duty of care is owed, especially in relation to public bodies.

75   [2005] 2 AC 373. The blanket policy immunity for local authorities had also been eroded in *W v Essex County Council* [2001] 2 AC 592 where a known child abuser was fostered with a family without their awareness of his history. The House of Lords decided that the parents had at least had an arguable claim for their psychiatric harm suffered as a result of feeling responsible for their children's sexual abuse. A similar view was adopted in *S v Gloucestershire County Council* [2001] 2 WLR 909. In *L and P v Reading BC and Chief Constable of Thames Valley Police* [2001] EWCA Civ 346, the Court of Appeal refused to strike out negligence claims brought by a father and his child against the local and police authorities where joint interviews were improperly conducted: see Jones, M., 'Child Abuse: when the professionals get it wrong', (2006) 14(2) *Medical Law Review* 264–76 for useful comment on some of these developments.

76   [2001] 2 AC 619.

77   *Blyth v Birmingham Waterworks Co.* (1856) 11 Ex 781. In the medical context the relevant circumstances include a consideration of the extent to which a patient must be

standard for any profession requiring particular levels of expertise, knowledge or experience[78] is the *Bolam*[79] test:

> A doctor is not guilty of negligence if he has acted in accordance with a practice accepted as proper by a responsible body of medical men skilled in that particular art.[80]

Equally:

> ... a doctor is not negligent, if he is acting in accordance with such a practice, merely because there is a body of opinion that takes a contrary view.[81]

The House of Lords has decided that this test applies to diagnosis,[82] disclosure of information,[83] as well as treatment.[84] It is worth noting that the standard has been adopted as relevant when determining the best interests of patients unable to make decisions[85] although this is now seen as but the first stage in making such an assessment.[86] The worry about this approach is that it is doctors who are setting standards, not the law. There is a perception doctors will be reluctant to criticize the practice of colleagues making it harder for patients to prove negligence. There has also been a worry that sub-standard practices would go unchecked by the law because of the support from professional bodies. The disillusionment with medical practice following such scandals as Shipman has led the GMC to emphasize the obligation on doctors to report concerns about their colleagues.[87]

As Pattinson points out,[88] McNair J.'s use of words such as 'responsible' suggests a normative standard of care prescribing what doctors ought to do. However, it is possible to read a descriptive standard of care into his direction elsewhere so that

---

protected from harming themselves (see the discussion in *Kirkham v Chief Constable of Greater Manchester* [1990] 2 Q.B. 283).

78   *Gold v Haringey HA* [1988] QB 481 at 489 per Lloyd LJ. Practitioners of alternative medicine will be judged by the standard of the particular 'art' rather than by those of orthodox medicine: *Shakoor v Situ* [2001] 1 WLR 410. This approach is essentially adopted by Article 4 of the European Convention on Human Rights and Biomedicine.

79   *Bolam v Friern HMC* [1957] 2 All ER 118.

80   Ibid., at 122 per McNair J.

81   *Bolam v Friern HMC* [1957] 2 All ER 118 at 122 per McNair J.

82   *Maynard v West Midlands RH* [1985] 1 All ER 635.

83   *Sidaway v Bethlem Royal Hospital* [1985] AC 871.

84   *Whitehouse v Jordan* [1981] 1 WLR 246.

85   See, for example *Re F (mental patient: sterilization)* [1990] 2 AC 1 at 73 where a decision had to be made whether the sterilization of a woman with learning disabilities was appropriate.

86   *Simms v Simms* [2002] 2 WLR 1465.

87   GMC, *Good Medical Practice*, 2006, paras. 43–5.

88   Pattinson, *supra*, n. 62 at p. 73.

actual professional practices determine what is negligent.[89] In reality, the *Bolam* test will be satisfied on a normative basis if the doctor complies with practices accepted by the profession. In applying the *Bolam* test, the actions of a doctor will be judged in light of the available knowledge at the time.[90] Accessibility of the information will be a consideration and given the increasing tendency for patients to explore the Internet,[91] the wise doctor will ensure that they meet the legal requirement to keep reasonably up-to-date.[92] Nevertheless, this test is problematic for claimants because the descriptive reading is unduly deferential to the profession in that they set the standards rather than the law.[93] This is underlined by cases where very low numbers of doctors supporting a particular practice have been deemed to constitute a 'body' of opinion[94] so that it has not been possible to establish a breach. The claimant can only be confident of having a strong case if they can find significant numbers to support their position. A pragmatic difficulty lies in the fact that it can be difficult to find other doctors willing to give evidence that the course of action was unacceptable to the profession as a whole although this is less of a challenge now with the prevalence of 'professional expert witnesses'.[95] The low rate of success in legally aided cases may reflect poor selection of cases but could also be the result of the *Bolam* test in operation.[96] These criticisms notwithstanding, judges are not medical experts who can make a judgment on appropriate medical practice and to soften the approach could lead to a significant increase in litigation. Without the protection of *Bolam*, doctors may become reluctant to try innovative ways of

---

89   The latter interpretation has predominated in subsequent cases: see, for example, *Maynard v West Midlands HA* [1985] 1 All ER 635 at 639 where Lord Scarman appears to equate 'responsible' body of opinion with one that is 'distinguished', a position he makes particularly clear in *Sidaway* at 881, *supra*, n. 83, when he summarized the *Bolam* test stating that 'the standard of care is a matter of medical judgment'.

90   *Roe v Minister of Health* [1954] 2 All ER 131.

91   Stevenson, F.A., Kerr, C., Murray, E. and Nazareth, I., 'Information from the Internet and the doctor-patient relationship: the patient perspective – a qualitative study', (2007) 8 *BMC Family Practice* 47; Helft, P.R., Hlubocky, F. and Daugherty, C.K., 'American Oncologists' Views of Internet Use by Cancer Patients: A Mail Survey of American Society of Clinical Oncology Members', (2003) 21(5) *Journal of Clinical Oncology* 942–7.

92   *Crawford v Board of Governors of Charing Cross Hospital* [(1953) *The Times*, 8 December, CA.; *H v Royal Alexandra Hospital for Sick Children* [1990] 1 *Med Law Rev* 297. See also, GMC *supra*, n. 87 at paras. 12–13 and Royal College of Paediatrics and Child Health (RCPCH), *Good Medical Practice in Paediatrics and Child Health: Duties and Responsibilities of Paediatricians*, 2002, paras. 10–12.

93   Brazier, M. and Miola, J., 'Bye-Bye Bolam: A Medical Litigation Revolution?', (2000) 8(1) *Medical Law Review* 85–114.

94   See, for example, *De Freitas v O'Brien* [1993] 4 *Med LR* 281 where the Court of Appeal held that it was not negligent to perform a spinal operation that was supported by only 11 doctors out of a thousand plus but these were particularly skilled surgeons and the courts will not want to stifle innovative practice.

95   Brazier, *supra*, n. 16, at p. 188.

96   Ibid., at p. 172.

delivering health care. Whether the use of innovative procedures can amount to negligence would be determined by assessing the risks and benefits in the light of available knowledge for the individual patient. In *Simms v Simms*,[97] the court supported the use of a highly experimental treatment on victims of Creutzveld-Jakob disease (CJD) because there were no alternatives and death was otherwise inevitable.

The decision in *Bolitho (Deceased) v City and Hackney HA*[98] confirms that the normative reading of *Bolam* is the accurate one. The medical opinion relied upon must have a 'logical basis'[99] having balanced risks and benefits, although on the facts of the case (discussed below in relation to causation) the court found in the defendant doctor's favour. Thus, the court reserved the right to prefer an alternative opinion. There is a view that all *Bolitho* has done is to restore *Bolam* to its proper limits the test having been too loosely applied by the courts and in too many situations.[100] The case was not the first to apply *Bolam* correctly but, as a House of Lords decision, will be the most influential and the development of new guidelines on clinical practice (discussed below) will assist the courts in finding intelligible sources of information when deciding whether standards have been breached.[101]

In practice, *Bolitho* has had limited impact,[102] as far as we can tell,[103] because judges are not medical experts[104] so that the opinion will have to be rather extreme before it is rejected.[105] Where *Bolitho* has been noted, it would seem that judges have been prepared to examine medical opinion more rigorously. For example, in *Marriott v West Midlands Health Authority*[106] the Court of Appeal supported the trial judge's finding that a failure to refer for further tests a patient who had suffered a fall was irresponsible even though the risk of a blood clot on the brain

---

97   [2002] 2 WLR 1465. Innovation is being encouraged by the Government in order to improve patient care and increase efficiency: DoH, *The National Plan for the New NHS*, 2000 *passim*.

98   [1998] AC 232. Note that the Australian courts exhibited a greater willingness to challenge the traditional usage of *Bolam* in *Rogers v Whittaker* (1992) 109 ALR 625 in which it was said that professional opinion would not necessarily be the sole determinant of an acceptable standard of care (at 631).

99   Ibid., at 242 *per* Lord Browne-Wilkinson.

100   Brazier and Miola, *supra*, n. 93.

101   Brazier and Miola, *supra*, n. 93.

102   McLean, A., 'Beyond *Bolam* and *Bolitho*', (2001) 5 *Medical Law International* 205–30.

103   Relying on law reports alone will not give the full picture because the NHSLA will want to settle cases likely to develop the law further and the NHS organizations concerned do not want adverse publicity to widen claims.

104   As acknowledged in *Maynard v West Midlands RHA* [1985] 1 All ER 635.

105   Lord Browne-Wilkinson noted in *Bolitho* itself that it will be a rare occurrence to make a finding that a professional opinion will not withstand logical analysis (at 10).

106   [1999] Lloyd's Med Rep 23.

was small. The Court took the view that notwithstanding the low level of risk, the consequences for the patient were very significant if it materialized. The language used in this case partly addresses the concern that logic is not a useful criterion in the case of clinical judgment[107] in that the conduct was discussed in terms of reasonableness.[108] The willingness to find a body of medical opinion unacceptable in this way is more likely where the issue is less technical.[109] That being said, if medical opinion is rejected it will require justification.[110] The *Bolitho* case does, however, have symbolic significance in signalling a move away from undue deference to medical opinion particularly when it is taken in conjunction with those cases that see the *Bolam* test as but the first step in determining the best interests of incapacitated patients.[111] Overall, a doctor will only have to demonstrate that his actions were above minimal standards so that a misdiagnosis[112] or a failure to highlight alternative treatment[113] will not *necessarily* be negligent. On the former point, provided a proper history is taken from the patient, appropriate investigations are undertaken and the symptoms are not such that a competent doctor should have recognized the underlying condition, liability is not likely to be established.

The standard of care expected from a professional will be determined by reference to the speciality or profession concerned, the circumstances in which the incident in question occurs and the level of information about a patient available. A patient with unusual symptoms should be referred to a relevant specialist by a general practitioner or general paediatrician in district general hospitals.[114] A general practitioner will not be expected to reach the level of expertise of a specialist consultant[115] but, equally, should not attempt to carry out an intervention that should be undertaken by a specialist.[116] This point has a particular resonance in relation to paediatrics where it is crucial that only suitably trained health professionals should undertake work with children, especially when this involves specialist interventions. It has become trite to state that children are not 'little adults'. The GMC[117] notes this and points out that good clinical care for children relies on specially trained clinical staff with suitable experience

---

107   Mason and Laurie, *supra*, n. 43, at pp. 315–16.

108   *Penney v East Kent Health Authority* (2000) 55 BMLR 63 does retain the language of illogicality.

109   *French v Thames Valley Strategic Health Authority* [2005] EWHC 459, para. 112.

110   *Elaine Ruth Glicksman v Redbridge NHS Trust* [2001] EWCA Civ 1097.

111   *Re S (adult patient: sterilization)* [2001] Fam 15; *Simms v Simms* [2002] 2 WLR 1465.

112   *Whitehouse v Jordan* [1981] 1 WLR 246, where it was held that errors in judgment may or may not be negligent and should be determined on the basis of the *Bolam* test.

113   *Thompson v Blake-James* [1998] *Lloyd's Rep Med* 187.

114   *Judge v Huntingdon HA* [1995] 6 Med LR 223.

115   *Stockdale v Nicholls* [1993] 4 Med LR 190.

116   *Defreitas v O'Brien* [1993] 4 Med LR 281.

117   GMC, O–18 years: guidance for doctors, 2007, at para. 73.

together with equipment, facilities and an environment appropriate to children's needs. Separate audits should be carried out with respect to children and young people's health care.[118] Employers have obligations to ensure the suitability of their staff to provide appropriate health care to children and young people.[119] It is also worth a reminder that, *inter alia*, children suffer from conditions peculiar to childhood, are anatomically different in some ways, may respond differently to drugs (including anaesthetics), may require different surgical techniques and need health professionals with appropriate communication skills. Should there be an allegation of negligence be made with respect to a child, a legal practitioner is sure to question whether the intervention was carried out by a suitably skilled health professional.

More generally, it must not be assumed that merely because a patient has been referred to a hospital that they will be given treatment by a health professional with an appropriate level of expertise. In the district general hospital setting in particular, but also in the tertiary specialist centres, doctors need to ensure they see and treat sufficient numbers of certain categories of patient, whether adults or children, to demonstrate required levels of expertise.[120] Where they do not have the requisite skills, they should refer further to someone who does. To do otherwise, and damage is suffered by their patient, any negligence action will be strengthened significantly, notwithstanding the guidance status of the standards concerned. Unfortunately, Trusts, which have some primary liability in this context to ensure safe systems of operation,[121] may not always provide adequate monitoring, nor will other doctors necessarily raise their concerns with the employers or the GMC even though there is a clear requirement to do so.[122]

Although a professional acting in a particular capacity will be expected to reach the standard of that post, an inexperienced professional may escape liability if the advice of a more experienced colleague had been followed.[123] It is likely that should it become apparent that the junior member of staff had not understood instructions they will not be able to avail themselves of this defence. Nor will this be possible in the light of *Bolitho*, if they had followed instructions that were obviously unusual or wrong.[124] The courts will not expect the same standard of

---

118   As required by the DoH, National Service Framework for Children, 2003, Royal College of Surgeon's of England, Children's Surgery – a first class service, 2000 and Department for Education and Skills, Common Core Skills for the Children's Workforce, 2005.

119   GMC, *supra*, n. 117 at para. 74.

120   See, for example, DoH, *A Policy Framework for Commissioning Cancer Services: A Report by the Expert Advisory Group on Cancer to the Chief Medical Officers of England and Wales* (Calman Hine Report), 1995.

121   This is an area that would be subject to Healthcare Commission scrutiny.

122   GMC, *supra*, n. 87, paras. 43–5.

123   *Wilsher v Essex AHA* [1988] AC 1074.

124   As in the earlier case of *Dwyer v Roderick* (1983) 127 SJ 806 where a pharmacist failed to confirm a prescription that was patently wrong.

care if the health professional is faced with an emergency[125] unless they are trained specifically to deal with emergencies.[126] Patients are expected to disclose relevant symptoms so that a doctor can proceed appropriately although they will need to be alert to the possibility that there will be circumstances where the patient is temporarily or permanently disabled and may be unable to do this.[127] Children may lack the skills to describe symptoms or be embarrassed to do so. This does not necessarily indicate incompetence but demonstrates the importance of having good communication skills and expertise in dealing with children.

Questions are often raised by health professionals as to the status of guidelines and protocols in determining standards of care and the following section attempts to establish what this might be.

The Role of Guidelines in Establishing a Breach of Duty

The guidelines such as those issued by the National Institute for Health and Clinical Excellence (NICE)[128] on best practice are not always acted upon because commissioners of health services fail to provide funding for them.[129] Indeed, there are specific concerns that guidelines may be used specifically as a rationing mechanism and NICE is charged with making cost-effective recommendations.[130] A lack of resources is unlikely to form the basis of a negligence action against a health professional because resource allocation decisions are generally challenged through public law mechanisms.[131] On the role of guidelines and their legal status more generally, there have long been arguments that they should inform, and, indeed, should not influence, the legal standard of care in clinical negligence litigation provided they have been developed rigorously.[132] As it is, they have been promoted by the DoH as a means of ensuring equitable access to high quality care

---

125   *Wilsher v Essex AHA* [1987] QB 730 at 749 per Mustill L.J. and *Watt v Hertfordshire CC* [1954] 2 All ER 368.

126   *Cattley v St John's Ambulance Brigade* (1998) (Lexis).

127   *Wood v Thurston, The Times*, 25 May 1951.

128   Established by S. I. 1999 No. 220 under s. 11 of the National Health Services Act 1977 and is accountable directly to the Secretary of State for Health.

129   For example, some Primary Care Trusts have not provided sufficient funds to ensure the *National Service Framework for Children, Young People and Maternity Services*, DoH, 2004 are fully implemented. See, also, Sheldon, T.A., Cullen, N., Dawson, D., Lanksher, A., Lowson, K. and Watt, I., 'What is the Evidence that NICE Guidance has been Implemented? Results from a National Evaluation Using Time Series Analysis, Audit of Patients' Notes and Interviews', (2004) 329 *British Medical Journal* 999 which notes other factors which may hinder the implementation of NICE guidance.

130   Syrett, K., 'Nice Work? Rationing, Review and the 'Legitimacy Problem' in the New NHS', (2002) 10 *Medical Law Review* 1–27.

131   See Herring, *supra*, n. 20, at pp. 513–42.

132   For a survey of these views see Tingle, J. and Foster, C., (eds), *Guidelines: Law, Policy and Practice*, London, Cavendish, 2002.

through NICE[133] and this is monitored by the Healthcare Commission. Professional bodies also require that established guidelines form the benchmark of acceptable practice.[134] Health professionals in the paediatric setting need to be aware of any available child-specific guidelines for particular conditions.

The evidence is that they are increasingly being used in such litigation and this looks set to continue not least because of the demands of the Civil Procedure Rules noted above and the clinical governance agenda within the NHS that aims to make its organizations accountable for safeguarding high standards of clinical care.[135] Guidelines are a key part of providing a benchmark against which clinical practice may be audited, and the Clinical Negligence Scheme for Trusts (CNST)[136] promotes their use as a means of reducing medical error through risk management strategies and the establishment of appropriate standards. Responsibility for this is at the highest level within organizations. More importantly, guidelines are perceived as influencing the court in a significant number of cases.[137] However, they were not seen as instrumental in determining liability perhaps because of differences in clinical and legal thinking.

The courts do need to be alert to the differing nature of the guidelines. Standard of care guidelines will be appropriate to consider. 'Appropriateness' guidelines may have been imposed to reduce variation in practice (all of which may be clinically acceptable) and possibly to reduce cost.[138] Courts may prefer the expert witness appearing in person rather than august medical opinion in learned journals.[139] This may particularly be the case if it is unclear the guidance has actually been adopted by clinical practitioners.[140] A robust conceptual model for the use of guidelines would help to address any reticence about the validity of their use. Samanta *et al.*[141] have suggested that a court should ask four questions about the use (or non-use) of guidelines: is the decision *Bolam* defensible? If it is, is it *Bolitho* justifiable? Is it *Daubert* valid (based on the US case,[142] which established that the admissibility of guidelines should be determined by reference to reliability and relevance)? Finally, how does the decision apply to the particular circumstances of the matter in question? The latter would import a need to consider whether the specific recommendations have been followed and whether

---

133 See e.g. *Making Amends*, *supra*, n. 10.

134 See e.g. GMC, *supra*, n. 87, paras. 12–13.

135 Samanta, A., Mello, M.M., Foster, C., Tingle, J. and Samanta, J., 'The Role of Clinical Guidelines in Medical Negligence Litigation: A Shift from the *Bolam* Standard?', (2006) 14 *Medical Law Review* 321–66.

136 *Supra*, n. 21.

137 Ibid., at p. 331.

138 Ibid., at p. 351.

139 See *Loveday v Renton* (1990) 1 *Medical Law Review* 117.

140 Sheldon et al., *supra*, n. 129.

141 *Supra* n. 135. Hurwitz, B., 'How Does Evidence Based Guidance Influence Determinations of Medical Negligence?', (2004) 329 *British Medical Journal* 1024.

142 *Daubert v Merrill Dow Pharmaceuticals Inc.* 509 US 579 (1993).

the approach was such that it is what would be expected from a reasonable doctor. At such a point the guidelines could inform the standard of care. This is seen as a halfway house between the traditional *Bolam* test and one where guidelines are the sole determinants of the standard of care to avoid the risk of using 'scientific evidence by rote'. Such an approach would bring evidence-based medicine into judicial decision-making but still allow the use of expert testimony in court thus maintaining clinical autonomy.[143]

Should a health professional depart from established protocols or policies adopted by their employing organization, then this may provide strong support for a negligence action given these will be based on recognized good practice. Any such departure in the individual case may be justifiable on clinical grounds[144] but this must be clearly recorded, thoroughly discussed with the patient where possible and colleagues. This will provide useful evidence that a body of responsible opinion would support the deviation. Conversely, following protocols and policies in all cases may not always be appropriate particularly if this will obviously harm a patient.[145] Guidance, whatever its source, does not have direct legal force but the courts will often refer to those published by professional bodies such as the GMC,[146] British Medical Association[147] or the Royal College of Paediatrics and Child Health (RCPCH)[148] to establish evidence of accepted standards of practice. Other organizations' guidelines are likely to be influential in specific circumstances. For example, the National Society for the Prevention of Cruelty to Children (NSPCC) guidance[149] on detecting thermal injuries that may be the result of abuse and/or neglect could be very influential if a health professional is accused of negligence on the basis that very obvious signs were ignored. Guidelines have been used in favour of both claimants[150] and defendants.[151]

The maxim *res ipsa loquitur* (the thing speaks for itself) will assist the patient in certain circumstances. The onus is on the claimant to prove, on the balance of probability, that the health professional concerned fell below the standard of a reasonably competent person exercising those skills. The doctrine helps patients in those cases where it is so obvious from the facts that the health professional

---

143   *Supra* n. 135 at pp.359–65.

144   Hurwitz, *supra*, n. 141.

145   *Barnett v Chelsea and Kensington HMC* [1968] 1 All ER 1068.

146   *Burke v General Medical Council (defendant) and Disability Rights Commission (interested party) and the Official Solicitor (intervenor)* [2005] EWCA 103.

147   In *Airedale NHS Trust v Bland* [1993] AC 789 at 871: Lord Goff took the view that the BMA's guidance on withdrawing treatment constituted a responsible body of medical opinion.

148   *Re C (a minor) (medical treatment)* [1998] 1 FLR 384, although this was a first instance decision.

149   NSPCC, *CORE-INFO: Thermal injuries on children*, 2008.

150   *DF (by her litigation friend and mother CF) v St George's Healthcare NHS Trust* [2005] EWHC 1327.

151   *Early v Newham Health Authority* (1994) 5 *Medical Law Review* 214.

will have to find an alternative explanation. Where the maxim applies, the court will be prepared to infer that the defendant was negligent without hearing detailed evidence from the claimant as to what the defendant did or did not do. To apply, the thing causing the damage must have been under the exclusive control of the defendant,[152] the accident must be of the sort that does not happen in the absence of negligence,[153] and there must be no explanation for the accident.[154] The classic illustration of this are the cases of *Cassidy v Ministry of Health*[155] where a patient had an operation to ease two stiff fingers but ended up with four stiff fingers, and *Mahon v Osborne*[156] where the plaintiff had an abdominal operation and later died with a swab left in his body. The doctrine will not assist where there may be a plausible, non-negligent cause.[157] In medical cases, it may be difficult to show who was actually negligent but the employing body will be vicariously liable for whoever was responsible. It may be relatively easy to establish the doctrine in obvious cases such as where the wrong limb is amputated, but less so in others. In more complex situations, a judge summing up would decide a case on the basis of inferences he was entitled to draw from all the evidence including expert opinion.[158] There seems to be a judicial preference for the term 'a *prima facie* case',[159] which indicates the courts' wish to restrict the maxim's use. The courts are reluctant to allow this to be argued early in cases where facts are in dispute.

In the event a breach of duty on the part of the defendant is established, there remains a not inconsiderable hurdle for claimants to overcome before they prove negligence: they must show that the breach factually and legally caused the damage they have suffered.

Causation

The starting point when addressing whether the causal link between the breach and the damage can be made out is the so-called 'but for' test. This asks whether 'but for' the defendant's negligence the claimant would have suffered the damage on the balance of probabilities. The classic illustration of this may be found in *Barnett v Chelsea and Kensington HMC*[160] where a doctor refused to examine a patient complaining of stomach pains telling him to see his own doctor in the morning if he still felt unwell. Five hours later he died of arsenic poisoning. Here, there

---

152 *Easson v London & North Eastern Railway* [1944] 1 KB 421.
153 *Mahon v Osborne* [1939] 2 KB 14.
154 *Barkway v South Wales Transport Co Ltd* [1950] 1 All ER 392.
155 [1954] 2 KB 343.
156 *Mahon v Osborne* [1939] 2 KB 14.
157 *Howard v Wessex RHA* [1994] 5 Med LR 57, QBD.
158 *Ratcliffe v Plymouth and Torbay HA* [1998] 4 Med LR 162.
159 Ibid., at 190.
160 [1968] 1 All ER 1068.

was a clear breach of duty but the patient would have died before diagnosis and treatment could have been carried out. Many situations are not this straightforward. For example, where alleged negligence means a condition is undiagnosed and therefore not treated properly, the claimant will have to show that had the doctor acted in a non-negligent manner the disease would have been diagnosed and that treatment, which is more likely than not to have made a difference to the outcome, was available.

The 'but for' test will not produce a sensible result when applied to situations where there is more than one possible cause of the harm of which one may be the professional's action. The courts have eased the difficulties for claimants seeking to establish a causal link between their damage and the defendant's behaviour where this was, in some way, reprehensible but not necessarily the cause of the harm. For example in *McGhee*,[161] the claimant developed dermatitis due to exposure to brick dust as a result of a lack of washing facilities that should have been provided by the employer. However, he would have been exposed to some dust that was outwith the employer's control. Thus, it was difficult to establish that the 'guilty' dust had caused the dermatitis. The court decided that he merely had to show the defendant had materially increased the risk of the damage occurring.

However, *Wilsher v Essex AHA*[162] seemed to signal a retreat from this claimant-friendly approach. In this case, a premature baby developed retrolental fibroplasias leading to significantly impaired sight. There were five possible causes of the baby's damage, all entirely separate and discrete, each of which was capable of producing the condition on its own. One such cause was that a junior doctor had measured the levels of oxygen in a vein instead of an artery so that the baby received excess oxygen. It could not be shown on a balance of probabilities that this negligent action had caused, or materially contributed to,[163] the damage so the action failed. The decision was distinguished from *McGhee* on the basis that there was insufficient evidence to allow an inference of a causal link between fault and damage, because an increase in risk is not enough.[164] This explanation was rejected in *Fairchild v Glenhaven Funeral Services.*[165]

In Fairchild workers had been negligently exposed to asbestos dust and, as a result, developed mesothelioma. The claimants could prove, on the balance of probabilities, that their condition was caused by the negligent exposure during the course of their employment but could not identify which defendant employer was responsible. One fibre was sufficient to cause the disease and further exposure did not worsen the condition. So, strictly, this was a discrete cause and *Wilsher* should have been followed. However, the House of Lords followed the earlier

---

161   *McGhee v National Coal Board* [1973] 1 WLR.

162   [1988] AC 1074.

163   As developed in *Bonnington Castings v Wardlaw* [1956] A. C. 613.

164   *Wilsher v Essex AHA* [1988] AC 1074 at 1090, where Lord Bridge stated that *McGhee* had taken a 'robust and pragmatic approach to the undisputed primary facts'.

165   [2002] Lloyd's Rep Med 361.

McGhee approach whilst specifically approving the *Wilsher* decision saying that all the employers were liable as they had materially increased the risk of harm to the employees. Here, there were no natural causes and the employers were clearly negligent. The majority dealt with the potential conflict between the two approaches on the basis that *McGhee* and *Fairchild* involved one causal agent, brick dust and asbestos respectively, whereas there were a number of competing causal agents in *Wilsher*. The suspicion has been that the courts are likely to be more restrictive in establishing liability in medical law cases as they are mindful of the impact on the NHS whereas other types of employers are more directly covered by insurance.[166] Lord Hoffman's remarks in *Fairchild*[167] confirm this suspicion because he explicitly referred to the potential huge increase in liability for the NHS if the case had been decided differently. For this reason, it is unlikely such a relaxed approach will be adopted in relation to medical law cases.[168]

The complexity involved in establishing causation is clearly demonstrated by *Bolitho (Deceased) v City and Hackney HA*.[169] In this case a registrar was called to attend a young boy of two who was suffering breathing difficulties, but she failed to do so. The registrar was unquestionably in breach for failing to attend but the court then looked at what would have happened had she attended. It was contended that had she done so and performed an early intubation, this would have prevented the serious harm that the claimant suffered. The counter-argument proposed was that, regardless of the failure to attend, the causal link could not be established because the registrar may not have intubated and would have had good reasons for her decision. The House of Lords set a two-stage test. First, it should be asked what the registrar would have done had she attended. As a factually-based question, the court would have to make some sort of a prediction. If she would have intubated, then negligence would be made out. If she would not have intubated, whether she should have done would be decided by reference to the *Bolam* standard, that is, is this a course of action that would be supported by a body of responsible medical opinion? The registrar escaped liability because she would not have intubated had she attended and there was evidence that to do this to such a young child carried serious risks. This line of reasoning involves the court in a degree of 'second guessing' with hindsight what the actions of the registrar might have been, which

---

166   Lord Woolf, 'Are the Courts Excessively Deferential to the Medical Profession?', (2001) 9 *Medical Law Review* 1.

167   [2002] Lloyd's Rep Med 361, at para. 69.

168   In *Fairchild* there was only one employer to sue as the other had gone out of business. It was possible that the remaining employer had caused no damage but nevertheless had to pay all of the awarded damages. The subsequent case of *Barker v Corus UK Ltd* [2006] 3 All ER 785 upheld the *Fairchild* principle but the apportionment of damages was held to be in proportion to the likelihood of the damage being caused. The ensuing discomfort with this decision was satisfied with the enactment of the Compensation Act 2006 which re-established the principle of joint and several liability in these cases.

169   [1998] AC 232.

is hardly ideal. Certainly it can be seen as a conflation of the tests for breach and causation and Bolitho remains a contentious decision.

The need to establish that, on the balance of probabilities, the negligent conduct caused or materially contributed to the injury has been confirmed by cases raising the possibility of a claim for depriving the claimant of a chance of treatment (the so-called 'loss of a chance' cases). Where there is a failure to diagnose a condition so that potentially curative treatment is not offered, a number of cases highlight the difficulties the claimant is likely to face. In *Hotson v E Berkshire*[170] a 13-year-old boy fell out of a tree, injured his hip and was taken to hospital where he received a negligent diagnosis. However, even with a proper diagnosis, there was a 75 per cent chance that the hip impairment would have materialized in any event. He maintained that a proper diagnosis would have resulted in treatment that carried a 25 per cent chance of providing a recovery. As it was, he suffered impairment of his hip function with a strong likelihood of osteoarthritis setting in at a later date. The court of first instance awarded the boy 25 per cent of the damages he would have received had the health authority been fully responsible for his condition. The House of Lords disapproved of this approach stating that damages could only be awarded if it could be shown that after proper diagnosis available treatment would have offered a 50 per cent chance of success. At 25 per cent, it had not been shown, on a balance of probabilities, that had the health authority not been negligent, he would not have suffered his eventual damage. Given these odds, he might have still suffered to the same extent even with the correct treatment.[171] Lords Mackay and Bridge left the idea open that there might be recovery for a loss of less than 50 per cent chance of a full recovery in some cases without indicating which type of case could give rise to such liability.

The loss of a chance issue was revisited in *Gregg v Scott*[172] where Dr Scott negligently diagnosed a lump in Mr Gregg's armpit as benign. A year later he was diagnosed with cancer of the lymph nodes and had to undergo chemotherapy but was left with a poor prognosis. Gregg argued that an earlier accurate diagnosis would have given him a much-improved chance of recovery. The trial judge thought Gregg's chances of surviving for more than ten years were now reduced from 42 per cent to 25 per cent on the evidence but that it was more likely than not that there would not be a complete cure. On this basis it could not be shown that the negligence caused the loss. Upon reaching the House of Lords the appeal was dismissed on a majority of three to two. The decision took eight months to materialize and was very controversial.[173] Adopting a very similar line of reasoning as in the *Hotson* case, the majority thought that it had not been demonstrated on a

---

170   [1987] AC 750.

171   For criticism of this approach see Stapleton, J., 'The gist of negligence: Part 2 the relationship between "damage" and causation', (1988) *Law Quarterly Review* 389.

172   [2005] 2 AC 176.

173   Burrows, A., 'Uncertainty about uncertainty: damages for loss of a chance' (2008) 1 *Journal of Personal Injury Law* 31–43.

balance of probabilities that the delay in treatment had caused a loss. Had Gregg been diagnosed properly it was likely he would suffer the same loss and the loss of a chance of a more favourable outcome could not form the basis of a tortious action. Lord Hoffmann's remarks indicate that legislation would be required for such a change in the law and, again, show a clear concern for the impact on the NHS and their insurers.[174] Hale L.J.'s remarks, in particular, established a bright line, no recovery rule in suggesting that there was no place for loss of a chance claims in clinical negligence cases.[175] By contrast, the minority considered that the claimant should be able to sue for the significant reduction in the possibility of survival on a principled basis that was clearly due to the negligence of the defendant.[176]

The following discussion indicates where the courts have reached a rather surprising conclusion given the context of negligence actions but a welcome one given the fundamental importance of informed consent.

An Ethical Approach?

Despite a largely defendant-oriented approach to causation in negligent cases, the courts have shown a willingness to support claimants in the important case of *Chester v Afshar*[177] where the judges were keen to emphasize the importance of informed consent. The salient points here were that Ms Chester suffered from very severe back pain and her consultant neurosurgeon, Mr Afshar, recommended surgery without informing her of the 1 to 2 per cent risk of significant nerve damage. She had the surgery and, unfortunately, the risk materialized and she was left partially paralysed. The trial judge found that had she been informed of the risk, she would have sought a second opinion but probably would have had the surgery at a later date with Mr Afshar. This would not normally have satisfied the traditional causal burden in that usually she would have had to prove that she would never have had the surgery. However, in Chester, the House of Lords found a sufficient causal link between the surgeon's advice and the patient's harm. By a majority of three to two, the House of Lords held that it was not necessary for Ms Chester to show that she would never have had the surgery relying on the fact that she would not have had the operation at that specific time. There was a recognition that this conflicted with normal causation principles because whenever the operation was carried out it carried the same risk although the exact nature of the injury may have differed. The main rationale for the decision was that patients have the right to be informed about risks and this would become meaningless if it

---

174   [2005] 2 AC 176, at para. 90.
175   Ibid., at paras. 223–7.
176   *Per* Lord Nicholls, at paras. 3–4 and 20–25.
177   [2004] 4 All ER 587.

was disregarded.[178] The dissenting judges took the view that most doctors comply with the right and the law did not need to reinforce this by awarding a large sum of money in a case where the defendant's breach of the right did not actually worsen the claimant's condition.[179] The dissenting views have, not surprisingly, found some support. For example, it has been said that Ms Chester 'lost nothing of value'.[180] Such comments notwithstanding, there are powerful justifications for a strong commitment to informed consent.

As Wicks has pointed out, what Ms Chester lost was the 'right to make an autonomous choice about medical treatment' though its rationale was under-articulated and over-compensated.[181] If autonomy is to be given the emphasis proposed throughout this book, then a much clearer enunciation of the importance of informed consent needs to be provided. For consent to be meaningful, the patient needs to understand the possible risks and benefits of an intervention as well as the implications of not having it at all, or of having an alternative procedure. This is easier said than done. Explaining sometimes complex and technical medical information clearly to someone who may be worried, and/or feeling unwell, is challenging. In addition, levels of risk and benefit may be difficult to establish. The patient may also state that they do not want all the details.[182] Nevertheless, attempts should be made even if all that can be realistically achieved is an avoidance of coercion and deceit.[183] Using a human rights approach will allow a balancing of the patient's rights with other interests. In the case of children, this will allow information to be withheld to protect them where appropriate. This accords with the legal provision for therapeutic privilege'.[184] This suggests that information may be withheld where it may harm the patient. In such a case information would be provided to their parents. A human rights framework would also offer an opportunity for resource matters to be considered. Unduly onerous requirements to impart information could be detrimental to others given the constraints in the

---

178   See Meyers, D., '*Chester v Afshar*: Sayonara, Sub Silentio, *Sidaway*?', and Jackson, E., '"Informed Consent" to Medical Treatment and the Impotence of Tort', in McLean, S.M.A. (ed.), *First Do No Harm*, Aldershot, Ashgate, 2003, 255–71 and 273–86 respectively for useful comments on *Chester* and the inadequacy of Tort in dealing with complaints about a lack of information from doctors.

179   *Chester v Afshar* [2004] 4 All ER 587 at para. 9.

180   Green, S., 'Coherence of Medical Negligence Cases: A Game of Doctors and Purses', (2006) 14 *Med L Rev* 1 at p. 14.

181   Wicks, E., *Human Rights and Healthcare*, Oxford, Hart Publishing, 2007, at pp. 49–50.

182   Whether there is a 'right' not to know is a moot point. It could be argued that having inadequate levels of information invalidates consent and is an unreasonable burden for health professionals to bear. See further Pattinson, *supra*, at n. 62, at pp. 119–20.

183   O'Neill, O., 'Some Limits of Informed Consent', (2003) 29 *Journal of Medical Ethics* 4–7.

184   See *Sidaway* at para. 887 *per* Lord Scarman, *supra*, n. 83 and GMC, *Seeking Patients' Consent: The Ethical Considerations*, London, GMC, 1998 at para. 10.

NHS setting. For children, there might be a danger that in ensuring they fully understand what is being proposed, fewer will be deemed competent to make decisions. Using the approach advocated in the Mental Capacity Act 2005 for all age groups whereby assistance is offered to help people make decisions could help to address this potential difficulty.[185]

The cases of *Chester v Afshar*[186] and *Fairchild v Glenhaven Funeral Services*[187] with their departure from established rules of causation highlight how the aim of tort law can be as much about identifying the wrongdoing of the defendant (although this is not reflected in the level of damages awarded) as it is about compensating the victim.[188] In *Gregg v Scott*,[189] there may have been concern about under- or over-compensation depending on when Mr Gregg died but this could be addressed by a sensible compensation arrangement.

Legal Causation and Remoteness

Even if the not inconsiderable hurdles of factual causation are overcome, the courts will not necessarily treat the breach of duty as the legal cause of the damage where there is more than one independently sufficient cause of harm to the claimant. If another's conduct intervenes between the negligent conduct and the harm, it could be decided that this is a *novus actus interveniens* breaking the chain of causation provided it is 'unreasonable' and 'unforeseeable'.[190] If the harm is such that it was very unpredictable, the court may decide that it is 'too remote' from the negligent conduct. Provided the type of harm was reasonably foreseeable, the event is unlikely to be too remote.[191] The extent of damage principle is also demonstrated by the 'egg-shell skull rule' that states that the defendant must take the claimant as they find them with respect to their physical characteristics. In *Smith v Leech Brain Co*,[192] the plaintiff suffered a burn on his lip as a result of the defendant's negligence. The burn caused cancer to develop as his lip tissues were in a pre-

---

185   S. 1(3). There are onerous requirements contained in Part 2, Chapter 3 of the Code of Practice in some detail as to what might be expected including appropriate settings and the use of aids. Note the recent evidence that 36.1% of children surveyed stated that they were not given sufficient information to help them make decisions about their sexual health: Children's Right Alliance's report to the United Nations Convention on the Rights of the Child presented 11 June 2008 in Geneva: 'Get Ready for Change: Being a Children's Right Champion', Children's Rights and Participation Conference, Centre for Applied Human Rights, University of York, 1 July 2008 and www.getreadyforgeneva.org.uk.

186   [2004] UKHL 41.

187   [2002] Lloyd's Rep Med 361.

188   For a useful overview of the aims of tort law more generally see Steele, *supra*, n. 73, at Chapter 1.

189   [2005] 2 AC 176.

190   *Knightly v Johns* [1982] 1 WLR 349.

191   *The Wagon Mound (No. 1)* [1961] AC 388.

192   [1962] 2 QB 405.

malignant state. The defendants argued that they could not have foreseen his death three years later but the court stated that they had to take the plaintiff as they found him. The question for remoteness was whether the burn could have been foreseen not the cancer. The principle also applies where the claimant's damage is a combination of the defendant's negligence and the medical treatment to which they were allergic. In *Robinson v Post Office*,[193] the plaintiff fell down a ladder as a result of the defendant employers' negligence and cut his leg. The doctor gave him an anti-tetanus injection to which the plaintiff was allergic. He contracted encephalitis and the defendants were held liable for both this and the original injury because it was foreseeable that he would be given the injection. Had the doctor been aware of the allergy but continued to administer it, this negligent act would probably be treated as a *novus actus interveniens*, that is, an intervening act that breaks the chain of causation between the original harm and the eventual damage.

Faults in Drugs and Medical Devices

The Medicines and Healthcare Products Regulatory Agency[194] monitors approval mechanisms and controls licensing arrangements of drugs and medical devices. The use of monolateral frames in limb-lengthening programmes for children would fall within the remit of this Agency for example. The need to use many unlicensed drugs in paediatric care is discussed in Chapter 7. When dangers concerning drugs and medical devices come to light, the Agency issues rapid warnings throughout the NHS. Drugs and other medical products account for significant levels of harm in patients[195] and an action in negligence may be available on the basis of traditional *Donoghue v Stevenson*[196] principles. A common law action is less likely to be pursued given the availability of an action under the Consumer Protection Act 1987 (CPA) for products manufactured after 1 March 1988.[197] This presents fewer obstacles to the claimant. An action in negligence will require the claimant to show that the defendant manufacturer did not take reasonable care in the design, manufacture, labelling or marketing of a drug for example, and this may be difficult because of the difficulties in obtaining information that is purported to be commercially sensitive and thus confidential. The Act does not require the claimant to establish fault[198] and they can sue anyone in the chain of supply[199] but

---

193   [1974] 1 WLR 1176.

194   www.mhra.gov.uk.

195   See Teff, H., 'Products Liability' in Grubb, A., (ed.) *Principles of Medical Law*, (2nd ed.), (2004).

196   [1932] AC 562.

197   S. 6(3) of the CPA extends the 1976 Act to include ante-natal injury.

198   S. 3 (1) states '… there is a defect in the product … if the safety of the product is not such as persons generally are entitled to expect … .'

199   Ss. 9(2) and 2 generally.

an action must be brought within ten years of the product being on the market. Where drugs are concerned, claimants need to note that manufacturers will present a robust response to any claim because they have huge resources at their disposal and because the implications of a successful action against them are such that many other claims are likely to follow.

Section 3(2) sets out the factors to take into account when determining whether a product is defective including:

a. the manner in which, and purposes for which, the product has been marketed, its get-up, the use of any mark in relation to the product and any instructions for, or warnings with respect to, the doing of anything with or in relation to the product;
b. what might reasonably be expected to be done with or in relation to the product; and
c. the time when the product was supplied by its producer to another.

Apart from the difficulties in establishing that a drug rather than the underlying condition has caused the harm, there may be inevitable side-effects from its consumption. A court may have to weigh up the benefits of taking the drug against any unpleasant side-effects which can vary between individuals as can its effectiveness more generally. They may also have to weigh up whether it is appropriate to treat with a relatively untested drug in the absence of any alternative.[200] This will often be the case with paediatric medicines that have not had the opportunity to be tested on children.[201] Clear warnings of possible adverse side-effects may well undermine a claimant's case which is probably why US drug manufacturers go to such inordinate lengths to print any possible reaction on their information sheets supplied with most drugs.

As with negligence,[202] the manufacturer will have a defence if scientific and/or other knowledge at the time of production was such that they could not possibly have been expected to discover the defect (the development risks defence).[203] In the leading case of *A v National Blood Authority*,[204] the National Blood Authority tried to claim that the public should not have an expectation that blood is always clean because it is not possible to test the blood for all contamination. The claim

---

200 As in *Simms v Simms* [2002] 2 WLR 1465.

201 Discussed further in Chapter 7 on research with children where it notes that this position should improve.

202 For a useful summary of the complexities that arose with respect to knowledge about the risks of contamination from Human Growth Hormone in the CJD litigation see Mason and Laurie, *supra*, n. 43, at pp. 325–7.

203 S. 4(1).

204 *A v National Blood Authority* [2001] 3 All ER 289. Although blood is a naturally occurring substance, it is subjected to technical intervention so falls within the ambit of the CPA.

here concerned contamination by the Hepatitis C virus. The judge held that if the public were not informed about possible contamination, they did have a legitimate expectation that the blood was clean. Rather than claiming to have no duty for unforeseeable risks, the development risks defence was raised but the judge held that this could not be relied upon merely because it was not possible to eliminate the contamination. The relevant point was that the risk was known about and the public should have been warned.

It may be possible to bring an action in contract against the seller of non-prescription drugs where these have caused harm because under the Sale of Goods Act 1979, goods must be of satisfactory quality and reasonably fit for the purposes for which they were purchased.[205] This is relatively straightforward in that the seller cannot claim they had no way of knowing the drug was defective though the action will be restricted to the purchaser because of the doctrine of privity. Anyone else harmed by the drugs would have to rely on a negligence claim.

Damages

Although one of the aims of torts law is to identify wrongdoing, as noted above, this is not reflected in the level of compensation awarded should a victim succeed in their action. This is because the overarching objective of tort law is to put the victim in the position they would have been in had the tort not been committed. Its intention is not to punish the tortfeasor or to reflect the seriousness of the wrongdoing. Any award should merely reflect the claimant's losses, which is more difficult where this involves physical injury and not just financial losses alone.

In common with other tortious claims, medical cases may receive damages with one or more of the following elements: fair and reasonable compensation for the injury suffered which is determined on a tariff basis;[206] for pain and suffering;[207] loss of amenity for the inability of the claimant to engage in previously enjoyed activities; expenses incurred as a result of the injuries including private medical expenses even when the same treatment was available in the NHS;[208] loss of earnings suffered as a result of the harm up to the date of the hearing and future losses which will involve some level of intelligent prediction and sometimes

---

205   Ss. 13 and 14 respectively.

206   E.g. the loss of amenity tariff discussed by the Court of Appeal in *Heil v Rankin* [2000] 3 All ER 138.

207   The Court of Appeal agreed with the Law Commission Report No. 257 (1999) in *Heil v Rankin ibid.*, in that the levels were set too low and increased them by 50 per cent notwithstanding the potential impact on the NHS.

208   S. 2(4) NHS Law Reform (Personal Injuries) Act 1948 although under the Redress Act 2006 it is not thought that the Redress Scheme will allow recovery for private medical treatment.

complicated calculations in order to estimate likely levels of expenses and loss of earnings that are likely to be incurred.

The way damages are calculated can result in very controversial awards. Bereavement damages of only £10,000 are available for a parent losing a child[209] but it is difficult to see what figure could reflect such a loss. The high sums involved where there is very significant physical impairment, may not adequately compensate the victim from their perspective. The levels may be affected by levels of income and, more controversially, by socio-economic status since the courts will take into account the life-style enjoyed because the purpose is to put the victim into the position as if the tort had not occurred. The traditional approach of awarding lump sums, after calculating a probable lifespan, could result in under- and over-compensation if the claimant lived for a longer or shorter period respectively than was anticipated. There is an increased tendency to use structured settlements to deal with this problem. Here, a lump sum would be awarded for initial, quantifiable losses with an additional amount paid into an annuity which would provide flexible sums to be paid as requirements develop or not. Initially, courts could only order these arrangements where the parties agreed and some claimants would not because of the ongoing need for medical assessment. There has been a major change in the law so that courts are now required to consider whether to make an order for periodical payments of damages rather than a lump sum and permits it to do so regardless of the wishes of the parties.[210]

The Limitation Act 1980 precludes claims after certain periods of time have elapsed. The rationale for this is that it would be unfair for defendants to have potential claims against them existing for years ahead. For personal injury the claim must be brought within three years of the date of the negligent act or from the date where the claimant realized an action could be brought.[211] For financial or contractual claims the limitation period is six years[212] that will be relevant for those claimants bringing an action where they have received their treatment in the private sector potentially. There is some discretion under section 33 for these periods to be extended by the court if there is a legitimate reason for the delay and neither party will be unduly prejudiced. However, this section only applies to cases of personal injury or those arising under the Fatal Accidents Act 1976. This has created difficulties with respect to child abuse, which may take a number of years for the effects to be fully manifest and appreciated by the victim. In *KR v Bryn Alyn Community (Holdings) Ltd (In Liquidation)*,[213] the Court of Appeal drew a distinction between claims for systematic negligence that could be regarded as a personal injury claim and abuse, which could not. In order to succeed in a claim

---

209   S. 1A of the Fatal Accidents Act 1976.

210   S. 2 of the Damages Act 1996 as substituted by s. 100 of the Courts Act 2003 and S.I. 2005/841.

211   S. 11.

212   S. 2.

213   [2003] 3 WLR 107.

for abuse then, it will have to be framed as being negligently-incurred personal injuries which is seen as unjust and arbitrary and the recommendations of the Law Commission[214] to dispense with these distinctions should be implemented.[215] Under section 28, the six-year limitation period runs from the date when an individual has ceased to be under a disability, which is defined to include those under the age of majority or is of 'unsound mind'.[216] Thus, the time starts to run after the age of 18.

Once the relevant total is calculated there may be a reduction where the claimant has contributed to his own injury by, for example, not disclosing relevant information about an important medical fact that is not checked by the doctor as it should be.[217] In such an instance, the claimant's compensation will be reduced in percentage terms to a level thought to reflect his contribution to any resulting damage. Compensation may also be reduced where a claimant fails to mitigate their losses by not seeking timely treatment for example. It is expected that claimants should take reasonable steps to reduce or limit any harm.[218] For secondary victims of psychiatric harm who have not been directly involved as participants in the traumatic event, we have seen that it is notoriously difficult to achieve success in an action in negligence. There may be an exception to this if the claimant is in a close relationship with the primary victim, such as parent and child, and what is witnessed is particularly horrifying.[219]

This is not the place to discuss the calls for wholesale reform of the compensation system that is more than adequately dealt with elsewhere.[220] However, it is worth noting that although no-fault systems allow for recovery for harm suffered during medical treatment whether there has been negligence or not, naturally occurring

---

214	Law Commission, *Limitation of Actions*, No 270.

215	Discussed in Giliker, P. and Beckwith, S., *Tort*, London, Sweet and Maxwell, 2004, at pp. 434–5.

216	S. 38(2) and (3).

217	Law Reform (Contributory Negligence) Act 1945.

218	*Geest plc v Monica Lansiquot* [2002] 1 WLR 1311.

219	The special rules applying to secondary victims are to be found in *Alcock v Chief Constable of South Yorkshire Police* [1992] 1 AC 310. *Ward v Leeds Teaching Hospitals NHS Trust* [2004] EWHC 2106 provides an example of the operation of these in the medical setting. Another exception may arise where someone close to the primary victim is informed in a negligent manner (almost becoming a primary victim) about what has happened to the primary victim and suffers psychiatric harm. However, it is the person who communicates the news, rather than the person who caused the harm the news is about, who will be liable: see *AB v Tameside and Glossop Health Authority* (1997) 8 *Medical Law Review* 91 although on the facts of this case the means of communication was held to be legitimate.

220	See, for example, Brazier, *supra*, n. 16, at Chapter 10 where alternative approaches are discussed. Note, also, that the UK does have limited no-fault schemes: the Industrial Injuries Scheme, the Criminal Injuries Compensation Scheme and Vaccine Damage Compensation Scheme.

conditions would not fall within their remit. This is subject to criticisms.[221] Nor are the schemes as generous as they are often thought to be,[222] although this may change.[223] In effect, under such schemes, individuals who are responsible for poor practice are not held to account.[224] It is argued that the removal of fault may impair processes for learning from errors and reduce the risk of harm to future patients[225] but other systems to encourage the reporting and dissemination of adverse incidents go some way to address this.[226]

There is little appetite to embrace the no-fault approaches adopted in some jurisdictions perhaps because of the huge costs involved in establishing such schemes[227] and also because there is recognition that many medical mishaps are not the result of just one individual's failings. Nor is it likely that we will adopt a system whereby victims of medical mishaps receive no or minimal compensation for their injuries because of the ensuing drain on NHS resources.[228] However, the flaws of the current system alluded to throughout the preceding section has received acknowledgement and some reform is forthcoming. Building on the Chief Medical Officer's proposals in *Making Amends*[229] the NHS Redress Act 2006 is designed only to address some of the shortcomings of the torts system in that it focuses on claims less than £20,000 in value. The Act requires that providers and commissioners of health services provide a responsive and appropriate alternative to litigation. Its key tenets are thorough investigation of events followed by an explanation and/or apology, remedial care of the victim and compensation where necessary, thus signalling a move away from the adversarial approach inherent in the torts system. The NHSLA will oversee its operation and will decide whether there is liability and suitable remedies. The detail of how these issues will be determined will evolve over time but it is likely where awards are made in the event of a serious shortcoming that could have been avoided, these will be broadly

---

221   Ibid.

222   Ibid., at p. 249.

223   The Injury Prevention, Rehabilitation and Compensation Amendment Bill (No. 2) is currently being considered by the New Zealand Parliament: http://theyworkforyou. co.nz/bills/injury_prevention_rehabilitation_no_2_2007/2007/dec/13/d02 .

224   See Pattinson, *supra*, at n. 62 at pp. 88–9 for a summary of a range of no-fault compensation schemes available (the Nordic countries seem to have had more success than New Zealand for example) and pp. 90–93 for an assessment of the effectiveness of different approaches to compensation in meeting its ethical rationale.

225   Wicks, *supra*, n. 181 at p. 55.

226   *Supra*, n. 5.

227   Currently estimated at anything up to £28 billion: *Making Amends*, *supra*, n. 10 at p. 112, as compared to the £579.3 million paid out on clinical negligence in 2006–2007, *supra*, n. 20.

228   As suggested in Harris, J., 'The Injustice of compensation for victims of medical accidents', (1997) 314 *British Medical Journal* 1821 so that the victim only receives treatment for their condition.

229   *Making Amends, supra*, n. 10.

equivalent to those received in the judicial setting .[230] Whether the standard for 'serious shortcoming' noted in *Making Amends* will be any different from the common law remains to be seen and establishing causation will still be a hurdle for complainants. It is expected that internal complaints procedures would still operate in conjunction with compensation claims.

Unfortunately, the parallel scheme for babies born under the NHS system who suffer neurological impairment as a result of their birth as proposed in *Making Amends* is not specifically included. It had been planned that this would become available where the symptoms become apparent within the first eight years' of life.[231] A package of care and compensation would have been offered with initial lump sum payments to address pain and suffering and the need to adapt the home environment followed by periodical payments for ongoing care requirements. This would have helped to secure higher standards of care for affected children given many fail to establish a successful action in negligence and resources for support are such that many of the demands of these children fall upon their parents. The current financial ceiling for the compensation package precludes anything like effective provision for these children.[232]

While costs are likely to be higher in the short term as more patients receive compensation, in the longer term it is expected that the costs to the Government overall will reduce because of a concomitant decrease in litigation. An important rationale for the legislation is the intention to move away from the attribution of blame[233] and focus instead on the prevention of harm, the reduction of risks and learning from mistakes that should also have the effect of reducing the costs of claims. Currently, this system will not supplant the right to use judicial proceedings, although this would be precluded if the Redress Scheme is used initially. There will be the right to have free legal advice to evaluate any offer made under the Scheme.

The law on prenatal negligence that arises from faulty advice, diagnosis and treatment resulting in the birth of an unwanted child is an area worthy of especial

---

230   *Supra*, n. 10 at p. 4.

231   These cases account for 5 per cent of all clinical negligence compensation claims and 60 per cent of the total clinical negligence budget: ibid., at p. 9.

232   This may, in part, have been due to responses received to the *Making Amends* consultation. The Royal College of Obstetrics and Gynaecologists wanted the Government to see if DoH initiatives would have an effect of the incidence of birth-damaged babies before instigating such a scheme for them. See Bridgeman, J., *Children and Healthcare Law*, Cambridge, Cambridge University Press, 2007 at pp. 204–14 for an indication of how this experience affects families. S. 2(1) of the Redress Act 2006 allows the Secretary of State to determine the scope of the scheme as he sees fit. This should allow regulations to be conceived should the initiatives to improve standards fail to realize their potential.

233   See Mullender, R., 'Negligence law and blame culture: a critical response to a possible problem', (2006) 22 *Professional Negligence* 1–17 where he considers that the evidence that there actually is a blame culture is equivocal.

attention because it raises policy and ethical issues not in evidence in other clinical negligence cases.

Prenatal Negligence

Broadly, actions may be brought in the child's name (or on their behalf) for losses associated with being born injured because of negligent conduct, or in the parents' names. I have adopted Pattinson's terminology in setting out possible actions[234] but it should be noted that this differs in part from other academic commentators. The following decisions illustrate well the ethical tension between the full recognition of parents' autonomous interests in having, or not having, a child as their choice and a paternalistic, welfare approach.[235]

Actions by the Child

Pre-natal Injury

There is a range of injuries that may comprise prenatal harm from preconception, before implantation of an embryo during *in vitro* fertilization (IVF) treatment, during gestation and/or during birth. Examples of a negligent act or omission would include a negligent failure to offer appropriate preconception immunization, negligent IVF treatment, the negligent prescription of drugs to a pregnant woman or the woman's negligent use of drugs and/or negligent delivery. The Congenital Disabilities (Civil Liabilities) Act 1976 provides a cause of action for a neonate 'born disabled'[236] (which is broadly defined[237]) for those born after July 22 1976. They must have survived for 48 hours with respect to injury *in utero*. Those similarly affected before that date can rely on the common law by bringing a negligence action.[238] However, an action can only be brought after birth because a foetus only gains a legal personality at that moment after separation from the mother.[239] In both cases it should be noted that there might still be considerable difficulties in establishing fault and a causal link between any breach and the resulting damage. In the event of foetal death, the only direct protection of the foetus is provided by the Infant Life (Preservation) Act 1929 which defines the

---

234   Pattinson, *supra*, n. 62, at Chapter 9 *passim.*
235   Pattinson, *supra*, n. 62, at pp. 306–308.
236   S. 1(1).
237   S. 4(1).
238   *Burton v Islington Health Authority, de Martell v Merton and Sutton Health Authority* [1993] QB 204.
239   *Re MB* [1997] 2 FLR 426 at 444 and *A-G's Reference (No. 3 of 1994) ibid.* when Lord Mustill recognized only the foetus' limited status at 255–6.

offence of child destruction or 'destroying the life of a child capable of being born alive.'[240]

Under the Act, the child has to establish that a duty of care was owed to one of its parents[241] and that the conduct in question affected either parent's ability to have a healthy child, the mother during the pregnancy or the mother or the child during the birth.[242] Provided the doctor acted negligently towards the mother, the child may claim for the harm he suffered even though his mother may be unaffected.[243] This sounds claimant-friendly but, of course, any defects in the action the mother may have enjoyed will also affect the child. The injured child will benefit from there being no requirement to prove that the defendant knew or ought to have known his mother was pregnant. This is because of the derivative nature of the child's claim, which also allows an action for negligent advice given to the mother.[244]

A child can only bring a claim against their mother if he sustained injuries *in utero* as a result of her negligent driving.[245] It was thought that the number of potential claims would be significant[246] if this category was expanded and could be used to the detriment of matrimonial proceedings whereas the availability of insurance cover would help to minimize conflict in driving cases.[247] There is, perhaps, a balance to be struck between the unfettered liberty of pregnant women as represented by blanket immunity, and partial constraints that could be established by a lower standard of care. This could still be seen as giving unwarranted priority to the foetus.[248]

---

240   *A-G's Reference (No. 3 of 1994)* [1998] AC 245 confirmed that there is no offence of feticide in English law when the House of Lords was asked to rule whether a manslaughter charge could be brought when a severely premature infant's death could be shown to have been caused by injuries inflicted on the mother when pregnant.

241   S. 1(3).

242   S. 1(1) and (2).

243   S. 1(3).

244   Whitfield, A., 'Actions Arising From Birth', in Grubb, A., (ed.) *Principles of Medical Law*, Oxford, Oxford University Press, 2004 at pp. 789–851.

245   S. 2. Any legal challenge to this on the basis that it breaches the right to a fair trial for determinations of one's civil rights and obligations under Article 6 ECHR could result in a declaration of incompatibility with the Convention as provided by s 4(2) Human Rights Act 1998 which would put (possibly irresistible) pressure on the Government to making a remedial order under s. 10.

246   Thus unduly constraining the mother's conduct, which is an imposition that is not similarly placed on men, who could also harm the foetus: see Jackson, E., *Regulating Reproduction*, Oxford, Oxford University Press, 2001 at p. 143.

247   The Law Commission, *Report on Injuries to Unborn Children*, Report No.60 (Cmnd 5709) London, HMSO, 1974 at paras. 58 and 60.

248   See Pattinson, *supra*, n. 62, at p. 292 for a discussion of these points with suggestions as to how they may be resolved without resorting to blanket immunity and Mason and Laurie, *supra*, at n. 43 at pp. 202–5 for examples of how the US has approached

Defendants' liability is restricted to one level of duty for the same act and they are protected to an extent by the statutory enshrinement of the common law (that is *Bolam*) approach to the standard used to determine breach.[249] It is likely that the *Bolitho*[250] modification of requiring that medical opinion be subject to logical analysis will apply. The defendant's position may also be assisted by the defences under the 1976 Act which address parental knowledge about any risks,[251] exclusion and limits of liability[252] as well as any contributory negligence on the part of one or both of the parents.[253] An example would be where they ignored advice thus exacerbating any harm. If either parent knew of a risk this will constitute a defence unless the defendant is the father, in which case the defence will not apply if he knew of the risk but the mother did not.

For those children born before 22 July 1976 their right to pursue a claim might never become statute-barred[254] so that the common law remains relevant.[255] The ability to sue a mother for negligence other than that involved in driving seems as unlikely in this context as it does under the 1976 Act.[256]

---

this issue with civil rather than the criminal courts seemingly more receptive to the idea of maternal responsibilities towards the foetus; the preferred approach in Canada and the UK is to issue care orders once a child is born.

249   S. 1(5) encompassing the idea that the alleged breach will be addressed in the light of the knowledge at the time and noting that departure from received opinion will not necessarily imply a breach of the standard of care.

250   *Bolitho (Deceased) v City and Hackney HA* [1998] AC 232.

251   S. 1(4).

252   S. 1(6) subject to, for example, s 2(1) of the Unfair Contract Terms Act 1977 that prevents the exclusion or limitation of liability with regards to personal injury and death.

253   S. 1(7). Note that there is no defence of 100 per cent contributory negligence if the Court of Appeals interpretation of s 1(1) of the Law Reform (Contributory Negligence) Act 1945 in *Anderson v Newham College* [2003] ICR 212 applies and the claim would fail on causation in any event if the mother was wholly at fault by, for example, failing to heed medical advice, given the derivative nature of the child's claim.

254   S. 28(1) of the Limitation Act 1980 provides that time does not start to run while a claimant is 'under a disability', which is defined to include infants and 'those of unsound mind' (s. 38(2)).

255   Confirmed in *Burton v Islington HA and De Martell v Merton and Sutton HA* [1993] QB 204, following the decision of the Supreme Court of Australia in *Watt v Rama* [1972] VR 353, crucially rejecting the objection that the claimant was not a legal person at the time of the alleged negligence (a negligent gynaecological intervention on a pregnant woman and a negligent delivery respectively) because it pre-dated the birth.

256   In *Burton v Islington HA*, Joined Cases: *De Martell v Merton and Sutton HA* [1993] QB 204, it was noted that such an action could give rise to undesirable conflict between the mother and child but Dillon L.J.'s remarks (at 232) suggest it remains a theoretical possibility. It is Pattinson's view that the decision of the Supreme Court of Canada in *Dobson v Dobson* [1999] 2 SCR 753 that maternal immunity should be maintained, will be persuasive in our own jurisdiction: see Pattinson, *supra*, n. 62, at p. 290.

Wrongful Life

Parents may wish to bring an action for 'wrongful life' because of losses suffered as a result of a failed termination of pregnancy that was carried out because of a defect in the foetus. They may also want to establish liability where a detected defect has not been communicated to parents thus denying them an opportunity to have a termination that would be lawful in such circumstances.[257] The distinguishing feature of these claims is that they arise from conduct that was a necessary condition for the child's very existence. The child would claim compensation for its birth and unacceptable prospects when, without the alleged negligence, it would not have been conceived or born at all. Again, this could occur at any stage so there could have been an absence of advice about future children carrying a risk of a genetic defect that is increasingly likely given the rapid growth in genetic knowledge. The negligent selection of an embryo for implantation could also account for such an action.

McKay v Essex AHA[258] addressed whether a wrongful life action could be brought in English law. The claimant was born deaf and partially blind as a result of her mother contracting rubella during the early months of her pregnancy. The child's claim was for wrongful life because she would not have been born but for the failure to offer the diagnosis, advise the mother of the risks to her unborn child and the availability of a lawful termination. The doctor failed to present an opportunity to the mother to have an abortion duty thus allegedly breaching a duty to the child. The claim was struck out by the Court of Appeal for public policy reasons because it would violate the sanctity of life and devalue the life of a disabled child.[259] There has been difficulty in awarding damages for the cost of raising a child,[260] with a narrow exception,[261] and this sits uneasily with the legislative support in the Abortion Act 1967 for termination on the grounds of foetal disability.[262] It was stated that it would not be possible to construe a level of damages that would represent the difference between such a child's existence or non-existence.[263] Mason and Laurie have suggested that compensation could be formulated by reference to actual suffering caused from the perspective of a

---

257   There may be a public interest in the 'intergenerational justice' dimension to the preconception tort whereby there is a duty to future generations not to harm potential parents: see, for example, McLean, S. and Mason, J.K., *Legal and Ethical Aspects of Healthcare*, London, Cambridge University Press, 2003 at p. 124 and UNESCO *Declaration of the Responsibilities of the Present Generations towards Future Generations* (1997), Article 1.

258   [1982] 1 QB 1166.

259   Ibid., at 1180 per Stephenson L.J.

260   As in *McFarlane v Tayside Health Board* [2000] 2 AC 59 and *Parkinson v St James and Seacroft University Hospital NHS Trust* [2002] QB 266 (discussed below).

261   The conventional sum awarded in *Rees v Darlington Memorial Hospital NHS Trust* [2004] 1 AC 309 (also discussed below).

262   S. 1(1)(d).

263   *McKay v Essex AHA* [1982] 1 QB 1166 at 1181–2 per Stephenson L.J.

diminished rather than a wrongful life.[264] Notwithstanding these criticisms of the case and others,[265] the case has subsequently been approved.[266]

The view of the Court in *McKay* was that the same facts brought in an action under the 1976 Act would have reached the same conclusion, has also proved to be contentious. The wording of section 1(2) (b) requires that the 'occurrence' is one which affected the mother during her pregnancy 'so that a child is born with disabilities which would not otherwise have been present' was interpreted by their Lordships to mean that the negligent conduct leads to the child's disabilities not its existence.[267] This interpretation gives effect to the Law Commission's recommendation that wrongful life actions should be precluded,[268] the preference for which has been criticized.[269]

Two possible wrongful life claims remain. Section 1(2)(b) states that the 1976 Act covers the birth of a disabled child by an occurrence that 'affected either parent of the child in his or her ability to have a normal, healthy child' apparently allowing a child to claim for a pre-conception event that was a necessary condition for its existence subject to the usual defences and limitations.[270] An example would be where negligent genetic counselling has taken place leading to the birth of a disabled child. In addition, section 1A provides for a disabled child to sue for negligence in the course of infertility treatment. While damage caused by preserving techniques would be brought as a prenatal injury action, negligent selection of gametes or an embryo could constitute a wrongful life action because this was a necessary condition of its existence.

It is hardly surprising that wrongful life actions are controversial in many jurisdictions.[271] They are difficult to justify on an ethical basis because it is difficult

---

264   Mason and Laurie, *supra*, n. 43, at p. 196. They support the idea that the health professional failing to advise on a genetic risk, for example, may not have caused the harm, they have breached a duty to prevent the disability so should be held to account, a position reflected exceptionally in French and Dutch jurisprudence (at p. 197).

265   See Pattinson, *supra*, n. 62, at p. 294.

266   By Lord Steyn (*obiter*) in *McFarlane v Tayside Health Board* [2000] 2 AC 59 at 83. Note that the European Court of Human Rights in *Reeve v UK* (1994) 24844/94 had earlier found that the refusal of a claim for wrongful life fell within the State's margin of appreciation.

267   See, for example, *McKay v Essex AHA* [1982] 1 QB 1166 at 1187 per Ackner L.J.

268   The Law Commission, *supra*, n. 247 at para. 89.

269   Given the views expressed during Parliamentary proceedings: Pattinson, *supra*, at n. 62, at p. 295 noting Jackson, A., 'Wrongful Life and Wrongful Birth', (1996) 17 *Journal of Legal Medicine* 349–81at pp. 366–8.

270   Kennedy, I. and Grubb, A., *Medical Law*, London, Butterworths, 2000 at pp. 1551–2.

271   See, for example, Morris, A. and Saintier, S., 'To Be Or Not To Be: Is That The Question? Wrongful Life and Misconceptions', (2003) 11(3) *Medical Law Review* 167–93.

to identify the wrong for which negligence actions aim to compensate the victim. There are supporters of the idea that doctors have a duty to the claimant who has an interest in not being born in a disadvantaged position.[272] However, it will be problematic for some to argue that the wrong is being brought into existence or to have it continue[273] although others clearly see harm where an individual is put into a position of unavoidable disability.[274] To sue for compensation directed towards the claimant's needs rather than for being the victim of a wrong inflicted by the defendant is also challenging. It sits uneasily with normal common law principles, but would help to address the shortfall in the current provision for the disabled[275] notwithstanding recent legislation.[276] These issues are not merely philosophical niceties because a child may only have a wrongful life claim available to claim damages in the event a mother does not have a corresponding wrongful conception or wrongful birth claim or has given up the child for adoption.

Finally, where death occurs *in utero* as a result of any negligence, this would constitute a wrongful death action that is not available in our jurisdiction[277] although parents may be able to use normal negligence principles to bring a claim where a negligently caused still-birth causes the mother physical injury and/or either parent psychiatric harm.

Actions by the Parents

As Pattinson notes,[278] a combination of the following features could be present in one case. Parents may have wished to avoid pregnancy, have taken steps to do so by undergoing a vasectomy or sterilisation but the negligent performance of the relevant surgery has resulted in a child being conceived in any event. In such cases, an action would be unavailable to the child because they have not suffered the harm. Alternatively, the parents may have desired a child but not the one that transpires because probable risks of abnormality have not been disclosed either through counselling or appropriate diagnostic testing or because a termination was negligently performed. An action could also lie where a child is conceived as a

---

272   Mason and Laurie, *supra*, n. 43, at p. 196.

273   Pattinson, *supra*, n. 62, at p. 295 noting Parfit, D., *Reasons and Persons*, Oxford, Clarendon Press, 1984, Chapter 16 and Feinberg, J., *The Moral Limits of the Criminal Law. Volume 1: Harm to Others*, Oxford, Oxford University Press, 1984 at p. 102.

274   Harris, J., *Clones, Genes and Immortality: Ethics and the Genetic Revolution*, Oxford, Oxford University Press, 1998 at p. 109. Overall, he rejects the idea of wrongful life actions on the basis of wrongs done to a child or on the child's needs in the absence of a wrong preferring state compensation schemes to be triggered merely by need (at p. 119).

275   *Supra*, n. 265, at p. 170. For a useful survey of the complexities of finding ethically justifiable reasons for wrongful life actions see also pp. 296–300.

276   E.g. Children Act 2004.

277   S. 4(2) (a) of the 1976 Act.

278   Pattinson, *supra*, n. 62, at p. 285.

result of the negligent selection of an unsuitable embryo. The negligent conduct can frustrate parental wishes not to have children or not to have a child with the particular characteristics in question. There is an additional burden for claimants in wrongful birth actions in that they will have to demonstrate that, if the prenatal negligence had not occurred, they would not have had another child.[279] The pregnancy would have been terminated.

Where individuals become unwilling parents they may wish to claim the costs of a post-negligent pregnancy, the birth and the costs of rearing the child. If the concern is that a child with preventable, unwanted characteristics has been born, the parents will want to claim for the loss of an opportunity to have a child without these characteristics as well as the financial and emotional costs of raising *that* child given they did anticipate the costs of raising *a* child. The latter scenario will arise where there has been a failure to warn about a risk of congenital abnormality or to carry out a warranted diagnostic procedure properly or at all.

The hallmark of the courts' approach to these issues has been to focus simply on whether the alleged negligence has resulted in the birth of a healthy or an unhealthy child.

Prenatal Negligence Leading to the Birth of a Healthy Child

The Scottish case of *McFarlane v Tayside Health Board*[280] represents the current law where a healthy child is born as a result of prenatal negligence. An undesired fifth child was born to the couple following a failed vasectomy operation. They were only allowed to recover compensation for the pain, inconvenience and associated costs of pregnancy and birth, not the costs of raising the child to maturity. The majority provided a range of views, largely based on policy considerations, for their position including the public's likely abhorrence[281] and that birth of a normal healthy baby was a blessing.[282] The latter remark is an indication of a lack of understanding of the pressed nature of some people's lives and that the birth of another child could represent the breaking point with no possibility of financial alleviation in the light of this decision. The Court clearly took the view that to impose liability on a doctor in these circumstances was out of proportion to the harm done thus denying recovery that would normally be available under

---

279   In the case of a negligent failure to inform parents about a foetal defect, the parents will have to prove they would have had a termination had they known. If the negligence relates to a failed sterilization, the action rests on the fact that the parents would not have had another child.

280   [2000] 2 AC 59 overruling *Emeh v Kensington and Chelsea and Westminster AHA* [1985] QB 1012 indicating a concern about the effect on a child if an award is made for the cost of its upbringing notwithstanding a line of English and Scottish cases that suggested an appetite for the opposing view: Mason and Laurie, *supra*, n. 43 at pp. 175–6.

281   *McFarlane v Tayside Health Board* [2000] 2 AC 59 at 82 per Lord Steyn.

282   Ibid., 111–14 per Lord Millet.

negligence principles. Despite widespread criticism,[283] including a rejection of the decision by the High Court in Australia,[284] the Court of Appeal has resisted attempts to distinguish the case by formulating the claim for compensation in terms of loss of earnings while caring for the child rather than for the costs of rearing the child per se.[285] The House of Lords has refused to reconsider its position even though *McFarlane* was recognized as a departure from the normal rules of tort by all the judges suggesting justice may not have been done.[286] However, where the prenatal negligence has resulted in the birth of a disabled child, claimants have received a more sympathetic response.

Prenatal Negligence Leading to the Birth of a Disabled Child

In *Parkinson v St James and Seacroft University Hospital NHS Trust*,[287] it was the mother who was the victim of a negligently performed sterilization operation. The Court of Appeal allowed compensation for the extra expenses associated with raising a *significantly* disabled child to be determined on a case-by-case basis with reference to the definition in the Children Act 1989.[288] The definition is considerably narrower than that in the 1976 Act.[289] Hale L.J. highlighted how to cause a woman to become pregnant against her will was an invasion of her bodily integrity and affected her personal autonomy in that her caring role would persist through childhood. This argument could equally be used in relation to the birth of a healthy child. The same approach was later adopted by the Court of Appeal in relation to wrongful birth cases: the negligent failure to detect a foetal abnormality deprived the woman of an opportunity to abort the affected foetus allowed her to recover the additional costs of raising a disabled child.[290]

---

283   See, for example, *Parkinson v St James and Seacroft University Hospital NHS Trust* [2002] QB 266 per Hale LJ and Hoyano, L., 'Misconceptions about wrongful conceptions', (2002) 65 *Modern Law Review* 883 at p. 904 where she criticizes the lack of intellectual rigour in Lord Steyn's reliance on the predicted views of the new 'reasonable man', the commuters on the Underground; *cf*. Cane, P., 'Taking Disagreement Seriously: Courts, Legislatures and the Reform of Tort Law', (2005) 25 *Oxford Journal of Legal Studies* 393 who believes, absent established legal principles, that to consider issues of morality and distributive justice is a legitimate way forward.

284   *Cattanach v Mechior* [2003] HCA 38 discussed in Cane, P., 'The Doctor, the Stork and the Court: A Modern Morality Play', (2004) 120 *Law Quarterly Review* 23–6.

285   *Greenfield v Irwin* [2001] 1 WLR 1279.

286   *Rees v Darlington Memorial Hospital NHS Trust* [2004] 1 AC 309 at para. 8.

287   [2002] QB 266.

288   S.17(11).

289   S. 4 (1).

290   *Groom v Selby* [2002] Lloyd's Rep. Med. 1.

Where prenatal negligence has caused an unwanted characteristic through failure to offer appropriate counselling or diagnostic screening,[291] compensation will be awarded on the same basis, that is the costs of raising a healthy child will be deducted from the costs of raising a disabled child though determining quantum seems less settled.[292] For example, although *Catherine Urch v Hammersmith Hospitals NHS Trust*[293] settled before trial, the discussion suggests that it may be possible for parents to continue to claim for the costs of raising a disabled child, even after the age of majority. Given the disability is the very thing the claimant sought to avoid, there is a strong case for establishing liability.[294]

The status of *Parkinson* is unclear given an equal number of judges both approved and disapproved it in *Rees v Darlington Memorial Hospital NHS Trust*.[295] This case concerned the birth of an unwanted healthy child but the mother was disabled because she was almost blind. She had the sterilization operation, which was performed negligently, because she was concerned that she would not be able to care properly for any child. Refusing to overrule *McFarlane*, a bare majority of four to three judges in the House of Lords awarded compensation for the pain and inconvenience of the pregnancy and birth with an additional, rather arbitrary, conventional sum of £15,000 in recognition of the wrong that she had suffered not as compensation for the unplanned child. They would not award damages for the extra costs incurred in raising the child because of her disability. This is a difficult decision not least because of remarks made by Lord Scott. He suggested that it should be possible to recover for prenatal negligence where this leads to a child with preventable, unwanted characteristics but not where the child was unwanted[296] when the parents in the latter case did not accept the costs of raising a child at all.

The dissatisfaction with the outcomes of these cases has led to a suggestion for a new head of damages that would recognize a breach of autonomy in that there has been an interference with one's right to plan one's life as one wishes.[297]

---

291   The negligent use of pre-implantation genetic diagnosis would be relevant here: Pattinson, *supra*, at n. 62, at p. 303. This view is also supported by remarks made by Lord Scott in *Rees v Darlington Memorial Hospital NHS Trust* [2004] 1 AC 309 at para. 147.

292   Estimated on the basis of the parents' means in *Rand v East Dorset Health Authority* [2000] Lloyd's Rep Med 181 but on the child's needs in *Hardman v Amin* [2000] Lloyd's Rep Med 498 and *Lee v Taunton and Somerset NHS Trust* [2001] 1 FLR 419.

293   Discussed in Glancy, R., 'Damages for Wrongful Birth: Where Do They End?', (2006) 3 *Journal of Personal Injury Law* 271–9.

294   *Lee v Taunton and Somerset NHS Trust* [2001] 1 FLR 419.

295   [2004] 1 AC 309. See Steele, *supra*, n. 73, at p. 457 on this point.

296   *Rees v Darlington Memorial Hospital NHS Trust* [2004] 1 AC 309 at para. 147.

297   Mason and Laurie, *supra*, n. 43, at p. 184.

Conclusion

It should now be apparent that reform of the clinical negligence litigation system is long overdue given its cost, stresses, complexity, ambiguities, inconsistencies and unfairness, as well as the length of time it takes to resolve the dispute. The Redress Act 2006 has the potential to address some of the concerns raised throughout this chapter but it is only when the Redress Scheme becomes operational that we will see whether the change in culture envisaged is realized. The failure to address the needs of severely neurologically impaired children under the Scheme thus far is regrettable: this is particularly in light of the inadequate levels of support families receive in caring for these children. Some change in attitudes towards the reporting of adverse incidents is already evident under other initiatives and the Healthcare Commission's monitoring of standards of care provides another means whereby the likelihood of clinical mishap is reduced. Balancing the need to encourage transparency and dissemination of learning points with the need to hold people to account where they, rather than the system, are responsible is a significant challenge indeed.

Chapter 7
Children in Research

Introduction

Children need to be shielded from undue risk but deserve to receive the best medical interventions possible. This means children should be given the opportunity to benefit from the results of successful research. On the one hand it can be argued that competent children should be able to decide whether to be involved in research or not along the lines expounded throughout this book. On the other, there is a countervailing proposal that individuals' interests should be subordinate to the interests of society. This suggests that there should be more of a presumption about the willingness of everyone to participate in research given we can all potentially benefit from it. For this position, the focus on the individual is understandable but arguably short-sighted. The lack of child-specific research in the pharmaceutical arena could be used to add force to this particular line of reasoning. The questions arise therefore, of where the balance should lie and whether relevant law and ethical guidance have adopted an appropriate approach?

That medical research is needed to discover new ways of treating health conditions is a well-established and reasonably non-contentious principle, although the means by which this is achieved may be less so. Discussions about the methodologies used are, however, beyond the scope of this chapter.[1] The hope is that cures will be found or at least novel means to alleviate (sometimes distressing) symptoms. As with all research participants, there need to be adequate safeguards in place so that children are not exposed to undue risks and that they and their parents are fully aware of the nature of any projects in which they are involved. The vulnerability of the research participant needs to be acknowledged, in particular where a child is involved. The relationship between researcher and participant is unequal in power in any research protocol. It is the researcher who is likely to be seen as imbued with knowledge and status and will be the active partner rather than acquiescent recipient of intervention(s). These factors are exacerbated when considering that the participant may be ill, in unfamiliar surroundings and, if a child, already further unequal in the power stakes.

The research position with respect to children has been characterized in the past as one of exploitation.[2] Some researchers believe the regulation pendulum

---

1   See Pattinson, S.D., *Medical Law and Ethics*, London, Sweet and Maxwell, 2006, Chapter 11 for an outline of research definitions, methodologies and a discussion on the legitimacy of equipoise and placebos.

2   See *infra* nn. 29–33.

has now swung too far in the other direction, so that it is well nigh impossible to carry out appropriate research in children. Some take the view that this amounts to discrimination *against* children.[3] Conversely, some current professional guidelines in relation to research on children unable to consent have been censured for being too permissive. One commentator [4] has taken the view that those guidelines advocating that such intervention should be 'not contrary to the [incompetent] child's best interests' flies in the face of the Helsinki Declaration's[5] commitment to the individual's interest taking precedence over those of wider society and not being used as a means to an end. For Edwards, this is too lenient an approach and he argues that research must only ever be in the child's best interests. Of course, much can turn on the interpretation of best interests.

The reluctance to involve children in research in more recent times means that they are disadvantaged on a number of fronts. Unless there is a change in emphasis on the involvement of children as research subjects, they will continue to suffer the double jeopardy of not being accorded appropriate recognition of their autonomous interests and not being afforded the same opportunities to benefit from research as adult subjects. It is not advocated that children should be subjected to undue risk or that those close to them should not be involved in any decision-making process, but rather that the regulatory framework should not be unduly restrictive. A more balanced approach is necessary and timely because researchers need the confidence to justify robustly their research proposals, rather than avoid them because of fear of castigation at the ethic approval stage of a research protocol.

This chapter will discuss the extent to which children should be engaged in therapeutic and non-therapeutic research. Should research be conducted *with* them where appropriate, rather than *on* them which is more commonly the case?[6] It is notable that children's viewpoints were not considered at all during the extensive consultation process regarding the European legislation promoting paediatric

---

3   Webb, E., 'Discrimination against children', (2004) 89 *Archives of Disease in Childhood* 804–8. This point should be viewed in the context of criticism that the regulation of research is already denying patients, as a whole, the benefits of clinical trials: Henderson, M., 'Over-protective bureaucracy "is denying patients the benefits of clinical trials"', *The Times*, 17 October, 2008.

4   Edwards, S. 'The ethical concerns regarding guidelines for the conduct of clinical research on children' 31 (6) *Journal of Medical Ethics* 351.

5   The World Medical Association (WMA), Declaration of Helsinki, last adopted by the 52nd General Assembly, Edinburgh, 2000 with a Note of Clarification on para. 9 added by the WMA General Assembly, Washington, 2002 and on para. 30 in by the WMA General Assembly, Tokyo, 2004. The Declaration of Helsinki is currently under review: www.wma. net.

6   See e.g. Marshman, Z., Gibson, B.J., Owens, J., Rod, H.D., Mazey, H., Baker, S.R., Benson, P.E. and Robinson, P.G., 'Seen but not heard: a systematic review of the place of the child in 21st Century dental research' (2007) 17 *International Journal of Paediatric Dentistry* 320–27. See further discussion on broader rights of participation in Chapter 8.

clinical trials.[7] There is evidence that children wish to be involved in research,[8] can be altruistic[9] and are capable of understanding quite complex medical issues.[10] A higher level of engagement with research, together with the likely benefits that will accrue as a result, will avoid the accusation that children suffer a double jeopardy as a result of their current limited involvement. Of course, any right to decide whether to participate in research could result in a refusal to take part. This may have significant implications for other children and society more generally. Should this be allowed to stand? Some may argue that the social interests should prevail.[11] With this in mind, an alternative account of how research might be conducted will be proposed, noting that current consent requirements for research are less than satisfactory as a mechanism to ensure legal and ethical compliance. Where the line should be drawn between supporting children's autonomy *vis-à-vis* societal interests will be addressed together with an assessment of whether relevant domestic and international law and other instruments have established the most appropriate focus.

The following section sets why there is a pressing need for research involving children. This will be followed by a discussion of why research requires regulation, its potential effects, the current regulatory position and a suggested approach to children's participation in research.

Background

There has been significant publicity about the lack of research into drugs used to treat children. This is ethically untenable because children cannot be assumed to be receptive to adult drug formulations.[12] Up to two thirds of children in hospital may be taking unlicensed drugs.[13] Other estimates suggest that 40 per cent of drugs

7   Regulation (EC) No 1901/2006 of the European Parliament and of the Council of 12 December 2006 on Medicinal Products for Paediatric Use and amending Regulation (EEC) No 1768/92, Directive 2001/20/EC, Directive 2001/83/EC and Regulation (EC) No 726/2004 (Official Journal L378,27/12/2006 p. 1–19). Cherrill, J., Hudson, H., Cocking, C., Unsworth, V., Franck, L., McIntyre, J. and Choonara, I., 'Clinical trials: the viewpoint of children', (2007) 92 *Archives of Diseases in Childhood* 712–13.

8   Cherrill et al., ibid.

9   Wolthers, O.D., 'A questionnaire on factors influencing children's assent and dissent to non-therapeutic research', (2006) 32 *J Med Ethics* 292–7.

10   Cherrill et al., *supra*, n. 7.

11   Medical Research Council, *MRC Ethics Guide: Medical Research Involving Children*, 2004 (last accessed at: http://www.mrc.ac.uk/Utilities/Documentrecord/index. htm?d=MRC002430) suggests that a child's refusal to participate or continue in research should always be respected.

12   This may be due, for example, to differences in metabolism.

13   Personal communication from Professor N. Bishop, Consultant Paediatrician, Sheffield Children's NHS Foundation Trust.

prescribed to children have never been tested on them and that the figure rises to 65 per cent where newborn babies are concerned.[14] As will be seen below, some commentators believe even these figures are conservative. The Government has committed additional funding to encourage research in this area.[15] Its position has been bolstered by the European Commission's legislation[16] forcing drug companies to undertake appropriate research on children so that their therapeutic needs are more directly addressed. That legislation followed a period of consultation with relevant stakeholders and is similar to that current in the United States,[17] which was also driven by ethical concerns.[18] These provisions are designed to promote studies in children to ensure the safety of medicines.[19] They will increase information available to the patient/carer and prescriber about the use of medicines in children, including clinical trial data. These objectives will be achieved through a system of requirements and incentives, overseen by the Paediatric Committee sited at the European Medicines Agency, to consider new products and certain changes to the marketing authorization for products still covered by patent protection. These initiatives are to be welcomed but could have improved the approach taken in the US by ensuring that paediatric research is genuinely directed at serving children's needs rather than merely extending patent protection in pharmaceutical companies' interests.[20] Also, they will be to no avail if other regulatory frameworks governing the ethical conduct of research are insufficiently permissive.

---

14   'Children in research: a risk of double jeopardy?', *The Times*, 21 August 2004.

15   Transforming Health Research: the first two years, National Institute for Health Research Progress Report, 2006–2008 at p. 7: £20 million has been allocated over five years to the Medicines for Children Research Network so that children can be treated with medications tailored to their specific needs.

16   *Supra*, n. 7.

17   Personal communication on the US and EU position in this section from Professor N. Bishop, Consultant Paediatrician, Sheffield Children's NHS Foundation Trust: Recent US paediatric studies, conducted in response to US legislation, the Paediatric Exclusivity and the Paediatric Research Equity Act 2002, led to 64 labels containing new paediatric information for established medicines between July 1998 and February 2004. In 41 cases, the new labels included important new dosing/pharmacokinetic information, lack of efficacy or safety information that had an impact on the safe and effective use of the medicine in children. The Act also established a fund of US$ 200 million for the fiscal year of 2002 and such sums as were necessary for each of the succeeding five years for the study of the use in the paediatric population of medicinal products for which there was no patent protection or market exclusivity.

18   Personal communication from Professor A. Plomer, School of Law, University of Sheffield.

19   Whereby an approved drug is permitted to be used in ways not specifically sanctioned although it is likely to be supported with scientific evidence, as is often the case with children's medication: http://archinte.ama-assn.org/cgi/content/full/166/9/1021.

20   Permanand, G., Mossialos, E. and McKee, M., 'The EU's new paediatric medicines legislation: serving children's needs?', (2007) 92 *Archives of Diseases in Childhood* 808–11.

These paediatric-specific provisions work alongside the framework that regulates the use of modern, biotechnological medicinal products.[21] From the marketing perspective, an EC Regulation, which has direct effect so needs no further implementation by Member States,[22] is now in place. It potentially allows faster and safer access to treatment for patients who suffer from diseases that have until now been incurable. This Regulation will cover new forms of treatment that are neither drugs nor surgery as traditionally understood: as well as advanced therapy medicinal products, such as gene therapy and somatic cell therapy,[23] tissue engineering is also now included. It creates a single European authorization process for the placing of advanced therapy medicinal products on the market. It will have a major impact on the biotechnology and medical research industries, and will play a large part in determining the direction that European medical research takes in the future. European market authorization for products can be gained through a single procedure that will obviously be far more commercially attractive than those which continue to require 27 different national authorizations.

The Regulation presents another opportunity to exclude unethical therapies from the marketplace: the European Medicines Agency will only grant market authorization if the product satisfies scientific evaluation of quality, safety and efficacy. It will also have to reach the high ethical standards of the Clinical Trials Directive[24] (implemented in the UK by the Medicines for Human Use (Clinical Trials) Regulations 2004 (Clinical Trials Regulations))[25] at its clinical trial stage. This is discussed further below. The product will also have to provide considerable detail about its provenance while respecting donor anonymity.[26] There will be a need for rules to be developed to ensure good clinical practice in investigations involving advanced therapy medicinal products because of their specific technical characteristics.[27]

---

21 Regulation (EC) No 726/2004 which established the European Medicines Agency responsible for the authorization and supervision of medicinal products for human and veterinary use following scientific evaluation of the quality, safety and efficacy of the product.

22 Art. 4(1) of Regulation (EC) No 1394/2007 addresses clinical trials with respect to tissue engineering.

23 Arts. 6(7) and 9(4) and (6) of Directive 2001/20/EC deal with clinical trials with respect to these therapies. The Clinical Trials Regulations are discussed *infra* in the text accompanying nn. 103–34.

24 Directive 2001/20/EC.

25 Preamble of the Regulation (EC) No 1394/2007, para. 16. The Clinical Trials Regulations 2004 were amended by the Medicines for Human Use (Clinical Trials) Amendment Regulations 2006 as a result of the Good Clinical Practice Directive 2005 and by the Blood Safety and Quality (Amendment) Regulations 2008) and are discussed *infra* at nn. 103–34.

26 See e.g. para. 19.

27 Ibid. and Art. 4(2).

If there is such a pressing need for these enabling provisions, why do we need regulation of paediatric research?

The Need for Regulation

The main impetus for ethical and legal regulation of medical research came from the appalling abuses perpetrated by the Nazi regime during World War Two internments.[28] As a result of the prosecutions that took place in response to these, the Nuremberg Code established a number of principles to guide future medical research. These have been built upon in numerous national and international ethical guidance and laws. Nevertheless, abuses have continued to come to light where financial and other incentives play a powerful role in addition to any more dubious psychological factors.[29] It is important to recognize society's responsibility to protect the vulnerable. The criticism of research carried out on especially defenceless children such as orphans, the learning disabled and state looked-after children, is entirely legitimate.[30] These children were given unproven vaccines that were accepted as risky and not approved for general use without parental consent. Some children suffered significant pain and were left with brain damage. Some research on children has been likened to child abuse.[31] Given historical incidences of the deliberate infection of children with syphilis and other diseases,[32] this conclusion is hardly surprising.

Abuse of children in research was perhaps possible because of the relative social invisibility of children at the time.[33] As attitudes to children changed, it might have been expected that these abhorrent practices would have ceased. However, this has not been the case. Unethical research has continued to be discovered, although not on such a scale. In 2000, it was alleged that research was carried out on premature babies at North Staffordshire Hospitals without parental consent about a decade previously.[34] Fortunately, now, controls are such that no Research

---

28   Annas, G. and Grodin, M., (eds), *The Nazi Doctors and the Nuremberg Code, Human Rights in Human Experimentation*, New York, Oxford University Press, 1992.

29   Pattinson, *supra*, n. 1 at pp. 336–7 and Plomer, A., *The Law and Ethics of Medical Research: International Bioethics and Human Rights*, London, Cavendish Publishing, 2004 at pp. 3–4 and 29–30 for some examples of these.

30   *Supra*, n. 14.

31   Henderson, R.A., *Consent, Choice and Children in Research*, University of Newcastle, 2008, Unpublished PhD Thesis.

32   Ibid.

33   Ibid. and James, A. and James, A.L., *Constructing Childhood: Theory, Policy and Social Practice*, Basingstoke, Palgrave: Macmillan, 2004.

34   NHS Executive, *West Midlands Regional Office Report of a Review of the Research Framework in North Staffordshire Hospital NHS Trust* (http://www.doh.gov.uk/wmro/nrthstaffs.htm); Editorial, 'Babies and Consent: Yet Another NHS Scandal', (2000) 299 *British Medical Journal* 1253. Not all the allegations were proven and the General Medical

Ethics Committee (REC) would approve such trials in the UK that effectively preclude them from taking place.[35] Yet, ethical and legal principles have struggled to keep pace with scientific developments and this has been particularly evident where biotechnological advances are concerned. The focus here will be on those most relevant for the debate concerning children's involvement in research in the European Union though it should be noted that there is a complex mosaic of measures regulating this area.[36]

The following section highlights some of the key ethical considerations in relation to children in research before evaluating the extent to which the current law and ethical guidance adopts an appropriate focus.

An Ethical Framework for Children's Participation in Research

Privacy and confidentiality, discussed in Chapter 4, have relevance in the research context but the main ethical focus in this chapter is on consent. Duty and rights-based theories are likely to be more cautious in their approach to medical research than utilitarian and communitarian theories. In their application, all moral theories will adopt an approach towards medical research that best protects the research participant from avoidable harm while striving for beneficial scientific results. Aside from the difficulties of establishing whether there has been a valid consent to medical research as determined by capacity, voluntariness[37] and sufficient information, some moral theories would prohibit research that has the potential to detrimentally affect the individual even with valid consent. This is on the basis that there are non-waivable constraints on conduct from either a communitarian or duty-based perspective. The former would wish to uphold certain community values and the latter, the duties one owes to oneself: these are collectively

---

council (GMC) dismissed claims against three paediatricians involved for professional misconduct ('Paediatricians cleared', *The Times*, 5 July 2008 at p. 4).

35 Pattinson, *supra*, n. 1 at pp. 362–7.

36 In addition to the Medicinal Products for Paediatric Use Regulation and its associated provisions discussed *supra*, nn. 15–26, the interplay amongst the Declaration of Helsinki, the Medicines for Human Use (Clinical Trials) Regulations 2004, Council of Europe's Convention on Human Rights and Biomedicine, (Oviedo Convention), 1997 (see also Additional Protocol to the Oviedo Convention, concerning Biomedical Research, 2005 (Protocol on Biomedical Research)), the Human Rights Act 1998, the Mental Capacity Act 2005 and the Human Tissue Act 2004 (HTA) are noted in relation to research. Further, professional guidance such as that of the GMC, *The Role and Responsibility of Doctors*, London, GMC, 2002 will be relevant. Breach of professional guidance can result in disciplinary action.

37 See Pattinson, *supra*, n. 1 at pp. 347–9 for a discussion as to whether inducements offered to research participants affects voluntariness, scientific validity and creates exploitation; compromise positions of payment at modest levels are usually adopted by relevant instruments.

described by Beyleveld and Brownsword as 'dignity as constraint'.[38] Their idea of 'dignity as empowerment' focuses on individual choice and autonomy that is only limited by the rights of others. Consent from the 'dignity as empowerment' position is a more powerful justificatory mechanism and accords with the human rights approach advocated here.

With this in mind, what should be the scope for children in deciding whether they wish to be involved in research? This question becomes even more important when we consider non-therapeutic research, where the research subject does not stand to gain directly from the research in which they are participating. Why is this ever necessary? Non-therapeutic research on children is necessary not least because they respond differently to drugs and suffer from illnesses that do not affect adults. A case in point is Duchenne Muscular Dystrophy (DMD), a very rare single gene condition, affecting only boys and resulting in premature death. It is only relatively recently that boys with DMD have survived to adulthood. The nature of this disease means that there is a need for research at all stages of the disease, but particularly on children, and in circumstances where such research may not benefit participants. This is because potential treatments arising out of any research may not be available before these children succumb to their disease. As it is, clinical trials are now taking place with adolescent sufferers of DMD whereby a 'molecular patch' should repair damaged DNA given the promising results from animal trials.[39] It is hoped that the disease will be stopped in its tracks or at least slowed down significantly. Clinicians advocate using younger children because the main potential benefit would be to those whose disease is not yet too symptomatic. However, the risks are perceived as being too great for younger children given the significant lack of knowledge about the effects of the intervention in human subjects.[40] Parents and research groups argue that, given the relentless deterioration in those affected, younger children and their families should be given the choice to participate in this research. Not to permit this could be seen as unduly harsh when there is no alternative treatment and when there is significant evidence that even very young children can understand the implications of what is being proposed.[41] Some further ethical complexities of DMD research is discussed below.[42]

---

38   Beyleveld, D. and Brownsword, R., *Human Dignity in Bioethics and Biolaw*, Oxford, Oxford University Press, 2001, particularly Chapter 2.

39   Personal communication from Professor F. Muntoni, lead researcher in TREAT-NMD (Translational Research in Europe – Assessment and Treatment of Neuromuscular Diseases) which is an international initiative bringing together some of the world's leading neuromuscular specialists in a pan-European 'network of excellence' aimed at improving treatment and finding cures for patients with neuromuscular disorders. See further Muntoni, F., 'Are we any further in the treatment of muscular dystrophies?' (2007) 17 (9–10) *Neuromuscular Disorders* 898 and 'Patch' test for boys' wasting disease', *The Times*, 18 September 2007.

40   Ibid.

41   See the discussion in Chapter 2.

42   DMD discussed *infra* in the text accompanying nn. 46–50.

Obtaining consent is seen as pivotal in ensuring research is legitimate. Children are placed in double jeopardy by a lack of enthusiasm to carry out paediatric research (particularly non-therapeutic research) and a reluctance to allow *them* to make decisions about participation in research thus failing to acknowledge their autonomy. There should be a greater recognition of the diversity that exists amongst children with respect to their capacities. The perception of the child as a vulnerable individual has been the metric for regulation and legislation, and is precisely the paternalistic presumption that should be challenged. It is important to establish that children are not a single, homogenous group. The legal concept of the child includes only a somewhat begrudging recognition of the older child's right to self-determination by a limited recognition of certain capacities to consent.[43] Nor is research a homogenous activity. There are very marked contrasts between the 'straightforward' clinical trial for a new drug and complex, longitudinal, genetic research or epidemiological research projects. For these reasons, ethical guidelines that facilitate research on children with a more permissive approach should be supported.

Empowering children to make decisions could result in their refusal to participate in research. Is there ever a case for allowing their autonomous interests to be overridden in the interests of others? This argument may be easier to sustain where the effect on the individual is minimal but the benefit to others is significant. Society needs to be more explicit about the need for research potentially to benefit everyone. There may also be an argument that there should be an expectation that all citizens should be willing to participate along the lines discussed in Chapter 5. This cannot be left to the individual consenting procedure as this could be coercive and invalidate the consent. To be part of a broader education however, would create the right climate for promoting engagement with research. Where a competent child or a parent nevertheless refuses to take part, the presumption of participation could facilitate any ethical consideration about overriding this refusal. Where there is no disproportionate risk to the individual but a potentially great benefit to others, this may a legitimate approach to contemplate. This has particular resonance when we consider the paucity of research with children.

In any event, consent is problematic for adults as well as children, being generally relied upon to do too much of the ethical work in the context of research. Some examples may help to demonstrate the complexity and range of issues inherent in some research and how consent is not always the appropriate mechanism enabling it to take place.

---

43   Given the retraction from the recognition of children's autonomous interests in *Gillick v West Norfolk and Wisbech Area Health Authority* [1986] AC 112 in the subsequent cases of, for example, *Re R (a minor) (wardship: consent to medical treatment)* [1991] 4 All ER 177, CA and *Re W (a minor) (medical treatment)* [1993] Fam. 64.

Case Examples

The difficulties of using consent as a mechanism for ensuring legal and ethical compliance in certain research projects has been described elsewhere.[44] Essentially, these projects involved the collection of biological samples from mothers and their newborn infants together with lifestyle information about the mothers and their partners. This was held in databases and may be made available to other research studies. Although parents have properly consented on the child's behalf, concerns have been raised about the fact that they are likely to become unwitting participants in further research during a time period in which they will develop an *actual* voice. They are unwitting because it was agreed that further decisions to use these data in anonymized form would be made by the REC. Recommendations may, but equally may not, include a requirement to seek further consent. With the development of the power of speech, there is also the voice, evidence of the burgeoning capacity to form an opinion, to have a viewpoint, and, in legal parlance, to have the competence to decide. Even though they may be able to withdraw their samples once they reach the age of 16, they are, until that age, essentially silent donors to medical research during a period in which they could feasibly give or withhold their consent at a much earlier point. Whether this is an injustice or not must be a judgment balanced against the merits of the project as a whole and the actual risks posed to the individual by continued participation.

Some dissenting children may be coerced into continuing to participate either because parents impose their will on the child or children do not feel empowered to speak. Add to this these facts that initial and continuing involvement in these studies relies upon the mother's consent the purposes of which may not be understood,[45] and we can see some of the complexity that surrounds the issue

---

44   See Hagger, L. and Woods, S., 'Children in Research: a Risk of Double Jeopardy' (2005) 13 *International Journal of Children's Rights* 47–68 where the Avon Longitudinal Study of Parents and Children and the North Cumbria Community Genetics Project are discussed.

45   See Haimes, E. and Whong-Barr, M., 'Levels and styles of participation in genetic databases: a case study of the North Cumbria Genetics Project' in R. Tutton and O. Corrigan (eds), *Genetic Databases: socio-ethical issues in the collection and use of DNA*, London, Routledge, 2004 and Haimes, E. and Whong-Barr, M., 'Key issues in genetic epidemiology: lessons from a UK based empirical study', (2004) 8 *TRAMES* 105–63 where they describe a number of concerns in their evaluation study of the NCCGP project. For example, some mothers regarded the cord blood and placental tissue as waste and therefore not significantly attached either to themselves or their child. This raises doubts as to whether they understood that agreeing to donate such tissue was in fact agreeing to their child's participation in the study. Some respondents reported that they would have asked more questions if the sample had been of a different type, such as venous blood or a cheek swab. Some respondents also reported being uncertain as to whether they donated tissue or not. Of course, if a more invasive sample had been requested, this does not necessarily mean that women's understanding of the gene bank would have been greater.

of presumed competent adults to consent for themselves and their children. This illustrates the unequal burden placed upon the role of consent to do most of the moral work in the context of research. It should be noted that many of those involved in these particular research projects remained enthusiastic about their participation, reporting motives, which included altruism and the wish to contribute something back to society. This supports the idea that there is a need to develop the richer notion of inclusive citizenship that was outlined in Chapter 5.

Henderson[46] has also examined the role of consent and found it wanting.[47] In his study, he interviewed parents of children with DMD as they contemplated whether to allow their sons to take part in preclinical and clinical trials aimed at developing gene-based treatments. They were chosen because these families often face difficult decisions about research and treatment participation. Currently, research projects are being developed which appear to promise great hope to families but also involve significant risks to participants. Most studies indicate that personal benefits, such as access to new treatment or better care, are prioritized over societal benefits when making decisions about research participation.[48] In addition, Henderson notes that informed consent is problematic in the way it is perceived. Decisions about research participation are made on the basis of life experience and social frameworks as well as medical information. Decisions are deliberative and interactive processes embedded in emotional and social contexts. Parents discussed the importance of families, health care professionals and researchers as well as the wider community in how they made decisions. Consent needs to be negotiated with this in mind. The idea that people genuinely 'choose' to participate might, nonetheless, be misleading. Parents may not want full information in their attempts to hang on to hope.[49] Some studies have indicated that consent may not be truly voluntary, in that parents feel obliged to agree. The emotional state of parents at the time of consenting may have meant that they were unable to assimilate the information they were being given.

'Therapeutic misconception', presents particular challenges with respect to DMD research. This is where there may be a mistaken belief that (even very early) research will offer some direct benefit, thus further undermining consent; this is

---

46 Henderson, *supra*, n. 31.

47 The following section is drawn from his work unless otherwise stated.

48 Ibid.: children themselves generally view trial participation as a positive experience, citing altruistic reasons, age-appropriate incentives and seeking a fun experience as motivations. However, a dislike of needles, blood tests and bad-tasting medicines may militate against the giving of assent to participation. Their final decision is likely to be influenced by relationships with their parents, the researchers and perceptions about the resolution of disagreements. Good communication is essential.

49 While this is entirely understandable, it sits uneasily with the view that where assent on behalf of others is concerned, and especially in relation to non-therapeutic research, only *full* disclosure of relevant information is satisfactory and justified: see e.g. Sch. 1, Part 4, para. 7 (for children under 16) and Sch. 1, Part 5 (for those aged 16 or more who lack capacity) of the Clinical Trials regulations.

more prevalent where DMD is concerned.[50] This is because the concept has been more often observed in cases of life-limiting illness, where there are few other treatment options and where there are highly publicized, novel agents. There is also an increased risk of therapeutic misconception where a researcher's stake in the success of a project affects the way in which they portray it. This can lead to children being entered into very gruelling trials because there is an assumption that researchers have already carried out an appropriate risk assessment. Pressures to consent to research also come from parents wishing to make their child's suffering 'meaningful' by hoping to benefit other children and from wanting to 'do something'. For these reasons, it is suggested that parents should not even be asked whether their children can participate in research where there are more than minimal risks, that is, such research should be prohibited.

Importantly, Henderson notes that it is not always possible for parents to make best interests decisions with respect to research on their children. There are numerous unpredictable variables implicit in research and best interests assessments can conflict with other family interests. He supports a modified principle of respect for persons that permits parents to use their child as a means as long as they simultaneously respect the child as a developing person. This permits wide parental autonomy in directing their child's future according to their own perception of the good. Parents have an obligation to provide for their child's basic needs, so compromising their health by allowing participation in research that carries more than minimal risk would be unacceptable. Henderson believes that such broad parental autonomy allows the accommodation of others' interests and more accurately reflects the reality of family life where other members may be affected by decisions made. It also accords with the legal standard of 'not acting against a child's interests'.[51]

These examples of research demonstrate not just the range of issues, but the moral ambiguity that can arise. The complexity of a research project, its context, and the uncertainty surrounding the aims of the research, sometimes make the ideal of informed consent as the ultimate ethical safe-guard an improbable, if not impossible, aspiration, not only for children but even for competent adult proxies. This is a complexity that should be both recognized and accepted. This is not an argument for abandoning consent, but rather that we should both recognize and be realistic about its limitations. One implication, perhaps, is that we should be more willing to allow children an active role in consenting to research recognizing that children are sometimes no more vulnerable than their adult proxies or other adults who are in a similar disease position. Of course, consent cannot legitimize an ethically flawed or unethically executed research project. Therefore, whilst widening the community of those deemed able to consent, we should redouble our

---

50   Ibid.
51   *S v S* [1972] AC 24.

efforts to ensure that research is properly governed and regulated.[52] This should include less of a focus on obtaining informed consent for research and more on moral dilemmas as they arise throughout the course of the study.[53] Above all, there needs to be a more 'socially nuanced' concept of consent.

It is with this final point in mind that we can return briefly to the idea that society can legitimately expect its citizens to promote the interests of others as outlined in Chapter 5. Participation in research would fulfil this function. The best medical treatment and care can only be achieved with proper research. For research to be of most benefit it requires the co-operation of a significant number to ensure validity and generalizability. Can we take participation in research as an activity whereby we express our concern for humanity as a whole?[54] Everyone stands to gain important benefits from health care and expects that their care will be of the highest standard. So how should a society that values these benefits characterize the expectations it has of its citizens if they are to enjoy these benefits? One could talk of a moral *duty* based on an equal expectation of reciprocity from the beneficiaries. The preference here is for the proposal that there should be a moral *expectation* that each person, the young, the old, the infirm and the healthy, will contribute to medical research.[55] The claim is proposed in this way because, although there may be a justified expectation of participation in research, that this expectation should be converted into an obligation that may be unilaterally enforced would be a step too far.[56]

For Harris and Woods,[57] the moral expectation that all citizens will contribute to medical research rests upon a number of considerations. The first is that it is part of the general morality that each person should refrain from harming others. The second is that we all have positive duty to do good. The third is that research is in everyone's interests and it therefore seems only fair to expect everyone to contribute to a service from which each expects to benefit.[58] Caplan[59] expounds a similar theme based on Rawls' concept of 'fair play'[60] and notes further:

---

52 Chadwick, R. and Berg, K., 'Solidarity and equity: new ethical framework for genetic databases' (2001) 2 *Nature Review Genetics* 318–21.

53 Henderson, *supra*, n. 31.

54 See the discussion in Chapter 5.

55 Harris, J. and Woods, S., 'What are the responsibilities of the individual when participating in medical research?' in Doyal, L. and Tobias, J., (eds), *Informed Consent in Medical Research*, BMJ Books, 2000 at pp. 286–92.

56 Ibid.

57 Ibid., at pp. 286–92.

58 Harris and Woods, *supra*, n. 55.

59 Caplan, A.L., 'Is there a duty to serve as a subject in biomedical research?' (1984) 6(5) *IRB: Ethics and Health Research* 1–5.

60 Rawls, J., *A Theory of Justice*, Cambridge, Harvard University Press, 1971 discussed in Chapters 2 and 5.

> Fair play seems to require that those who reap the benefits of greater therapeutic knowledge and skill that are derived from biomedical research should be called upon to bear the burdens and costs of pursuing such activities. There is no more reason for tolerating free riding in research contexts than there would be in any other voluntary social cooperative.[61]

Teaching hospitals as research institutions can be seen as a scientific social cooperative. In Caplan's view this approach should not be restricted to knowing participants: fair play requires that where the benefits of better care, closer attention and higher levels of medical skill that are often available in a teaching hospital are knowingly and willingly sought out by patients, they incur an obligation to participate in research. Of course, participation should be subject to fair play, so that it is not unduly onerous, including the right to refuse to participate.[62] Such a refusal sits uneasily with a moral *obligation* to participate in research that suggests a commitment from which one cannot demur, hence the preference here for an *expectation* of participation. It could be observed that these claims are too demanding[63] given that people who turn to the health care services do so out of need and are inherently vulnerable as patients. It may be argued that patients in the UK may not consciously choose which institution they attend. However, GPs are increasingly offering their patients a choice of where to attend for treatment. Caplan's points about the benefits of teaching hospitals will be factors that will be taken into account, and that will include paediatric services.[64] It should be emphasized that this obligation, or rather expectation as is preferred here, to participate in research does not diminish the moral importance of each individual patient, including the right to have his or her personal interests taken into account. Nor does it give licence to health professionals to pursue their research interests without due consideration of their moral and legal responsibilities. Existing legislation and ethical guidance is designed to afford protection to individuals who participate in research. However, the existence of specific legislation does not alter the fact that, first and foremost, all people, patients and health professionals alike, have moral responsibilities. This is particularly apposite with regard to children where there has been historical reluctance to engage with paediatric research, even where children will be the direct and sometimes the only beneficiaries.

Having an expectation that everyone, including children, will contribute to research should be construed as part of the initiation into good citizenship. Children should grow up socialized into a world in which the society in which they thrive has legitimate expectations in return. To expect participation in research is to

---

61   Caplan, *supra*, n. 59 at p. 4.

62   Ibid.

63   See e.g. MacKillop, W.J. and Johnson, P.A., 'Ethical problems in Clinical Research: the Need for Empirical Studies of the Clinical Trials Process', (1986) 39(3) *Journal of Chronic Diseases* 177–88 at p. 179.

64   www.nhs.uk/Coices/Pages/Aboutpatientchoice.aspx.

presume willingness to do what any reasonable, moral person should be prepared to do, at least where the risks of serious harm are small or non-existent. These arguments stand independently of the issues associated with consent. Failure to obtain consent from the child or their parent, may present a circumstance in which one feels that the expectation of participation remains legitimate, but for pragmatic reasons it would be politic not to insist. The sight of a child dragged kicking and screaming from their parent's arms is not an image that could conceivably contribute to an argument about good citizenship.

Bearing in mind that there could reasonably be an expectation rather than an obligation to participate in research, where should the balance lie when a competent child refuses to take part? It will be assumed that all efforts have been made to present a suitably persuasive case but if the child remains adamant, should their wishes be disregarded? Each case will have to be determined on its merits by an appropriate REC subject to the demands of current legal and ethical guidance. Do they allow for such a consideration?

The Legal and Ethical Instruments: International

In general terms, a key difficulty of achieving ethical research, lies in the problems of obtaining universally acceptable principles that are enforceable during an era of unprecedented scientific and biotechnological development. The World Medical Association (WMA) was established in 1947 to represent and promote the freedom of the medical profession and medical ethics after the abuses suffered by human subjects during the Holocaust came to light.[65] The following year the WMA issued the Declaration of Geneva and the International Code of Medical Ethics in 1949,[66] both of which set out the duties of physicians in relation to their patients. Subsequent revisions are notable for their change in emphasis to a prescriptive rather than a normative approach as well as the requirement to respect the rights of patients and colleagues.[67] However, it is the Declaration as a statement of moral ideals and adopted by the WMA in 1964[68] that has been the most influential document in relation to the regulation of biomedical research. Key principles include the need to obtain informed consent (or appropriate proxy consent in the case of incapacity),[69] for participation in research that is designed to be scientifically valid and productive,[70] conducted by qualified and experienced

---

65 Annas and Grodin, *supra*, n. 28.

66 International Code of Medical Ethics, WMA adopted by the 3rd WMA General Assembly, London 1949 and amended by the 22nd WMA General Assembly, Sydney, Australia, 1968 and the 35th WMA General Assembly, Venice, Italy, 1983.

67 Ibid.

68 Declaration of Helsinki (1964) based on the principles of the Nuremberg Code extracts of which are set out in Annas and Grodin, *supra*, n. 28 at p. 2.

69 Ibid., at para. 20 and 22–6

70 Ibid., at para. 11.

personnel,[71] and protective of the participant's rights.[72] The right to confidentiality and to withdraw at any time should be conveyed to the participant.[73] Research should be commenced, and continued, only where *minimal* risks are justified by the projected benefits.[74] It must also be reviewed by an independent ethics committee.[75]

The Declaration has gone through a number of iterations and the current version[76] does not possess the paternalistic notions evident in the original Declaration. Controversies remain however. One concern is the removal of the distinction between therapeutic and non-therapeutic research, because this is seen as lowering the protection of research subjects.[77] Another is the inadequacy of the Declaration's standards when applied to clinical trials conducted in developing countries where charges of exploitation have been made, although these countries have argued that it is for them to determine whether the research is ethical or not.[78] This particular issue highlights well the difficulties of obtaining sufficient consensus about the applicability of the Helsinki standards which is essential if they are to be seen as legitimate. Without this, widespread adherence becomes potentially problematic. The relatively recent development of public consultation on standards should help in this regard.[79]

The Declaration and other international instruments such as the Oviedo Convention[80] provide guidance only, although adherence to these may be achieved by the actions of, *inter alia*, ethics approval bodies, such as RECs and MRECs in the UK, which must take account of relevant policies and legislation which may well be drafted with these in mind.[81] Without approval from an ethics committee and

---

71   Ibid., at para. 15.

72   Ibid., at paras 21–2.

73   Ibid.

74   Ibid., paras 16–17.

75   Ibid., para. 13.

76   WMA, *Declaration of Helsinki* adopted by the 52nd WMA General Assembly, Edinburgh, Scotland, October 2000.

77   Ibid., A new category of 'research combined with medical care' was introduced although the concepts remain broadly the same: Brazier, M. and Cave, E., *Medicine, Patients and the Law*, London, Penguin Books, 2007 at p. 411. One argument against 'therapeutic' research is that very dangerous toxic drug trials can be approved as 'therapeutic' whereas 'non-therapeutic' research into children's views about good standards of care can be dismissed: personal communication from P. Alderson, Professor of Childhood Studies, Institute of Education, University of London.

78   Plomer, *supra*, n. 29 at pp. 3–4.

79   Plomer, *supra*, n. 29 at pp. 13–14.

80   Oviedo Convention and additional Biomedical Research Protocol, *op. cit.*, n. 35.

81   See Pattinson, *supra*, n. 1 at pp. 362–7 for a description of how these bodies function.

the Medicines and Healthcare Products Regulatory Agency (MHPRA),[82] research into pharmaceutical products cannot take place. However, the weakness of the Declaration is particularly evident when invoked in legal proceedings where it may be undermined by procedural and substantive rules of law as well as the more general points about lack of enforcement procedures and penalties for breach.[83]

The Oviedo Convention

The Oviedo Convention is seen as a significant development in its attempts to establish fundamental, overarching and universal values as they apply to biomedicine, incorporating a human rights perspective.[84] Given the diversity of international approaches to the regulation of these matters, dependant to some extent on whether the state adopts a liberal or conservative stance, [85] the Convention opted for general definitions of key concepts in order to gain early acceptance. Specification was to come later through Protocols. The concern is that ethical standards become diluted in attempt to be all-embracing. An example of this is how the UK's liberal position on embryo research compares to its continental neighbours yet does not breach the Convention's provisions.

One area that created most difficulty in terms of drafting was in relation to admitting the possibility of non-therapeutic research on those unable to consent where the individual does not stand to benefit directly.[86] This controversial aspect of research created difficulties for the Declaration of Helsinki in earlier revisions as well as the US Advisory Committee on Human Radiation Experiments (ACHRE) Report, which attempted to establish six basic ethical principles that could be universally acceptable and/or applicable. That one ought not to use a person merely as a means to others' ends; not deceive; not inflict harm or risk of harm; promote welfare and prevent harm; treat people fairly and with respect, and respect the self-determination of others, is not especially contentious whatever moral theory is used. However, the concepts are not without criticism.[87] For present purposes, a key difficulty does lie in the lack of specificity in the term 'welfare', because it fails to stipulate whether this refers to the individual or society. There is an

---

82   The MHRA is responsible for licensing procedures, market authorization and implementation.

83   Plomer, *supra*, n. 29 at pp. 5–7 where she discusses the US *Pfizer* case in which even very reprehensible behaviour of the pharmaceutical company during clinical trials failed to breach the 'universal concern' standard required for legal sanction.

84   Plomer, *supra*, n. 29 *passim.*

85   Plomer, A., 'Participation of Children in Clinical Trials: UK, Europe and International Perspectives on Consent', (2000) 5(1) *Medical Law International* 1–24.

86   Plomer, *supra*, n. 29 at p. 26 and see Hagger and Woods, *supra*, n. 44 for a discussion of how the term 'non-therapeutic' could be addressed.

87   Collated by Plomer, *supra*, n. 29 at pp. 32–4.

inherent tension between the idea that everyone should promote the interests of society given they receive its benefits, against a Kantian view which sees no such obligation. The ACHRE approach, given that there is no ranking of the principles, allows the possibility of society's interests 'trumping' those of the individual without justification. This is a particular concern in relation to the incapacitated. It is the lack of a robust framework that could establish the scope, meaning and justification of the principles within a hierarchy of priorities that ultimately means they cannot claim to be universally applicable.

Bearing these conceptual difficulties in mind, Plomer assesses whether the Oviedo Convention manages to avoid them.[88] The overarching, fundamental values include the protection of dignity and identity of all human beings;[89] the primacy of the human being;[90] equitable access to health care,[91] and the requirement that any intervention in the health field should be carried out in accordance with relevant professional obligations and standards.[92] Where specific areas are concerned, these must be read in accordance with these values. It could be charged that these values are less determined than ACHRE's principles, but other parts of the Convention elucidate the concepts. Human dignity, for example, incorporates the Kantian notion of respecting the individual's right to make autonomous choices. The Oviedo Convention introduces the notion of respecting the individual as a member of the human species. The human species is ascribed rights and dignity, thus allowing the possibility of conflict between these rights and those of the individual. In that progress in biology and medicine should be used for the benefit of present and future generations, the Convention offers more determinacy than the ACHRE Report. In addition, the Convention is very explicit that the interests of the individual must prevail over those of society in the event of a conflict.[93] However, in reality, the specific rules on scientific research appear to adopt the converse position in some cases: where mentally incompetent individuals are concerned, the Convention allows their legal representative to volunteer them to be participants, even when the research will be of no direct benefit to them and could carry minimal risk.[94] For these categories of participant, both ACHRE and the Oviedo Convention fail to provide a rigorous ethical justification for allowing society's interests to prevail over those of the individual, thus allowing the potential for abuse that 'a human rights instrument should be seeking to avoid'.[95]

---

88 Plomer, *supra*, n. 29 at pp. 37–42.
89 Article 1.
90 Article 2.
91 Article 3.
92 Article 4.
93 Article 2 and para. 21 of the Explanatory Note.
94 Article 17 *passim.*
95 Plomer, *supra*, n. 29 at p. 42. See also pp. 18–21 where a major criticism of the Convention could be raised with respect to the fact that individuals do not have the right of petition to the European Court of Human Rights (Article 29) but must rely on, *inter alia,*

That there should be free and informed consent to any biomedical intervention has widespread agreement in international ethical codes, human rights instruments and, in some jurisdictions, domestic law.[96] As far as medical research is concerned, the Oviedo Convention is particularly strong on this requirement given the detailed information researchers are expected to provide to prospective participants.[97] The right to physical and mental integrity of the person under Article 3 of the EU Charter of Fundamental Rights[98] has particular relevance here. It notes that, in the fields of medicine and biology, the following must be respected in particular: the free and informed consent of the person concerned, according to the procedures laid down by law; the prohibition of eugenic practices, in particular those aiming at the selection of persons; the prohibition on making the human body and its parts as such a source of financial gain, and the prohibition of the reproductive cloning of human beings. Article 24 includes, *inter alia*, the right of children to have the protection and care necessary for their well-being; to express their views freely, and to have such views taken into consideration on matters which concern them in accordance with their age and maturity. These themes are echoed in the Regulations,[99] which should strengthen any claims made by a participant that this requirement has been breached, given that such a breach may result in criminal liability. It should be noted, however, that the Regulations do not require that participants are given information about sources of funding, affiliations of the researcher, or potential conflicts of interest.[100]

Oviedo Convention Protocol on Biomedical Research

Of particular note is the Oviedo Convention Protocol on Biomedical Research.[101] Article 15 states that research on a person without the capacity to consent may be undertaken only if *all* the following specific conditions are met:

- the results of the research have the potential to produce real and direct benefit to the participant's health
- research of comparable effectiveness cannot be carried out on individuals capable of giving consent

---

governments to seek advice as to the interpretation of its provisions. However, Plomer argues that it could be used as a guide when an action is brought under the ECHR, as in *Glass v UK* [2004] 39 EHRR 15.

96   For example, Declaration of Helsinki, Oviedo Convention and, in the UK, the Clinical Trial Regulations.

97   Article 16, Protocol on Biomedical Research, *supra*, n. 35.

98   EU Charter of Fundamental Rights, 2000. See also the commitment to human dignity under Article 1 where it states that this is inviolable and must be respected and protected (http://www.europarl.europa.eu/charter/pdf/text_en.pdf).

99   Schedule 1, Part 3.

100   *Cf.* the Declaration of Helsinki 2000 and GMC, *supra*, n. 36.

101   Chapter V of the Protocol on Biomedical Research refers to persons unable to consent.

- the person undergoing research has been informed of his or her rights and the safeguards prescribed by law for his or her protection, unless this person is not in a state to receive the information
- the necessary authorization has been given specifically and in writing by the legal representative or an authority, person or body provided for by law, and after having received the information required by Article 16, the taking into account of the person's previously expressed wishes or objections
- an adult unable to consent shall, as far as possible, take part in the authorization procedure
- the opinion of a minor shall be taken into consideration as an increasingly determining factor in proportion to age and degree of maturity
- the person concerned must not object
- exceptionally, and under protective conditions prescribed by law, where the research does not have the potential to produce results of direct benefit to the health of the person concerned, such research may be authorized in some circumstances and will be subject to the preceding conditions (apart from the direct benefit criterion) with the following *additional* conditions:
- the research must have the aim of contributing, through significant improvement in the scientific understanding of the individual's condition, disease or disorder, to the ultimate attainment of results capable of conferring benefit to the person concerned, or to other persons in the same age category, or afflicted with the same disease or disorder, or having the same condition
- the research entails only minimal risk and minimal burden for the individual concerned, and
- any consideration of additional potential benefits of the research shall not be used to justify an increased level of risk or burden[102]

The stipulation for exceptional circumstances, allowing non-therapeutic research where there is minimal risk and limited burden to the participant, fits well with the proposals contained in Chapter 5, suggesting that there should be a greater

---

102   The approach adopted in the US is instructive. Here, research on children is allowed where it poses no greater than minimal risk; where it involves greater than minimal risk and offers direct benefit to the individual research subject; where it involves greater than minimal risk but offers no prospect of direct benefit to the subject but may yield information about their condition and where understanding may be advanced about a serious health problem in children. This last category of research requires that any risks must be only a minor increase over minimal risk; the research interventions are reasonably commensurate with those inherent in [the subject's] actual or expected medical, dental, psychological, social or emotional situations; the expected knowledge is of vital importance for the understanding or amelioration of the subject's disorder or condition and the parents consent and the child assents to participation (National Institutes of Health, section 46.405). Specific approval at federal level is also required following advice from a panel of experts (*Code of Federal Regulations*, paras 46–50).

focus on the familial and social context. It is a relatively generous provision in comparison with other ethical guidance and legislation such as the Clinical Trials Regulations, to which the discussion now turns.

The Clinical Trials Regulations

The Clinical Trials Directive is exceptional in that it is legally binding on European Union Member States and their non-compliance may result in a reference to the European Court of Justice.[103] The Clinical Trials Regulations, which implement the Directive in the UK, attempt to approach the conduct of medical research on humans on a par with the detailed provisions for embryo and animal experimentation.[104] Clinical trials must be carried out in accordance with the Declaration of Helsinki 1996[105] rather than the 2002 version. This is important because the earlier document provides, *inter alia*, a stronger emphasis on the precedence of the interests of the individual over those of society and draws a distinction between therapeutic and non-therapeutic research.[106] This is one example of the restrictive nature of their provisions.

For the individual researcher, it is a criminal offence to commence a clinical trial without obtaining authorization from the MHPRA and the approval of the relevant REC.[107] So not only do the Regulations embrace the ethical principles of international instruments, such as the Declaration of Helsinki, they have force, in that sanctions may be applied by the regulatory body, including the termination of the clinical trial.[108] The Good Clinical Practice Directive[109] supplements the Clinical Trials Regulations with further detailed guidance on the conduct of clinical trials, including appropriate documentation, and the authorization of the manufacture and importation of medicinal products to be used.

The focus of the discussion now will be on the consent provisions of the Clinical Trials Regulations. They add no further detail to the concept of voluntariness than the common law. This suggests that pressure would have to be very significant to vitiate consent.[110] Schedule 1 sets out the conditions of good clinical practice in

---

103   For an overview of the mechanisms of sanction in relation to EU law see Hervey, T.K. and McHale, J.V., *Health Law and the European Union*, Cambridge, Cambridge University Press, 2004, at pp. 63–7.

104   The Human Fertilisation and Embryology Act 1990 (until the Human Fertilisation and Embryology Bill 2008 is enacted) and the Animals (Scientific Procedures) Act 1986 respectively.

105   Sch. 1, Part 2.

106   Plomer, *supra*, n. 29 at p. 3 and Pattinson, *supra*, n. 1 at p. 360.

107   For a useful account of how these operate in the UK, see Pattinson, *supra*, n. 1 at pp. 362–7.

108   Regulation 31.

109   2005/28/EC.

110   *U v Centre for Reproductive* Medicine [2002] EWCA Civ 565.

relation to research participants with capacity, or who have had capacity, and these include a provision on informed consent. These do not require the same level of detail as the some professional guidance[111] and the Declaration of Helsinki 2000[112] but could incur criminal liability if breached, in addition to any civil liability.

The Clinical Trials Regulations require that a legal representative, selected sequentially from a hierarchy, must give informed consent on an incapacitated person's behalf.[113] Such a legal representative must not be connected with the trial.[114] For children under 16, this will be someone with parental responsibility[115] and for incapacitated adults someone who is willing to act as a legal representative or who has been nominated by the person while competent to do so.[116] Where such individuals are unavailable or unwilling to act in this capacity, the participant's doctor may act as the legal representative provided they are unconnected with the trial. If this is not possible, the relevant NHS Trust may nominate someone else to act as the legal representative, typically their treating doctor provided they, too, are unconnected with the trial. A parent or legal representative must act on the basis of the 'presumed will' of the incapacitated patient[117] with all the inherent difficulties this concept entails, given that it may not be based on past or current expressed will. In common with the 'substituted judgment' approach prevalent in the US, this necessarily imports a level of fiction into the calculation although the child's perspective may be more likely to be taken into account than with the application of the best interests' approach.

The proxy must be given all the information that would be provided to a person with capacity[118] and the incapacitated participant must be provided with a level of information about potential benefits and risks to the extent that they can understand it.[119] This does not introduce any requirement for assent on the part of the incapacitated participant and any previously expressed dissent only has to be considered by the researcher.[120] The researcher, or legal representative, cannot overrule any refusal that was expressed prior to the onset of incapacity.[121]

---

111   See e.g. GMC, *supra*, n. 36, at paras 19–21.

112   Which require, *inter alia*, that prospective candidates should be given information that includes the '… aims, methods, sources of funding, any possible conflicts of interest, institutional affiliations of the researcher.' (para. 22).

113   Sch. 1, Part 1, para. 2 (incapacitated adults) and Sch. 1, Part 4 (children).

114   Sch. 1, Part 4 (child) and Sch. 1, Part 5, para. 4 (incapacitated adult).

115   As provided by s. 3(1) Children's Act 1989.

116   Ss. 30–34 Mental Capacity Act 2005 noted in particular at n. 181 *infra*.

117   Sch. 1, Part 4, para. 13 (child) and Sch. 1, Part 5, para. 13 (incapacitated adult).

118   Sch. 1, Part 4, para. 7 (for children under 16) and Sch. 1, Part 5 (for those aged 16 or more who lack capacity).

119   Sch. 1, Part 4, para. 6 (child) and Sch. 1, Part 5, para. 6 (incapacitated adult).

120   Sch. 1, Part 4, para. 7 (child) and Sch. 1, Part 5, para. 7 (incapacitated adult).

121   Sch. 1, Part 1, para. 1(5)(b).

The research trial must be 'designed to minimize pain, discomfort, fear and any other foreseeable risk',[122] and must be essential to validate data obtained by other methods.[123] For incapacitated adult research participants, the trial must relate directly to a life-threatening or debilitating clinical condition from which they are suffering and there must be grounds for believing that it will produce a benefit that outweighs any risk should it exist.[124] Where children are the research subjects, the trial must relate directly to a clinical condition from which the child suffers, or only be capable of being carried out on children; additionally, some direct benefit must be obtained by the group of participants involved in the trial.[125] The requirement that clinical research may only be carried out on children where it is therapeutic[126] apparently rules out non-therapeutic research unless a very wide reading is taken of the term 'therapeutic', such that it may include psychological and other benefits,[127] including the enhancement of skills as they engage in decision-making processes.[128] The courts have adopted a broad reading of best interests in the context of treatment (and there is no expectation that the standards would be any less rigorous where research is concerned), which encompass medical, emotional and other welfare factors,[129] including the psychological and social benefits to the child.[130] So there are potential benefits to the child, albeit of a different order.[131] Of course, research must not be against their interests, as it would be if there is a risk of more than minimal harm. We saw that it is possible for parents to consent to non-therapeutic medical treatments: by analogy it should be possible for them to consent to non-therapeutic research. This seems unlikely in the current, cautious climate. This position is to be regretted because it undermines children's autonomy by not allowing them to be involved in any decision-making process, and may over emphasize the importance of the individual. The overarching principle that the interests of the child must prevail over the interests of science and society,

---

122   Sch. 1, Part 4, para. 14 (child) and Sch. 1, Part 5, para. 13 (incapacitated adult).

123   Sch. 1, Part 4, para. 11 (child) and Sch. 1, Part 5, para. 10 (incapacitated adult).

124   Sch. 1, Part 4, paras 9 and 11.

125   Sch. 1, Part 4, paras 9 and 10.

126   Schedule 1,Part 4, para. 10 discussed *infra*, nn. 99–125.

127   Schedule 1,Part 4, para. 10, discussed in Hagger and Woods, *supra*, n. 44. Cf. Post-script, p. 211.

128   Noted in Chapters 2 and 8, in particular.

129   We have very clear statements to the effect that best interests are more than medical best interests and include social, welfare, emotional and other factors: *Re A (male sterilization)* [2000] 1 FLR 549 *per* Dame Butler-Sloss P. at 555 and *Simms v Simms*[2003] 2 WLR 1465, para. 42 where Butler-Sloss P. states that *Bolam* is only the first stage in determining a patient's best interests. See Hagger and Woods, *supra*, n. 44 for a discussion on this point. See also Cherrill, et al., *supra*, n. 7.

130   *Re Y* [1997] 2 WLR 556 at 562.

131   Discussed in Hagger and Woods, *supra*, n. 44.

echoing the sentiments of other relevant instruments,[132] underlines this point.[133] The approach advocated by the Clinical Trial Regulations is in line with both international instruments and professional guidelines, although the latter are more supportive of non-therapeutic research in some cases.[134]

The Clinical Trials Regulations offer a statutory basis governing the protection of the participant in clinical trials. However, in common with other legal and ethical instruments, reference to a range of guidance, especially the common law, will be necessary for interpretive purposes.[135] *Non-clinical* research, such as psychological and epidemiological research, will continue to be predominantly governed by case law and ethical guidelines. Does the domestic setting offer opportunities to empower children in their decision-making, yet consider when others' interests might prevail?

The Legal and Ethical Instruments: Domestic

Other forms of intrusive research[136] will now be regulated by the Mental Capacity Act 2005 (MCA), Department of Health Guidance (DoH)[137] and other ethical guidance:[138] this is largely confined to the investigation of new surgical techniques and psychological research. It will be remembered that those under 16 years of age do not fall within the MCA's remit.[139] Its provisions are broadly in line with the approach taken by the Clinical Trials Regulations. However, it states that the benefits of the research must justify the risks to the individual in therapeutic research, or the risks must be negligible; the research must not interfere significantly with the participant's freedom or privacy, nor be unduly intrusive or restrictive thus allowing non-therapeutic interventions.[140] In this way, the Act owes more to Article 17(2) of the Oviedo Convention in allowing non-therapeutic research that carries minimal risks. With respect to research using human material

---

132   E.g. WMA, Declaration of Helsinki, 2000, para. 5.

133   Schedule 1, Part 4, Principle 16, Clinical Trials Regulations 2004.

134   British Medical Association (BMA), *Medical Ethics Today. The BMA's handbook of ethics and law*, London, BMA, 2004, Royal College of Paediatric and Child Health (RCPCH), 'Guidelines for the ethical conduct of medical research involving children' (2000) 82 *Archives of Disease in Childhood* 178–82 and the Council for International Organizations of Medical Sciences, *International Ethical Guidelines for Biomedical Research Involving Human Subjects,* Geneva, 2002, p. 5.

135   Schedule 1, Part 4, paras 1–8 and Principles 13–15.

136   Defined in s. 30(2) to mean any research that would be deemed a trespass, unless lawfully justified.

137   DoH, *Research Governance Framework for Health and Social Care*, 2005, that was introduced to address the limited governance of research not covered by the Clinical Trials Regulations 2004.

138   E.g. RCPCH, *supra*, n. 134.

139   See Chapter 2.

140   S. 31(5)(b)(6).

after death, section 2 of the Human Tissue Act 2004 provides that where a child is competent, they can make an advance decision concerning their consent to the removal and use of their human material. Such a decision must be respected. If the child was incompetent, the person with parental responsibility can consent for the child, apart from the use of the body for anatomical examination. This requires consent from the child. Where the child has died leaving no one with parental responsibility, someone in a 'qualifying relationship' can consent to the removal, storage and use of the material.[141]

The interpretation of legal requirements will be subject to the rules of statutory interpretation and, where relevant, the common law. Ethical guidance will also be interpreted through the common law where necessary. Where the common law is engaged, the principles established in case law on medical treatment will need to be distilled and applied by analogy to the research context, given the paucity of directly relevant cases. We have seen that the common law in the UK has eventually recognized the rights of competent patients to consent to and refuse *treatment*, in recognition of the fundamental principle of the right to self-determination.[142] Without valid consent, a health professional will be liable in the tort of battery and consent can be vitiated by fraud and the misrepresentation of information given prior to the intervention.[143] The level of information disclosed should be in broad terms as to the nature and purpose of the intervention.[144] Where research is concerned, the threshold of disclosure will be higher.[145]

Where a legal claim is based on a failure to disclose sufficient information about the procedure, for example, any known risks, then action will lie in negligence.[146] Such an action is more challenging for claimants as has been demonstrated in Chapter 6. Where there has been a failure to disclose risks an action in clinical negligence will only succeed if the doctor has breached the *Bolam*[147] standard as to what a reasonable doctor would have disclosed in the same circumstances, subject to the *Bolitho*[148] requirement that medical opinion should be capable of withstanding logical analysis. Such a doctor should now disclose a significant risk of harm that would affect the judgment of a reasonable, prudent patient.[149] It is likely that there would be liability in battery and negligence if the researcher failed to disclose the intervention was experimental or mainly for research purposes:

---

141   Section 2(7). The hierarchy of qualifying relationships is set out at s. 27(4).

142   *Re T (adult: refusal of medical treatment)* [1993] Fam 95 and *Ms B v An NHS Hospital Trust* [2002] 2 All ER 449m respectively and discussed in Chapter 2.

143   *Re T*, ibid., at 663.

144   *Chatterton v Gerson* [1981] QB 432.

145   Discussed *infra* at text accompanying nn. 150–154.

146   *Sidaway v Board of Governors of the Bethlem Royal and the Maudsley Hospital* [1985] AC 871.

147   *Bolam v Friern Management Committee* [1957] 2 All ER 118.

148   *Bolitho (Deceased) v City and Hackney Health Authority* [1998] AC 232.

149   *Pearce v United Bristol Healthcare Trust* [1999] PIQR 53 at 59.

the courts have exhibited a growing tendency in favour of patient's rights to information.[150] In addition, doctors cannot possibly rely on their 'therapeutic privilege' to decide it would not be in a patient's best interests to be made aware of research information.[151] In deciding the appropriate standard of disclosure, courts are likely to take account of national and international guidance, that are very clear on the need for detailed disclosure.[152]

Notwithstanding this trend, difficulties remain in the research context. These include ascertaining what was known about risks at the time the research was conducted and the degree of latitude allowed to health professionals on disclosure by the *Bolam* standard even with the *Bolitho* caveat. Establishing the causal link between the undisclosed risks and the eventuating damage is always problematic. Proving the research subject would have opted not to participate had they been aware of the risks is also difficult.[153] Overall, there is widespread agreement that in the case of non-therapeutic treatment, the level of disclosure should be much higher than that expected with respect to treatment.[154]

Of course, full information needs to be understood, and General Medical Council (GMC) guidance[155] is particularly helpful in this regard. It stipulates that the information that the patient wants or, importantly, 'ought to know', should be 'presented in terms and a form that they can understand' with detailed guidance as to what this might be, including allowing for time to deliberate on the implications of participating in research.[156] The guidance is also useful in that it stipulates that doctors must not put pressure on volunteers to participate in research and must ensure that no real or implied coercion is put on those in a dependant relationship.[157] The GMC has now published specific guidance on ways in which communication with children may be enhanced.[158] It must not be forgotten that professional guidance provides a useful benchmark for the courts to consider in any allegation of breach, and referral to the GMC is an option for the aggrieved

---

150   *Chester v Afshar* [2005] 1 AC 134.

151   *Sidaway supra*, n. 146.

152   See, for example, Declaration of Helsinki 2000, paras 20, 22 and 32.

153   Notwithstanding *Chester v Afshar supra*, n. 150 and discussed in Chapter 6.

154   See, for example the US case of *In Re Cincinnati Radiation Litig* 874 F Supp 796 (SD Ohio 1995) where the failure to disclose risks has even been held to violate their fundamental right to life and liberty under the due process clause of the Fourteenth Amendment of the Constitution which is a more rigorous legal response than the UK's reliance on torts and the Canadian case of *Weiss v Solomon* (1989) Carswell Que 72 discussed in Plomer, *op. cit.*, n. 29 at pp. 55–60

155   GMC, *supra*, n. 36.

156   Ibid., at paras 19–21.

157   Ibid., at paras 8 and 21.

158   GMC, *0–18 years: guidance for doctors*, 2007 which adopts an empowering approach to doctors' dealings with children and young people, including capacity-maximizing provisions in the section on communication (paras 14–21).

who cannot or do not wish to pursue litigation. Breach of this guidance may result in disciplinary action.

The Incompetent Child and Research

For research that falls outside the ambit of the Clinical Trials Regulations, the law affecting incompetent children lies in the common law and, in the case of those aged 16 and 17 years, in the MCA. To allow research on the incapacitated, the voluntary consent provisions of ethical and legal instruments as they apply to competent individuals have to be suspended. As far as the common law position in relation to children is concerned, we know that someone with parental responsibility may consent for the child in relation to treatment[159] provided they act in the child's best interests.[160] Where the child is deemed incompetent, parents will be able to consent to *therapeutic* research, although professional guidelines suggest obtaining the child's assent would be good practice in addition even where experimental treatment is concerned.[161] In *Simms v Simms*,[162] it was held that parents could consent to novel treatment for their 16-year-old daughter suffering from new variant CJD. Given there was no alternative therapy available, it was thought that the treatment might halt the deterioration in her condition and would not increase her suffering, this was seen as entirely reasonable and is consistent with approaches elsewhere.[163] It should be noted that the Institute of Medical Ethics[164] recommends assent of children over seven years old should be obtained for research and that the Medical Research Council[165] has suggested that the child should be able to refuse. Where they are too young to give consent, proceeding in accordance with parental consent should be undertaken with caution. It is certainly arguable that parental consent should be seen as only one factor to take into account. Parental consent may satisfy legal requirements but not be necessarily ethically justifiable: this could arise where the research is still distressing to an incompetent minor, for example. Here, ethical practice would require the researcher not to enter or to withdraw the child.

---

159   S. 3(1) Children Act 1989.

160   *Simms v Simms, supra,* n. 129.

161   E.g. BMA, *supra,* n. 134.

162   [2003] 2 WLR 1465.

163   See Badcott, D. and Wingfield, J., 'Access to experimental drugs: legal and ethical issues of paternalism', (2008) 280 *The Pharmaceutical Journal* 86–7 which describes the successful challenges in the US by the AIDS lobby to regulatory orthodoxy and the 'compassionate use' approach adopted in Canada and Europe: this dispenses with the normally strict requirements of the licensing process.

164   Institute of Medical Ethics, 'Medical Research with Children: Ethics, Law and Practice' (1986) Bull. No. 14, p. 8 usefully defines the acceptable risk levels in relation to death, major and minor complications.

165   Medical Research Council, *Medical Research Involving Children*, 2004.

Probably the area of greatest contention concerns the incompetent child and non-therapeutic *clinical* research. Should parents be able to authorize their child's participation in these cases, or even to a randomized controlled trial, given the child will not necessarily stand to gain directly from this? It is suggested that they should, given the other benefits that could accrue to the child and to society more broadly.[166] In the absence of clear legal guidance in the case of *non-clinical* research, such authorization *may* be legitimate even if the child does not stand to gain directly. Where the courts have been asked to assess whether proposed interventions are in a child's best interests, they *generally* do not consider the wider interests of those caring for the child or of society.[167] These other interests might however be considered where this may have an indirect benefit to the child.[168] In *S v S*, [169] the courts said that interventions may be permissible provided they are not against the child's interests.[170] Although this case could be confined to the facts and has been criticized for the dilution of the best interests' principle,[171] there is at least an argument that such an approach could render non-therapeutic interventions lawful, provided they do not cause significant harm. A child should be involved in any decision-making about non-therapeutic research to the extent of their capacity as an acknowledgement of their autonomous interests. A consideration of their views, where possible, even where they are deemed to be legally incompetent, acknowledges that they still bear interests that should be taken into account.[172] In this way, they gain a psychological benefit that would be in their best interests.[173] On this basis, so-called clinically non-therapeutic interventions where the child does not stand to benefit directly, in the commonly accepted sense, could be viewed as personally therapeutic. Further, it may be possible to rely on other-

---

166   Along the lines discussed *supra*, nn. 127–31 and nn. 54–64 respectively, for example. *Cf.* Kennedy, I. and Grubb, A., *Medical Law*, London, Butterworths, 2000 at p. 1718.

167   *Re D* [1976] 1 All ER 326 and *Re B* [1987] 2 All ER 506 but note the decision in *Re T (wardship: medical treatment)* [1997] 1 WLR 242, where the court did defer, unusually, to the mother's wishes over those of the medical team who considered a liver transplant to be in the child's best interests.

168   *Re Y*, *supra*, n. 130: although this case concerned an incapacitated adult, a very broad reading was given of her best interests so that the benefit of saving her sister's life meant that her mother would maintain more positive contact with her.

169   *S v S* [1972] AC 24 where it was considered that to allow paternity testing against the mother's wishes would not be against the child's interests and was justifiable in the general public interest.

170   Ibid.

171   Fox, M. and McHale, J., 'In Whose Best Interests?' (1997) 60 *Medical Law Review* 700–709.

172   See the discussion in Chapter 3.

173   See e.g. Carnegie United Kingdom Trust, *Measuring The Magic? Evaluating and Researching Young People's Participation in Public Decision-Making*, 2002 and the discussion in Chapter 8 more generally.

regarding ethical approaches to justify proceeding with non-therapeutic research of all kinds where there is minimal risk.[174]

Of course, guidelines have an important role in assisting the courts to interpret the demands of the law. This would especially be the case should a research issue be presented for legal resolution given the absence of significant, relevant case law. The DoH has provided an overarching view of policy and operational matters as well as the broad requirements for ethics approval, where it is noted that children will require information about a proposed research project to be presented in an accessible format and a useful illustrative example is given of how this might be done.[175] Otherwise, detailed ethical guidance is to be found in National Research Ethics Service (NRES) guidance.[176] The intention is that the approach of the Clinical Trials Regulations will apply to all research more generally so that RECs will assess applications on that basis.[177] Nevertheless, NRES notes the position of the Royal College of Paediatrics and Child Health (RCPCH): this has a more permissive approach as well as particular expertise in relation to children. The College takes the view that, provided non-therapeutic research cannot be carried out on adults and an appropriate risk/benefit assessment is undertaken, non-therapeutic research is legal and ethical.[178] The claim that non-therapeutic research

---

174   *Supra*, nn. 54–64, for example. *Cf.* Lewis, P., 'Procedures that are Against the Medical Interest of Incompetent Adults' (2002) 22(4) *Oxford Journal of Legal Studies* 575–618 where she discusses the tension between maintaining the dignity of the incapacitated adult (which is equally relevant to non-competent children) and benefiting society when they are used in non-therapeutic interventions.

175   DoH, *Research Governance Framework for Health and Social Care: Second Edition*, 2005 at p.12 for example, where suggestions are made about how to respond simply to a child's questions such as how long an interview will take, who will be present, whether information will be identifiable, recorded and shared, and whether they can change their mind about participating in the study cited.

176   The NHS Patient Safety Agency, as part of its NRES, developed an Integrated Approval Process for Research in the NHS in 2007. NRES, Consent Forms and Information Sheets: Guidance for Researchers and Reviewers, 2007. There is detailed guidance on the information to be provided to various age groups and parents at pp. 35–47 and a summary of a range of ethical approaches to research with children (including the permissive regime suggested by the RCPCH) at Annex H; available at: http://www.nres.npsa.nhs.uk/rec-community/guidance/#InformedConsent. The guidance suggests the study should include a simple, explanatory title and that there should be an invitation to take part in the research looking at a drug, procedure or medical device (all of which should be described in simple language). The information should explain why the research needs to be done, why they are being asked to participate and how many other children will be involved or have been in the past. Children also need an explanation of what will happen if they participate and their responsibilities if they take part.

177   Central Office for Research Ethics Committees (now NRES) 2004, introduction, para. 3.

178   RCPCH, *supra*, n. 134. The support for the term 'non-therapeutic research' was not accepted by some of the authors of the 1992 version of the Report who saw all research

may be legal appears somewhat categorical. Although there is an ethical argument that may be mounted to support the contention that it is permissible to conduct non-therapeutic research on children, this would only be lawful if accepted by the courts. Parental consent cannot be seen as sufficient to render such research lawful, nor would it be necessarily ethically justifiable. When considering harm, rather than the lack of possible benefit, the RCPCH starts with a broad, cautious statement:

> ... childhood is a vulnerable, formative time, when harms can have serious impact. Potential harms should be assessed carefully before children are put at risk.[179]

Overall, it recognizes that some ethical research may subject children to some harm but that

> ... [t]he attempt to protect children absolutely from the potential harms of research denies any of them the potential benefit.[180]

The RCPCH usefully defines levels of risk. Questioning, observing and measuring children, collecting urine samples but not by aspiration, and using 'spare' blood obtained for clinical use, would all constitute minimal risk. Low risk might involve procedures that cause 'brief pain or tenderness'. For the RCPCH, examples of high risk might include lung or liver biopsy or arterial puncture. The National Institutes of Health's research protocols for paediatric research in the US, describes 'minimal risk' where:

> The probability and magnitude of harm or discomfort anticipated ... are not greater ... than those ordinarily encountered in daily life or during ... routine or psychological examinations or tests.[181]

These terms suggest a helpful, broad framework but ones that require further close contextual definition. 'Mere inconvenience' has been suggested but fails to encompass the 'likelihood' variable.[182] Note must also be made here about

---

as being non-therapeutic nor was there agreement about acceptable levels of risk: personal communication from P. Alderson, Professor of Childhood Studies, Institute of Education, University of London.

179　　Ibid., at p. 178.

180　　Ibid.

181　　45 CFR 46, Subpart D, section 46.404.

182　　Freedman, B., Fuks, A. and Wijer, C., '*In loco parentis*: Minimal Risk as an Ethical Threshold for Research upon Children' in *Ethical and Regulatory Aspects of Clinical Research: Readings and Commentary*, Emanuel, E.J., Crouch, R.A., Arras, J.D., Moreno, J.D. and Grady, C., (eds), Baltimore, John Hopkins University Press, 2004, 247–52 at p. 248.

the lack of agreement amongst researchers about levels of risk.[183] By anchoring research involving a 'minor increase over minimal risk' as a categorical judgment that focuses upon the comparison of new experiences to those of a child's actual, everyday life, some commentators consider that this represents a reasonable approach to such research.[184] Further, the RCPCH states:

> We believe that research in which children are submitted to more than minimal risk with only slight or uncertain benefit deserves serious ethical consideration.[185]

This represents an acceptable position. Part of any ethical consideration should be the extent to which children should be engaged in decision-making about participation in research and the circumstances in which it may be permissible to dispense with consent requirements in the broader interests of society.

The law is still unclear about non-therapeutic research. A court declaration as to the lawfulness or otherwise of any proposed non-therapeutic research where *non-clinical* research is concerned should be sought where there is concern that risks may be more than minimal. Of course, in light of the apparent statutory prohibition on non-therapeutic *clinical* research, the courts may be influenced by this in relation to other types of research: approval may now be less likely to be given.

The Competent Child and Research

In theory, competent children should be able to decide whether they will participate in research or not. However, while the Clinical Trials Regulations are clear that parents must consent to their child's participation in *clinical* research, it is not always as straightforward as it might be in other cases. If a child is over 16 their competence is now determined under the MCA,[186] which largely enshrines the common law approach and this will continue to be used for interpretative purposes. Section 8(1) FLRA also allows 16 and 17 year-olds to consent to therapeutic and diagnostic interventions.[187] If they are under 16, they will need to be *Gillick* competent.[188] For those children under 16, the decision in *Gillick*[189]

---

183   Freedman et al., ibid., at pp. 248–9.

184   Ibid., at p. 250.

185   Ibid., at p. 179. Note that NRES, *supra*, n. 176, at p. 13 seems to suggest that this is at least a possibility in stating that, in long term studies where the child may reach the age of majority, it will have to be considered if it would be appropriate or feasible to obtain their consent to continue in the study or use samples already obtained.

186   S. 2(5).

187   See the discussion in Chapter 2.

188   *Gillick v West Norfolk and Wisbech Area Health* Authority [1986] AC 112. See Chapter 2 for a discussion of *Gillick* competency.

189   Ibid.

in relation to treatment suggests implicitly that those who are deemed to be of sufficient maturity and understanding would be able to consent to participation in *therapeutic* research where they stand to benefit directly from it. This means that they will need to understand fully the implications of what is proposed.

Allowing competent children, of any age, to consent to non-therapeutic research is problematic given Lord Donaldson's remarks in *Re W.*[190] He doubted that 16 and 17 year-olds under section 8(1) FLRA could ever be seen as sufficiently mature and comprehending to consent to a non-therapeutic procedure.[191] This is still likely to be the case notwithstanding the MCA, although a better view might be that the latter prevails on the basis of normal statutory principles.[192] If that is found to be the case, perhaps 16 and 17 year-olds should be able to consent to participation in clinical research under the Clinical Trials Regulations. Research was not considered in *Gillick*, but the same interpretation is likely to apply so that competent children under 16 will also be unable to consent to non-therapeutic research as it is currently conceived.

Guidance from the RCPCH suggests that the consent from a child with 'sufficient understanding and intelligence to understand what is proposed' is adequate.[193] Should a researcher attempt to rely on the consent of a sufficiently mature minor to participate in non-therapeutic research, they may need to employ robust arguments to justify this. Lord Donaldson's views are challenged here on the basis of the empirical evidence and human rights arguments employed in Chapter 2, particularly the right to private and family life under Article 8(1) of the ECHR that protects autonomy. Nevertheless, the practice is likely to be that consent is obtained from the child *and their parents*. The DMD study referred to earlier[194] highlights the difficulties inherent in obtaining consent in the case of potentially competent children. Commitment may be expressed to the idea that their children should decide whether to participate in trials by a parent. However, if this does not concur with their own views, the temptation to intervene and reassert their authority may be irresistible.[195] The ultra-cautious researcher should seek judicial clarification.

Given that there is no direct precedent, in the event of conflict, the courts are likely to refer to professional guidance to set the appropriate ethical standards in

---

190   *Re W (a minor: medical treatment)* [1993] Fam 64.

191   Ibid., 78–9.

192   I.e. later law takes precedence. See Chapter 2 where it was noted that both Acts are currently on the statute books and there may be uncertainty about consents to treatment (and, it may reasonably be assumed, consent to research) that is not personally therapeutic by 16- and 17-year-olds. There is a view that the common law will still be used for this age group because the courts' inherent jurisdiction over minors continues until the age of 18 and applications under this jurisdiction are likely to be more flexible than the MCA system, although the latter is likely to be used as a guide: See Bartlett, P., *Blackstone's Guide to the Mental Capacity* Act, Oxford, Oxford University Press, 2005 at pp. 94–5.

193   RCPCH, *supra*, n. 134 at p. 180.

194   *Supra*, nn. 46–50.

195   Henderson, *supra*, n. 31.

such a situation. These broadly advocate the rights of such children to consent to therapeutic treatment, but some guidelines specifically recommend that the assent of parents should also be obtained unless, in the case of 16- and 17-year-olds, it would not be in the child's best interests for the parents to be informed in this way.[196] This is not the position of the RCPCH's view that a *Gillick* competent child should be able to consent to participation in research with no reference to their parents.[197] There is some concern that researchers may not be equipped to assess competency and perhaps should not in any event because of their vested interest in the project and the possibility of benefiting from the outcome.[198] For those who are cautious about using the consent of a *Gillick* competent child, it is clearly justified when the research may generate significant advantages for the participants while exposing them to relatively minor risks, depending on the phase of the trial: earlier studies may have generated some promising results. It may also be appropriate to rely solely on *Gillick* consent when there is a potential to generate societal benefit and pose minimal risks for the participants but parents object.[199] An example of this may be found in social psychology research that is exploring the effects of networking on children suffering from spinal muscular atrophy. In the US, some parents are blocking access to these sites to prevent their children gaining information about the condition that they think would be harmful.[200]

Autonomy must be genuinely respected and protected against vested, personal interests. With this in mind, *Gillick* competency should be assessed rigorously by someone who has no interest or involvement in the research.[201] There are suggestions that, since we allow mature minors over the age of 14 to make medical decisions, such as seeking contraceptive advice that carries minimal risk, they should certainly be permitted to consent to research that involves no more than minimal risk.[202] This relatively progressive stance is to be welcomed but needs to be more radical. Relying on the age of 14 as a benchmark by which it can reasonably be assumed that children can understand research[203] is unacceptable in the light of empirical evidence of children's abilities generally,[204] and specifically in relation to research, where studies

---

196　DoH, HSG (91)5, para. 4.

197　RCPCH, *supra*, n. 134 at p. 180. See Edwards, *supra*, n. 4 where he has commented that these guidelines are out of step with the Declaration of Helsinki, the cornerstone of approaches to be taken to ensure the protection of research subjects.

198　Hunter, D. and Pierscionek, B.K., 'Children, Gillick competency and consent for involvement in research' (2007) 33(11) *Journal of Medical Ethics* 659–62.

199　Ibid.

200　Personal communication from Dr. S. Woods, member of the TREAT (*supra*, n. 39) Ethics Committee.

201　Ibid.

202　Leikin, S., 'Minors' Assent, Consent, or Dissent to Medical Research' in Emmanuel 252–8 at pp. 257–8.

203　Wendler, D.S., 'Assent in paediatric research: theoretical and practical considerations', (2006) 32 *Journal of Medical Ethics* 229–34.

204　See Chapter 3.

indicate that children as young as nine-years-old may well have sufficient cognitive capacity to be involved in decision-making about participation in most research.[205] Interestingly, NRES does consider the possibility that a child may be deemed *Gillick* competent from the age of 10 upwards.[206]

In view of Lord Donaldson's remarks in *Re W*, it is probable that researchers will prefer to gain the assent of parents in such a case as recommended more generally by professional guidelines.[207] Even where parental assent is forthcoming, it is considered such research should only be undertaken where the risk is minimal.[208] Chapter 2 illustrates that the HRA offers opportunities to challenge the boundaries of the common law, but it is also worth noting again that Article 3 of the ECHR, the right, *inter alia*, not to be subject to inhuman and degrading treatment, is particularly pertinent to the issue of research. Strasbourg case law suggests that only the more extreme examples of inhuman and degrading treatment will breach Article 3.[209] In *R (Burke) v GMC*,[210] Munby J. noted that dignity is protected by Article 3[211] and there needs to be an enhanced degree of protection and increased vigilance in reviewing whether the Convention has been complied with in the case of the vulnerable.[212] Further, there may be incompatibility with the standards imposed by Article 3 in the protection of fundamental human dignity, even though that person may not be able, or capable of, pointing to any specific ill-effects.[213]

In Munby J.'s view, treatment is capable of being 'degrading' within the meaning of Article 3, whether or not it arouses feelings of fear, anguish or inferiority in the victim as judged by right-thinking bystanders.[214] By analogy, similar arguments can be made with respect to research. Currently, absence of appropriate consent to research may constitute a breach of Article 3, particularly if this is then followed by very significant levels of suffering and/or humiliation. An example of the latter might arise in some obesity studies that involve classroom work.[215]

There is a need to be alert to the fact that it is possible to interfere with the right to private and family life under Article 8(1) ECHR under Article 8(2), broadly in

---

205   Leikin, *supra*, n. 202 at p. 256.

206   NRES, *supra*, at n. 176 at p. 42: 'It is unwise to use this for children younger than ten years of age' referring to the use of the *Gillick* test.

207   Annex H.

208   Along the lines suggested by the RCPCH, *supra*, at n. 134. See also the Institute of Medical Ethics, *supra*, at n. 164.

209   *Z v UK* [2001] 2 FLR 612.

210   [2004] EWHC 1879 (Admin) where Munby J. provides a useful survey of relevant cases, notwithstanding the overruling of his substantive decision.

211   At para. 63.

212   At para. 67.

213   Ibid.

214   At para. 149.

215   *Supra*, n. 200.

the interests of others.[216] This can undermine its potential strength in supporting children's autonomy if not cautiously employed. However, it does provide a useful device with which to consider whether it may be legitimate to override autonomy in some compelling circumstances. A prime example is where the competent child refuses to consent to research that promises great benefit to others with minimal risk to themselves. So, for example, where there is already a sample of blood, it should be possible to use it without further consent.[217] NRES guidance[218] seems to suggest that this is at least a possibility. It states that, in long term studies where the child may reach the age of majority, it will have to be considered if it would be appropriate or feasible to obtain their consent to continue in the study or use samples already obtained.[219] The more restrictive instruments, such as the Clinical Trial Regulations where relevant, seem to preclude this possibility: although a child's refusal to participate in research or objection to continuing participation merely needs to be considered by the researcher,[220] the interests of the individual should always prevail over science and society.[221] Competent children should be able to make such decisions. Given its importance, consideration should be given to the need for legislative amendment so that its substantive content is in line with more permissive ethical guidance and the law in other jurisdictions. The less restrictive instruments, such as the Biomedicine Research Protocol, have sufficiently flexible wording to allow the tension between individual autonomy and wider interests to be explored. Any changes should merely be to ensure that that each argument is given a fair hearing. The human rights approach as provided by the HRA offers a mechanism with which to undertake this exercise.

Conclusion

The fact that there are some conditions that only affect children and that a significant proportion of drugs prescribed for them are untested on the paediatric population, means that research for children should be increased urgently. This must be carried out within strictly circumscribed limits to ensure children are not exposed to undue

---

216   The Oviedo Convention may be used as a means of interpreting the ECHR and an insufficient disclosure of risk could amount to breaches of Articles 5, 16 and 17. These broadly accord with the traditional notions of therapeutic and non-therapeutic research on those unable to consent; the latter category requires additional authorization from a legal representative in writing and carrying only minimal risk and burden on the incapacitated participant.

217   RCPCH, *supra,* n. 134, at p. 179.

218   NRES, *supra,* at n. 176, at p. 13.

219   Ibid.

220   Part 4, para. 7.

221   Part 4, para. 16. However, para. 5 refers to the right of the person with legal responsibility for the child to be able to withdraw the child from the research at any time however.

risk. However, safeguards to ensure ethical research should not be so rigorous that they make it impossible to recruit sufficient numbers of children for a study to be feasible, and children should be as fully engaged in the decision-making processes as possible, otherwise they will remain in the bind of double jeopardy.

Instruments, such as the Clinical Trial Regulations, should be interpreted robustly in their assessment of what is meant by 'direct benefit', so that it includes the psychological benefit of taking part in research, even where no clinical benefit is likely to accrue. The fact that those with legal responsibility for the child must assent to any participation is to be regretted. Who consents to any research should actually be determined on the basis of a robust assessment of *Gillick* competence. For those who believe the consent or assent of parents provides an additional and useful safeguard for child participants, the child is either competent or they are not. In the former case, they should have the definitive say in whether they participate in research not. Whether the research is ethical or not is for the REC to determine. The Clinical Trials Regulations should be amended to accommodate this position.

It is hoped that, with appropriate education about the importance of contributing to research programmes, competent children or parents will agree to participate to further the interests of society. Where, despite best endeavours no consent to take part is forthcoming, this should be respected. There may be exceptional circumstances where the burden and risk of participation is minimal but the potential benefits to society are great. Although there will always be disagreement about such notions as 'minimal risk', independent scrutiny of proposals from experts in a relatively relaxed framework might be one adopted by RECs in the UK. We already have some clear guidance as to what this might be.[222] Where a committee experiences difficulty as it grapples with the ethical issues raised by complex new technologies, a national expert body may be able to assist. For example, the Gene Therapy Advisory Committee in the context of genetic research, could be the source of such advice. The problem with both RECs and national bodies is the distance between them and potential research participants if they try to fulfill their gatekeeper role for research participation decisions. For this reason, clinicians who have ongoing relationships with patients and families should be routinely involved. Where children are concerned, it should be mandatory that a paediatrician and/or other relevant professional should be called upon to advise RECs. They are used to considering the best interests of children and parents want clinicians to have this role.[223] Brazier[224] has also argued that judges should not be the final arbiters of acceptable practice. She suggests the establishment of a code of practice underpinned with statutory force detailing when consent can be given and by whom, and overseen by independent expert scrutiny.[225]

---

222 RCPCH, *supra*, n. 134.
223 Henderson, *supra*, n. 31.
224 Brazier, M., *Medicine, Patients and the Law*, London, Penguin, 2003.
225 Ibid. at p. 408.

The proposal that it is acceptable to dispense with consent has particular force in those circumstances where there is no physical invasion and likely to be minimal psychological distress. This will be a matter for RECs to decide where the law permits. Alternatively, they may have to consider whether to accept parental consent where it is not forthcoming from a competent child or an incompetent child objects. The arguments for and against overriding the need for consent must be thoroughly explored and a justifiable conclusion reached. Using the balancing approach provided by the HRA should result in an ethical resolution. Where the law is inflexible and does not provide a competent child with the opportunity to consent to all types of research, or where there is no consideration of whether it is legitimate to interfere with their decision, it should be amended. The proposals contained in this chapter seek to strike an acceptable balance between the appropriate protection and empowerment of children, together with the needs of the research community by assuming everyone wishes to make a contribution to the overall welfare of wider society.

Post-script

There is a view that research cannot be justified for such psychological benefits because these cannot be assured or direct and they are not the purpose of the research (which is to collect, analyse and report data), and so it would be unethical to use them as an incentive: personal communication from P. Alderson, Professor of Childhood Studies, Institute of Education, University of London. Some of these points could be addressed by careful, skilled exploration of the issues with the prospective child research participant. We should not also presume that research is a burden or will inevitably have negative side-effects because this is not known either. As a matter of empirical fact, there is evidence that children wish to be involved in research, can be altruistic and are capable of understanding quite complex medical issues as discussed at nn. 8, 9 and 10 and have found participation in research beneficial: see, e.g. the Avon Longitudinal Study of Parents and Children project discussed at n. 44.

Chapter 8

Children's Participation and Foundation Trusts: Some New Opportunities?*

Introduction

As we have seen, the call for children to be allowed to make decisions for themselves in recognition of their autonomous interests is not new in the health care setting.[1] The suggestion in this chapter that they should be offered opportunities to make other-affecting decisions through involvement in health policy formulation is a relatively recent phenomenon, but one that can be supported by human rights arguments. It is accepted in other contexts that policies that affect children will be improved by involving a wide range of participants in general decision-making and there are many examples elsewhere of children being meaningfully engaged in decision-making, but there are few examples in the health care context. Where there is participation, it tends to be at a consultative rather than at a decision-making level in any real sense. Although NHS institutions may be willing to adopt child-participation initiatives, many lack confidence in their ability to do it properly. The establishment of the new NHS Foundation Trusts, requiring the adoption of governing bodies representing broad constituencies of patients, the public and other stakeholders, means that this involvement can be expedited. The learning curve is likely to be steep, but there is considerable excitement that efforts to grant young people a greater role in determining policy will reap considerable rewards for everyone. This chapter argues that the current age restriction on Foundation Trust governors unnecessarily undermines children's human rights, is indefensible in law and weakens health care policies. There is a theoretical case for involvement and the governance arrangements for Foundation Trusts offer a model for such engagement.

Children possess a human right to participation, which has received recognition in international quasi-legal instruments, and, more recently, in UK policy

---

*A version of this chapter first appeared as Hagger, L., 'Foundation Trusts And Children's Participation: Some New Opportunities?', (2007) (8) 4 *Medical Law International* 325–48 and is reprinted with the kind permission of A B Academic Publishers.

1   See, e.g. Hagger, L., 'Some Implications of the Human Rights Act 1998 for the Medical Treatment of Children' (2003) 6 *Medical Law International* 25–51 and the discussion throughout this book.

documents and legislation.[2] The child's right to participate is further strengthened by the Human Rights Act 1998 (HRA). There is a general case for a wide range of participants in policy-making, rather than leaving professionals to determine the policy. Where policies affect children, they should be based on children's and young people's narratives of their lived experiences so that they are more relevant to their needs. Inclusion of children recognizes their autonomous interests and the process itself enhances their competence to participate more broadly as they gain confidence and knowledge.[3]

Even though there is a statutory requirement to obtain the views of children in the planning, delivery and evaluation of services,[4] if the child's voice has been heard at all it is primarily through that child's parents and carers.[5] There are examples elsewhere of children's participation, but such involvement tends to be limited.[6] The position is the same in the health care setting in that children's participation tends to take the form of parental views.[7] The development of health care services is inclined to take the form of adaptation of national policies by managers and local clinicians.[8] It could be argued that children can have influence through, for example, in focus groups and questionnaires, but this is no substitute for being more directly influential in decision-making bodies.[9]

Monitor, the regulatory body for Foundation Trusts, is currently resisting the call for children under 16 to be allowed to adopt some of these enhanced participatory roles on the basis that the issues under consideration are potentially

---

2   The United Nations Convention on the Rights of the Child 1989, Department for Education and Skills (DfES) and Department of Health (DoH), *Every Child Matters: Change for Children* – joint planning and commissioning framework for children, young people and maternity services, 2004 and the Children Act 2004, respectively.

3   Carnegie United Kingdom Trust (2002) Measuring the Magic? Evaluating and researching young people's participation in public decision-making at p. 2 and Yates, M. and Jouniss, J., (eds) *Roots of Civic Identity: International Perspectives on Community Service and Activism in Youth* (Cambridge, Cambridge University Press, 1998) *passim*.

4   *Every Child Matters supra*, n. 2. The extent of this compliance is one of the measures used by the Healthcare Commission when it inspects NHS organizations and ranks their standards.

5   National Children's Bureau (2005) *Children and Young People's Views on Health and Health Services: A Review of the Evidence*.

6   Hill, M., Davis, J., Prout, A. and Tisdall, K., 'Moving the Participation Agenda Forward' (2004) 18 *Children and Society* 77–96 *passim*.

7   *Supra*, n. 5.

8   See, for example, the implementation of the NHS National Plan (DoH, 2000): the author has 20 years' experience in the NHS as a member of the now defunct Community Health Councils and as a Non-executive Director of NHS Trusts, latterly as Chairperson of the Sheffield Children's NHS Foundation Trust.

9   *Supra*, n. 5.

too serious.[10] This is an unsustainable position for the reasons that will be discussed below. One argument worth highlighting at the outset is that children have a stake in the future development of health services. To limit their involvement is short-sighted and legally challengeable.[11] Of course, there are examples where children have no rights even where their present and future interests are at stake,[12] but it will be argued that health care policy-making presents a special case.

This chapter will seek first to examine why participatory rights, particularly those of children, are important before examining the legal framework that supports these claims, some are theoretical models of participation and some practical illustrations of good participatory practice. It will be argued that the new governance structures for Foundation Trusts present an opportunity to expand children's involvement which should be embraced by their regulatory body by allowing them to become governors.

The Rationale for Participation

There are strong normative arguments that citizens have a democratic right to be involved in decisions that affect their lives[13] and such involvement can legitimize decisions made.[14] Exclusion may hamper regulation because of resistance.[15] Accountability is largely achieved through the constitution of decision-making bodies and/or public consultation. There is evident commitment by the Government to have greater public involvement in determining national and local policies by increasing the numbers of participants in formal decision-making roles at all levels.[16] The Government empowers patients further with the emphasis on

---

10   Moyes, W., 'The kids are alright, but are they ready to be governors?' 31 August 2006 *Health Service Journal* and personal communication from W. Moyes, Executive Chairman of Monitor, Foundation Trusts' regulatory body, to the author.

11   Discussed *infra*, at nn. 129–30.

12   Exclusion from Parliamentary elections would be a case in point.

13   Daniels, N. and Sabin, J., 'Limits to health care: fair procedures, democratic deliberation, and the legitimacy problem for insurers.' (1997) 26(4) *Philosophy and Public Affairs* 303–50 and Doyal, L., 'Rationing within the NHS should be explicit: The case for.' 314 *BMJ* 1114–18.

14   Ham, C., 'Priority setting in the NHS: Reports from six districts' (1993) 307 (6901) *BMJ* 435–8.

15   Mullen, P.M., 'Public involvement in health care priority setting: are the methods appropriate and valid?' in Coulter, A. and Ham, C., (eds) *The Global Challenge of Health Care Rationing*, Buckingham, Philadelphia, Open University Press, 2000.

16   See, for example, the recent consultation exercises discussed *infra* at n. 30 and the inclusion of lay representatives on bodies such as the National Institute for Clinical Excellence discussed by Syrett, K., 'Nice Work? Rationing, Review and the 'Legitimacy Problem' in the New NHS' (2002) 10 *Medical Law Review* 1–27.

enhanced choice initiatives.[17] This inclusive approach helps to make the process more explicit, enhancing the public's trust as well as using their perspective to inform decisions made.

Acceptable justifications for decisions must be accessible to the public.[18] Given our pluralistic society, consensus will be difficult to achieve. Nevertheless, decisions need to be morally defensible not least because this makes them more widely acceptable.[19] As part of broad public deliberation, ethically justifiable decisions should be available in addition to the information provided on options and performance. Participation is seen as being essential to legitimate decision-making[20] and this also offers the opportunity of educating the public.

Jasanoff[21]argues that the most powerful argument for wider lay participation in decision-making is not that the public possesses some mysterious reservoir of lay expertise that is equal to the knowledge of experts, but that all decisions should, as far as possible, be public in democratic societies. She characterizes the public's role as one of 'critical supervision':

> [E]xpertise is constituted within institutions, and powerful institutions can perpetuate unjust and unfounded ways of looking at the world unless they are continually put before the gaze of laypersons who will declare when the emperor has no clothes.[22]

Overall, whatever approach is adopted, a fair process of decision-making needs to be established noting that unfair and predictable decisions are more acceptable than those that are unfair and unpredictable.[23] The involvement of laypersons helps to make the process fairer by holding those responsible for establishing the decision-making process to account.

If we accept only some of the reasons outlined above and note the international examples of good practice,[24] the case for public involvement is persuasive and it is argued below that such involvement should include children.[25] However, concerns may remain about the legitimacy of public involvement. These include

---

17   DoH (2006): www.dh.gov.uk/PolicyAndGuidance/PatientChoice/fs/en.

18   Daniels, N., 'Accountability for Reasonableness in Private and Public Health Insurance' in Coulter and Ham, *supra*, n. 15.

19   Ibid. and Norheim, O.F., 'Increasing demand for accountability: is there a professional response?' at p. 227 in Coulter and Ham *supra* n. 15.

20   *Supra*, n. 14.

21   Jasanoff, S., 'Breaking the waves in science studies: comment on Collind, H.M. and Evans, R., "The Third Wave of Science Studies"' (2003) 33 *Social Studies of Science* 389–400.

22   Ibid., at p. 398.

23   Hope, A., 'Resource allocation decision-making: reasons and process', UK Clinical Ethics Network 5th Annual Conference, May 2005.

24   Coulter and Ham *supra*, n. 15 *passim*.

25   *Infra*, at nn. 33–48.

questions about whether participants are representative and whether that always matters, lack of expertise in a context populated by professionals, risk of populism, compensatory attempts to balance the lack of democracy elsewhere in the system, the lack of democracy in an appointments-based rather than an electoral system and the risk that those involved may be unrepresentative because of a reluctance of some groups to participate.[26] There is always disquiet that those individuals who are empowered, educated, vocal and assertive are more likely to have their issues addressed than more vulnerable members of society.[27] Being alert to these pitfalls is essential and it will be necessary to attend to, *inter alia,* empirical research that highlights methods to engage with all relevant parties to the best effect.

In the UK, apart from the limited participation within the National Institute for Health and Clinical Excellence,[28] participation has been mainly at a local level.[29] There has been increased public involvement in relation to the location of health service provision and non-medical matters such as appointment systems, but little public role in the larger question of determining the scope of the NHS.[30] Health authorities have used a multiplicity of methods to gather public views and values and also to enhance understanding about the need to set priorities.[31] The Healthcare Commission is building networks of community-based and user groups through consultation processes so that they can engage with local people on issues that concern them.[32] The Citizen's Summit of one thousand people in October 2005 was organized on behalf of the Government following a large-scale questionnaire exercise, but the range of issues was limited and cynics might believe that they were manipulated to suit the political agenda. More recently, regional citizen's juries were held to discuss developments in health care.[33] Valuable though these exercises might be, they are unlikely to produce a representative and accountable infrastructure for public and patient involvement and suspicions remain that they are somewhat tokenistic.[34] Public involvement remains limited because it is largely

26   *Supra*, n. 15 at p. 164.

27   Hurst, S., 'The views of primary care physicians on ethical issues in resource allocation: A European Comparison' UK Clinical Ethics Network 5th Annual Conference, 2005. There is an expectation that Foundation Trusts will attempt to reach 'hard to reach groups': DoH, *A Guide to Foundation Trusts*, 2002, *passim.*

28   Syrett *supra*, n. 16.

29   Newdick, C., *Who Should We Treat? Rights, Rationing and Resources in the NHS*, Oxford, Oxford University Press, 2005, at pp. 42–3.

30   Ibid., at pp. 211–20.

31   Ibid.

32   Healthcare Commission, Annual Report, 2005.

33   http://www.timesonline.co.uk/tol/comment/columnists/alice_miles/article 2388130.ece.

34   Ibid.

locally-based and restricted to consultation rather than actual decision-making. In particular, there is no public engagement in questions of resource allocation.[35]

There are personal benefits to individuals from participation, including the personal satisfaction of making a contribution and any direct benefit that may be conferred from relevant policies. Children gain additional benefits. Engaging children in all types of decision-making to the extent of their capacity recognizes their autonomous interests and the process itself enhances their competence to participate. Meaningful involvement increases:

> ... confidence, self-belief, knowledge, understanding and changed attitudes, skills and education attainment.[36]

This point is particularly important in relation to children from deprived backgrounds who may not have a tradition of engaging in participatory activities so strategies are needed to encourage these children to participate. Interestingly, empirical studies demonstrate that young people may become involved initially because they perceive personal advantages in doing so, but take a broader view over time. Young participants begin to see the wider benefits to the community of their enhanced decision-making skills.[37]

Notwithstanding these encouraging developments, the voices of children generally remain excluded and participation activities are under-resourced: children are still likely to be passive recipients rather than true partners in participatory activities.[38] Children do care about policies as they affect them and even quite young children can articulate their views.[39] They can develop to the point where they also care about issues by which they are less directly affected[40] so they must be seen as full partners listened to as they are now, as possessors of valid perspectives and rights to be heard and not merely because of the person they will become.

---

35 Edgar, W., 'Rationing Health Care in New Zealand – How the Public Has a Say' in Coulter and Ham, *supra*, n. 12 shows that public participation in the bigger health questions is feasible even within a restricted health budget.

36 Carnegie *supra* n. 3 at p. 2.

37 Koller D., '"Making a Difference": Youth Participation in Education and Health Care' presentation at the University of Sheffield, Centre for the Study of Childhood and Youth: 'Childhood and Youth: Choice and Participation International Conference', 2006; see, also, Cherrill, J., Hudson, H., Cocking, C. Unsworth, V., Franck, L., McIntyre, J. and Choonara, I., 'Clinical trials: the viewpoint of children', (2007) 92 *Archives of Diseases in Childhood*, 712–13 where the authors cite evidence of children's willingness to behave in altruistically in relation to research.

38 Davis, J.M. and Watson, N., 'Disabled children's rights in everyday life: problematizing notions of competency and promotion self-empowerment' (2000) 8 *International Journal of Children's Rights* 211–28.

39 Borland, M., Laybourn, A., Hill, M. and Brown, J., *Middle Childhood*, London, Jessica Kingsley, 1998.

40 *Supra*, at. n. 37.

Although there are examples of children being consulted about health care issues,[41] this does not involve decision-making in its fullest sense. The mainstreaming of children's health needs into public health debates is vital to make children visible and integrated, rather than marginalised, isolated or ignored. Gaining children's perspectives of the services they use or may use in the future can give invaluable insight into the best means of enhancing the quality of interventions, particularly where they are used on a long-term basis. It is increasingly apparent that almost all children, whatever their age and circumstances, can provide valuable perceptions that can improve clinical care.[42] With appropriate techniques, children as young as four can make helpful comments about their experiences of health services[43] and like to be involved in this way.[44] More importantly, children's views about health and health services differ from those of their parents and the professionals with whom they are in contact.[45] For these reasons alone, children's views should be taken into account, together with those of their parents, carers and professionals, in order to gain a different perspective acknowledging they are likely to know best about their needs and feelings.

A pragmatic rationale would include current concerns about health conditions such as obesity, substance abuse and mental and sexual health. These conditions are costly now and, in the case of obesity in particular, will have huge implications for the NHS given the propensity for the later onset of other diseases such as diabetes and heart conditions. Involving children fully in the formulation of relevant policies is more likely to result in effective policies to which children will adhere.[46] Such engagement should be carried out against 'an explicit and shared normative framework against which to assess existing laws, policies, programmes or social relations',[47] which the United Nations Convention on the Rights of the

---

41   *Supra*, n. 5 at pp. 6–7.

42   Chesney, M., Lindeke, L., Johnson, L., Jukkala, A. and Lynch, S., 'Comparison of child and parent satisfaction ratings of ambulatory pediatric subspeciality care' (2005) 19(4) *Journal of Pediatric Health Care* 221–9.

43   Curtis, K., Liabo, K., Roberts, H. and Barker, M., 'Consulted but not heard: a qualitative study of young people's views of their local health service.' (2004) 7(2) *Health Expectations* 149–156.

44   Elliott, E. and Watson, A., 'But the doctors aren't your mum' (1997) 30 *Health Matters* 8–9.

45   Meade, J.A., Lumley, M.A. and Casey, R.J., 'Stress, emotional skill and illnesses in children: The importance of distinguishing between children's and parents' report of illness' (2001) 42(3) *Journal of Psychology and Psychiatry* 405–12, Chesney, *supra* n. 42 and Percy-Smith, B., Burns, D., Weil, S. and Walsh, D., (2003) *Mind the Gap: Healthy Futures for Young People in Hounslow*, University of the West of England and Hounslow Community Health Council, respectively.

46   *Supra*, n. 5.

47   Piron, L., 'Rights-based Approaches and Bilateral Aid Agencies: More than a Metaphor?' (2005) 36(1) *IDS Bulletin*, 19.

Child (UNCRC) can fulfil given its wide acceptance and recognition that children have entitlements.[48] This is explored further below.[49]

The inception of Foundation Trusts has highlighted an appetite to engage with the public, and, in some cases, younger people, where this is seen as relevant, but it involves considerable effort, not least to change cultural attitudes. The Government's commitment to enhanced user-involvement generally will aid the cause of specifically engaging young people[50] and, in the context of policy formulation, some organizations have developed a track record in working with participants who are not expected to cope with traditional, formal approaches.[51] Experience has shown that strategies can be developed to ensure fuller participation in more meaningful decision-making[52] and a wide range of participants will mean better policies that affect children. The involvement of young people is essential to increase knowledge about their views and needs in order to enhance the quality of decision-making that affects them. Not only are they more likely to act in accordance with the decisions made, but will have a perspective other participants may not have. This has particular resonance where children suffer from long-term conditions.[53]

In sum,

> ... in order for children's rights to become a social and legal reality, they must be firmly rooted in social policies that command the support of the adult population.[54]

These are clearly desirable outcomes in an era in which the call for greater involvement of citizens and consumers has become commonplace. However, the specific engagement of children in the citizenship agenda has been encouraged on

---

48   Tobin, J., 'Beyond the Supermarket Shelf: Using a Rights Based Approach to Address Children's Health Needs' 14 (2006) *The International Journal of Children's Rights* 275–306.

49   *Infra*, n. 64–76.

50   See, for example, DoH, *Creating a patient-led NHS: Delivering the NHS Improvement Plan*, 2005.

51   *Infra*, at nn. 100–120.

52   Badham, B., 'Participation – for a Change: Disabled Young People Lead the Way' (2004) 18 *Children and Society* 143–154.

53   Eiser, C., 'Changes in understanding of illness as the child grows' (1985) 60 *Archives of Disease in Childhood* 489–92; Fielding, D. and Duff, A., 'Compliance with treatment protocol: interventions for children with chronic illness' 80 *Archives of Disease in Childhood* 196–200; Alderson, P. and Montgomery, J., 'What about me?' (1996) *Health Service Journal* 22–4.

54   James, A. and James, A.L., *Constructing Childhood: Theory, Policy and Social Practice*, Basingstoke, Palgrave: Macmillan, 2004.

the basis of preparing them for the appropriate exercise of adult rights, rather than to empower them to exercise political influence in their own right.[55]

Earlier it was noted that there are examples where children have no rights, even where their present and future interests are at stake such as in Parliamentary elections.[56] The age restrictions for this and other activities such as marrying and purchasing and consuming alcohol may be seen as arbitrary, but a pragmatic response to try and ensure children do not make foolish decisions. Where health and life choices are concerned, the aim is to protect what Feinberg would call the child's right to an 'open future'.[57] Using age as a rough assessment of competence here is generally acceptable since assessing individual abilities is clearly not practicable. The lack of wide experience and political activity could be used to justify the lack of suffrage in democratic processes, but it was suggested earlier that health care policy-making is a different case. Here, children do have experience, as patients or users of health services, with particular insights and perspectives not shared by adults. This unique perspective will be lost if we insist they must reach a certain age because children are normally transferred to adult services on attaining the age of 16.[58]

In addition, health may be singled out as a special case because of its importance as a condition of achieving autonomy. It is a domain in which children can act autonomously when they achieve sufficient maturity and understanding in that they can consent to medical interventions for themselves.[59] While they may be unable to refuse life-saving treatment,[60] allowing them rights to participate in general decision-making is more difficult to deny when such vivid implications do not apply. Public interest contentions in not allowing children to make flawed decisions that may affect others are weak when reality would dictate that these would be made in conjunction with adults (not necessarily wise) and with the support of, *inter alia*, full, accessible information and mentors.[61]

---

55   *Supra*, n. 6.

56   *Supra*, n. 12.

57   Feinberg, J., 'The Child's Right to an Open Future' Reprinted in Feinberg, J., *Freedom and Fulfillment: Philosophical Essays*, Princeton, Princeton University Press, 1992, at pp. 76–98.

58   It is worth noting that Article 23(1) of the UNCRC, discussed *infra* at n. 68 includes a recognition that a mentally or physically disabled child has the right to have their active participation in the community facilitated.

59   *Gillick v West Norfolk and Wisbech Area Health Authority* [1985] 3 All ER 402.

60   *Re R (a minor) (wardship: consent to medical treatment)* [1991] 4 All ER 177, CA and *Re W (a minor) (wardship: consent to medical treatment)* [1993] Fam 64.

61   Governors in Foundation Trusts contribute to the setting of strategy in conjunction with boards of directors who take account of views expressed but make the final decisions. Dissatisfaction with any decisions taken may mean removal of non-executive directors by governors and, in practice, any cuts in services would require the sanction of Monitor. Foundation Trusts are discussed in more detail *infra* at n. 123–42.

Allowing participation in this way can be an important staging post on the route to citizenship.[62] Part of the notion of citizenship must surely be the idea that we all contribute to the public good of the NHS. It is a reasonable expectation within any developed society to receive the best medical treatment and care. The *raison d'être* of the NHS is to provide this. It is in everyone's interests that health care delivery is of the highest possible standard and participation in determining health policies can help to achieve this.[63] Encouraging children to participate in this way can improve the policies that affect them and improve their ability to contribute more generally, now and in the future. Managed well, the involvement can be the springboard to more effective, broader participatory activities.

The Legal Framework

In the context of children's involvement in policy making, it is worth noting again that children as persons are entitled to the rights that attach to persons, although these are constrained as a result of their dependent nature.[64] The UNCRC is the global human rights instrument relating to children. It confirms that children have human rights and attempts to disaggregate these from the rights of families and the state by ensuring they are seen as independent actors who should be given every opportunity to make decisions. As indicated, these rights are limited by capacity and the cultural context, but States are obliged to treat children's interests as a primary consideration in all actions concerning them[65] and to undertake measures to implement children's economic, social and cultural rights to the extent of their available resources.[66] The United Kingdom acceded to the Convention in 1991. Although the UNCRC underpins the UK's legal framework, it is arguable that some of its key Articles are not fully reflected in law, policy and practice, in common with most other jurisdictions.[67]

---

62   *Supra* at n. 6. See also the discussion in Chapter 5 on the citizenship agenda.

63   For a further discussion of how this argument runs in relation to research see Harris, J. and Woods, S., 'What are the responsibilities of the individual when participating in medical research? in: L. Doyal and J. Tobias (eds), *Informed Consent in Medical Research.* (London: BMJ Books, 2000) 286–92.

64   Discussed *supra*, n. 57 as an example.

65   Article 3.

66   Article 4.

67   UN Committee on the Rights of the Child (2002) *Concluding Observations of the Committee on the Rights of the Child: United Kingdom of Great Britain and Northern Ireland* http://www.unhchr.ch/html/menu2/6/crc/doc/past.htm; Joint Committee on Human Rights, House of Lords/House of Commons, Westminster, 2003. *The Government's Response to the Committee's Tenth Report of Session 2002–3 on the UN Convention on the Rights of the Child.* Eighteenth Report of Session 2002–3. HL Paper 187/HC 1279; Children's Rights Alliance for England, 2003. *Convention on the Rights of the Child:*

The UNCRC is seen as pivotal in the call for greater recognition of children and young people not only to express their views but also to have them acted upon. Article 12, in particular, may be viewed as the basis for arguing that children and young people have the right to be consulted about issues that affect them directly or indirectly:

> ... the child who is capable of forming his or her own views has the right to express those views freely in all matters affecting the child: the views of the child being given due weight in accordance with age and maturity of the child... the child shall in particular be provided with the opportunity to be heard in any surgical or administrative proceedings affecting the child directly; or through a representative body.

Article 13 also has some relevance here:

> ... the child shall have the right to freedom of expression, (including) freedom to seek, receive and impart information and ideas regardless of frontiers, either orally, in writing or in print, in the form of art, or through any other media of the child's choice.

While local differences may require flexible interpretation, some variations are wholly unacceptable particularly where this indicates a lack of adherence to the Convention's principles at all. These Articles must be read widely so that there is also a right to be involved in policy making that may not benefit children so directly in the spirit illustrated by Article 23(1) which states that:

> States Parties recognize that a mentally or physically disabled child should enjoy a full and decent life, in conditions which ensure dignity, promote self-reliance and *facilitate the child's active participation in the community.*[68]

To do otherwise would be inconsistent. Of course, the language used here suggests opportunities should be optimized for engagement in civic society only to the extent possible. The UNCRC can provide an agenda and has been used as a tool to justify children's participation.[69]

Policy documents, written with the UNCRC in mind, now specifically note making a positive contribution as one of the five key policy objectives of the Government[70] and this is now enshrined in legislation. The Children Act 2004,

---

Review of UK Government Action on 2003 Concluding Observations of the UN Committee on the Rights of the Child: London.

68   Author's emphasis.

69   *Supra*, n. 52.

70   *Every Child Matters*, *op. cit.*, at n. 2 establishes being healthy, staying safe, enjoying and achieving, making a positive contribution and securing economic well-being

inter alia, established the office of the Children's Commissioner to give a national voice to all children and young people, especially the disadvantaged and the vulnerable. The Commissioner has an independent remit to promote awareness of views and interests of children within the framework of the five *Every Child Matters* outcomes[71] that complement the rights under the UNCRC to which the Commissioner must have regard.[72] The Act refers to 'the contribution made by children to society'[73] and 'social and economic well-being'[74] respectively as being key concerns of this role both of which necessarily import notions of civic participation. While the Children's Commissioner is an encouraging development, the office is still rather new to be able to assess its overall impact. As will be demonstrated, the Office has yet to take up the cause of children in health care policy-making.[75]

The lack of enforcement measures, that undermines the effect of the UNCRC, may be counteracted to some extent by the European Convention on Human Rights (ECHR)[76] even though it is not specifically concerned with the rights of children. It is the first international instrument of its kind to provide the mechanisms for its own interpretation and enforcement. Notwithstanding its focus on human rights rather than children's rights *per se*, it has had an impact on important children's issues throughout Europe, but there is still little domestic case law acknowledging that children have recognizable rights under its auspices although there are some cautious judicial comments that are encouraging as far as self-regarding decision-making is concerned[77] and anecdotal evidence suggests that pockets of good practice abound,[78] but that it is inconsistent.[79]

---

as important policy outcomes.

71   Ibid.

72   S. 2(11) Children Act 2004.

73   S. 2(3)(d).

74   S. 2(3)(e).

75   Discussed *infra*, at n. 141.

76   Fortin, J., *Children's Rights and the Developing Law*, (2nd ed.), London, Lexis-Nexis, 2003, Chapter 2.

77   Ibid., and Fortin, J., 'Accommodating Children's Rights in a Post Human Rights Act Era' (2006) 69(3) *Modern Law Review* 299–326 and see the discussion in Chapter 2 regarding *Mabon v Mabon and others* [2005] 3 W.L.R. 460, *Re Roddy (a child) (identification: restrictions on publication)* [2004] 2 FLR 949 and *R (Axon) v Secretary of State for Health (Family Planning Association intervening)* [2006] EWHC 37 in particular.

78   See, for example, Brook, G., 'Children's competency to consent: a framework for practice' (2000) 12 *Paediatric Nursing* No. 5, 31 in which she discusses the framework of practice established at the Liver Unit, Birmingham Children's Hospital NHS Trust which allows the child every opportunity to engage in the process of deciding their optimum treatment, at all stages, decisions big and small, with all the disciplines involved in their care in accordance with their levels of competence.

79   Alderson, P. and Montgomery, J., *Health Care Choices: Making Decisions with Children*, London, IPPR, 1996, discovered this to be the case based on a 1993 research

In Chapter 2 the development of Article 8(1) was highlighted. For our purposes here, Munby J's comments on 'physical and psychological integrity' point raised in *Botta*,[80] in *R (on application of A, B, X, & Y) v East Sussex County Council (No. 2)*,[81] are worth emphasizing. He took the view that this embraced the concepts of human dignity and the right to participate in community life, the former described along the lines of the Golden Rule accepted by most major religions whereby you must 'treat your neighbour as you wish your neighbour to treat you'.[82] Kantian ethics offers more rigour to this in that this is concerned with what may be rationally willed.[83] Beyleveld and Brownsword draw a distinction between 'dignity as constraint' and 'dignity is empowerment'.[84] The former encapsulates Kantian concepts and would include a communitarian perspective of working towards a particular vision of society. The idea of 'dignity as empowerment'[85] focuses on individual choice and autonomy that is only limited by the rights of others. Adopting human rights approaches offers an opportunity to balance these sometimes competing claims and the HRA can help to support the right of children to participate in civic society. The law needs to adopt a robust position because it can change cultures.[86] Others argue that there remains a need for executive functions, including extra-judicial mechanisms, to pay greater attention to promoting rights-based decision-making with respect to children given the uneven approach adopted by legislation and the judges.[87]

Where the ability to influence policy-making is concerned, the picture is more disappointing.[88] This is so despite developments such as the Children Act 1989, which was seen as giving statutory recognition to children's rights formulated

---

project generally and more recent evidence suggests this is still so: BMA working party on children's consent, http://www.bma.org.uk/ap.nsf/Content/consenttk2. This seems to be the case even in specialist children's settings: see Healthcare Commission's *State of Healthcare*, 2007 at p. 71 and personal communication from Dr J. Wales, Consultant Paediatrician, Sheffield Children's NHS Foundation Trust.Healthcare Commission

80   *Botta v Italy* (1998) 26 EHRR 241.

81   [2003] EWHC 167 (Admin).

82   Ibid., at paras. 85–99 in particular.

83   Kant (1948) *Groundwork of the Metaphysics of Morals*: translated by Paton, H.J., as *The Moral Law*, London, Routledge, 1948, at pp. 83–4: 'Act only on that maxim through which you can at the same time will that it should become a universal law.'

84   Beyleveld, D. and Brownsword, R., *Human Dignity in Bioethics and Biolaw*, Oxford, Oxford University Press, 2001, particularly Ch. 2.

85   Ibid.

86   *The Human Rights Act: Changing Lives*, British Institute for Human Rights, 20 April, 2007.

87   Williams, J., 'Incorporating children's rights: the divergence in law and policy' (2007) 27(2) *Legal Studies* 261–87. It is worth noting that the Employment Equality (Age) Regulations 2006 could also be used to strengthen legal claims made even though it is generally thought that these will be prayed in aid of the older generation.

88   *Supra*, n. 54 *passim*.

in case law, and policy documents such as *Youth Matters*,[89] which are rich in the rhetoric of the child's voice being heard. This lack of influence is mirrored in the health care context.[90] There are examples where young people offer significant levels of contribution to issues that affect them, but more consistent approaches are required in relevant contexts for greater coherence and strong judicial pronouncements could encourage this.

Frameworks for Children and Young People's Participation

There is a number of participation 'frameworks' and benchmarking tools for working with children and young people. These include the Youth Council for Northern Ireland which developed '*Seen and Heard*',[91] Hart's Ladder of Youth Participation,[92] which is used by UNICEF, and the Carnegie Young People's Initiative 'circular model' of participation.[93]

The Youth Council for Northern Ireland's '*Seen and Heard*' promotes a range of principles to guide organizations wanting to work with young people. There should be genuine intentions, organizational support from key decision makers, vision and clarity about what youth involvement is for, versatility and a willingness to use a variety of approaches with appropriate timing, adequate preparation and sufficient staff and budgetary resources. The strategic intent should have youth involvement as a long-term commitment with the inclusion of disadvantaged or 'difficult to reach' young people. There should also be equality of opportunity amongst young people, who are not a homogenous group, and trust developed through valuing and respecting them. This requires the provision of capacity-building for them and the staff that work with them. Organizations need to be responsive, offering recognition and feedback to young people yet being aware of welfare issues such as child protection.

Hart's Ladder of Youth Participation sets out the range of levels of involvement by young people in decision-making. These range from optimal levels where decision-making is shared with adults, initiated and sponsored by young people and where young people are consulted, to tokenism where young people are seen as decoration and/or may be manipulated. At this end of the spectrum, the levels would count as non-participation. It perhaps ought to be noted that this model is somewhat linear and that progress along the 'rungs' will depend upon the context in which young people are operating. The pinnacle of Hart's ladder does not

---

89   National Children's Bureau, *Consultation with Young People The Green Paper – Youth Matters* (A Report for the Office of the Children's Commissioner, 2005).

90   *Supra*, n. 5.

91   http://www.ycni.org/downloads/publications/takingtheinitiative.pdf.

92   Hart, R., *From Tokenism to Citizenship*, Florence, UNICEF Innocenti Research Centre, 1992.

93   http://cypi.carnegieuktrust.org.uk/cypi/news_and_events?from=14.

necessarily translate in all settings where it may not be possible to allow such a significant level of involvement from young people.[94]

The Carnegie Young People's Initiative also sets out degrees of participation. Projects may be designed and run by adults but children are consulted, having a full understanding of the process and their opinions are taken seriously. The next degree would be a project assigned by adults with children volunteering on the basis of information given. The children understand the project, know who decided to involve them and why. Adults respect their views. The next step up would be an adult-initiated project but with young people involved in every step of the planning and implementation. Not only are their views considered but children are also involved in taking the decisions. To take this approach further, children would have the initial idea and decide how the project is to be carried out, adults would be available to assist, but would not take charge. A variation would have adults available for advice, discussion and support, offering expertise where necessary but not directing.

Before exploring how Foundation Trusts may further this agenda, some examples of where children and young people's participation has been seen as meaningful would be helpful in illustrating how they could be applied in the health care setting.

Policy Changes in the Representation of Young People

Policy changes in the representation of young people have taken place within the context of international developments such as the UNCRC.[95] The Carnegie United Kingdom Trust established the Carnegie Young People Initiative in 1996 as a research project using those between the ages of ten and 25 years with the aim of improving the quality and increasing the breadth of young people's participation in public decision-making.[96] *Taking the Initiative* combines two reports summarizing the state of youth involvement work in the US and the UK. It concludes:

> In the UK in recent years it has become increasingly acceptable to describe as a right young people's participation in the key decisions that shape their lives. In the US the major policy influence has been the idea of *personal development,* seeing young people as assets or resources and emphasising their ability to make judgements for themselves.[97]

It has promoted the evaluation of good practice and developed standards for the public and voluntary sectors at national and local levels to involve young

---

94   *Supra,* n. 37.
95   *Supra,* n. 2.
96   Carnegie United Kingdom Trust *supra,* n.3 at p. 2.
97   Carnegie United Kingdom Trust, *Taking the initiative,* 2004.

people. There is growing evidence of the benefits to the young persons themselves and to the wider community of encouraging such participation but tangible results in improved services and policies are limited. Further work needs to be carried out using qualitative and quantitative methodologies to ensure rigorous evaluations are conducted on relevant initiatives that are more than mere monitoring.[98] This is particularly true when considering why certain young people do not become involved, for participants do not always represent target populations. What is recognized is that a range of consultation methods should be used to gain maximum benefit with appropriate support for young people and the adults working with them in a context of minimal bureaucracy and accessible information.

The establishment of a Children and Young People's Unit in 2001 within the Department for Education and Skills (DfES) which, until July 2007, advised the Government on the development of policies for children and young people, has been welcomed as providing a key impetus for their involvement in policy, service design and delivery.[99] Ten key national Government departments are now expected to adopt such an approach that is reflected in local government practice.[100] The Government's 2004 policy overview Green Paper, *Every Child Matters*[101] was followed in 2005 by Youth Matters[102] and the Report of the Russell Commission on youth volunteering which emphasized the need for activity to be led by young people themselves.[103]

The Children and Youth Board was set up in June 2004 to advise the DfES and the Minister for Children, Young People and Families, on policy issues and to be involved in recruiting the Children's Commissioner.[104] The 25 Children and Youth Board members are aged between eleven and nineteen, have a wide range of backgrounds and are recruited from all over the UK. They were responsible for appointing the Children's Commissioner in England, helping to produce the job advert, designing and marking written tests for the candidates, producing a short-list and questioning candidates face-to-face about how they would tackle the issues affecting children and young people.

In its first year of operation, the Office of the Children's Commissioner has listened to and engaged with children and young people to formulate priorities for research and development and to develop policy positions. A key plank of the Commissioner's media profile was to emphasize the importance of children

---

98   Pinkerton, J., 'Children's participation in the Policy Process: Some Thoughts on Policy Evaluation Based on the Irish National Children's Strategy' (2004) 18 *Children and Society* 119–30.

99   Sinclair, R., 'Participation in Practice: Making It Meaningful, Effective and Sustainable' (2004) 19 *Children and Society* 106–18.

100   *Supra*, n. 52.

101   *Supra*, n. 2.

102   DfES and the DoH, *Youth Matters* Green Paper, 2005.

103   Russell Report (2005): http://www.russellcommission.org/report/index.html.

104   http://www.dfes.gov.uk/rsgateway/DB/RRP/u014969/index.shtml.

and young people participating in society and decision-making.[105] To highlight one important report commissioned by the Children Commissioner's Office, *Children and Young People's Views on Health and Health Services: A Review of the Evidence*,[106] it is clear that there has been a large amount of consultation with children and young people and there is good knowledge of how they think services should be improved. There now needs to be implementation of their suggestions and an effort to engage them in policy-formulation at a higher level than the development of services that directly affect them.

Sceptics suspect that these initiatives have less to do with concern about the rights of children and the impact of the UNCRC than with the lack of participation in the democratic process.[107] Nevertheless, progress does appear to be being made although evaluation is necessary to ensure the commitment is more than superficial. Children should also help to determine what these rights might be.

To illustrate a general point about the advantages of engaging users in non-traditional roles, the Charity Commission provides a useful example.[108] It promotes diverse representation amongst charity trustees and has discussed widening trustee memberships to users and highlights an example of good practice in involving them in governance. Doing so has acted as a catalyst for enhancing the charity's effectiveness and efficiency by providing more responsive, better services to users, notwithstanding the time and financial resource implications for the charity. As far as young people go, in 2004, the Commission made a watershed decision to register some types of charities with trustees under 18 years old.[109] For the Commission the test is whether the person understands their duties and responsibilities. The Commission has recognized 'Funky Dragon'[110] as a charity requiring young people as trustees because of its nature. As a peer-led organization whose aim is to give 11 to 25-year-olds the opportunity to have their voices heard on issues that effect them, it is cited as an exemplar by the Children's Commissioner.[111] So, the issue of young people's representation in decision-making bodies is clearly live and is leading to changes in policy.

In some areas then, there are good examples of a genuine commitment to children's rights of participation, so that practice is changing in social policy as society becomes more aware of the need to ensure equal opportunities and

---

105   Children's Commissioner, Annual Report 2005/06.

106   National Children's Bureau, *Young people on NCB's Board of Management: An Evaluation of the First Three Years*, 2005.

107   *Supra*, n. 6.

108   Charity Commission, *RSI – Trustee Recruitment, Selection and Induction*, 2006, *passim*: (http://www.charitycommission.gov.uk).

109   http://www.charity-commission.gov.uk/supportingcharities/under18scc30.asp.

110   The Welsh Youth Council and the Children and Young People's Assembly for Wales also known as the Welsh Youth Parliament): http://www.funkydragon.org.

111   Sir Al Aynsley-Green, Children's Commissioner, Implementing the Children's Bill Conference, Royal Society of Medicine, 19 April 2006.

to encourage participation from groups that have traditionally been excluded.[112] However, this is not yet widespread particularly in the healthcare context.[113] The legal framework increasingly tends towards participation and engagement rather than exclusion. In light of the changing social framework, the guidelines available and examples of good practice, it is to be hoped that the appetite of Foundation Trusts to play a full role in developing this strategy in relation to young people is maintained. The following sets out the new Foundation Trust regime to illustrate how it may further the participatory rights of children and young people as well as enhancing policies.

Foundation Trusts

The central proposition in this chapter is that Foundation Trusts are ideally placed to help deliver effective participation through the democratic mandate provided by their large membership constituency. The legal framework of Foundation Trusts[114] provides mechanisms for addressing the participatory deficit in health care policy-making through its governance structures. The engagement of significant numbers of the public in Foundation Trusts to inform strategic development provides an unprecedented opportunity to deal with, *inter alia*, policy formulation in a more ethically justifiable way. Children and young persons need to be involved in decisions about how services aimed at them as a group are shaped.

Currently, although there are obligations to involve the public in NHS service provision by, for example, patient and public involvement in the acute and primary care setting,[115] such involvement is on a very small scale compared to the potential for it within the Foundation Trust system where community participation is transferred to the boards of governors.[116] All Foundation Trusts have been concerned to learn from emerging good practice about how to make their wider governance structures as inclusive and representative as possible.[117] Although still part of the NHS as their name suggests, these organizations will be controlled and run locally as public interest organizations through a form of social ownership modelled on co-operative societies and mutual organizations. As such, they will be non-profit organizations, *supposedly* freed from Whitehall control. The freedoms should allow innovations in service delivery, asset use and human

---

112 *Supra*, n. 117.

113 *Supra*, nn. 41–8.

114 Established by the Health and Social Care Act 2001.

115 *Supra*, n. 29.

116 DoH, *Guide to Foundation Trusts*, 2002, *passim*.

117 As Chairperson of the Sheffield Children's NHS Foundation Trust, the author was elected to the Foundation Trust Network Board (the Foundation Trusts' representative body) from 2005–6 where Information was canvassed from all Foundation Trusts providing children's services.

resources together with increased options for capital funding.[118] Patients and the public have an interest in all these fundamental issues and need to be aware of the rationale for this new regime if they are to hold the Trust to account. Only those NHS trusts able to demonstrate high performance and sufficient financial rigour to be viable over a five-year projected period will be approved by the regulator (Monitor) and be given a licence to operate as a Foundation Trust. Overall, Foundation Trusts must operate within a statement of purpose which makes clear that it is established to provide health and related services for the benefit of NHS patients and the community, upholding as it does so the values of the NHS, such as the Core Principles contained in the *NHS Plan*.[119]

The scrutiny provided by the membership of Foundation Trusts and their governors will be a key mechanism for accountability allowing for public involvement in setting the agenda for the health care community. Local democracy will be improved and decision-making will be further legitimized. This is where young people have a key role. Local people, patients and staff interested in the development and well-being of their local NHS Foundation Trust can register as members. To ensure there is real stakeholder commitment, there should be wide advertising of eligibility for membership and proactive, innovative approaches to ensure those groups who do not traditionally become involved in running public services are encouraged to do so. The benefits include the fact that the board of directors will be accountable to them by developing the organization in line with local needs, albeit within the wider NHS context, and ensuring it operates within the terms of its licence so that the membership can promote its public service purpose. Members must receive regular information about the Trust and be consulted on such matters as how provision of NHS clinical services could be improved.[120]

Members will be able to elect a board of governors with representatives from the public, patients and staff with appointments of certain other local stakeholders. This is likely to include the local authority, commissioners of services in the form of primary care trusts and universities where the trust has a teaching dimension so that the full range of members' interests are reflected with a proper balance between different interest groups. The board of governors will be directly accountable to members for ensuring the Foundation Trust operates within its objectives as set out in its constitution and within the terms of its licence. It will act as a trustee for the welfare of the organization as it was originally established and as a vehicle for influencing change and development replacing the public interest responsibilities exercised by the Secretary of State for Health for other health bodies.[121] The fact that members elect governors avoids the impression of the selection of a 'favoured few'. There is often an impression that where efforts are made to involve young people in policy-making, for example, it is only the 'usual suspects', i.e. those

---

118   *Supra*, n. 125.

119   DoH, Preface of the *NHS Plan*, 2000, Cm 4818–1.

120   Ibid.

121   *Supra*, n. 125.

who have become known to the establishment, who are approached often at the expense of the hard-to-reach groups.[122] Children's participation should be meaningful, effective and sustainable.[123] The younger age group are a less obvious choice when considering the involvement of children because of the additional challenges presented in ensuring, for example, that information is accessible and they receive appropriate encouragement to voice their views.

Although the Health and Social Care Act 2001 is silent about the need to consult with children specifically, the interpretation of the governance requirements means that, in practice, arrangements to do this must be in place. Monitor has to approve their constitutions and demands children and young people's representation in memberships where relevant i.e. where there is provision for children's services.[124] This gives a real opportunity for young people to become 'specialist insiders' who can make an effective contribution to policy-making.[125] How this is achieved needs serious attention, not least some level of audit, to ensure opportunities are maximized.

A number of Foundation Trusts wish to pursue greater diversity by having children as *governors* particularly where the Trust provides paediatric care.[126] It is worth re-iterating that it is important to include the patients' unique perspective. To do otherwise presents a negative message about the potential usefulness of children's contributions. Being involved in other ways, including attendance at governors' meetings, is no substitute for being more directly influential with voting rights and access to full information. Children who are members of Foundation Trusts *do* have potential suffrage. The legislation should be interpreted so that there is nothing to prevent children being governors in the spirit demonstrated by the Charity Commission.[127] Governors are elected by their constituency after a manifesto pledge. This process will have established that the young person has the competence to represent constituency views and the ability to make important decisions.

However, Monitor is adamant that children should be 16 before they become governors because of concerns about the serious decisions to be made, even though this group would constitute only a small part of the whole body.[128] Robust representations by the Sheffield Children's Hospital NHS Trust asking for younger

---

122   McNamee, S.A., 'The Consequences of visibility for children's participation' presentation at the 'Childhood and Youth: Choice and Participation' International Conference, *supra*, n.36.

123   Sinclair, R., 'Participation in Practice: Making It Meaningful, Effective and Sustainable' (2004) 19 *Children and Society* 106–18.

124   *Supra*, n. 125.

125   Maloney, W.A., Jordan, G. and McLaughlan, A.M., 'Interest Groups and Public Policy: the Insider/Outsider Model Revisited' (1994) 14(1) *Journal of Public Policy* 17–38.

126   *Supra*, n. 126.

127   *Supra*, nn. 117–20.

128   *Supra*, n. 10.

members be allowed to adopt this role has been resisted despite appeals to Articles 8 and 14 of the Human Rights Act 1998 in particular, the Employment Equality (Age) Regulations 2006 (Regulations) and the National Service Framework for Children.[129] As indicated earlier, the broad reading of Article 8 can support children's right to participate in general decision-making and, once this Article is engaged, the right not to be discriminated against under Article 14 may be employed. The Regulations could equally be used to argue against age discrimination for the younger age group as for those of more advanced years. Although the *National Service Framework for Children* has less force as policy, regulatory bodies must recognize that there is an obligation on the part of public bodies to comply with such Government initiatives particularly where its aims are enshrined in legislation.[130] Given that the learning disabled have been allowed to become governors in Mental Health Foundation Trusts,[131] it is likely that these arguments will be pursued given the lack of a consistent approach to the competence issue. Sheffield Children's NHS Foundation Trust has referred the matter to the Children's Commissioner in the hope that his influence can be brought to bear on Monitor.[132] Thus far, he has not responded. Monitor's approval of Foundation Trust *membership* encompassing a younger age group is to be welcomed but if the possibility of becoming a governor remains removed from this category this will add to the difficulties of 'selling' the already limited advantages of becoming a member.[133]

Conclusion

In theory, the only requirement for eligibility for the office of a Foundation Trust governor should be the ability of the child member to convince their constituency that they can make a meaningful contribution. In practice, Foundation Trusts' boards of directors may draw a line at an age where they consider the child can make an effective contribution determined by empirical research and whether there are the resources available to support that child. There is widespread support from Foundation Trusts for the proposition that their governing bodies should have representation of children under 16[134] and Monitor's opposition to this is regrettable. If this issue were resolved, it would give a strong message that the UK is finally taking children's rights more seriously, is matching rhetoric with reality and provide a very visible example that can be followed elsewhere.

---

129   DfES, *supra*, n. 1; for example, Standard 3 on Child, Young Person and Family-centred Services at p. 87.

130   *Supra*, nn. 71–4.

131   *Supra*, n.10.

132   *Supra*, n. 126.

133   Ibid.

134   *Supra*, n. 126.

Chapter 9
Concluding Remarks

It has been argued throughout this book that children's autonomy should be promoted but constraints may need to be applied in some circumstances. This may be because some children lack the capacity for autonomy and require protection. There might also be legitimate reasons to interfere with their autonomy in the interests of others. No individual, child or adult, can be seen in isolation from their relationships with others in their immediate familial and social circle or in the broader socio-political context.[1] Aside from third party considerations, a protective position gradually needs to give way by allowing children to determine what happens to them on their journey to competent adulthood where this is possible. Children need to be empowered by giving them optimal opportunities to acquire knowledge and experience life at an appropriate rate. This includes involvement in health care decision-making. Clearly, in the case of younger children, this is a key function for those exercising parental responsibility, but should also be given attention by anyone involved in children's decision-making. Familiarity in working with children and developing communication skills[2] with younger patients will facilitate recognition of whether the child possesses the level of reflective thinking required for competence. It is only where there is a disagreement between parents, or between parents and health professionals, about a proposed medical intervention that a court will be required to determine what is in the best interests of the child. Only then is the child given a *certain* opportunity to have their needs and wishes addressed.

Chapters 2 and 3 in particular, propose that the law should adhere to a strong notion of children's right to autonomy. A presumption of autonomy will help to redress the current imbalance in the way children are dealt with when decisions are made in the health care setting. The law has a key role in changing cultures. The increasing recognition of children's rights and persuasive empirical evidence that children are more capable of making decisions than is generally thought to be the case should encourage judicial decisions that support sophisticated assessments of children's autonomy. To adopt traditional, cautious approaches in the way we engage with children in the health care setting flies in the face of this evidence.[3] Competent children should be permitted to refuse life-saving treatment where they

---

1   See, in particular, Chapters 5 and 7.

2   See e.g. Kinnersley P., Butler C., 'Context bound communication skills training: development of a new method', (2002) 36 *Medical Education* 377–83.

3   See e.g. the discussion in Chapters 2 and 8 in particular where they discuss the evidence about children's capacities and the limits of consent respectively.

suffer from, for example, debilitating, chronic conditions provided they understand the implications of what they are deciding. Their experience as an 'expert patient' can mean they possess higher levels of maturity than would normally be expected in children of the same age.[4] Experience of illness, disability and treatment is a more indicative factor in assessing competency than age.[5] As Alderson[6] states:

> Many children exceed many adults in, for example, intelligence, ability, prudence, size ... the difference between adults and children lies mainly in social beliefs.[7]

Legal scholarship ignores this fact at its peril: if the law does not reflect 'reality', it will lose credibility. Strong judicial statements about children's autonomy would also encourage their involvement in policy making in the way suggested in Chapter 8. Thus far, the law has failed to fulfil its potential in recognizing children's autonomous interests: the Mental Capacity Act 2005 (MCA) does not include the under 16s within its remit and the common law remains cautious in its approach notwithstanding some welcome developments.[8]

I have maintained throughout this book that a human rights approach can establish the parameters of autonomy to the extent that this is possible. The Human Rights Act 1998 (HRA) can balance competing claims. There are realistic notions of autonomy that can recognize the position of children. Where children are concerned, we must balance any right to autonomy with parental and societal interests in protecting that child. The current position of children requires the use of rights language to ensure that their interests are not neglected, partially or otherwise. It is worth reiterating that whether discussions about rights is constructive or not will depend partly on the skill of those involved. The key point is that the HRA allows a full consideration of everyone's interests including those of the child in their familial and wider social networks. Ethical challenges cannot be reduced to a focus on the individual. As a living instrument, the HRA is also sufficiently flexible to extend the law in accordance with evolving social mores.

---

4   Eiser, C., 'Changes in understanding of illness as the child grows' (1985) 60 *Archives of Disease in Childhood* 489–92, Fielding, D. and Duff, A., 'Compliance with treatment protocol: interventions for children with chronic illness' (1999) 80 *Archives of Disease in Childhood* 196–200 and Alderson, P. and Montgomery, J., *Health Care Choices: Making Decisions with Children*, London, IPPR, 1996.

5   Hammond, L., *Children's Decisions in Health Care and Research*, London, Institute of Education, 1993.

6   Alderson, P., *Children's Consent to Surgery*, Oxford, Oxford University Press, 1993.

7   Ibid. at p. 190.

8   See the discussion in Chapter 2 on *R (Axon) v Secretary of State for Health (Family Planning Association intervening)* [2006] EWHC 37 and *Bro Morgannwg NHS Trust v 'P' and others* [2003] EWHC 2327 (Fam) (*Re P*).

Given children are more capable than we usually give them credit for,[9] the concept of autonomy as it pertains to children does require further development.

As noted in Chapter 1, self-determination, self-government, sense of responsibility and sense of development are overlapping aspects of autonomy. The individual cannot be seen as an abstraction from the socio-political context or from their relationships with others. Dworkin's account of autonomy, that is supported here,[10] can accommodate this reality. Autonomy is an ideal towards which we should strive for optimal functioning while acknowledging the impact this can have on the autonomous interests of others.[11] As far as the effect on families is concerned, we should acknowledge that, generally, parents will have their children's interests at heart.[12] However, the temptation to be overly protective may prove to be irresistible and inappropriate at times. Attributing rights to children provides a security net that can ensure their interests are appropriately assessed. Ideally, disagreements can be resolved constructively in the family or any other setting. Should this not be possible, asserting children's rights ensures their interests receive appropriate recognition albeit in a context that acknowledges undue demands should not be placed on other members of the family. Relying on an application of the welfare principle, which may be seen as unpredictable, lacking in substance and susceptible to bias, can mean a child's interests are insufficiently acknowledged.[13] On the road to realizing their full autonomous potential, children can be encouraged to develop a sense of familial and social obligation. This should pre-empt some of the potential difficulties highlighted in this book: this sense of obligation should mean that individuals are happy to share their genetic information with family members[14] and participate in research designed to help others.[15]

The preceding chapters demonstrate how a human rights approach can be used to protect children's autonomy in the health care setting[16] while recognizing that there may be circumstances when it is legitimate to override this right in the interests of others. The disclosure of genetic information and participation in crucial research are cases in point. Rights-based approaches are often perceived in a negative light. For some, rights-based discourse reflects an impoverished society in which individuals' duties and virtues fail to receive sufficient recognition.[17]

9　See the discussion in Chapters 2 and 7 in particular.

10　See the discussion in Chapter 2.

11　Downie, R.S., Fyffe, C. and Tannehill, A., *Health Promotion: Model and Values*, Oxford, Oxford University Press, 1990, at pp. 138–9.

12　Jonas, M., 'The baby MB case: medical decision-making in the context of uncertain infant suffering', (2007) 33 *Journal of Medical Ethics* 541–4.

13　Reece, R., 'The Paramountcy Principle: Consensus of Construct?', (1996) 49 *Current Legal Problems* 267 at p. 303.

14　See Chapter 5.

15　See Chapter 7.

16　This is also true in other settings. See Fortin, J., *Children's Rights and the Developing Law* (2nd ed.) London, Butterworths, 2003, *passim*.

17　Laws, J., 'The Limitation of Human Rights', (1998) *Public Law* 254 at p. 255.

It is seen as inherently confrontational and unable to accommodate the realities of caring relationships, particularly with respect to children who are inevitably dependent on others.[18] It is alleged that a rights-based approach can undermine parental authority and family autonomy[19] as well as being inadequate for the task of protecting children.[20] This hostility is misplaced. The focus of modern law and policy has been one of protection partly as a response to historical and more current abuse,[21] as well as recognizing that children lack adult capacities at certain stages of their development. While entirely understandable, this has arguably been at the expense of children's interests, especially that of having their autonomy acknowledged appropriately.

Whatever discomfort there may be about rights-based discourse, the fact is that we have the HRA and children fall within its remit. The growing recognition of the United Nations Convention on the Rights of the Child (UNCRC)[22] means that increasing account will be taken of children's rights. The HRA must be taken into account in judicial decision-making, policy formulation and practice. This is as true in the health care setting as anywhere else. The HRA provides a mechanism that is sufficiently flexible to address the concerns about the potential lack of acknowledgement of the familial and social context the child inhabits. The HRA can attend to individual's and others' rights. The ECHR was established to enhance life and should be interpreted accordingly. On this basis, a child cannot assert a right to harm themselves. Of course, there are some decisions, which will, on the face of it, be perceived as harmful. An example would be the case of the refusal of life-saving treatment. However, in the exceptional circumstances discussed in Chapter 2, where a mature child has just had enough of challenging interventions in a life dogged by chronic illness, those caring for them, be they family or professionals, may see the child's wish to refuse an intervention as being in their 'objective' best interests, whatever that is taken to mean in these contexts. Even where there is no such concurrence and it is only what *the child* believes is in their best interest, that view should prevail if the child is competent.

Whether balancing the interests of individuals' and others' interests is successful lies partly in the hands of those interpreting its provisions be that policy makers, judges and/or health professionals. This takes confidence and skill but there is sufficient jurisprudence to act as a springboard for a more robust approach

---

18   Bridgeman, J., *Parental Responsibility, Young Children and Healthcare Law*, Cambridge, Cambridge University Press, 2007, *passim*.

19   O'Brien Steinfels, M., 'Children's Rights, Parental Rights, Family Privacy, and Family Autonomy' in Gaylin, W. and Macklin, R. (eds), *Who Speaks for the Child?* Plenum Press, 1982 at p. 240 cited in Fortin, *supra*, n. 16.

20   See e.g. Herring, J., 'The Human Rights Act 1998 and the welfare principle in family law – conflicting or complementary?' (1999) at p. 233.

21   See e.g. Fortin, *supra*, n. 17, Chapter 15 and the discussion in Chapter 8 in this book on unethical research in children.

22   See e.g. *Axon, supra*, n. 8 discussed in Chapter 2.

to children's autonomy. By having to balance in this way, a rigorous consideration of all the issues should result in a workable decision or policy. Much then will be determined by the resolve of those who implement them. What we need is a more enthusiastic embracing of the principles enshrined in the UNCRC by the judiciary, policy makers, and those who implement them. This would strengthen the position of children and lend coherence to the various strands of medical law, ethical guidance and policy documents as it affects them. Powerful messages from the judiciary about allowing children a greater say in their medical treatment would have a significant impact and further change a culture where lip-service tends to be paid to the autonomous interests of children. Rhetoric is beginning to change[23] but a significant test of judicial commitment to children's autonomy has yet to take place.

We have seen that the law clearly fails to protect *fully* the interests of children and could adopt a more robust position to help change current cultures.[24] It can be argued that there remains a need for policy-makers, including extra-judicial bodies, to pay greater attention to promoting rights-based decision-making with respect to children given the uneven approach adopted by legislation and the judges.[25] *The Human Rights Act: Changing Lives* report by the British Institute for Human Rights shows how the language and ideas of the Human Rights Act 1998 (HRA) are being used to change the approach taken by health and social care workers in dealing with more vulnerable members of society.[26] Yet we have also seen that these changes have yet to extend to children in any coherent way in practice. The assessment of children's competence to be involved in their treatment options can be conservative and inconsistent across individual instances or institutional settings.[27] This may be the result of a lack of confidence on the part of health care professionals in assessing competence in children, rather than reflecting a lack of commitment to children's rights: inevitably, health professionals will be cautious when decisions may have very significant implications for that child. The 'informed' aspect of informed consent means that information may be provided to

---

23   See e.g. the comments in *Axon* and *Re P*, *supra*, n. 8 discussed in Chapter 2, the discussion of children's participatory rights in Chapter 8 and the terminology in the GMC, *0–18 years: Guidance for Doctors*, 2007.

24   See Chapter 2 in particular.

25   Williams, J., 'Incorporating children's rights: the divergence in law and policy' (2007) 27(2) *Legal Studies* 261–87.

26   British Institute for Human Rights, *The Human Rights Act: Changing Lives*, 2007.

27   Alderson and Montgomery, *supra*, n. 4, discovered this to be the case based on a 1993 research project generally and more recent evidence suggests this is still so: BMA Working Party on Children's Consent, http://www.bma.org.uk/ap.nsf/Content/consenttk2. This seems to be the case even in specialist children's settings: see Healthcare Commission's *State of Healthcare*, 2007 at p. 71 and personal communication from Dr J. Wales, Consultant Paediatrician, Sheffield Children's NHS Foundation Trust.

children about proposed interventions but this can become a restricted exercise if the child is later deemed unable to consent inappropriately.

Given the *ad hoc* nature of judicial development and inconsistent approaches in practice, Children's Commissioners could further champion the cause of children. Clear and very detailed guidance about the need to recognize children's autonomy using a human rights perspective and how that might be done would be helpful. Courts frequently refer to ethical guidance and this would give them confidence to adopt a rigorous position with respect to children's rights. Unfortunately, the Children's Commissioners of the UK have expressed disappointment to the UN yet again about the lack of progress on developing children's participatory rights in the UK in their 2008 Report.[28] Indeed, in some areas, there has been a retreat from some of the advances made.[29] However, the Commissioners believe that the responsibility for raising awareness of, providing accessible information to and disseminating the UNCRC lies primarily with the Government.[30] Their calls for the adoption of a Bill of Rights and Duties would enhance further the position of children.[31] Their other suggestion, that a children's rights impact assessment should be carried out with respect to all legislative and policy developments at national and local levels,[32] is also very useful. The idea that all those who work with young people, including relevant policy makers, be trained in children's rights and the incorporation of the UNCRC into the school curriculum would go a long way in changing the culture to benefit children. The UN Committee on the Rights of the Child has wholly endorsed the recommendations made by the Commissioners.[33] However, even the Children's Commissioner in England has not responded to calls for key lobbying opportunities.[34] As we saw in Chapter 8, the inception of NHS Foundation Trusts offered the prospect of giving younger children the chance to adopt high profile roles in the new governance structures. This evidence of a commitment to the empowerment of children would carry a more significant message than any number of specious policy documents.

What steps could be taken in practice to further empower children? Health professionals could, for example, use the services of Participation Works. This is a consortium of national children and young people agencies who work together to ensure that every child and young person can influence decisions affecting their lives.[35] Their *Hear by Right Self-Assessment Tool* enables organizations to map

---

28   See e.g. UK Children's Commissioners' Report to the UN Committee on the Rights of the Child, 2008 at p. 4.

29   Ibid.

30   Ibid., at p. 10.

31   Ibid.

32   Ibid.

33   Following its meeting in Geneva, September, 2008: http://www.unicef.org.uk/press/news_detail_full_story.asp?news_id=1203.

34   See the discussion in Chapter 8.

35   www.participationworks.org.uk.

the extent of children and young people's participation within an organization and agree a strategic plan for change. This could be used for ensuring involvement at a policy-making level but there is no reason it could not be used by clinical directorates as a means of sharing ideas about good practice in decision-making with children. Such practical proposals about the way in which children's health care decision-making will help to challenge prevailing understandings about young children's abilities that underestimate these.[36] To ensure that decision-making concerning children's medical treatment is carried out more appropriately, how might this be done?

Decision-making and the Mature Minor

Decision-making is enhanced when as broad a range of views as possible is taken into account by drawing on different areas of expertise. Health professionals clearly have skill in clinical matters but have no especial insight into a person's life and what it means for them unless they are heavily involved in their long-term care. Relatives and carers may be able to provide a useful perspective but may not be sufficiently objective or may even have conflicting interests. Providing an optimal procedural environment for decision-making is more likely to protect human rights notions of autonomy and dignity as they affect the individual: human rights instruments, such as those contained within the HRA, allow the interests of all relevant parties to be taken into account and balanced with each other. Human rights have an instrumental as well as a substantive value in that they can act as a bulwark for children where there are parental or other disputes. Human rights give children, in what has become somewhat a cliché but pertinent nevertheless, a 'voice'. Any concern that the engagement of the HRA is inevitably and necessarily confrontational should be challenged.[37] Policy makers, judges and/or health professionals, when interpreting human rights provisions, should be sufficiently skilled to optimize the chances that discussions will be constructive. It is the responsibility of parents, carers, health professionals and the law, to ensure that the child is a central part of the process to ensure their interests are fully safeguarded. In this way, children will be better protected. There needs to be a more appropriate evaluation of adolescent autonomy: this should recognize its importance and take account of empirical evidence that children's competence is often underestimated.[38] This will determine the level of their engagement in the decision-making at the outset. Involving the child in this way and giving credence to their views will empower children and their carers as they are helped to face difficult decisions, adding to their confidence and competence, as well as providing a thorough means of assessing the child's capacity.

---

36 Alderson and Montgomery, *supra*, n. 4.
37 See Bridgeman, *supra*, n. 18 at p. 19 for example.
38 Discussed in Chapter 2.

In more routine cases, DoH consent forms provide a useful approach in that they provide a useful synthesis of law and ethics as they relate to children in an accessible way and provide an excellent format for determining competence. They remind the assessor not to make assumptions based on age or apparent ability alone and to make appropriate levels of disclosure of risk.[39] Although the assessment of competence in practice tends to be impressionistic, further support is available in formal tests. It is arguable that these should be used, by those qualified to use them, when issues have significant implications for the child or there are disagreements amongst relevant parties.

Given the frequency with which competency issues arise in the medical context, protocols for assessing capacity would be advisable. These could include wide-ranging factors to be considered and could form part of an integrated care pathway which is 'a multi-disciplinary approach to assessing, planning, implementing, monitoring and evaluating care in collaboration with the patient and family'.[40] Where children are deemed incompetent, it is important that they should be as involved in the decision-making process as much as possible. They could, for example, give or withhold their *assent*. To clarify by example, this might entail a young person choosing between an invasive or less invasive treatment on the basis of likely pain, discomfort and/or inconvenience. Indeed, such an approach reflects the experience of many in the paediatric setting.[41] Many health professionals consider that refusal of such assent can mean treatment becomes impossible and should neutralize parental consent: consider the case of a large child refusing injections for a chronic condition. How is this to be administered in the face of non-cooperation? However, where the withholding of assent becomes life-threatening or otherwise significantly impairs health, moves to overcome this through rigorous means is likely.

There will inevitably be medical involvement in the decision-making process and a particularly rigorous approach would be to adopt Alderson and Montgomery's call for legislation supported by a code of practice covering all aspects of children's health care decision-making.[42] The code could be drafted after consultation with those involved with children and with children themselves.[43] The basic principles

---

39   The MCA makes similar provisions: see e.g. sub-sections 1(3) and 1(4). See, also, Turner, D.C. and Sahakian, B.J., 'Neuroethics of Cognitive Enhancement' (2006) 1 *Biosocieties* 113–23 where they discuss the topical example of the use of cosmetic psychopharmaceutical drugs to enhance performance where the long-term implications of such usage is yet to be discovered.

40   Murray, Y., 'Integrated Care Pathways for Paediatrics: A Guide for Nurses', Paediatrics 2000 Conference, Olympia, London.

41   See e.g. Brook, G., 'Children's competency to consent: a framework for practice' (2000) 12(5) *Paediatric Nursing* 31 in which she discusses how such a framework of practice was established at the Liver Unit, Birmingham Children's Hospital NHS Trust.

42   Alderson and Montgomery, *supra*, n. 4.

43   Ibid. at pp. 66–71. Further evidence that children are capable of contributing to policy-making may be found in Chapter 8.

would be contained in the framework legislation with the code providing the more detailed guidance and checklists of appropriate questions particularly in difficult cases. It would require procedures and policies to be in place to deal with potential problems. Any departure from the standards of good practice in the code could provide evidence of a breach in a negligence action unless this could be justified in the individual case. This approach would be supplemented by the usual internal complaints procedures, professional disciplinary action and be overseen by the courts. Most importantly, central to Alderson and Montgomery's proposals is the participation of the child in the decision-making process, one that is given wholehearted support here. However, this approach is unlikely to be forthcoming given the MCA failed to include children under 16 within its remit, which would have provided an ideal opportunity to ensure as demanding an approach to decision-making with this group as with older children.[44]

In cases where there is no evidence of mental disability, society will need to decide whether it will countenance decisions being made by the adolescent that many may see as defeating their self-interest, but leaving such determinations to others is harder to sustain in cases where a cure is unlikely, an inevitable, early death is merely being postponed and/or the treatment is burdensome. Adopting the approach advocated here in cases such as *Re E* [45] would have resulted in a different outcome. Decisions about refusal of life-saving treatment should be based on principles adhering to strong notions of children's autonomy not post hoc rationalization in the light of anecdotal evidence. This has particular force where children who have proved to be competent hold long-term beliefs, may suffer from chronic life-limiting conditions or feel deep abhorrence at the thought of having another person's body part placed in their own. In the case of *Re E*, the young man could have died peacefully not believing he was involved in an ungodly act. It is often argued that mature, devout young people lack experience of the wider world that may affect their beliefs in due course. This is, of course, possible. Equally, such core values often persist. Where potentially life-limiting decisions are being made, clearly there is a need to ensure the child is truly competent on the basis of formal assessments rather than any impressionistic account (no matter how informed and widely drawn) and that they do not suffer from the defects apparent in the cases of *Re R*[46] *and Re W*.[47] Children also need to be in receipt of all relevant information and the decision-making process should be facilitated in the ways suggested in

---

44   See, for example, the MCA, Code of Conduct, Chapter 3 for the onerous requirements to provide every assistance to incapacitated individuals to make decisions.

45   *Re E (a minor) (wardship: medical treatment)* [1993] 1 FLR 386.

46   *Re R (a minor) (wardship: consent to medical treatment)* [1991] 4 All ER 177.

47   *Re W (a minor) (medical treatment)* [1993] Fam 64.

the MCA's Code of Practice.[48] The protective approach epitomized by Feinberg[49] is entirely understandable and appropriate in many cases but must be subject to close scrutiny. Mature minors must be given extended opportunities to make their own decisions. The potential approach discussed in *Re P*,[50] where Johnson J was prepared to acknowledge that there may be cases where older children would be permitted to refuse treatment, is a welcome development and one to be further considered in similar cases, even where the child is under 16.

It is clear that I am a strong proponent for the promotion of children's autonomy and for the freedom for them to exercise this, therefore children should be given every opportunity to participate in decision-making to the extent of their capabilities. This should include appropriate assessments of their competence taking account of evolving multi-disciplinary data that provides evidence of children's capabilities.[51] In difficult cases, the use of psychological tests by those qualified to administer them should be mandatory. Where there is evidence of competence, allowing children to refuse even life-saving treatment should be considered, especially where the child has experience of long-term debilitating illness. It should also be clear that that I acknowledge that children's autonomy should be fettered in some circumstances. Some children lack the capacity for autonomy so there is a need to ensure children's welfare is promoted and maintained. However, constraints may also be applied to those who do have capacity. A protective approach needs to subside so that children can determine what happens to them on their journey to competent adulthood. To empower children, they need to acquire knowledge and experience life. In sum, the use of rights-based language carries a strong rhetorical message in itself. It alerts us to the autonomous interests of children that can easily be overlooked in a world geared to a focus on adults.[52] Of course, rights need to be carefully delineated so that they are not dismissed for being too prevalent, trivial or unreal. Children's right to autonomy does now have legal recognition but this needs strengthening by the law to further define its scope. The HRA is an ideal mechanism with which to ensure children, as vulnerable patients, receive appropriate protection and empowerment.

---

48   MCA, Code of Practice, Chapter 3: e.g. a suitable environment (para. 3.13 in particular).

49   Feinberg, J., 'The Child's Right to an Open Future' in *Freedom and Fulfilment*, Princeton, Princeton University Press, 1992 at pp.76–98 in Chapter 2 for his proposals for protecting children so that they may enjoy an 'open future'.

50   *Re P*, *supra*, n. 8.

51   See e.g. the discussion in Chapters 2 and 7 in particular where they discuss the evidence about children's capacities and the limits of consent respectively.

52   Bainham, A., 'Can we protect children and protect their rights?', (2002) *Family Law* 279 at p. 282 and 284.

Index

Note: information contained within the footnotes is indicated by 'n' followed by the foot-note number.

0–18 Years: Guidance for Doctors (GMC, 2007) 39n200, 52n282, 56n14, 85n71, 86n75, 94–5, 103n172, 103n175, 146–7, 149n134, 200, 239n23

Abortion Act 1967 168
abuse of children 10, 142, 161–2
    arising from research 180–81
    disclosure of information 102–5
access to medical records 108–11
Access to Health Records Act 1990 109
Access to Medical Records Act 1988
    109–10
Access to Justice Act 1999 134n19
ACHRE (Advisory Committee on Human
    Radiation Experiments) 191–2
adverse events 132n10, 133, 138–9
Age of Legal Capacity (Scotland) Act 1991
    48
AIDS *see* HIV/AIDS
Alder Hey Report (Royal Liverpool
    Children's Enquiry Report) 10n50,
    70–71, 119
Anatomy Act 1984 71
anonymization of data 79, 86, 91, 92–3,
    106–8, 124, 184
Attorney, Lasting Power of 26, 49n266
Australian Anti-Cancer Council of Victoria
    Report 122–4
autonomy of children and the law 5–7, 9,
    13–14, 52–3, 235–6, 239–44
    children's rights 17–24, 237–8
    critique of the current legal position
        44–7
    and the HRA 38–44, 236–7, 238–9
    future developments 48–52

legal competence to consent 22–4
    aged 16–18 years 24–7
    aged under 16 27–38
    nature of autonomy 14–17

babies, neurological impairment resulting
    from birth 164
    see also pregnancy
battery (tort) 29, 61, 137n43, 199
bereavement counselling 73
'best interests' principle 55, 59, 62, 74
blood products 159–60
    right to refuse 43, 51–2, 68
BMA (British Medical Association):
    *Consent, Rights and Choices for
        Healthcare for Children and Young
        People* (2001) 28n110
    guidance on genetic information 124
Brazier, M and Bridge, C, 'Coercion
        or caring: analysing adolescent
        autonomy' 34n160, 35n164,
        35n169, 36n172, 36n182, 37,
        47n252
Bristol Royal Infirmary, inquiry into
        children's heart surgery 3n14,
        10n50, 70, 73, 119, 131n4, 132n10,
        133
British Medical Association *see* BMA
'but for' test (negligence) 151–2

Caesarian section, refusal of 33–4
*Caldicott Report on the Review of Patient-
        identifiable Information* (NHS
        Executive, 1997) 78, 102
    Caldicott Guardians 79, 85
cancer, Australian Anti-Cancer Council of
        Victoria Report 122–4

FAP (familial adenomatous polyposis)
      123, 124, 125, 128
care:
   duty of *see* negligence
   ethic of 119–21
Carnegie United Kingdom Trust 50n267,
      51n274, 202n173, 214n3, 218n36
   Carnegie Young People's Initiative
      226–8
Charity Commission 229, 232
child abuse 10, 142, 161–2
   arising from research 180–81
   disclosure of information 102–5
Children and Young People's Unit (DfES)
      228
Children Act 1989 22n54, 24n70, 29, 30,
      41, 55n1, 57, 61, 67n90, 68, 82n45,
      172, 196n115, 225–6
Children Act 2004 19n30, 170n276,
      214n2, 223–4
Children and Young Person's Act 1933
      57n16
Children (Scotland) Act 1995 19n29
Children's Commissioners (UK) 19,
      223–4, 228–9, 240
   *Report to the UN Committee on the
      Rights of the Child* 6n29, 48n259,
      69n107, 240n28
Children's Right Alliance *Report to the
      UN Committee on the Rights of the
      Child* 1n4, 157n185
circumcision:
   female genital mutilation 59–60
   male 55n4, 59–62
citizenship 118–9, 185, 188, 222
civic friendship 118–9
Civil Liability (Contribution) Act 1978
      137n42
Civil Procedure Act 1997 135n24
CJD (Creutzveld-Jakob Disease) 145,
      159n202, 201
Clinical Trial Regulations 181n36,
      185n49, 195–8, 201, 203, 205, 206,
      210
communitarian philosophy 16, 115–18,
      122–3, 181, 225
compensation *see* damages

competence of children to make decisions
      about their care 9, 22–4
   aged 16–18 24–7
   aged under 16 27–38
   Fraser guidelines for assessing 43, 83,
      85
   threshold for 44–5
   see also consent
complaints *see* negligence
confidentiality 10–11, 42–3, 75–7, 110
   access to medical records 108–110
   breach of privacy 87, 90n90
   common law 82–6
   disclosure 10, 11, 95
      child protection 102–5
      genetic information 111, 114–30,
         237
      HIV infection 98–102
      police and legal enquiries 105–6
      threat of violence 96–8
   forms of consent 77–9
   and HRA 81, 82–3, 87–92, 98–102
   legal liability 86–7
   medical research 106–8
   ownership of health information 92–5
   statutory obligations and permissions
      80–81
Confidentiality Code of Practice (DoH,
      2003) 76n4, 79n24, 94, 96,
      107n202
*Confidentiality and Disclosure of
      Information* (DoH, 2004) 83, 85,
      106n199
*Confidentiality: Protecting and Providing
      Information* (GMC, 2004) 76n4,
      78, 85n71, 87n81, 91n96, 94n123,
      94n124, 95n129, 96–7, 99,
      103n171
Congenital Disabilities (Civil Liabilities)
      Act 1976 165, 167, 169, 170n277,
      172
consent:
   and Clinical Trial Regulations 195–8
   forms of 77–9
   informed 11, 131, 155–7, 239–40
   research involving children 177,
      181–2, 183, 195–8
   see also competence of children...

Consent, Choice and Children in Research
(Henderson) 180n31, 185–7,
206n195, 210n223
Consent, Rights and Choices for
Healthcare for Children and Young
People (BMA, 2001) 28n110
Consumer Protection Act 1987 158–60
contributory negligence 167n253
Coroners Act 1988 71
'cosmetic' procedures, parental consent to
59, 74
counselling, genetic *see* genetic testing and
counselling
Courts Act 2003 161n210
Courts and Legal Serices Act 1990 134n17
Creutzveld-Jakob Disease (CJD) 145,
159n202, 201
Crime and Disorder Act 1998 105n191

damages 131–2, 160–5
Damages Act 1996 161n210
Data Protection Act 1998 see DPA
death of children 70–73
decisions about care:
competence of children to make 9,
22–38, 43, 44–5, 83, 85
parental responsibility 10
patients' involvement in 3
role of teams in 9
Disability Discrimination Act 1995 112n6
disabled children 172–3
disabled people, quality of life 65–6
disclosure of confidential information 10,
11, 95
child protection 102–5
genetic information 114–22, 237
HIV infection 98–102
police and legal enquiries 105–6
threat of violence 96–8
DMD (Duchenne Muscular Dystrophy)
182, 185–6, 206
DoH (Department of Health):
Confidentiality Code of Practice (2003)
76n4, 79n24, 94, 96, 107n202
Confidentiality and Disclosure of
Information (2004) 83, 85,
106n199

Every Child Matters (DfES/DoH)
103n177, 214n2, 214n4, 223n70,
224
Making Amends: A Consultation
Paper Setting Out Proposals
for Reforming the Approach to
Clinical Negligence in the NHS
(2003) 132n10, 133n14, 135n22,
138n48, 149n133, 163–4
Protection and Use of Patient
Information (1996) 78, 82n47, 93,
105
Research Governance Framework for
Health and Social Care (2edn,
2005) 198n137, 203n175
Seeking Consent: Working with
Children (2001) 28n110
Donaldson, Lord 15n8, 24n67, 27n103,
29, 34, 37n183, 50, 63, 205, 206,
208
double jeopardy (research involving
children) 176, 177, 178n14, 183,
184n44, 209
DPA (Data Protection Act 1998) 77n11,
78n16, 79, 80–81, 106–7, 108, 109,
110
driving, negligent 166
drugs:
faults in 158–60
research 177–8, 179–80
Duchenne Muscular Dystrophy *see* DMD
Dworkin, G 15–17, 24n65, 46n245,
116n30, 237

ECHR (European Convention of Human
Rights) 6, 36, 61, 76–7, 128–9,
192n95, 206, 208, 224–5
Eekelaar, J. 19–20
embryos, use for research 8
ethics 4–5
clinical practice 6–7
ethic of care 119–21
ethic of justice 119–21
framework in research 181–3
RECs (Research Ethics Committees)
180–81, 184, 189, 190, 195, 210
European Convention of Human Rights see
ECHR

European Convention on Human Rights
    and Biomedicine *see* Oviedo
    Convention
European Court of Human Rights 65–6
European Medicines Agency 178, 179
euthanasia, Netherlands law 45–6
Every Child Matters (DfES/DoH)
    103n177, 214n2, 214n4, 223n70,
    224
express consent *see* consent

fair play 187–8
familial adenomatous polyposis see FAP
families, as the patient 73, 75
    'family model' of genetic information
    111, 125–6
Family Law Reform Act 1969 see FLRA
Fatal Accidents Act 1976 161n209
FAP (familial adenomatous polyposis)
    123, 124, 125, 128
Feinberg, J. 14n4, 17n20, 18, 20, 47,
    48n258, 170n273, 221, 244
Female Genital Mutilation Act 2003 59,
    60
FLRA (Family Law Reform Act 1969) 25,
    26–7, 29, 205, 206
Foundation Trusts, participation of children
    in 12, 220, 230–33
Fraser guidelines for assessing competence
    43, 83, 85
Freedom of Information Act 2000 109
Freeman, M. 15n5, 20n40, 21–2, 50n270,
    69n105

General Medical Council *see* GMC
genetic testing and counselling 11, 75,
    111–13, 125–9, 169, 173
    Australian Anti-Cancer Council of
    Victoria Report 122–4
    BMA guidance 124
genetic databases 184–5
genetic information:
    nature of 113–4
    disclosure of 114–22, 237
    research 210
Gillick competence 26n93, 29–30, 31–2,
    35, 37–8, 48, 62, 82, 108, 205–8,
    210

Gilligan, C. 119–21
Glass, David 65–6
GMC (General Medical Council) 56,
    60n42, 61, 91n96, 138, 150,
    180n34
    0–18 Years: Guidance for Doctors
        (2007) 39n200, 52n282, 56n14,
        85n71, 85n73, 86n75, 94–5,
        103n172, 103n174, 103n175,
        146–7, 149n134, 200, 239n23
    *Confidentiality: Protecting and
        Providing Information* (2004)
        76n4, 78, 85n71, 87n81, 91n96,
        94n123, 94n124, 95n129, 96–7, 99,
        103n171
    Good Medical Practice (2006)
        39n200, 60n42, 94n123, 98n145,
        140n61, 144n92, 147n122
    Role and Responsibility of Doctors
        (2002) 181n36, 193n100,
        196n111, 200
    *Seeking Patients' Consent: The Ethical
        Considerations* (1998) 39n200,
        156n184
*Good Medical Practice in Paediatrics
    and Child Health: Duties and
    Responsibilities of Paediatricians*
    (RCPCH, 2002) 91n100, 98n145,
    144n92
Great Ormond Street Hospital 14n3
guidelines, role in establishing breach of
    duty of care 148–51
*Guidelines for the Ethical Conduct of
    Medical Research Involving
    Children* ((RCPCH, 2000)
    198n134, 198n138, 203–5, 206–7,
    208n208, 209n217, 210n222

Hart's Ladder of Youth Participation
    226–7
Health and Social Care Act 2001 106, 108,
    230n114, 232
Health and Social Care Act 2008 138n46
Health, Department of *see* DoH
health information, ownership of 92–5
    see also confidentiality
health professionals:
    fear of litigation 132, 133

intuition 7–8
relationship with parents 65–6
relationship with patients 6–7, 73
Healthcare Commission 77–8, 132n9, 138,
  139n52, 147n121, 149, 174, 214n4,
  217
  State of Healthcare (2007) 14n2,
    225n79, 239n27
heart transplants, refusal of 32–3
Henderson, R.A., *Consent, Choice and
  Children in Research* 180n31,
  185–7, 206n195, 210n223
HIV/AIDS
  patient confidentiality 80, 88–9, 91
Hippocratic Oath 76n3
HRA (Human Rights Act) 6, 7, 36, 53, 68,
  69, 233, 241, 244
  and children's autonomy 38–44,
    236–7, 238–9
  and confidentiality 81, 82–3, 87–92,
    98–102
  and genetic information 128–9
  and participation 214
  and research 181n36, 208, 211
Human Fertilisation and Embryology Act
  1990 3n17, 8n40, 80n31, 80n35
Human Fertilisation Embryology
  (Disclosure of Information) Act
  1992 80n35
Human Genetic Commission 124
human rights:
  of children 1–2
  of participation 213–4
Human Rights Act *see* HRA
human tissue:
  Human Tissue Act 1961 71
  Human Tissue Act 2004 3n17, 181n36,
    198
  non-regenerative 63
  retention 70–73
Huntingdon Disease 125–6

immunization 55n4, 63
implied consent *see* consent
Infant Life (Preservation) Act 1929 165–6
informed consent *see* consent
insurance cover, and genetic information
  112n6

intuition, of health professionals 7–8
IVF (in-vitro fertilization) 165

Jain faith 62
Jehovah's Witness faith 30–32, 51–2, 68
Jewish faith:
  and male circumcision 60
  and medical treatment 67
  and tissue retention 72
justice, ethic of 119–21

Kymlicka, W. 116–8, 120–21

Lasting Power of Attorney 26, 49n266
Law Reform (Contributory Negligence)
  Act 1945 167n253
learning disabilities 62n51, 143n85, 180,
  233
legal liability for confidentiality 86–7
liberalism 115–18
life-saving interventions, children's right
  to refuse 9, 13–14, 21, 37, 51–2,
  221, 235–6
limb-lengthening procedures, parental
  consent to 59
Limitation Act 1980 161, 167n254
litigation:
  cost to NHS 134
  fear of among healthcare professionals
    132, 133
liver transplants 63–4
'loss of a chance' cases (negligence)
  154–5

*Making Amends: A Consultation Paper
  Setting Out Proposals for
  Reforming the Approach to
  Clinical Negligence in the NHS*
  (DoH, 2003) 132n10, 133n14,
    135n22, 138n48, 149n133, 163–4
malpractice *see* negligence
mature minors *see* minors
MCA (Mental Capacity Act 2005) 3n17,
  25–7, 31n128, 36, 37, 38, 46, 49,
  51, 70, 82, 181n36, 196n116, 198,
  201, 205, 236, 242n49, 243
  Code of Practice 44, 52–3, 244

medical equipment, proper functioning of
        136, 158–60
medical research *see* research
Medical Research Council *Medical
        Research Involving Children*
        (2004) 177n11, 201n165
Medicines and Healthcare Products
        Regulatory Agency *see* MHPRA
Mental Capacity Act 2005 *see* MCA
mental disturbance, inability to make
        decisions due to 36
MHA (Mental Health Act 1983) 29, 30,
        36, 97
MHPRA (Medicines and Healthcare
        Products Regulatory Agency) 158,
        195
minors, competence of 22–4
        mature 9, 14, 26, 29, 34, 36, 43,
                49–50, 63n52, 85, 110, 207, 241–2,
                244
        refusal of life-saving treatment
                14n3, 37, 45–6, 51–2, 68
Monitor (regulatory body for Foundation
        Trusts) 214–5, 221n61, 231, 232,
        233
Muslim faith:
        and male circumcision 60, 61–2
        and tissue retention 72
mutations *see* genetic testing and
        counselling

National Blood Authority 159–60
National Children's Bureau, *Youth Matters*
        (2005) 226, 228n102
National Health Service *see* NHS
National Health Service Act 2006 107
National Institute for Health and Clinical
        Excellence *see* NICE
National Research Ethics Service see
        NRES
negligence (tort) 11, 86, 131–2, 139, 174
        damages 131–2, 160–5
        duty of care 139–42
                breach of 142–51
                causation 151–5
        ethical approach to 155–7
        faults in drugs and medical devices
                158–60

legal causation and remoteness 157–8
        medical malpractice context 132–5
        other forms of liability 135–9
        prenatal:
                actions brought by the child
                        165–70
                actions brought by the parents
                        170–73
Netherlands, euthanasia law 45–6
NHS, failures within 138
NHS and Community Care Act 1990
        134n21
NHS Law Reform (Personal Injuries) Act
        1948 160n208
NHS Litigation Authority 99n152, 134–5,
        136, 137n45
no-fault system of compensation 132n10,
        135n26, 162–3
NICE (National Institute for Health and
        Clinical Excellence) 148–9, 217
non-therapeutic procedures, parental
        consent to 59, 74
non-therapeutic research, and children
        177n9, 182–3, 190, 191, 197–8,
        201–3, 205–6, 208n216
notifiable diseases 80
NRES (National Research Ethics Service)
        203, 205n185, 208, 209

obesity 219
organ retention 10, 70–73
Oviedo Convention (European
        Convention on Human Rights and
        Biomedicine) 39, 63n52, 143n78,
        181n36, 191–3, 198, 208n216
        Protocol on Biomedical Research
                181n36, 190n80, 193–4, 209

parental responsibility 22, 55–7, 73
        actions of the responsible parent 63–7
        consideration of children's views
                55–6, 69–70
        death of the child 70–73
        legal obligations 57–63
        religious/cultural dimensions 67–9
parents:
        relationship with children 6–7

relationship with health care
professionals 65
participation of children 213–5
and Foundation Trusts 12, 220,
230–33
frameworks for 226–7
legal framework for 222–6
policy changes in 227–30
rationale for 215–22
Participation Works 240–41
paternalism 15, 21, 31, 43, 46, 52, 165,
183, 190, 201n163
paternity testing 55n6
Patient Information Advisory Group *see*
PIAG
permitted disclosure *see* disclosure
Physical Signs of Child Sexual Abuse:
an Evidence-based Review and
Guidance for Best Practice
(RCPCH, 2008) 102, 103n171,
103n178, 104n179
PIAG (Patient Information Advisory
Group) 107–8
port-mortems, tissue retention 71–3
posthumous disclosure of information 87
pregnancy:
pre-natal injury 165–7
wrongful life 168–70
press freedom 89–90, 100, 101–2
privacy, breach of (tort) 87, 90n90
see also confidentiality
Protection and Use of Patient Information
(DoH, 1996) 78, 82n47, 93, 105
psychiatric injury, liability for 140–41,
142n75, 162
Public Disclosure Act 1998 80
Public Health (Control of Disease) Act
1984 80n34

quality of life 66

Rawls, A. 21, 115, 117n35, 120, 187
RCPCH (Royal College of Paediatrics and
Child Health) 150
Good Medical Practice in Paediatrics
and Child Health: Duties and
Responsibilities of Paediatricians
(2002) 91n100, 98n145, 144n92

Guidelines for the Ethical Conduct
of Medical Research Involving
Children (2000) 198n134,
198n138, 203–5, 206–7, 208n208,
209n217, 210n222
Physical Signs of Child Sexual Abuse:
an Evidence-based Review and
Guidance for Best Practice (2008)
102, 103n178, 104n179
Responsibilities of Doctors in Child
Protection Cases With Regard to
Confidentiality (2004) 95n128,
103n171, 104n182
RECs (Research Ethics Committees)
180–81, 184, 189, 190, 195, 210
redress *see* damages
Redress Act 2006 160n208, 174
religious beliefs and medical interventions
30–32, 63
female genital mutilation 59–60
male circumcision 60–62
remedies under common law 93–4
Report to the UN Committee on the
Rights of the Child (Children's
Commissioners) 6n29, 48n259,
69n107, 240n28
Report to the UN Committee on the Rights
of the Child (Children's Right
Alliance) 1n4, 157n85
research and children 12, 175, 209–11,
237
and the competent child 205–9
confidentiality 106–8
consent requirements 177, 181–2, 183,
195–8
drugs research 177–8, 179–80
ethical framework 181–3
and health information 106–8
and the incompetent child 205–9
legal and regulatory framework 175–6
international 189–98
UK 198–209
moral expectation of participation
187–9
need for regulation 180–81
non-therapeutic research 177n9, 182–3,
190, 191, 197–8, 201–3, 205–6,
208n216

*Research Governance Framework for
    Health and Social Care* (DoH,
    2edn, 2005) 198n137, 203n175
*Responsibilities of Doctors in Child
    Protection Cases With Regard to
    Confidentiality* (RCPCH, 2004)
    95n128, 103n171, 104n182
rights of children 17–24
    and the HRA 38–44
Road Traffic Act 1988 105n189
Role and Responsibility of Doctors (GMC,
    2002) 181n36, 193n100, 196n111,
    200
Royal College of Paediatrics and Child
    Health see RCPCH
Royal Liverpool Children's Enquiry Report
    (Alder Hey Report) 10n50, 70–71,
    119

Sale of Goods Act 1979 160
Scotland:
    Age of Legal Capacity (Scotland) Act
        1991 48
    Children (Scotland) Act 1995 19n29
    Scottish Report on Retained Organs at
        Post-mortem 72
Seeking Consent: Working with Children
    (DoH, 2001) 28n110
*Seeking Patients' Consent: The Ethical
    Considerations* (GMC, 1998)
    39n200, 156n184
Seen and Heard; Youth Council for
    Northern Ireland 226
Shipman, H. 138n46, 143
Silber J. 3, 42–3, 50n271, 83–5
Skene, L. 125–6, 127–8
State of Healthcare (Healthcare
    Commission, 2007) 14n2, 225n79,
    239n27
sterilization 25n80, 27, 55n4, 57n21,
    143n85, 146n111, 170, 171n279,
    172, 173, 197n129
Supreme Court Act 1981 110

Taylor, C., 'social thesis' 116–7
Terrorism Act 2000 105n190

testing, genetic *see* genetic testing and
    counselling
therapeutic misconception 185–6
therapeutic privilege (withholding of
    information) 156–7, 199–200
Thorpe, Katy 62n51
threshold for competence 44–5
tissue retention 10, 70–73
tort 86, 90, 157, 160–61, 172
    battery 29, 61, 137n43, 199
    breach of privacy 87, 90n90
    flaws in law of 131–2
    of negligence *see* negligence
transplant surgery:
    heart transplants 32–3
    liver transplants 63–4

Unfair Contract Terms Act 1977 167n252
UNRC (United Nations Convention on the
    Rights of the Child) 12, 17–18,
    48–9, 55n8, 84, 214n2, 219–20,
    221n58, 222–4, 238, 239, 240
    Children's Commissioners' Report to
        6n29, 48n259, 69n107, 240n28
    Children's Right Alliance Report to
        1n4, 157n185
United States, research involving children
    178, 194n102

vasectomy 170–71
vicarious liability 135–6
violence, duty to disclose threat of 96–8

WMA (World Medical Association) 76n4,
    176n5, 189–90
    Declaration of Helsinki 176n5,
        181n36, 189n68, 190n76, 191,
        193n96, 193n100, 195–6, 197n132,
        200n152, 207n197
women, moral reasoning 119–20
wrongful life 168–70

Youth Council for Northern Ireland *Seen
    and Heard* 226
Youth Matters (National Children's Bureau,
    2005) 226, 228n102